Coercion and Conciliation in Ireland

1880-1892

A Study in Conservative Unionism

PRINCETON STUDIES IN HISTORY, 13

Coercion and Conciliation
in Ireland

1880-1892

A STUDY
IN CONSERVATIVE UNIONISM

By L. P. Curtis, Jr.

PRINCETON UNIVERSITY PRESS
PRINCETON, NEW JERSEY
1963

Publication of this book has been aided by
the Ford Foundation program to support
publication, through university presses, of
work in the humanities and social sciences.

❖

L. P. Curtis, Jr., a member of the History
Department at Princeton University from
1959 to 1963, is an Assistant Professor of
History at the University of California,
Berkeley.

Printed in the United States of America
by Princeton University Press, Princeton, New Jersey

TO ALISON

The moment the very name of Ireland is mentioned, the English seem to bid adieu to common feeling, common prudence, and common sense, and to act with the barbarity of tyrants and the fatuity of idiots.   SYDNEY SMITH

The repeal of the Union we regard as fatal to the Empire, and we will never consent to it—never, though the country should be surrounded by dangers as great as those which threatened her when her American colonies and France and Spain and Holland were leagued against her, or when the armed neutrality of the Baltic disputed her maritime rights—never, though another Buonaparte should pitch his camp in sight of Dover Castle, never till all has been staked and lost, never till the four quarters of the world have been convulsed by the last struggle of the great English people for their place among the nations.

THOMAS MACAULAY

PREFACE

IN RECENT YEARS the origins, tactics, and aims of the Home Rule movement have received much attention from British and Irish scholars. Gladstone's pilgrimage toward the grail of Irish nationhood—what Tim Healy once referred to as "Gladstone and the Western Question"—as well as the character of Parnell and his "constitutional agitation" have long fascinated historians and politicians alike. The years between 1880, when the New Departure first began to affect the course of British politics, and 1892, when Gladstone won his last lease of office, embrace a period of acute turmoil both in Ireland and at Westminster. One indication of the virulence of the Irish Question was that in little more than a decade ten different men served as chief secretary for Ireland. Lord Salisbury was not exaggerating when he declared in March, 1887: "All the politics of the moment are summarised in the word 'Ireland.'" And the dismembering of both the Liberal and Irish parties within a span of five years provides conclusive proof, if any is needed, of the turbulence that marked this era of prolonged depression in trade and agriculture.

In view of the crucial nature of Anglo-Irish relations in the 1880's, it is curious that one side of the story has either been neglected or, worse, widely misunderstood. The forces dedicated to maintain the Act of Union, and in particular the dominant section led by Lord Salisbury, have not been treated to the attention that their long tenure of office would seem to merit. Admittedly, biographies of the leading Conservative politicians abound, but too often they are the devoted productions of relatives or disciples. In the absence of any unifying essay on Conservative Unionism during its formative phase I have tried to examine the premises on which the Conservative leaders opposed Home Rule, to appraise government policy in Ireland from 1885 to 1892, and, lastly, to explore the impact of the Irish Question on Conservative tactics and thought. The scope of this book, therefore, is not merely confined to administrative details in Dublin Castle but encompasses the interaction between Irish and English politics in an age of increasing party organization and effective mass agitation. Any attempt to analyze the complex structure of the Unionist alliance would require a separate study. The Liberal Unionists, for example, have been considered only insofar as they influenced Irish legislation and officials in Dublin. This inquiry, in short, is primarily concerned with private or ministerial, as opposed to public, opinion.

For centuries English policy toward Ireland had consisted of an erratic alternation between coercion and conciliation, while the virtues inherent in these two remedies were canceled out by the circumstances in which each was conceived and applied. When Salisbury accepted office in the summer of 1885, Ireland had just endured three years of stringent coercion under Lord Spencer. Using Lord Carnarvon as a goodwill ambassador, the Caretaker ministry tried its hand at conciliation but failed either to appease the nationalists or to reduce agrarian crime. The Conservatives did succeed, however, in misleading many Liberals about their views on Irish self-government, and when Gladstone decided to champion the Parnellite cause, he gave his opponents an ideal issue with which to exploit the prejudices and fears of a majority in Parliament. After defeating the Home Rule alliance in the general election of 1886, the Conservatives, now re-enforced by the secessionists from the Liberal party, again tried to govern Ireland without coercive power. But Hicks Beach's strenuous efforts to cope with agrarian crime and intransigent landlords ended in failure and a physical collapse. Only after Arthur Balfour had become chief secretary were the two elements of coercion and conciliation fused into a policy designed to kill, once and for all, the demand for Home Rule. The dimensions of Balfour's achievement at the Irish Office have never been adequately gauged, while too many historians have ignored the incessant friction within the Unionist coalition between Conservative and Liberal Unionists as well as between ministers and Irish landlords. Only a few of the many facets of the Irish Question could have been illuminated without access to such collections as the Salisbury Papers, the Balfour Papers, and the official records in the State Paper Office, Dublin Castle. Even though several tantalizing questions remain unanswered, especially in the areas of the Special Commission and the O'Shea divorce case, the abundance of manuscript sources has helped to dispel many of the myths concocted by the enemies as well as the champions of Home Rule.

It should be added that restrictions imposed on certain archives while I was writing this book dictated the terminal date of 1892. But the period under consideration contains two intrinsic forms of unity. The first is Parnell's unchallenged ascendancy until December, 1890; the second comprises the foundations of a Unionist policy for Ireland, which were laid down in the years 1887-1892. However brief this span of twelve years may appear in retrospect, few periods of equal length in the Victorian era can compete in the magnitude of issues involved and the intensity of feeling aroused.

Many people have helped me at each stage of this book, and mention here cannot repay the debt of gratitude I owe to the following: John Mason, Charles Stuart, Steven Watson, and the Treasurer of Christ Church; David Butler, the Warden and Fellows of Nuffield College; Herbert Nicholas; the Dean of Balliol; Miss W. D. Coates; the Keeper of Manuscripts, British Museum; R. B. McDowell and Professor T. W. Moody; T. P. O'Neill of the National Library of Ireland; the Keeper of the State Paper Office, Dublin; also Miss Cohalan of the American Irish Historical Society; Herbert Cahoon of the Pierpont Morgan Library; William Gaines; and Donald and Mary Hyde. In addition, I am grateful for encouragement and advice to Professors Norman Cantor, Gordon Craig, Charles Gillispie, Arno Mayer, George Nadel, and Wallace Notestein. To F. S. L. Lyons of Trinity College, Dublin, Piers Mackesy of Pembroke College, Oxford, and my father I am especially indebted for valuable criticism of the final draft.

For permission to publish from their family papers I must thank the Earl of Balfour, the Earl of Carnarvon, the Earl of Iddesleigh, the Marquess of Salisbury, the Earl St. Aldwyn, the Hon. David Smith, Lord Tollemache, and Francis Wyndham. The State Paper Office in Dublin kindly granted me access to documents up to 1892.

For editorial *expertise*, I owe much to Mrs. Alan Smith and Mrs. James Holly Hanford. The main burden of typing the manuscript was patiently borne by my wife, with the help of Miss Jan Logan.

Last but not least, generous grants from the Four Oaks Foundation, the trustees of the Gladstone Memorial Exhibition, Nuffield College, the Princeton University Research Fund, and the Ford Foundation have aided the writing and publication of this book.

L. P. CURTIS, JR.

Princeton, New Jersey
September 1962

ABBREVIATIONS

Add. MS 49683-49962	Balfour Papers, British Museum
AIHS	American Irish Historical Society
DICS	District Inspector Crime Department, Special Branch
HC	Parliamentary Papers
IHS	Irish Historical Studies
ILPU	Irish Loyal and Patriotic Union
PML	Pierpont Morgan Library
SPO	State Paper Office, Dublin Castle

Contents

Contents

List of Illustrations

Coercion and Conciliation in Ireland

1880-1892

A Study in Conservative Unionism

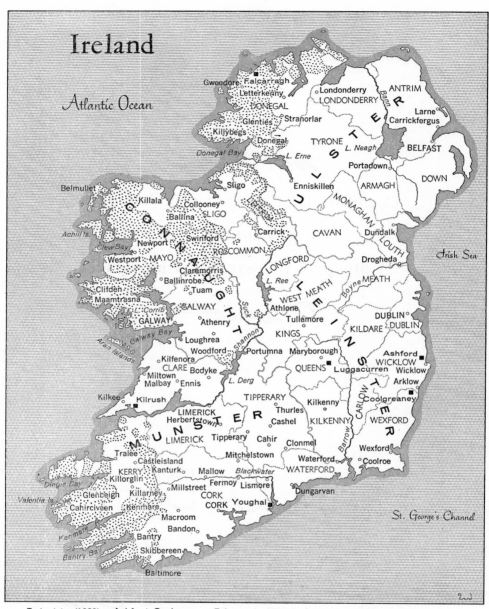

Ireland

Atlantic Ocean

Gweedore Falcarragh
Letterkenny
DONEGAL
Glenties Stranorlar
Killybegs
Donegal
Donegal Bay

Londonderry
LONDONDERRY
ANTRIM
Larne
Carrickfergus

TYRONE *L. Neagh*
BELFAST

Portadown
DOWN

Enniskillen
ARMAGH

Sligo
L. Erne

MONAGHAN

Belmullet
Killala
Collooney
Ballina SLIGO
Achill Is.
Newport Swinford
Clew Bay
Westport MAYO
Claremorris
Ballinrobe
Clifden Tuam
Maamtrasna
GALWAY
L. Corrib
GALWAY
Athenry
Aran Islands
Galway Bay Loughrea
Woodford
Kilfenora
CLARE Bodyke
Miltown
Malbay Ennis
Kilkee Kilrush

CONNAUGHT

ROSCOMMON

Carrick
CAVAN
Dundalk
LOUTH

LONGFORD
L. Ree
Drogheda

WEST MEATH
MEATH
Boyne
Athlone
DUBLIN
Tullamore
DUBLIN
KINGS
KILDARE

Portumna Maryborough
Shannon
Suck
L. Derg

QUEENS Luggacurren

LEINSTER

Ashford
WICKLOW
Wicklow

Arklow

Coolgreaney

CARLOW

TIPPERARY
Kilkenny
Thurles
KILKENNY
WEXFORD
Cashel
Barrow

Herbertstown
LIMERICK
Tipperary Cahir
Clonmel
Wexford
LIMERICK
Mitchelstown
Coolroe
Tralee
Castleisland
WATERFORD
Kanturk Mallow *Blackwater*
KERRY
Killorglin Millstreet Fermoy Lismore
Dungarvan
Dingle Bay
Glenbeigh Killarney
CORK
Valentia Is.
Cahirciveen Kenmare
CORK Youghal
Macroom
Bandon
Kenmare
Bantry
Skibbereen
Bantry Bay
Baltimore

MUNSTER

Irish Sea

St. George's Channel

Test estates (1889): Ashford, Coolgreaney, Falcarragh, Kilrush, Luggacurren, Youghal ■

Congested Districts (1892)

CHAPTER 1

The Irish Question

THE IRISH QUESTION, as Sir Ernest Barker once observed, is as old as Oxford University. From the time of the first Anglo-Norman invasion of Ireland in 1169 down to the twentieth century, the problem of maintaining satisfactory political and commercial relations with the "other island" vexed and bewildered English governments. By no means their least difficult task during this span of seven centuries was to define the precise meaning of the Irish Question. Whether native rebellions and agitations sprang from economic, political, social, or even spiritual causes became a matter of the utmost importance to ministers, whose careers often depended upon the accuracy of their guess. No single Irish question has ever existed, least of all in the nineteenth century, when, in an age of increasing democracy and political organization, the number and complexity of Irish problems brought into full view the incompatibility of these two islands.[1]

What then was the Irish Question? How many pieces were there to the puzzle? Every man had his own answers, and the trouble was that Englishmen disagreed among themselves as often as they disagreed with equally contentious Irishmen. To Edmund Burke it was more than a matter of religious oppression by the Protestant ascendancy. As he wrote to his son: "Alas! It is not about Popes but about potatoes that the minds of this unhappy people are agitated. It is not from the spirit of zeal, but the spirit of whisky that these wretches act."[2] Half a century later Disraeli thought he had the answer when he told the House of Commons: "I want to see a public man come forward and say what the Irish question is. One says it is a physical question; another, a spiritual. Now it is

---

[1] E. Barker, *Ireland in the Last Fifty Years, 1866-1918*, Oxford, 1919, p. 5. For further details see P. N. S. Mansergh, *Ireland in the Age of Reform and Revolution, 1840-1921*, London, 1940.

[2] T. H. D. Mahoney, *Edmund Burke and Ireland*, Cambridge, Mass., 1960, p. 322. THE ABBREVIATIONS USED THROUGHOUT ARE GIVEN ON P. X.

1

the absence of the aristocracy, then the absence of railroads. It is the Pope one day; potatoes the next." And then, having dwelt on the evils of overpopulation and poor diet, he arrived at the heart of the matter: "That dense population in extreme distress inhabits an island where there is an Established Church which is not their Church, and a territorial aristocracy the richest of whom live in distant capitals. Thus you have a starving population, an absentee aristocracy, and an alien Church, and in addition the weakest executive in the world. That is the Irish question."[3] Armed with shrewd intuition and anxious to vilify Peel, Disraeli came closer to understanding both the Irish Question and its significance for British political life than did most of his contemporaries or successors in the Conservative party. Nevertheless, this quixotic figure scarcely lifted a hand to help that "damp island contiguous to the melancholy ocean" during a time of mounting economic distress. Gladstone's diagnosis, on the other hand, was both apocalyptic and ominous. "Ireland, Ireland!", he wrote to his wife in 1845, "that cloud in the west, that coming storm, the minister of God's retribution upon cruel and inveterate and but half-atoned injustice! Ireland forces upon us these great social and great religious questions—God grant that we may have courage—to look them in the face and to work through them."[4] And yet, while Gladstone prescribed surgery to remedy Irish complaints, Disraeli was content to recommend long periods of convalescence or legislative inactivity after the "drastic" cures of his rival.

Perceptive Englishmen watched with dismay the impact of the Irish Question upon domestic politics. Besides the amount of parliamentary time used by Irish members to discourse on all matters under the sun, Ireland had a lethal effect upon the lives of English ministries. Lord Carnarvon, who played a leading role in the political drama of 1885, counted at least eight ministries in the nineteenth century that had been "destroyed" by the Irish nemesis.[5] And had Carnarvon lived longer he would presumably

[3] W. F. Monypenny, *The Life of Benjamin Disraeli, Earl of Beaconsfield*, New York, 1917, II, pp. 191-92.

[4] J. L. Hammond, *Gladstone and the Irish Nation*, London, 1938, p. 51.

[5] A. H. Hardinge, *The Life of Henry Howard Molyneux Herbert, Fourth Earl of Carnarvon, 1831-1890* (hereafter cited as *Carnarvon*), London, 1925, III, p. 215 n. 1.

have added to his list the Conservative defeat in 1892, Gladstone's resignation in 1894, and Lord Rosebery's fall in 1895. The attempts of English ministers to solve the riddle of Ireland thus had a marked effect upon their own careers; and whenever they offered conciliation to the native populace, their motives were impugned in both countries while their measures were usually mangled in Parliament. Mutual resentment, mutual ignorance, mutual suspicion: these were the obstacles that lurked in waiting for any reformers who tried to reconcile England and Ireland.

For generations after the Act of Union the cycle of government policy in Ireland was all too easy to discern and to ridicule. Agrarian crime or the agitation of self-styled patriots would lead first to coercion or summary justice and restrictions upon arms, speeches, and the press. When these measures had failed to quell the disturbances, ministers would relent, perhaps even listen to the voices of reform, and with reluctance make concessions. Invariably these concessions would be too little and too late. The native population for whom they were intended would mock them as the last gasp of a moribund government. To Irish leaders the rules of the game seemed simple enough: the fiercer the agitation, the larger the concession. And in the wake of renewed protest— expressed by shootings, dynamitings, cattle maiming, vandalism, and other acts of terrorism—came coercion again, at the bidding of disillusioned ministers and irate landlords. Repression, needless to say, never cured an Irish grievance, and any new concessions that might follow would arrive in an atmosphere already poisoned by previous doses of coercion. In short, this two-phase cycle of coercion and conciliation, this haphazard alternation of "kicks and kindness," punctuated by long periods of indifference or apathy, characterized British policy until the last years of the nineteenth century.

The Irish Question occupies a unique place in English history. No other single issue so embittered feeling at Westminster in that century. Indeed, from an English point of view the Irish Question had much in common with a plague. It came and went mysteriously, maiming or destroying its victims in both countries. For years there was no known cure, no antibody that would guarantee immunity either to landlords or to politicians. In the decade of the 1880's the Irish "disease" broke out in a more virulent form; and it was this new epidemic that permanently scarred the British party system, obliterating political landmarks and loyalties, and leaving the parliamentary process considerably weakened in all its parts.

Irish grievances in the nineteenth century varied as much in content as in expression. There was the Act of Union itself, engineered by means of flagrant bribery and unredeemed promises of Catholic emancipation, which gave Ireland representation in the imperial Parliament at Westminster. And when O'Connell, the "Great Liberator," first articulated the demand for repeal of the Union, he was not creating a new spirit of national self-consciousness but merely endowing that existing sentiment with "a distinct form, a steady action, and a constitutional character."[6] The economic restrictions imposed on Ireland after 1660 constitute a familiar story of exploitation, and even staunch defenders of the Union were forced to admit that British commercial policies had inflicted irreparable damage on the Irish economy. Then, too, there was the anachronism of the Protestant ascendancy in a predominantly Catholic country; and the sectarian passions it aroused were not to be expunged by Catholic emancipation or commutation of tithes alone.

For most Irishmen the great famine of 1845-1848 epitomized the nature of the connection between England and Ireland. The Act of Union and Whitehall were blamed for this catastrophe, which came closer to a "final solution" of the Irish Question than even the pogroms of the seventeenth century. Death through starvation or disease, and emigration as well, reduced the population of the country by over two million in less than a decade; and the hundreds of thousands who emigrated during this period created a new Irish nation overseas.[7] Concentrated in the industrial centers of the new world, this nation in exile, its patriotism made more extreme by distance and the difficulties of assimilation, contributed to the Home Rule movement not only money and men but ideas.

[6] W. E. H. Lecky, *The Leaders of Public Opinion in Ireland*, London, 1871, p. 229.

[7] W. P. O'Brien, *The Great Famine in Ireland, 1845-1895*, London, 1896, pp. 1-251; *The Great Famine: Studies in Irish History, 1845-1852*, ed. R. D. Edwards and T. D. Williams, Dublin, 1956; and G. Locker Lampson, *A Consideration of the State of Ireland in the Nineteenth Century* (hereafter *Ireland*), New York, 1907, pp. 275-76.

The famine that marks the great divide in Irish history between the old Ireland and the new also brought into prominence the conflict between landlord and tenant, which had bedeviled Anglo-Irish relations for centuries. Arthur Balfour once declared that the history of Ireland was nothing more than a history of the land question; and if this was an oversimplification, it was also true that the agrarian problem lay at the root of much Irish discontent. In a country where agricultural pursuits supported two-thirds of the population, the land question obtruded into almost every phase of life. Three factors in particular aggravated landlord-tenant relations. First, the peasantry still cherished the belief that the land belonged to all. Under the sept system prevalent before the Anglo-Norman invasions, "absolute" property was unknown and the right to hold land in a community was inseparable from the right to cultivate it. Second, the Encumbered Estates Act of 1849 had created a new class of landlords, almost exclusively composed of Irish speculators from the cities and towns who were interested primarily in profit. After the mid-century many Anglo-Irish squires who had spent their lives accumulating debts, hunting foxes, and fighting law suits were supplanted by these urban speculators and "gombeen men"; and the tenants thus affected soon found the new landlords far more exacting in the enforcement of their legal rights. Lastly, Irish agriculture was distinguished by primitive methods, rackrents, and absentee ownership, by insolvent landlords and the denial outside Ulster of a tenant's legal interest in his holding, and by the proliferation of small holdings incapable of sustaining the occupier and his family. Such conditions meant chronic shortage of capital and mounting arrears of rent. The primacy of landlords' over tenants' rights and a precarious margin between subsistence and famine conditions characterized the Irish land system, which J. S. Mill described in 1868 as without doubt "the worst in Europe."[8]

[8] J. S. Mill, *England and Ireland*, London, 1868, p. 15. See also Mill, *Chapters and Speeches on the Irish Land Question*, London, 1870; J. E. Pomfret, *The Struggle for Land in Ireland, 1800-1923*, Princeton, 1930; and R. D. C. Black, *Economic Thought and the Irish Question 1817-1870*, Cambridge, 1960, *passim*.

I. GLADSTONE, DISRAELI, AND THE IRISH QUESTION

Throughout the nineteenth century relatively few Englishmen crossed the Irish Sea as tourists, and those who did usually stayed within the pale of Anglo-Irish civilization, whose center was Dublin or the viceregal lodge and whose outermost limits were prescribed by the "smart" hunts of the midland counties. The rare Englishman who ventured beyond this familiar, affluent, and safe world required a strong stomach and a taste for scenes of squalor and utter desolation. In the south and along the wind-swept western littoral the peasant could escape from his grim existence only through death, drink, or emigration.

Because ignorance of the "condition of Ireland" question was so widespread in English political circles, it was all the more remarkable that Gladstone, who had never braved the Irish Sea, should have addressed himself to Irish as well as administrative reforms in his first ministry. Determined to atone for Ireland's "historic wrongs," he began by disestablishing the Irish Church and ended by providing safeguards for tenants' holdings in the Land Act of 1870. Taken together, these two measures may have alienated churchmen, landlords, and the Queen, but they stand as a landmark in Anglo-Irish relations; and after 1870 no responsible English politician could safely afford to repudiate the precedent set by Gladstone in Irish affairs.[9]

The shortcomings of the Land Act of 1870 are well known. So complex were the provisions extending the custom of Ulster tenant right throughout the country that few lawyers, let alone tenants, fully understood the act. Besides protecting tenant improvements in the land, the measure (in several clauses named for their sponsor, John Bright) also tried to encourage land purchase. But few tenants bothered to buy their holdings under these terms; many land reformers felt that the act barely touched the evils of the system; and no material relief reached the great body of Irish peasants. If the Land Act served a useful purpose in England by educating a minority in the inequities of Irish land tenure, the political implications in Ireland were more important. The im-

[9] For an account of Gladstone's "mission to pacify Ireland," see Hammond, *op.cit.*, pp. 83-131; and J. Morley, *The Life of William Ewart Gladstone* (hereafter *Gladstone*), New York, 1903, III, pp. 237 ff.

pression was widespread that only Fenian dynamitings had steered Gladstone into a reforming frame of mind; and as R. Barry O'Brien, the prominent Irish publicist, once remarked, so long as English ministers gave the appearance of yielding only to force, then nationalist leaders were virtually compelled to adopt forceful methods.[10]

Gladstone's great ministry came to an end in the general election of 1874, having already foundered on the reefs of higher education for Catholics in Ireland. His successor was shrewd enough to realize that reforms in Ireland were not worth many votes in England, and the British electorate was soon treated to a dazzling display of social reform at home and imperial self-assertion abroad. Disraeli was a masterhand at conjuring away unpleasant realities that might endanger the appeal of his "new" Conservatism. In public he steadfastly ignored the ominous signs that pointed to a depression in trade and agriculture, while he sought to distract Englishmen from domestic anxieties by visions of grandeur in India and the Near East. When Disraeli became prime minister, the Irish Home Rule League had been functioning for a year under the direction of Isaac Butt, a mild-mannered Protestant lawyer who led some fifty-nine supporters in the Commons. It was all too easy for ministers to ignore this group of moderate Irishmen drawn in part from the professional classes who mixed freely in English society and were reviled as "whigs" by the more extreme nationalists. Lacking verve and organization, Butt's party constituted no real threat either to the government or to the Act of Union. Unfortunately for both Conservatives and Liberals, Butt was only a transient figure in the rapidly changing political landscape of Ireland.

Toward the end of Beaconsfield's regime an agricultural depression struck Ireland with devastating force, leaving thousands of tenants in the south and west on the verge of starvation and precipitating wholesale evictions by unsympathetic landlords. Two factors, the blight and cheap grain imported into England from Russia and North America, were the principal agents of this distress. While the rate of agrarian crime increased in proportion to evictions in Ireland, English industry was experiencing

[10] R. Barry O'Brien, *The Life of Lord Russell of Killowen*, London, 1902, p. 216.

the throes of depression accompanied by high unemployment and labor unrest. When confronted with the stark reality of famine in Ireland, Beaconsfield indulged in gloomy prophecies about the imminence of rebellion, but he did little to prevent this contingency. Such despondent moods rapidly gave way to elation, and the aging, almost senile premier would dismiss Irish discontent with a wave of his hand: "There! if you say 'Bo!' loud enough to a goose—the goose will go away."[11]

Needless to say, the Irish party that emerged out of the economic and social dislocation of the late 1870's did not behave like a flock of geese. Safely ensconced in the House of Lords, Beaconsfield tended to underestimate the disruptive force that had entered Parliament in the form of Parnell and his party. Lord Salisbury, in the days when he had not forgiven Disraeli for carrying the Reform Bill of 1867, confided to a friend that the Conservative leader enjoyed playing "the old game of talking Green in the House and Orange in the Lobby."[12] Apart from lending his support to two funds for famine relief in the distressed areas of Ireland, the prime minister did not try to compete with Gladstone in the field of Irish reform. Sir Michael Hicks Beach, chief secretary for Ireland, had carried an important measure in the Intermediate Education Act, which assigned one million pounds out of the Irish Church surplus to improve facilities at the secondary level. But after 1878, when Hicks Beach moved to the Colonial Office, the Government made no effective attempt to eliminate the causes of Irish distress.[13]

The Conservative defeat in 1880 was as unexpected as it was resounding. Those voters whom Disraeli had enfranchised in 1867 once again proved ingrates; public health acts, "peace with honor," and jingoistic diplomacy had failed to stimulate the slumping British economy; and the premier's warning in his electoral manifesto about the menace of resurgent nationalism in Ireland held no attraction for the unemployed and for those who could not forget his support of the infidel Turk. As Beacons-

[11] Lady John Manners to Salisbury, 27 Dec. 1880 and 28 Jan. 1881, Salisbury MSS.

[12] Salisbury to Carnarvon, 6 March 1868, *ibid.*

[13] Lady Victoria Hicks Beach, *The Life of Sir Michael Hicks Beach, First Earl St. Aldwyn* (hereafter *St. Aldwyn*) London, 1932, I, pp. 52-56.

field walked away from Downing Street after his resignation, he was heard to mutter something about the troubles brewing in Ireland. To all intents this Delphic utterance was not only too cryptic, it was also too late.

The condition of Ireland in 1880 defies description. The ruinous harvest of the previous year had helped to produce some 2,500 agrarian outrages, over 105,000 cases of pauperism, and the eviction of more than 2,000 families. By 1882 evictions had increased to 5,201 cases and agrarian crime to 3,432. It took facts of this kind to awaken Englishmen to the size and potential danger of the Irish Question. Reports reaching London were far from reassuring. The wealthy Lord Ardilaun, who lived in Ashford Castle, Cong, believed that Ireland was "on the verge of a rebellion" in 1880 and expected to be shot during the winter. And this landlord had a clean record as far as evictions were concerned. Ardilaun carried "a six-chambered revolver" at all times, even while in London; and many landlords as well as English officers quartered in Ireland never went out hunting without loaded weapons.[14] John Gorst, who had overhauled the Conservative party machinery after 1869, visited Ireland in December, 1881, and witnessed the seizure of some cattle from a tenant in arrears. The forces of the law were represented by a sheriff, half a dozen Property Defence men, forty members of the Royal Irish Constabulary, fifty soldiers "all armed to the teeth, and a resident magistrate who appears to go about with the Riot Act pasted in the crown of his hat ready for an emergency. The tenant and his friends," Gorst reported to Lord Salisbury, "looked on with the appearance of deadly hatred and would have murdered any one of us if they could. How long is such a state of things to last?"[15]

Such a question was not easily answered. John Morley encountered an Irishman in 1882 who said that Ireland was "literally a society on the eve of dissolution"; and Gladstone came to a similar conclusion soon after returning to power. What Ireland needed was a drastic cure, and the cost—both political and financial—was irrelevant to Gladstone. Conciliation was the first order

[14] Lady John Manners to Salisbury, n.d. Oct. 1880 and 11 Jan. 1881, Salisbury MSS.

[15] Gorst to Salisbury, 30 Dec. 1881, *ibid*.

of the day, and after introducing the abortive Compensation for Disturbance Bill, the premier decided to pacify Ireland with the famous Land Act of 1881. This measure revolutionized the laws of land tenure by guaranteeing tenants the famous "3 F's": fixity of tenure, fair rents, and free sale. Once again Gladstone proved that the path of inconsistency held no terror for him. Or, as the youthful Arthur Balfour expressed it: "Gladstone is Gladstone no longer if he is bound by his previous utterances—or if he cannot, when it suits him, drive a coach and six through any principle ever invented."[16] The Land Act not only deprived landlords of their right to decide arbitrarily upon rents, evictions, and sale, but set up an elaborate apparatus to adjudicate rents. Despite orders from the nationalist leaders to limit their applications for fair rents to a few test cases, the tenants flocked to the land courts in such numbers that the legal machinery almost broke down under the strain. Although the act did not safeguard the tenants against eviction and rackrents in any final sense, the land and county courts together fixed over 150,000 "fair rents" in the first three years of operation, with reductions averaging twenty per cent.[17]

II. THE NEW DEPARTURE

In the last years of Beaconsfield's ministry a new and daring leader, Charles Stewart Parnell, emerged to unite the various elements of Irish nationalism into a formidable, if restless, alliance. The New Departure was a hybrid of those forces opposed to English rule and landlordism, and it represented the most serious threat to the Union to date. Parnell once called it a "combination of the political with the agrarian movement." The man chiefly responsible for harnessing the enormous force of the land question and placing it at Parnell's disposal was Michael Davitt, an ex-Fenian and veteran of Dartmoor. A vigorous exponent of land nationalization, Davitt founded the Irish Land League in 1879 in order to prevent landlords from rackrenting and evicting their tenants. The main weapon of the league was the boycott, a term immortalizing the name of Lord Erne's land agent. This practice

[16] Balfour to Salisbury, 21 Jan. 1881, *ibid.*

[17] For details of the Land Act of 1881 see Pomfret, *op.cit.*, pp. 161-219; and Hammond, *op.cit.*, pp. 215-62.

amounted to the imposition of economic, social, and even spiritual sanctions on all who cooperated with harsh landlords. The new league recruited thousands of members across the country and was primarily responsible for launching a land war on a hitherto unknown scale.

Through the agency of the Land League Davitt proved that it was possible to merge the forces behind Fenianism and Home Rule into "a parallel action between the revolutionary and constitutional movements." Some of the traditional distrust that had long separated these two elements was bound to survive, but the ascendancy of moral force over dynamite was inherent in Davitt's movement, and Parnell did not ignore this fact. The exact antithesis of the conventional Irish patriot, Parnell was one of the supreme political tacticians of his age. In 1878 he took part in a series of delicate negotiations with Davitt and other leaders of the Irish and Irish-American world. Their goal was a united front, but the supreme council of the Irish Republican Brotherhood continued to disapprove of a purely constitutional agitation, and it was not until after the disastrous harvest of 1879 that the "grand coalition" was finally realized. Parnell's acceptance of the presidency of the revitalized Irish National Land League in October, 1879, effectively sealed the understanding that had been reached between the revolutionary and constitutional forces. The new leader was a man in a hurry: in 1877 he had displaced Butt as head of the Home Rule Confederation of Great Britain, only two years after his election to Parliament, and in May, 1880, he became chairman of the Irish parliamentary party. Having gained control of both the Land League and Butt's old party, Parnell was justly called "the uncrowned king of Ireland."[18]

An able Chief Secretary for Ireland, Chichester Fortescue, who assisted Gladstone in his Irish reforms up to 1885, once said: "Conceive the curse it would be to have a body of moral-force Fenians or Nationalists returned to Parliament." Parnell fully intended his party to be such a curse for English legislators at

[18] This account is based on T. W. Moody, "The New Departure in Irish Politics, 1878-1879," in *Essays in British and Irish History in Honour of James Eadie Todd*, ed. H. A. Cronne, T. W. Moody, and D. B. Quinn, London, 1949, pp. 303-33. See also C. C. O'Brien, *Parnell and His Party, 1880-1890*, Oxford, 1957, pp. 1-10.

Westminster so long as Home Rule was withheld. From America he drew some of the inspiration for his party machine. He was the first "party boss" in Ireland, relying on the caucus, paying some of his followers, and pledging all of them to uphold the principles of the New Departure. In Parliament the New Departure soon left its mark. According to Joseph Biggar, the exuberant patriot who resembled a gargoyle, "The first thing you have got to do with an Englishman on the Irish Question is to shock him. Then you can reason with him right enough." From Biggar Parnell learned the art of obstructing debate, and the motto of the Irish parliamentary party became: "Never talk except in Government time." The brilliant, if wearisome, use of obstructionist methods exposed all the inadequacies of procedural rules in the House and made it impossible for ministers to conduct even the routine business of government.

The emergence of an Irish leader with such exceptional talents transformed the Home Rule agitation from an abstract issue to a practical reality. Parnell's credentials, in fact, were far more presentable by English standards than were those of O'Connell. A Protestant landlord who had studied for two years at Cambridge, Parnell possessed that note of respectability which was essential for one dealing with English politicians. That he was also a man of deep, even volcanic, passion concealed beneath many layers of reserve was a fact known to only a few. His non-Celtic origins and haughty bearing impressed many Englishmen, who had always associated Irish nationalism with bellicose demagogues drawn from the peasantry or lower middle class. Throughout his career Parnell's overriding ambition was to divert the forces of the land question and of Fenianism into the main channel of Home Rule. Nourished by an Anglophobia more profound than that of most nationalists, he spent over five years creating a party that would arouse all Englishmen from their complacency and force Parliament to admit the urgency of the Irish Question.

What then was the Irish Question in the 1880's? In one sense Burke and Disraeli were right: it was still a "bread and butter" question. Despite the population decline after the famine, the pressure upon the resources of the land was still too great to free the people from substandard living conditions or to remove the threat of recurrent famine. But it was also a question of constitutional arrangements. Memories of Irish autonomy, of the pre-Tudor Irish parliament, and of Grattan's achievements could never die. To establish a parliament in Dublin with jurisdiction over all internal affairs—however these might be defined, but including the right to protect Irish industries—was Parnell's aim. Not that he ignored the land question: he could not afford to do so. What he advocated was not outright confiscation but the creation of a peasant proprietary class through generous loans from the British Treasury. If the landlords had to leave Ireland, then they must go adequately compensated for their "disturbance."

There were other facets to the Irish Question. In the realm of Catholic higher education English governments had been singularly remiss. Plans for a Catholic university equivalent to Trinity College, Dublin, failed to materialize; and until 1908 the only concession granted in this field was a skeletal institution called the Royal University of Ireland, which set examinations and awarded degrees after 1879. Unfortunately for Ireland, concessions to Catholic education always put the British electorate, whether Anglican or nonconformist, into a sullen and resentful mood. Then, too, there was the Ulster question, created by the enterprising population of Presbyterians, Methodists, Quakers, and other Protestant denominations that made up a bitterly anti-Catholic colony in the northeast corner of the island. The presence of a large minority of Catholics in parts of Ulster only aggravated the difficulties inspired by religious bigotry and fear. The list of Irish grievances also included the fact—sentimental, no doubt, but nonetheless important—that British sovereigns had spent a total of twenty days in Ireland in the two centuries from 1660 to 1860. Queen Victoria did not atone for this oversight by shunning the island herself and vetoing plans to send the Prince of Wales to Dublin as "permanent" viceroy. And the Fenian outrages in England in 1867 did not improve matters. As the Queen wrote at the time: "These Irish are really shocking, abominable people—not like any other civilised nation."[19]

Almost all the ingredients of the Irish Question were old. What

[19] Queen Victoria to Sir Stafford Northcote, 2 Oct. 1867, Iddesleigh MSS.

was new was their fusion and expression in Parnell's constitutional movement. The New Departure was helped immeasurably by the introduction of the secret ballot in 1872, the Reform Acts of 1867 and 1884, and by the prolonged depression that disrupted the economy of the British Isles in the last decades of the century. The uniqueness of the New Departure lay not only in the mechanics of political organization, but also in the qualities of its leader and in the group of highly talented men who served as his lieutenants in the House of Commons. And thanks to a combination of personal ability, electoral reforms, agricultural distress, and a steady flow of funds from the Irish world overseas, the Irish Question returned to haunt British politics with a vengeance for another two generations.

CHAPTER II

The Origins of the Caretaker Ministry

DURING the first years of Parnell's ascendancy most Englishmen saw nothing constitutional about the agitation for Home Rule. The invocation to "Captain Moonlight," who did not confine his brutal work to the nocturnal hours, and the Land League's campaign of organized boycotting seemed to imply that the national question had once again been subordinated to that of the land. The extent of disorder in Ireland forced Gladstone to adopt a policy of alternating coercion and conciliation, and much of the goodwill engendered by the Land Act of 1881 was soon undone by the imprisonment of the League's leaders in October of that year. Soon after the disclosure of the so-called Kilmainham Treaty, by which the nationalist leaders were released on promises of good behavior, there came the shocking murders in Phoenix Park. The Invincibles' surgical knives had also jeopardized Parnell's cause, and the Irish leader even offered to resign. A Draconian crimes act was the result, and for the next three years many Irishmen had firsthand experience of what amounted to martial law.

I. MINISTERIAL WOES

Gladstone's cabinet was soon preoccupied with crises in Egypt, South Africa, Afghanistan, and the Sudan; but after 1884 the Irish Question again loomed large as ministers tried in vain to solve that ancient riddle. In the way of remedial legislation Ireland had received an Arrears Act in 1882, relieving tenants' arrears in certain cases of insolvency, the Labourers Act of 1883, which promoted working-class housing, and the Tramways Act of the same year, which authorized the extension of narrow-gauge railways in specified districts. But these measures were only gestures at conciliation: something far more substantial was required.

The Franchise Bill of 1884 was the first great hurdle of the year for the Liberal ministry, and it took them some ten months to clear it. The Opposition's refusal to countenance franchise reform without a simultaneous redistribution of seats almost touched off a popular campaign against the Conservative peers, whose leader Lord Salisbury angrily accused the Government of trying to rig the forthcoming elections in their own favor. Only a joint conference between Government and Opposition leaders, at the request of an anxious Queen, allayed party feeling sufficiently to permit a compromise settlement. One of the most controversial features of the Franchise Bill was its application to Ireland. Informed observers predicted that the removal of distinctions between the borough and county franchise in Ireland would have a decisive effect on the Home Rule movement. Estimates on the precise number of seats Parnell would gain by such a concession varied widely; but most Conservatives and especially the Irish landlord class agreed that the Irish agricultural laborer would endorse the nationalist party whether for reasons of expediency or principle.[1] When a group of prominent landlords moved an amendment omitting Ireland from the measure altogether, Gladstone defended the concession on the grounds of decency and justice to Ireland, stressing the need to maintain England's moral position in the eyes of the world. Although there was some talk of reducing the Irish representation to a number commensurate with the country's depleted population, neither Conservatives nor Liberals dared to press this issue for fear of either permanently alienating the Parnellites or inciting rebellion in Ireland. Eventually the landlords' amendment was defeated by 332 to 137; and the Irish electorate rose from 222,000 to 740,000.

In recent years the effects of this concession upon Parnellism have been more critically appraised, and some of the Unionist exaggerations on this score have been exposed.[2] Both Chamberlain and Parnell estimated that the measure would make a difference of only ten seats in the nationalists' favor; and this figure comes much closer to the truth. By 1884 Parnell already controlled the votes of most Catholics in Ireland; nevertheless, the franchise extension did increase his support, and, even more important, it added much weight to his bargaining power in Great Britain.

[1] See Lord George Hamilton to Salisbury, 18 Dec. 1884, Salisbury MSS.
[2] C. C. O'Brien, *Parnell and His Party*, p. 87, and p. 150 n. 3.

Gladstone was not the only English politician to appreciate the mandate that Parnell could now claim. From an English point of view, therefore, the importance of the electoral change in Ireland ought not to be underestimated.

Meanwhile, military reverses in the Sudan, culminating in the death of General Gordon at Khartoum, diminished both the Government's majorities in the Commons and British prestige on the continent. It was against this background of approaching disaster abroad that Gladstone embarked on a new Irish adventure. The prospect of local government reform in Ireland brought into full view the animosities of Whigs, Liberals, and Radicals in the cabinet, and ultimately led to its downfall. In the first place, ministers could not agree on a scheme that would guarantee the proper administration of the law. If the justices of the peace were to be supplanted by elective councils, how could the Catholic majority be prevented from turning the courts into instruments of oppression for the Protestant or loyalist minority? The second, and closely related, dilemma concerned the renewal of the Crimes Act, which was due to expire in August, 1885. The Radical element, composed of Joseph Chamberlain and his astute colleague Sir Charles Dilke, disliked coercion in any form, and insisted that a bold local government bill take precedence over any coercive measure, however mild; and Gladstone tended to agree.

Opposed to this view was Lord Hartington, secretary for war; a Whig to the core, and heir-apparent to the party leadership, Hartington objected to any major concessions to the Parnellites. Having lost a brother to Irish cutthroats, he had no qualms about coercion, and wished to extend the land purchase clauses in the Act of 1881. Sir William Harcourt, the home secretary, and Lord Spencer, the Irish Viceroy, also took this position, the latter consenting to a scheme that limited the powers of Dublin Castle, but only on condition that certain clauses in the Crimes Act be renewed. Undaunted by Whig coolness toward concession, Gladstone urged Chamberlain to draft a plan for local government reform. Seeing his chance to "dish the Whigs" and outflank the Parnellites at the same time, Chamberlain welcomed this commission. So too did Dilke. The curious spectacle thus emerged of the president of the Board of Trade, aided by the president of the Local Government Board, assuming full responsibility for policy-planning in Irish affairs.

After several months of tortuous negotiations with Parnell, conducted through the agency of the unscrupulous Captain O'Shea, Chamberlain arrived at a plan of elective county boards coordinated by a central board in Dublin that would have control over such affairs as land laws, elementary education, the poor law, and public works. The central board, composed of members elected by the county boards, would have no judicial functions but would supplant most of the administrative departments in Dublin Castle. Parnell objected to the legislative functions of the central board and sought to confine its operations to public works and education: the national parliament that he had in mind would assume all legislative powers. Thanks to the duplicity of O'Shea, however, Chamberlain was left with the false impression that Parnell would accept his plan, with only a few changes, as a final settlement. The fact was that throughout the discussions Parnell never allowed the prospect of local government reform to distract him from the primary objective of an Irish parliament.

Chamberlain's central board scheme had a mixed reception both in the cabinet and in Ireland. Lord Hartington repudiated the plan as a typically democratic product of the Birmingham caucus. All the peers in the cabinet except Granville, who was more loyal to Gladstone than to Ireland, opposed it, and the leading Parnellites were hardly enthusiastic. On May 9 the scheme was rejected in cabinet by a narrow margin. Gladstone, saddened by the dissension of his colleagues and anticipating greater trouble to come in default of a concession, began to consider the advantages of resigning from office on some issue far removed from Ireland.[3]

The cumulative strains of heading a ministry that could not escape the stigma of Kilmainham or Khartoum, of trying to deal with Parnell, whose ambivalent position at home required him to denounce the administration, and of acting as arbiter between quarrelsome ministers had left their mark on the aging prime

[3] Hammond, *Gladstone and the Irish Nation*, pp. 340-75; C. C. O'Brien, *op.cit.*, pp. 90-97; C. H. D. Howard, "Joseph Chamberlain, Parnell, and the Irish 'Central Board' Scheme 1884-1885," *Irish Historical Studies*, 1953, Vol. 8, No. 32, pp. 324-61.

minister. The prospect of an early release from these afflictions held nothing but pleasure for him.

The first few months of 1885 saw all the incompatibilities of the Liberal ministry rising to the surface. More sensitive than ever to Whig slights, Chamberlain and Dilke rejected a compromise solution in the form of an Irish land purchase bill and shortly thereafter tendered their resignations over a misunderstanding with Gladstone. For several days the fate of the ministry hung in the balance. To make matters worse, the dilemma of the Crimes Act still remained. Once again Hartington condemned the Radical position, arguing that Lord Spencer could not continue to govern the country without special powers. Bristling with resentment against the Viceroy and his Whig friends, Chamberlain replied that coercion was both demoralizing and unnecessary. On May 15 the cabinet discussed the draft of a modified crimes bill, and that afternoon Gladstone announced in Parliament the Government's intention to renew a milder form of coercion. It did not take him long to perceive that even an adulterated measure would meet stiff resistance in the Commons.[4] Although Chamberlain and Dilke were still living in a state of suspended resignation, the cabinet finally agreed on the main provisions of a new crimes bill. But the appearance of accord was deceptive. After months of dissension and much hard feeling only coercion was left as a practicable policy, and even that prospect divided the Government. By June, 1885, Gladstone was exhausted from the effort of trying to hold his ministry together, and the urgent problem of Irish national aspirations seemed further from solution than ever.

II. AN ACT OF "HARA-KIRI"[5]

The Government's fall came suddenly and, to all but a few, unexpectedly. On the night of June 8 a listless debate on the spirits clauses of Childer's budget was lulling members into drowsiness. The Opposition had, in the name of Sir Michael

[4] Morley, *Gladstone*, III, pp. 170-98; B. Holland, *The Life of Spencer Compton, Eighth Duke of Devonshire* (hereafter *Devonshire*), London, 1911, II, pp. 60-61.

[5] This term was used by T. M. Healy to describe the fall of Gladstone's ministry. See his *Letters and Leaders of My Day*, New York, 1929, I, pp. 207-11.

Hicks Beach, moved an amendment against any increase in duties. A leading Parnellite T. P. O'Connor has described the Commons' temper that night as one of "utter forlornness," dispelled only by a lively, witty speech from Gladstone. When the division bell sounded, the Parnellites as usual walked into the Opposition lobby with the Conservatives. So far nothing out of the ordinary had occurred. Then word began to spread that the ranks filing into the Government lobby were thinner than those of the Opposition. An air of nervous expectancy settled upon the House. Even before the tellers could declare their numbers, the news of the Government's defeat was out. Lord Randolph Churchill, half-mad with joy, jumped up and down on the bench waving his handkerchief and yelling like a master of hounds who has sighted game. While pandemonium reigned among the Opposition benches, and with the Irish members joining in with shouts of "Coercion!" and "Buckshot!", Gladstone, oblivious to all, calmly scratched away on his writing pad, reporting the night's proceedings to the Queen.[6]

The defeat stunned most of the House and all the public. It was hard enough to account for the division, but harder still to explain Gladstone's behavior. He made no effort to save his ministry by moving the adjournment. Instead, amidst the dying tumult, he walked over to shake hands with the Liberal chief whip Lord Richard Grosvenor. Three days later he formally announced the Government's resignation. Since that night the question has been asked many times: what caused the Government's collapse? Tim Healy, the razor-tongued Irish nationalist, always something of a gamin at heart, called it an act of "hara-kiri." The Liberal whips, on the other hand, protested—perhaps a shade too vehemently—that the result was entirely unforeseen, the product of an unfortunate coincidence of events. This testimony did not corroborate the evidence of many Liberal members, who complained of having received no "whip" before the division. Over seventy Liberals were absent from the House and only fourteen of these were paired.

Healy's explanation strikes closer to the mark than any other.

[6] W. S. Churchill, *Lord Randolph Churchill* (hereafter *Churchill*), London, 1906, I, pp. 399-400; T. P. O'Connor, *Memoirs of an Old Parliamentarian*, London, 1929, I, pp. 351-57.

As in so many political crises of this period, the presence of Chamberlain hovers in the background, powerful and secretive, seen in fleeting glimpses here and there. And yet the evidence is never quite sufficient to convict him. This time, however, all signs indicate that the Government courted defeat in order to end their anguish and to prevent a split between the two wings of the party. The main burden of proof comes from Lord Acton, an intimate friend and counselor of Gladstone, and a Home Ruler to boot. According to Acton, who learnt it on "the best Birmingham authority," the division was arranged by the "Birmingham wire-pullers" so as to save the party from an irreparable breach. Acton's source, needless to say, was none other than Chamberlain, who happened to be his tenant at Princes Gate.[7]

Everyone close to the cabinet early in 1885 sensed that ministers dreaded the prospect of a longer stay in office. Hartington had written revealingly to Spencer: "When is this damned Government going out?"; and Gladstone needed no reminding that his Whig and Radical colleagues had been at loggerheads for months, if not years. In addition, Dilke had already promised Parnell's lieutenant Tim Healy that the Government would not renew the Crimes Act but would "ride for a fall" instead; and during the debate on June 8 he had warned the House that ministers intended to treat the spirits clauses as a "question of life and death."[8] After May 9 Chamberlain, according to his biographer, wished the Government to topple "as soon as its voluntary demise could be arranged with tolerable decency." The large number of Radicals abstaining from the division is further evidence of his contribution to the ministry's fall. Less than a year later Chamberlain openly admitted to Balfour: "It is no particular secret now that what destroyed the last Liberal Government was not the Budget but the proposal of a National Council for Ireland."[9] Other Liberal members, who were apathetic about or hostile to the budget and hopeful of a fresh lease of life come

[7] Selections from the Correspondence of the First Lord Acton, London, 1917, I, p. 265.

[8] Healy, op.cit., I, pp. 208-09.

[9] J. L. Garvin, The Life of Joseph Chamberlain (hereafter Chamberlain), London, 1932-1934, I, p. 605; B. E. C. Dugdale, Arthur James Balfour, First Earl of Balfour (hereafter Balfour), London, 1936, I, p. 99.

November, helped to make up the abstentions necessary for defeat. As far back as January, Hicks Beach had suspected that the Government might try to "ride cleverly for a fall"; and as J. L. Hammond pointedly observed, some ministers considered the end of cabinet strife well worth the price of defeat.

The official Liberal version of the defeat rests on the theory that the Conservatives and the Parnellites conspired together in secret to overthrow the Government. James Bryce, a staunch Home Ruler after 1885, elaborated an account of Tory subterfuge, based on his discovery of Parnell in deep conversation with the Conservative chief whip Rowland Winn in a corridor of the House of Commons only a few hours before the crucial division. On the lookout for collusion, Bryce interpreted the results of the division as final proof of Opposition skulduggery.[10]

The story of the Parnell-Winn interview is cluttered with half-truths. More than two years later Winn, by now Lord St. Oswald, sought Salisbury's advice on the best way to dispel the rumor of a Conservative compact with Parnell in June, 1885. In the newspapers Winn firmly denied having had an interview with Parnell about Irish affairs on that or on any other occasion. In private, however, he reminded Salisbury that he had seen the Irish leader at least twice on February 28, 1885, the night of the vote of censure over Khartoum. On that occasion the Parnellites had voted with the Opposition, reducing Gladstone's majority to fourteen, but only after receiving assurances from the Conservative leaders about the Irish clauses of the Franchise Bill. Winn had promised Parnell, who showed much anxiety on this score, that his party would stand by their pledge not to tamper with the Irish representation of 103 members. Nothing was said about Home Rule; and Winn, as Salisbury later confirmed, gave no pledges on the subject. The former chief whip, whose memory was fallible, insisted that no "official interview" with Parnell took place on June 8; and Salisbury, after searching his papers, affirmed that he had not authorized any communications with the Parnellites on the eve of the division.[11]

[10] H. A. L. Fisher, *James Bryce*, New York, 1927, I, pp. 209-10.
[11] St. Oswald to Salisbury, 28, 31 Oct. and 4 Nov. 1887, 15, 19 Dec. 1890; Salisbury to St. Oswald, 30 Oct. and 1, 5 Nov. 1887, 18 Dec. 1890, Salisbury MSS. See also St. Oswald's memorandum for 28 Feb. 1885, *ibid.*

In spite of Bryce's allegations, the Conservatives had no need to bargain with Parnell on that particular date. An unofficial agreement between the two parties had been arranged late in May by Lord Randolph Churchill under circumstances shortly to be explained. By voting with the Conservatives on June 8 the Parnellites were only continuing a tradition established by Spencer's coercive regime. The point is important because Home Rulers later accused the Conservatives of having promised Parnell Home Rule in return for his aid in upsetting Gladstone's ministry. In view of the Liberals' own connivance at defeat in June, their subsequent recriminations about the "Tory-Parnellite alliance" have a somewhat hollow ring.

III. THE CONSERVATIVE PARTY, 1880-1885

The Conservative party as of June, 1885, was in no position to boast of party solidarity and strength. Like the Liberals they had experienced discord, the only difference being that their quarrels had become public knowledge, well advertised and embellished in the national press. Since 1880 the Conservatives had passed through a series of internal crises damaging both to morale and to their position in the country. In the first place, the party had no official leader after Lord Beaconsfield's death in April, 1881. None of the ranking members possessed sufficient respect or experience to fill the huge gap left by his passing. In the hope of avoiding ill-feeling, the party leaders agreed to leave the chief position in abeyance and to substitute a duumvirate consisting of Sir Stafford Northcote in the Commons and Salisbury in the Lords.[12]

For the next four years the party labored under this double yoke. The conduct of the Opposition towards the Arrears Bill in August, 1882, exposed the disadvantages of divided leadership. When Salisbury prepared to move some hostile amendments against the measure in the Lords, a large number of Conservative peers adopted Northcote's conciliatory attitude and decided to vote against the amendments at the last minute. Salisbury was left high and dry, and could only inveigh in private against the weak-

[12] For an account of the duumvirate see W. S. Churchill, *Churchill*, I, pp. 145 ff.; and Lady Gwendolen Cecil, *Life of Robert Marquis of Salisbury* (hereafter *Salisbury*), London, 1921-1932, III, pp. 38-124.

hearted behavior of his party. On such occasions only personal ties of affection and loyalty between the Conservative leaders held the partnership together.

The dual control had lasting repercussions. Few Conservatives questioned Salisbury's qualifications to lead in the Lords: besides being their most forceful speaker in the House, he surpassed them all in his grasp of foreign affairs. But Northcote's conduct in the Commons as well as his poor health prompted sharp criticism from Conservatives, who resented his habit of truckling to the prime minister. Sir Stafford's proverbial respect for Gladstone was in their opinion seriously impairing his effectiveness as leader of the Opposition.

The resultant disaffection in the party was not just spontaneous: it received organized expression and a stimulus from Lord Randolph Churchill, who never suffered timid or mediocre men gladly. Dubbing his leader "the Goat," Churchill made a great show of flouting the party whips; and his increasing irritation over Northcote's tactical errors found an outlet in the sallies of the famed Fourth party. The public soon received the impression that Lord Randolph was not merely opposing Northcote but was actively campaigning in favor of his own candidacy for the leadership. This suspicion gained currency in two ways. First, Churchill appealed in print for a leader fit to inherit "Elijah's Mantle"—preferably someone not drawn from the overstuffed chairs of the Carlton Club, where the "old gang," an epithet inspired by his gerontophobia, sought refuge from decisions. And second, he set out in 1883 to capture the party's popular organization, or "handmaid," the National Union of Conservative and Constitutional Associations. The details of Churchill's campaign to undermine the party's central committee are not strictly relevant. Suffice it to say that, even after the compromise of July, 1884, many party members neither forgot nor forgave Churchill's gibes about "double-barrelled mediocrities," bourgeois backgrounds, and "Hibernian legal minds." Relying on his popularity in the constituencies, Churchill was already preparing to inject a large dose of Tory democracy into the hardening arteries of the party when the Liberal ministry collapsed.[13]

[13] A partisan account of Lord Randolph's bid for power is contained in R. R. James, *Lord Randolph Churchill*, London, 1959, chaps. 3-6. See also W. S. Churchill, *op.cit.*, i, chaps. 5-10.

The Conservative party lacked ideas as well as cohesion. However suspect the ideology of *"omnia sanitas"* and empire that Disraeli constructed, at least it provided the party with slogans and measures attractive to the urban voter. But after 1880 the Conservatives continued to lose ground, and showed little imagination in refurbishing the party platform. Only Churchill—who inspired distrust, if not aversion, among his older colleagues by methods and language reminiscent of Chamberlain—understood the policies that would appeal to an electorate who were tired of outworn shibboleths and platitudes. Salisbury, whose real passion was foreign affairs, served as a storm anchor in domestic politics, exerting a steady drag on the forces of change. Unlike Disraeli, he never trusted the working classes: he assumed that if given the chance they would gladly redistribute the country's private wealth among themselves and subscribe to the "new Radicalism" of Chamberlain and Dilke by pulling down the hallowed structure of the established church. To Salisbury, who happened to believe that good churchmen also made good Conservatives, the cry for disestablishment represented all the destructive or leveling forces in society: it had to be resisted at all costs. Resenting democracy, especially the American variety, he warned against the menace of the caucus, which, if unchecked, would sooner or later appropriate the functions of Parliament.

If the party was deficient in policies, it suffered also from a paucity of talent in the House of Commons. After 1880 the Opposition front bench contained few men with enough calibre to answer the heavy artillery on the ministerial side. Churchill had established his reputation as a first-class speaker, but his barbed taunts were aimed at his own colleagues almost as often as they were at the official enemy. Another Conservative of merit was Sir Michael Hicks Beach, who had impressed the House with his firm and incisive manner. A man of considerable political experience, devoid of affectation and eloquence, Beach was an able administrator rather than leader. Obstinate in his convictions and cautious in his politics—Tory democracy never excited him—he arrived at decisions only after long deliberation with his conscience. Although sympathetic with Churchill, he had kept clear of the Fourth party and the National Union imbroglio. Familiarly known as Black Michael, he possessed a fierce temper, which, when aroused, drove all before it. But a genuine sensitivity, even shyness, underlay this formidable exterior; and many colleagues admired his reserve if not his frugal tastes. A less generous critic once described him as having "the manners of a pirate and the courage of a governess";[14] but few saw the pusillanimous side of Beach.

Apart from these two luminaries and Northcote, there were a number of lesser lights. The veteran R. A. Cross, Disraeli's worthy but pedestrian home secretary, was one of Churchill's favorite targets in the "old gang." John Gorst, the shrewd and waspish party organizer, who had served with distinction in the Fourth party, had a gift for making enemies that deprived him of high office. Two other men destined for cabinet rank were reliable but never brilliant: W. H. Smith, whose fortune had not blemished his morality, and Lord George Hamilton, son of the Duke of Abercorn, the great Irish landowner. Last but not quite least, there was Arthur Balfour, the nephew of Lord Salisbury, who gave every appearance of preferring abstract ideas, repose, and parlor games to politics. In a parliamentary sense he had not yet come of age. Having toyed with the Fourth party, he gradually withdrew from the councils of this ginger group, once he divined Churchill's ulterior purpose in attacking the Conservative leadership. As the *Daily News* remarked about the relationship between Churchill and Balfour: "They were friends at first but afterwards became contemporaries." In general, the rank and file of the party were men better known for their sporting or brewing interests than for political acuteness. But it was the front bench that mattered, and for the poverty of talent there Beaconsfield was partly to blame. Not only had he failed to recruit enough able men, but he had elevated effective debaters like Gathorne-Hardy into the political limbo of the upper House. Fate had already deprived the party in the Commons of their most promising front bencher, Lord Cranborne, who was removed to the House of Lords on the death of his father in 1868.

The outlook for the Conservatives in June, 1885, was not without one redeeming feature. At least the party had the backing of the Queen, who had not recovered from Beaconsfield's heady flatteries. Having acquired a distaste for Liberals, whom she con-

---

[14] This was Balfour's appraisal. See Sir Austen Chamberlain, *Politics from Inside An Epistolary Chronicle 1906-1914*, London, 1936, p. 183.

sidered tainted with republicanism, the Queen welcomed a change of ministry. In her view Gladstone had made a shambles of British foreign policy, exposing the country to world-wide ridicule; and she feared lest concessions to Irish "vandalism" set a dangerous precedent in England. Queen Victoria never wasted any affection on the Irish, whom she had not forgiven for refusing to send a delegation to Prince Albert's funeral. And subsequent Fenian attempts to blow up the consort's statue in Dublin were hardly calculated to ease her mind on this score.[15]

Toward Ireland the Conservative party, in general, had displayed a consistently negative attitude. Accepting only a landlord's version of the land question, they blamed Irish unrest on professional demagogues who had scared Gladstone into making dangerous concessions. Like so many educated Englishmen of their day they regarded the Irish as a primitive people: uncivilized, unwashed, and deeply superstitious. And Ireland itself was England's backyard, which, with the exception of Dublin, the midlands, and Ulster, was a wasteland beyond either material or moral redemption. When forced to consider Irish legislation, the majority of Conservatives instinctively thought of coercion and famine relief. Parnellism struck them as another name for expropriation of the propertied classes. To deal with obstruction in Parliament they supported with some misgivings Gladstone's closure resolutions in 1882, even though Churchill and Hicks Beach condemned this "foreign practice" as an invasion of parliamentary custom. At first only the more enterprising members of the party advocated land purchase, and their chief concern lay with adequate compensation for the landlords. In a vengeful mood after Gladstone's invasions of property rights, they insisted that the state had acquired thereby an obligation to the landlord class that could be discharged only by loaning large sums on imperial credit to purchasing tenants. In 1883 Lord George Hamilton had introduced a bill that provided for the advance by the state of the whole purchase price, and although the measure was defeated, it served as the model for all future Conservative legislation in this field.

A more important question to be asked about the events of

[15] See *The Letters of Queen Victoria*, ed. G. E. Buckle, New York, 1926, 2d series, I, pp. 575-77, and II, pp. 136-38, 213-16.

June, 1885, is why Salisbury chose to accept office at all. The circumstances could not have been more inauspicious. Being in a minority, the Conservatives could form a government only with Irish support and on Liberal sufferance. Moreover, a general election based on the new voting registers was due to take place in November. The political situation bore a striking resemblance to that in March, 1873, when the wily Disraeli had refused to take office after Gladstone's defeat on the Irish University Bill.[16] That Salisbury was more than aware of the disadvantages of office in 1885 can be seen in some of his statements at the time.

In the first place, the obvious hunger of many Conservatives for office did not materially affect his decision. The division on June 8 he considered "anything but a subject for congratulation."[17] Appreciating the dangers of a minority government with only a few months left before the election, he could not share the joy of Churchill and his sympathizers at the Liberals' defeat. The alacrity with which Gladstone had resigned over a relatively minor issue, as well as the circumstances of that defeat, heightened his suspicions; and the party whips were asked to investigate why the Liberal majority had failed to materialize on that occasion.[18] In the previous month Salisbury had tried to warn Churchill about the folly of precipitate action. To turn Gladstone out, he wrote on May 7, would be a "nuisance" in view of the far more crucial "battle" to be fought at the general election. And a week later he reminded Lord Randolph: "Our chance in November will be all the better for our not winning now."[19]

Another factor weighing heavily on Salisbury's mind was the position of his co-leader in the House of Commons. Upon learning of Gladstone's intention to resign, the Queen had sent for Salisbury, not for Northcote; and feelings of loyalty to his friend made Salisbury reluctant to accept the premiership. But the majority of the party did not share these scruples. They wanted the vigorous leadership that Northcote had failed to give them. The strength of feeling against Sir Stafford among the rank and file

[16] See Disraeli's memorandum on the subject in G. E. Buckle, *The Life of . . . Beaconsfield*, London, 1920, v, p. 211.

[17] Cecil, *Salisbury*, III, p. 133.

[18] Viscount Chilston, *Chief Whip*, London, 1961, p. 44.

[19] Salisbury to Churchill, 7, 14 May 1885, Salisbury MSS.

surprised and even shocked some of his older colleagues, who blamed Churchill for this state of affairs. Even putting personal considerations aside, Lord Salisbury was reluctant to form a ministry. "To have to govern six months with a hostile but dying Parliament," he wrote, "is the very worst thing that can happen to us." The prospect of an Irish alliance and recollections of Lord Derby's precarious ministries increased his distaste for office.[20]

During the fortnight's interregnum that followed the Liberal defeat Salisbury received advice from various party members, who stressed the disadvantages of office. Some of the older Conservatives actually tried to foil any attempt to form a government. On June 15 a small band of "orthodox" Conservatives defied the party whips by joining Churchill and Hicks Beach in moving the adjournment. The resultant split in the party at division time astonished many, but none so much as Northcote. As Lord Eustace Cecil explained to his brother, he and his friends had supported Churchill's motion against Northcote in order "*purposely* to *accentuate* the apparent division of the Party in the eyes of the Public—and render its return to office impracticable."[21]

In the face of such omens why did Salisbury, against his better judgment, accept the hazards of leading a minority government? The answer lies in Salisbury's relationship with the Queen and his concern for foreign affairs. When Salisbury arrived at Balmoral on June 12, he found the Queen in a state of alarm over the prospect of Gladstone's return to power. The vehemence of her appeal overcame his initial aversion to taking office and also eased his feelings of conscience toward Northcote. With unconcealed reluctance he agreed to form a ministry, but only on condition that the Liberals give definite guarantees that they would not impede the ordinary business of Parliament before the dissolution. Apart from his susceptibility to the Queen's blandishments, what ultimately decided Salisbury to take office was the perilous state of foreign affairs. The Queen had appealed to him to pick up the pieces of Gladstone's diplomacy, and the temptation proved too great for him to surmount. As Balfour later observed, Salisbury accepted the Queen's commission in order to control foreign policy: ". . . home affairs were not what mainly interested

[20] Cecil, *Salisbury*, III, pp. 132-33.
[21] Lord Eustace Cecil to Salisbury, 16 June 1885, Salisbury MSS.

him at this particular moment, perhaps at very few moments."[22]
On June 24 the new prime minister kissed hands, and the Caretaker ministry formally came into being. Whether or not he
placed duty to the Queen above concern for his country's tarnished
prestige—and the two were not unrelated in his mind—the fact
remains that from a strictly party point of view Salisbury's action
proved a costly mistake.

The formation of the new government caused Salisbury endless
anxiety and trouble. Not only did the problem of extracting
adequate pledges from Gladstone confront him, but Lord Randolph's petulance, his extravagant demands about the composition
of the new ministry, caused much hard feeling. On the first score
delicate negotiations between the leaders of the two parties lasted
for almost a fortnight; and the Queen's private secretary Sir
Henry Ponsonby spent these days "diving backwards and forwards" between 10 Downing Street and Salisbury's residence in
Arlington Street. Although Gladstone objected to the principle of
guaranteeing such forbearance, he eventually agreed to an ambiguous pledge, which Salisbury accepted, albeit with misgiving.[23]

The second difficulty caused the Conservative leader even
greater vexation. Northcote, already upset by the Queen's choice,
refused to become first lord of the Treasury; Churchill, determined to exact a high price for his services, turned down the
offer of the India Office so long as Northcote remained leader of
the party in the Commons; and Beach, learning of Churchill's
decision, declined the Colonial Office. While Lord Randolph kept
aloof, privately ranting against the "old gang," Salisbury contemplated the perversities of human nature and decided that his
pledge to the Queen and party unity took precedence over personal
emotions. After a number of painful interviews and several meet-

[22] A. J. Balfour, *Chapters of Autobiography*, London, 1930, p. 193.
Salisbury's reluctance to form a ministry in 1885 was substantiated by
Lord Randolph Churchill who wrote a memorandum on the subject. But
this interpretation conflicts with that of Sir Henry Ponsonby who found
Salisbury "much pleased" at the prospect of office in June. Ponsonby
presumably based this misleading impression on Salisbury's anxiety over
Liberal failures in foreign affairs. See W. S. Churchill, *op.cit.*, i, pp. 402-
07; *Letters of Queen Victoria*, 2d series, iii, p. 660.

[23] Morley, *Gladstone*, iii, pp. 203-08; *Letters of Queen Victoria*, 2d
series, iii, pp. 662 ff.

ings of the "shadow cabinet," Northcote agreed to accept a peerage and the first lordship of the Treasury; Churchill went to the India Office after recommending his two henchmen in the Fourth party for office; and Hicks Beach emerged as chancellor of the Exchequer and leader of the House. The whole transaction was characterized by the indignation of the "old gang" against Lord Randolph for his extreme presumption. Under humiliating circumstances Sir Stafford Northcote had been elevated into virtual obscurity as the Earl of Iddesleigh, and Churchill had some grounds for believing that "Elijah's Mantle" might not be so remote after all.

IV. SALISBURY AND IRELAND

Although the life of the new ministry depended upon the co-operation of the Irish party, Salisbury was notably miscast in the role of Parnell's ally. His ignorance of Ireland was matched only by his antipathy for Irish national aspirations. Having been Indian secretary under Disraeli, he knew more about the problems of that country than he did about Ireland. He was not ignorant of land tenure practice in the other island, but his landlord instincts did not allow him to feel much sympathy for the tenants' point of view. The Foreign Office opened fascinating vistas to his mind, and he preferred international affairs to the more mundane pursuit of domestic politics. The Irish Question, being an issue neither wholly domestic nor foreign, had been a blind spot in his political periphery, and in this respect he resembled the vast majority of his countrymen. In spite of his travels as a young man halfway round the world to the gold fields of Australia, Salisbury had never visited Ireland. Disraeli managed to avoid Ireland altogether; and Gladstone made the trip only once, for three weeks in 1877. Salisbury, in fact, never showed much desire to see what he considered an uncivilized country with a moist climate, where the priests vied with the Fenians for the allegiance of the people. Like many other Englishmen he found St. George's Channel a serious inconvenience. When refusing an invitation to visit Ulster in 1882, he confessed: "Moreover there is the four hours sea passage."[24] And yet he endured the rigors of the English

[24] Salisbury to Northcote, 12 Sept. 1882, Iddesleigh MSS.

Channel several times a year on his way to his summer retreat at Puys, near Dieppe, or to the Riviera.

Ignorance of the topography and customs of a country does not necessarily preclude interest in its problems. As an English landowner he wished to protect the rights of the same class in Ireland and to prevent the tenant agitation from spreading to England. In Opposition he had used Irish distress and unrest as an excuse to belabor the Liberals. Twenty years earlier, as Lord Robert Cecil, he had supported a motion calling for relief measures in Ireland. The Liberal chief secretary had blandly denied the existence of any distress, and this display of complacency moved Lord Robert to deplore the record of English exploitation in Ireland. "It is a mere mockery," he declared, "first to bind her hand and foot and then to tell her to run a race with other countries which depend on their own resources." And he urged ministers to "repair the evils your fathers have done . . . to increase the general strength of the Empire, and to remove something like a moral slur from the honour of England."[25] On subsequent occasions he had spoken out in favor of stimulating the Irish economy and suppressing agrarian crime. Although vehemently opposed to Irish disestablishment, he had voted for Gladstone's bill in 1869 because "the nation" had been consulted on this issue at the general election.

Salisbury, however, drew the line at Gladstone's tampering with the land laws in Ireland. In 1870 he condemned the arbitrary manner in which the prime minister was trying to transfer the rights of landlords to their tenants. Conciliation to Salisbury meant moderate grants to promote native industries and relief funds in time of famine. It did not mean abrogating property rights in the hopes of reducing the inveterate hatred of the Irish for England; and it did not preclude coercion to cope with lawlessness. At times Salisbury candidly admitted his scepticism about the efficacy of conciliatory legislation. If anything, concessions or the "incessant doctoring and meddling" of English politicians had aggravated rather than alleviated disorder in Ireland. As he wrote in the *Quarterly Review* of October, 1872, recent events had convinced the Irish peasantry that violence always produced concession: by blowing up Clerkenwell prison, the

---

[25] Hansard, *Parliamentary Debates,* 3d series, Vol. 177, pp. 721-22.

Fenians had brought down the Irish Church, while the systematic murder of landlords and land agents had led to the Land Act of 1870. The next demand would be for political separation, and the widening appeal of the slogan "Ireland for the Irish" gave cause for serious alarm. In a brief but significant passage Salisbury summed up his feelings about the Act of Union. "On Tory principles the case presents much that is painful, but no perplexity whatever. Ireland must be kept, like India, at all hazards: by persuasion, if possible; if not, by force." The greatest single danger to the Union, he warned, lay in the sentimental notion of Liberals that Ireland ought to be governed in accordance with the desires of disloyal and irresponsible Irishmen.

The debates on the Land Act of 1881 revealed Salisbury's true colors as a champion of property rights. According to Sir Michael Hicks Beach the Conservative peer had declared that "as we had to deal with a mad man in Gladstone, it was necessary to have a mad man on the other side, and he offered himself for the purpose."[26] But even his sustained efforts could not stop Gladstone from implementing what was derisively called a system of "dual ownership" in Ireland. During the Arrears Bill contretemps of 1882 Salisbury showed his contempt for "weak-kneed" men. When the majority of Irish peers and the Ulster landlords in particular followed Lord Cairns and the Duke of Richmond in opposing the amendments to the measure, Salisbury regarded their behavior with disgust. Although aware that fear of a dissolution and electoral considerations in Ulster weighed heavily in their decision, he could not forgive them for having abandoned their principles over a bill that presumably had its origins in the Kilmainham Treaty. To Northcote he vented his anger: "Anyhow, it will be one consolation that in any future struggles we shall not be under any obligation to defer to the wayward tactics of Irish landowners. Their notion of self-defence is that you should fight for them under the condition of not causing them the slightest agitation of mind by your blows."[27]

The issue of franchise reform in 1884 showed that Salisbury was more worried about repercussions in England arising from an extended suffrage. Edward Gibson, the Conservatives' expert on

[26] Hicks Beach, *St. Aldwyn*, I, p. 201.
[27] Salisbury to Northcote, 10 Aug. 1882, Iddesleigh MSS.

Irish affairs, informed him in January: "Redistribution is needed in Ireland, but no scheme of Redistribution—if there is a lowering of the franchise, and *if* the present number of members is maintained—could avoid the strengthening of Parnell's party. I am satisfied that Harcourt and many others would like to have a substantial reduction of the Irish members—but . . . I question that the cabinet have courage *even* for this." Gibson also contended that "many" in Ireland and "everyone" in England and Scotland would welcome such a reduction, acting on the principle that "it is as well to be hanged for a sheep as a lamb."[28] But no responsible English politician dared to tamper with the Irish representation, and, as Lord Salisbury wrote to Northcote, the Irish landlords deserved their fate under the new measure for having failed to oppose effectively Gladstone's land legislation in the past. Far more alarmed by the "new Radicalism" emergent in England, he minimized the effects of the concession upon the nationalist cause. "As to the Parnellite members," he wrote, "are they worse than Radicals pledged to do all the Irish want? I think they are much better. They carry with them none of the moral weight which comes with the support of a sympathetic English Radical: and the Irish who would return such a member— everyone of them voted against us in 1880—never made Radical majorities."[29] He failed to foresee that Parnell might soon be in a position to make majorities of his own in Parliament, while bringing Ireland much closer to Home Rule.

Salisbury's views on the Irish Question were thus undistinguished by a spirit of altruism. As a politician he had used Ireland in order to embarrass the Liberals; and as a vigorous defender of landlords' rights he had fought against Gladstone's concessions to the tenantry. Several other factors in 1885 also restricted his approach to the Irish Question. The minority status of the Caretaker ministry provided no incentive for a bold departure in Irish policy. And Salisbury's inexperience as premier, added to his insistence upon combining that burdensome office with the foreign secretaryship, meant that there was little chance of his doing justice simultaneously to domestic problems, to Ireland, and to British interests abroad in the short time re-

[28] Gibson to Salisbury, 27 Jan. 1884, Salisbury MSS.
[29] Salisbury to Northcote, 4, 21 Dec. 1884, Iddesleigh MSS.

maining before the election. Lord Salisbury, therefore, began his first administration by underestimating the momentum that Parnell had imparted to the Irish Question. Anxious to repair the damage caused by Gladstone's foreign policy, he tended to ignore Ireland until events threatened to destroy his ministry on this very issue.

V. THE PARNELLITE ALLIANCE

The first major decision facing the new administration concerned the future of the Crimes Act. Ministers were not slow to realize that their survival in office depended upon their ability to offer the Parnellites a policy of conciliation. Even before the Liberal debacle Churchill and Hicks Beach had made up their minds on the subject. Early in May Beach advised Salisbury that he could see no excuse for continuing to coerce Ireland. If any doubts existed about the indispensability of the Crimes Act, then he considered it wiser to leave Gladstone in office. Only Lord Salisbury, he declared, had sufficient authority to persuade the party to abandon coercion. Lord Randolph had stated the case more forcefully. The Conservatives, he knew, had no chance of staying in power without Parnell's blessing; and he worked hard to convince the Irish leader that his party had nothing but good intentions toward Ireland. Churchill, in fact, made nonrenewal of coercion one of the two conditions of his accepting office; and he went so far as to intimate in public that if the Liberals were defeated, the Conservatives would allow the act to lapse.[30]

A closer study of the situation shows that the Conservatives had very little choice in the matter of coercion: renewal of the Crimes Act would automatically have lost them the Irish vote. Moreover, early in June Edward Gibson reported that the condition of Ireland justified the experiment of governing without special legislation. He admitted that the situation was delicate and that everything depended upon Parnell's mood. If the Irish leader chose to wring concessions from Parliament by force, he could easily incite the tenants to commit crimes. Gibson urged that an understanding with Parnell would calm the country as well as prolong the Conservative sojourn in office.[31]

[30] W. S. Churchill, *Churchill*, I, pp. 390-91.
[31] Gibson to Salisbury, 15 June 1885, Salisbury MSS.

Such an understanding already existed. Without Salisbury's permission Churchill had approached Parnell in the latter part of May and promised that the Conservatives would not coerce Ireland. It was no accident that Lord Randolph should have approached the Parnellites on this question. Not only did he count several friends and many admirers among the Irish members, but, as a politician more than usually concerned with power and its uses, he was one of the first Conservatives to recognize the New Departure and to advocate some understanding with this powerful third force in the Commons. Recalling his interview with Parnell, Lord Randolph wrote: "There was no compact or bargain of any kind, but I told Parnell when he sat on that sofa [in Connaught Place] that if the Tories took office and I was a member of their government, I would not consent to renew the Crimes Act. Parnell replied, 'in that case, you will have the Irish vote at the Elections.' "[32]

Whatever else was said at this meeting, which was more decisive in its effects than Carnarvon's famous interview, the fact remained that a leading Conservative had promised to do away with coercion. Parnell was obviously impressed. But as rumors of the understanding spread through the political world, some of the older Conservatives grew apprehensive. The very idea of an alliance with such "unscrupulous" men as the Irish members, arranged by the *enfant terrible* of their party, appalled them.[33]

If Lord Salisbury shared some of these misgivings, he did not order Churchill to repudiate his unsolicited remarks. Instead, he asked Lord Carnarvon to accept the Irish viceroyship and sent him to Dublin to learn whether the condition of the country justified the acceptance of Churchill's pledge to Parnell. Carnarvon returned from Ireland on July 4 and informed his colleagues that the outlook was bleak but not hopeless. From talks with Sir Robert Hamilton, the permanent under secretary, he gathered that what the country needed most was relief from coercion. "Ireland," according to Hamilton, "has leant so much on special legislation

[32] W. S. Churchill, *op.cit.*, I, p. 395.
[33] Such was the reaction of Lord Cranbrook. See A. E. Gathorne Hardy, *Gathorne Hardy, First Earl of Cranbrook: A Memoir* (hereafter *Cranbrook*), London, 1910, II, p. 215.

that it has hardly appreciated how much she can walk alone." The influential under secretary, who had become a convert to Home Rule, argued that the attempt to govern Ireland without a crimes act would please everyone. Moonlighting and intimidation, in his opinion, could be checked by the ordinary law.[34] E. G. Jenkinson, head of the Irish CID, and another Home Ruler, also informed Carnarvon that the state of the country justified abandoning coercion.[35] The cabinet listened to Carnarvon's report and then formally approved the policy of conciliation. In view of the political circumstances, they had no real alternative.

[34] Excerpt from Carnarvon's memorandum on talk with Hamilton, 30 June 1885, Carnarvon MSS. See also Hamilton's memorandum on the Crimes Act of 1882, 8 June 1885, *ibid.*

[35] See Carnarvon's notes on talk with Jenkinson, n.d. June 1885, *ibid.*; and Jenkinson's memorandum, "On the organization of the United Brotherhood, or Clan-na-Gael, in the United States," 26 Jan. 1885, Salisbury MSS.

CHAPTER III

The Carnarvon Experiment

THE NEW lord lieutenant possessed most of the attributes of the scholar-statesman. Like the 14th Earl of Derby and Gladstone he was passionately devoted to the classics, and he found an outlet for his intellectual leanings in translating Homer and Aeschylus, in writing historical sketches for well-known journals or reviews, and in studying languages and the graphic arts. He was a man of unusual sensitivity and gentleness; his health was almost as delicate as his feelings. Although sharing Gladstone's humanitarian instincts, he lacked the latter's physical and intellectual resilience. His experience as colonial secretary had taught him the virtues of self-government and imperial federation. He had drafted a federal constitution for Canada, and had worked hard, if in vain, to accomplish the same feat in South Africa.[1] There were no aggressive traits in Carnarvon: he disliked political strife almost as much as war. From a party point of view his major defect was a proclivity for resignation. He had what Lord George Hamilton described as a "microbe of incurable fidgetiness" in his character.[2] In 1867 he had resigned with Salisbury in protest against extending the franchise; and in 1878 he abandoned office once again, this time over the decision to resist the Russian advance on Constantinople. For such reasons he made a poor "party man" and would have been far happier as a Whig living in the age of Melbourne. His second resignation led to some cooling of relations with Salisbury. The latter continued to respect Carnarvon's abilities; but their friendship, as Lady Gwendolen Cecil pointedly remarked, became a "shell of habit."[3]

An important proviso governed Carnarvon's appointment: he

[1] See Hardinge, *Carnarvon*, I, pp. 285-333; II, pp. 155-324.
[2] Hamilton, *Parliamentary Reminiscences and Reflections 1868-1906* (hereafter *Reminiscences*), London, 1917-1922, II, p. 10.
[3] Cecil, *Salisbury*, III, p. 153.

reserved the right to retire in December, no matter what the result of the general election. The rigors of the Irish climate were magnified in his mind by the poor state of his health. Reluctantly, Salisbury agreed to these terms, hoping to dissuade Carnarvon from his resolve when the time came. There were other reasons for Carnarvon's assignment to Ireland besides the friendship that had sprung up when he and Salisbury had been contemporaries at Eton and Christ Church, Oxford. The political situation required a man who could govern Ireland without the benefit of coercion. Hicks Beach could not be spared from the House of Commons or the Exchequer, and Churchill was considered too inexperienced and mercurial for the Dublin post. Only Carnarvon, Salisbury believed, could preserve the informal alliance with Parnell and at the same time conciliate the Irish people. For the post of chief secretary, without a seat in the cabinet, Sir William Hart Dyke was chosen. A proficient racquets player and a power in Kent politics, Dyke had served as chief whip in Disraeli's last administration and was thoroughly versed in the vagaries of party management. He lacked any special knowledge of Ireland and admired Carnarvon to the point of accepting his ideas on the Irish Question.

Salisbury knew perfectly well that Carnarvon advocated a federal solution to the problem of Anglo-Irish relations; no doubt he hoped that Carnarvon's reputation as an imperial federationist would ingratiate the new ministry with the nationalists and thereby keep Ireland calm until the election. Several months before his appointment, in fact, Carnarvon had opened his mind to Salisbury on the subject of Irish autonomy. It was his opinion that the Conservatives should prepare a rival Irish policy to match that of the Liberals during the election campaign. Deploring the past vacillation of English politicians on this issue, he argued that the alternation of concession and coercion had thoroughly demoralized the population. Convinced that Ireland deserved a chance to administer its own affairs, he had asked the distinguished Irish patriot Sir Charles Gavan Duffy to draft a plan for modified Home Rule along the lines of imperial federation. Gavan Duffy's proposals appeared in the *National Review* in February, 1885, and Carnarvon immediately drew Salisbury's attention to this article, which he believed would appeal to moderate nationalist opinion in Ireland. According to Carnarvon the Conservatives had three choices: they could "refuse, evade, or entertain" such a proposal.[4]

Lord Salisbury chose to evade. His reply, written before he had read the article, was guarded and vague. Writing from a purely hypothetical point of view he admitted that some form of Home Rule, with adequate safeguards for minorities, might be devised. But he had serious doubts about the practical application of any such plan; and he insisted that he would never consider any form of Irish self-government without the approval of a decisive majority on both sides of the Irish Channel. Even if Parnell returned from the next election with a party solidly pledged to Home Rule, that fact alone would not justify such a concession. Once he had read Gavan Duffy's article, Salisbury attacked the weakness of the proposed safeguards for the Protestant minority and suggested that what Ireland needed to counterbalance the nationalist majority in any decentralized scheme was a powerful authority, analogous to the United States Supreme Court, which would review the decisions of subordinate bodies.

The Carnarvon-Salisbury correspondence that preceded the fall of Gladstone's ministry thus served to clarify the views of both men on the Irish issue. Salisbury showed his readiness to discuss Home Rule only on a theoretical plane; and Carnarvon revealed his deep concern with Irish desires for self-government. The cabinet also knew of the viceroy's sentiments, but in their eagerness to get on with the business of government they were too apt to dismiss his arguments as whims of the moment.

I. PRESERVING THE ALLIANCE

On July 6 the Government announced their intentions at home and abroad. After referring to crises in Afghanistan and the Sudan, Salisbury denied the rumor that he and his colleagues wished to prolong the session as long as possible in order to enjoy the "sweets of office." No one was more anxious than he to finish the session, to dissolve, and to end the anomalous position the ministry occupied. Carnarvon followed this speech with a statement on Ireland. He reviewed the crime rate and expressed his regret that the country had, with a few brief interludes, lived

---

[4] Hardinge, *Carnarvon*, III, pp. 147-53.

under coercion since 1847. He called the Crimes Act not only inexpedient but obsolete. Some of its clauses had never been used, and the rise of boycotting and the National League proved only too clearly the deficiencies of the other provisions. The Government, he declared, were going to abandon coercion altogether in the belief that the Irish people would justify this confidence shown in them. He did not think that "the combination of good feeling to England and of good government to Ireland" was a hopeless task. Just as he had seen friendly relations in the colonies among English, Irish, and Scottish settlers, so he expected similar amity between England and Ireland.[5]

Carnarvon's announcement profoundly impressed Gladstone and his supporters, who suspected that the Conservatives had arranged a formal treaty with the Irish party. The Government were accused of "wooing Parnell"; and the rumor spread that Carnarvon was going to Ireland in order to draft a federal constitution. Two days after his speech in the Lords, Carnarvon wrote to Dyke from Ireland that his cordial reception in Dublin had contrasted strongly with the armed processions and jeers that had accompanied Spencer's departure. The success of the new administration, he believed, depended upon the Parnellites; and he asked the chief secretary as his spokesman in the Commons to do everything in his power to appease the Irish party. "It is the foundation and beginning of all improvement," he added.[6]

The Parnellites, however, made difficult allies; and the Maamtrasna debate gave them an ideal opportunity to test the nature of the new alliance. In the autumn of 1884 several Irish members had demanded an official review of capital sentences passed during Spencer's regime. Chief among the crimes involved was the notorious massacre of a family at Maamtrasna, in that desolate part of Connemara known as "Joyce's Country," in August, 1882.[7] At the time Churchill and his Fourth party had defended the Irish motion, while the majority of Conservatives had upheld both the sentences and Spencer's administration of the Crimes

[5] *Hansard,* 3d series, Vol. 298, pp. 1658-62.

[6] Carnarvon to Dyke, 8 July 1885, Carnarvon MSS.

[7] The ruthless murder of both parents and two children, which arose out of a local feud, shocked public opinion in both countries. See Hammond, *Gladstone and the Irish Nation,* pp. 315-24.

Act. Early in July, 1885, Parnell revived the controversy; and the cabinet met to discuss his demand for the appeal of sentences. Ministers were fully aware that any concession might undermine the Irish judiciary. But complications arose when Churchill and Hicks Beach decided to support Parnell's motion, in the belief that a refusal would endanger the Irish alliance. Both ministers felt that a simple guarantee of appeal would satisfy the Irish party; and Churchill added that he could not consistently refuse a motion he had once supported.

With a cabinet schism already defined, Beach asked Carnarvon on July 13 to give some assurance that cases involving the discovery of new evidence would qualify for the ordinary process of appellate review. But the viceroy hedged on the question, fearing lest the public receive the impression that the Government would entertain every Irish demand for review of capital sentences. Attaching great importance to the issue, he advised Salisbury that discredit, if not disaster, would follow any such concession. Only with reluctance would he agree to an official statement in Parliament that the administration would not deviate from the usual practice in such cases. The whole controversy unnerved Carnarvon; and Salisbury had to warn Beach against making any promises to the Irish party without the cabinet's consent.[8]

Beach, for his part, had no intention of pledging the administration to review the Maamtrasna sentences and other cases. On the contrary, he wished only to assure the Parnellites that the Irish judiciary would consider any future appeals without prejudice. In his brief statement on July 17, he informed the House that the viceroy would give his "personal attention" to any appeal properly forwarded. He also intimated that he found it impossible to approve much of Spencer's repressive policy in Ireland. Churchill, however, and his accomplice Gorst went much further. Reverting to the language of Fourth party days, Lord Randolph criticized the Government's narrow view of the situation; and Gorst's reference to "reactionary Ulster members" did not help matters. Recriminations followed rapidly. The Queen lectured Lord Salisbury about the dangers of indulging either the Parnellites or Churchill; and Salisbury confessed his annoy-

[8] W. S. Churchill, *Churchill*, I, pp. 436-44; Hicks Beach, *St. Aldwyn*, I, pp. 242-48; Cecil, *Salisbury*, III, pp. 144-49.

ance to Lady John Manners, his devoted confidante and the wife of a senior member of the Government: "I was very much vexed with what passed on Friday night. I fear it bodes ill for the cohesion of the party. I had spoken and written to Sir Michael and I thought I had persuaded him to pursue a more reasonable course. But the influence R. C. exerts over him is very perilous. If we hold together till the prorogation, it is as much as we can do."[9] Hart Dyke apologized to Carnarvon for having failed to limit the debate; and Beach promised to reprimand Churchill and Gorst. In the end Carnarvon, having been consoled by Salisbury, received and rejected the memorials of appeal with which the motion was concerned.

The repercussions of the debate were wholly disproportionate to the nature of the controversy. Lord Randolph, in trying to cement the Parnellite alliance, had succeeded in alarming his own party as well as the Liberals; while Parnell was amused by the Government's consternation. If the crisis proved nothing except that some ministers were willing to go further than others in bidding for the good will of the Irish party, the Liberals interpreted the Maamtrasna debate as tangible proof of an alliance between Conservatives and Parnellites. A new "Kilmainham Treaty," it seemed, was in the making, with Churchill filling the role formerly played by Chamberlain.

The Government soon recovered from the Maamtrasna affair and turned to more important matters. Several useful measures became law during the five weeks remaining in the session. But it was not long before a crisis developed in Ireland: on July 15 the Munster bank failed. After a fortnight of increasing anxiety about the state of the bank's finances, it was discovered that one of the managers had embezzled a sum amounting to £70,000. Having bungled an attempt "to smother up his own defalcations," the culprit fled the country, converted the money into diamonds, and disappeared. For some time the bank had been in difficulties, and not even a large loan from the Bank of Ireland had restored confidence in its credit. The majority of shareholders were small farmers and tradesmen, and in the event of a "run" on the bank's resources serious hardship would have ensued. In his eagerness to prevent such a panic Carnarvon acted promptly, but rather

[9] Salisbury to Lady John Manners, 19 July 1885, Salisbury MSS.

too generously for his colleagues' peace of mind, by assuring the directors that he would arrange to secure open credit at either the Bank of Ireland or Bank of England for the £500,000 needed to keep the bank solvent. The cabinet strongly disapproved any such undertaking, however, and Carnarvon was forced to back down in public by refusing the directors' request for aid. When the fraud came to light, the Munster bank had to enter into liquidation proceedings, and it was eventually reconstructed as the Munster and Leinster bank.[10] From Carnarvon's point of view the cabinet's coolness to his appeal for special measures proved a bitter disappointment. The *Freeman's Journal* had already advised the viceroy that he must not be deceived "into imagining that mere good intentions upon his part can bridge the chasm" between the two countries. And Salisbury had written to Carnarvon on July 22: "The hopelessness of managing England and Ireland together was never brought into such startling relief. . . . The old crucial question is still there. How is England to be made to swallow measures that Irish authorities consider necessary for Ireland?"[11]

One piece of legislation welcomed by the Irish tenantry was the Land Purchase Bill, which Gibson, by now Lord Ashbourne, introduced in the House of Lords on July 17. The Irish lord chancellor claimed no originality for the idea of creating peasant proprietors, but hoped that this measure, which was based on earlier plans proposed by Lord George Hamilton and Sir George Trevelyan, would end the serious block in the land market. Ashbourne's bill provided for a Treasury grant of £5 million, thereby enabling tenants to borrow the whole purchase price, which would be repaid in annuities at four per cent interest over a period of forty-nine years. The security for this loan consisted of one-fifth the purchase price deposited with the Irish Land Commission, which was responsible for administering the measure. In case of default the tenant's holding would be confiscated. The most important features of the bill were the guarantees that the tenant need no longer provide some fraction of the purchase money and that the annuity would not exceed the original rent. Ashbourne admitted that the grant was modest because the scheme

[10] *Times*, 17-30 July 1885; *Freeman's Journal*, 15 July-18 Aug. 1885.
[11] Hardinge, *Carnarvon*, III, p. 173.

was somewhat experimental, but he assumed correctly that most landlords and tenants considered the land purchase clauses of Gladstone's two acts completely inadequate.

Lord Salisbury, in defending the new measure, confessed that it was no panacea for Ireland's ills. But he trusted that this would be the first of many land purchase bills. No scheme of purchase could possibly succeed, he added, unless the cause of law and order was vigorously upheld. In the Commons the Irish members opposed some of the safeguards, but Parnell called the bill a step in the right direction and affirmed that the land question ought to be settled "permanently upon the basis of an occupying ownership." After several amendments had been carried, the bill passed its third reading on August 11.[12]

There were a number of Irish landlords who protested at the eagerness of ministers to promote tenant ownership of the land. And Churchill argued that since the landlords presented a formidable obstacle in the way of Parnell's ambition, it might not be "good policy to clear . . . [his] path with British gold."[13] Lord Salisbury, however, adhered to the principles of land purchase because he was convinced that it offered the only solution to the land question acceptable to tenants, Parnellites, and to the majority of landlords. As he declared in 1882, only the creation of a peasant proprietary class would end the anomaly of dual ownership, which Gladstone had established by his Land Act of 1881.

The Government was not so generous with regard to Irish education. Protestant opinion in Ireland, not to mention England, did not welcome the endowment of Catholic institutions, and most cabinet ministers shared this view. When Carnarvon asked for a grant of £6,000 to the Catholic University of Ireland, Salisbury replied that the cabinet opposed any such subsidies for the present, and Ashbourne estimated that such a concession would lose the party some thirty or forty seats at the election.[14] Carnarvon gave way; and the whole problem of Catholic higher education was indefinitely postponed. One small concession to

[12] *Hansard,* 3d series, Vol. 299, pp. 1042-46; Vol. 300, p. 1105, 1854.

[13] Churchill to Salisbury, 11 Dec. 1885, Salisbury MSS.

[14] Hardinge, *Carnarvon,* III, pp. 171-72; Ashbourne to Carnarvon, 22 July 1885, Carnarvon MSS.

Irish education was made, however, thanks to the personal intervention of Lord Randolph, who was always interested in placating the Irish hierarchy. Churchill departed from Indian affairs long enough to assist the Irish Educational Endowments Bill through the House of Commons. Originally introduced in the House of Lords in May, the measure inspired little enthusiasm among Conservatives, who resented such a burden at the close of the session. Churchill collaborated with the Irish Attorney General Hugh Holmes in redrafting the bill and removing several features to which the Parnellites objected. The Educational Endowments Act became law on the last day of the session, August 14, and it proved a boon to primary, intermediate, and higher education in Ireland.

A third measure on the Irish agenda was the Labourers' Bill, another Liberal measure left over from the change of ministry. Designed to improve the living conditions of the poorer agricultural laborers and to establish compulsory leases of land for workers' housing sites on a ninety-nine years' basis, the bill passed at the end of the session in spite of objections by Ulster members, who continued to sulk over the Maamtrasna debate.[15]

Meanwhile, in Ireland, Carnarvon was re-enforcing the Parnellite-Conservative alliance. Wherever he went the viceroy distributed the spirit, if not the substance, of conciliation. After three years of Lord Spencer's coercion, the populace enjoyed the presence of this sympathetic viceroy. The whole success of the Carnarvon experiment, in fact, depended upon his ability to convince the Parnellites, the hierarchy, and the tenantry that their best interests lay in cooperating with the Conservative party. Searching for evidence with which to support his ideas of self-government, Carnarvon interviewed numerous officials, talked with nationalists as well as loyalists, and went out of his way to cultivate the Catholic hierarchy. Particularly anxious to befriend the militant nationalist Archbishop of Dublin William Walsh, the viceroy worked to promote vocational training in such industries as fishing and weaving.[16] With the approval of the hierarchy he asked Hicks Beach for £14,000 with which to endow and improve technical schools. But Beach was sceptical about the project and insisted on numerous safeguards in order to prevent the familiar

[15] Dyke to Salisbury, 30 July 1885, Salisbury MSS.
[16] Hardinge, *Carnarvon*, III, pp. 183-84.

spectacle of jobbery and waste. What Ireland needed, in Beach's opinion, was legislation on the whole educational question, and he advised Carnarvon to use the grant for industrial schools as a "sugar plum" with which to bribe the hierarchy to support the other measures that the Government wished to introduce.[17]

Carnarvon, however, did not approve of bribes; and he asked only for the grant to technical education. Having implored Beach not to behave like a chancellor of the Exchequer, but to look upon the request both "liberally and exceptionally," he finally secured half the desired amount from the Treasury. Hart Dyke enthusiastically described the award as "the most successful Treasury assault of modern times."[18] But educational subsidies alone scarcely satisfied the viceroy's desire for constitutional reform in Anglo-Irish relations.

Not even Carnarvon's good works succeeded in reducing the main threat to peace and prosperity in Ireland. The National League was indeed a formidable organization. Although in parts of the country this association actually worked to discourage outrage, this was not the case in the south and west. Parnell had dedicated the new league, which supplanted the proclaimed Land League in October, 1882, to the cause of Home Rule first and foremost; and it soon became an integral part of his parliamentary machine.[19] By 1885 over 1,200 branches of the league were in operation, and many of these depended upon some form of intimidation to enforce obedience to its will. A self-constituted authority with powers parallel to those of the established government had thus emerged.

The character of the league's branches varied greatly: in some districts their activities were innocuous, in others violent. As Carnarvon reported in a cabinet memorandum, those branches over which the younger priests presided usually caused the greatest amount of "mischief." And he singled out as the most pernicious feature of the league the existence of secret courts, "which assumed to revise and judge the relations of landlord and tenant,

[17] Beach to Carnarvon, 26 Sept. 1885, Carnarvon MSS.

[18] Carnarvon to Beach, 30 Sept. 1885; Dyke to Carnarvon, 7 Oct. 1885, *ibid.*

[19] For details of the National League, its aims and organization see C. C. O'Brien, *Parnell and His Party*, pp. 126-33.

to regulate differences between tenants, to decide even beyond these limits upon the right or wrong of boycotting in particular instances." As for boycotting, "The name was comparatively new, but the practice very old"; and where the parish priest directed the activities of the league, this form of agitation took on a religious as well as political character.[20] From a legal point of view boycotting proved difficult to curb because witnesses refused to testify in court. The Crimes Act had failed to check the practice, and Carnarvon knew that the evil would not stop of its own accord. Aware of the difficulties facing the Irish administration, he ended his first report from Dublin with the words: "The ice is very thin."[21]

Although Carnarvon boasted that he had allayed the hostility of priests and other nationalists in many parts of the country, the league remained impervious to his charm. Disruptive forces, he knew only too well, hovered close to the surface of society. In such counties as Cork, Kerry, Clare, and Galway, "local feeling" or resurgent Fenianism exceeded the "central control" of the league, and he feared that serious outrages might result if the extremists lost their patience. The future was full of uncertainty. He stood, "as the Mohammedans would say, on *el serat*—on a foothold so narrow that the slightest breath would overthrow me." The cabinet was informed that, although the temper of the people was "encouraging," the steady fall in prices and the number of impending evictions left no room for optimism. As the summer progressed, police reports showed a marked increase in minor crimes from cattle maiming to boycotting. But Carnarvon responded to this news by arguing that only renewal of the Crimes Act with special clauses aimed at boycotting would relieve this situation, and since the Government had renounced coercion, he saw no alternative other than conciliation.[22]

Without a Crimes Act Dublin Castle could do little to relieve the numerous victims of intimidation beyond listening to their complaints. As a result, Carnarvon tended to ignore the problem of social disorder. In his reports to the Queen, for example, he omitted reference to the rise in agrarian crime, emphasizing

[20] Hardinge, *Carnarvon*, III, pp. 251-54.
[21] Carnarvon to Salisbury, 1 July 1885, Carnarvon MSS.
[22] Carnarvon to Salisbury, 23 July, 7, 10 Aug. 1885, Salisbury MSS.

instead the goodwill encountered on his tours through the country: "Everything may be described as favourable. Lord Carnarvon has met only with respect and friendliness; there is a distinct tendency to better relations than have existed for a long time, and from many persons and classes there come communications which are kindly and well-disposed in their nature. It would of course be imprudent to build upon this as a reliable or permanent foundation; but so far as it goes, it is a very great gain."[23] But in private he was full of misgivings about his ability to govern Ireland without a bold step in the direction of Home Rule.

II. THE PARNELL INTERVIEW

As the general election approached, both British parties selected a number of non-Irish issues with which to attract the recently enlarged electorate. Salisbury's achievements at the Foreign Office during the first months in office had left him little time to study the condition of Ireland. Reports from Dublin Castle did not appear to justify coercion, and in any case the cabinet could not consider a change in Irish policy until the election had shown whether or not the Parnellite alliance was indispensable.

In Dublin the process of softening the attitude of the nationalists with goodwill continued. What Salisbury and the cabinet did not know was the extent to which Home Rule sympathies pervaded the Castle. Sir Robert Hamilton, one of the most influential men in Ireland, led the group that favored a large measure of autonomy. The viceroy, pleased at finding several departmental chiefs sharing his views, commissioned Hamilton to discuss with Gavan Duffy various proposals for an Irish parliament. Ironically, Hamilton's breakfast-table conference with Gavan Duffy at the Shelbourne Hotel on August 1 coincided with a more important talk in London.[24]

Anxious to sound all opinions in Ireland, Carnarvon had long entertained the idea of meeting Parnell. The Government, he reasoned, would have to deal with Parnell sooner or later; and much might be gained from this interview. No pledges would be

[23] Carnarvon to Queen Victoria, 3 Aug. 1885, Carnarvon MSS.

[24] For an account of the conference with Duffy, see Hamilton to Carnarvon, 1 Aug. 1885, *ibid.*

given: the meeting would be only a symposium on possible remedies for Ireland. Parnell, on his part, wished to discover exactly how far the Conservatives were prepared to go toward satisfying Irish national aspirations. Although he knew Carnarvon's sympathies, he could not judge the feelings of other ministers, and he welcomed a chance to explore the Government's position. The delicacy of the situation made secrecy essential; and when the meeting was arranged by Justin McCarthy and Howard Vincent, every precaution was taken to guarantee privacy.[25]

At least two other cabinet members knew of the interview before it took place. Lord Salisbury gave his approval; and Ashbourne helped to settle the details of the meeting at which he was originally scheduled to act as third party. Recalling the furor that followed the disclosure of the Kilmainham Treaty, Salisbury cautioned Carnarvon against making commitments of any kind to Parnell. Because the viceroy was acting on his own initiative, it was decided not to inform the cabinet of the conference. Thus the blame, if any should be forthcoming, would fall entirely upon Carnarvon, and the Government would be spared the distressing repercussions that such a talk might easily entail. Or so Salisbury hoped.[26]

Like the Maamtrasna debate, the meeting that took place on August 1 in an empty house in Mayfair was more important for its long-range than for its immediate results.[27] When the two men met, Carnarvon made three stipulations: by a gentleman's agreement the conversation was to be considered strictly private; there was to be "no sort of bond or engagement," the purpose being merely to exchange opinions; and lastly, he could not entertain any plan that excluded the Act of Union. To these conditions Parnell readily assented. What Carnarvon did not say, and ought to have said, was that the cabinet had not been told of the meeting, and that most of his colleagues had serious doubts about his views on the question of a viable policy for Ireland. According to

[25] R. Barry O'Brien, *The Life of Charles Stewart Parnell*, London, 1899, II, pp. 51-95.

[26] Hardinge, *Carnarvon*, III, pp. 174-77; C. C. O'Brien, *op.cit.*, pp. 102-03; Cecil, *Salisbury*, III, pp. 155-58.

[27] The meeting was held at 15 Hill Street. See also Carnarvon to Salisbury, 20 March 1890, Salisbury MSS.

the viceroy, who afterward drew up a detailed report for Salisbury, the discussion ranged over the familiar ground of the Irish Question from fair rents to self-government. There was a good deal of diplomatic parrying on both sides; and yet Carnarvon found the Irish leader extremely reasonable and accommodating and "not so cold" as he had expected. After some general conversation, Parnell remarked on his efforts to curb violence in Ireland and to keep the National League "within the bounds of law." He dwelt at length on the problem of landlord-tenant relations, stressing the latter's willingness to pay his rent so long as the former behaved tolerantly. After agreeing on the need for some "reasonable" guarantee that private property should be respected, the two men arrived at the core of the problem. Parnell referred to an "Irish legislative body." Carnarvon countered with a suggestion for minority representation (to which Parnell acceded), and then warned that feeling in England ran strongly against anything like a central parliament in Dublin. Parnell acknowledged this fear, but insisted that a central body was essential. Whether it was called a council, board, or chamber made no difference: it was the centrality that mattered. This body, he continued, would have jurisdiction over education, railways, arterial drainage, native industries, and other strictly Irish affairs. The land question "in the first instance" could be left to the imperial Parliament for settlement. In retrospect, Carnarvon attached great importance to Parnell's acceptance of the principle of gradualism in any transfer of power.

On the question of local government Parnell proved more equivocal. He appeared to favor some scheme of elective county councils, but was anxious not to adulterate the powers of the Dublin assembly by excessive decentralization. Next, Parnell expressed concern about the improvement of Ireland's material condition, speaking, as Carnarvon recalled, "with greater emphasis than on any other point." Protection of Irish industries was nothing less than a "public necessity," he declared, simply because the country could never compete with England on any other basis. As to the removal of Irish members from Westminster in the event of a Home Rule solution, he would regret any such exclusion. Surely it could be arranged to forbid Irish members to speak or vote on certain reserved subjects. If, however, removal was a "necessary condition" of Irish self-government, then he had no choice but to accept it. In closing, Parnell confessed his anxiety about falling prices and the activity of extremists in Ireland.[28]

Such was Carnarvon's account of the famous meeting. He had no ostensible reason for distorting the facts, since his memorandum was intended for Salisbury's private perusal. That Parnell had an entirely different impression of the encounter would not be revealed for another ten months, and then at a time when the political atmosphere was highly charged, to say the least. Immediately after the interview, Carnarvon left for Hatfield in order to report the proceedings to the prime minister. Salisbury allegedly expressed his satisfaction with the viceroy's conduct. But precisely when he first showed dismay over Ashbourne's absence from the meeting is not known. It can be assumed, however, that his concern for the Government's welfare moved him to favor the presence of a third person at the conference from the moment he learned of its possibility. In any event Salisbury rejected outright Carnarvon's request that either the cabinet or the Queen be informed of the interview. Secrecy was essential, he felt, if the ministry was not going to be held responsible collectively for the interview.[29]

For several weeks after the meeting Carnarvon's optimism was unbounded. Apprehensions about the partisan forces at work in Westminster did not trouble this man of lofty ideals. He deluded himself into thinking that no real obstacles stood in the way of a final solution to the Irish Question. Unfortunately, the secret interview brought the Government no closer to their goal of a safe and practicable Irish policy. What the meeting did accomplish was of a more negative order. It deceived Parnell and his lieutenants into thinking that the Conservatives were seriously considering some scheme of Home Rule. And if this false assumption tended to promote more cordial relations between Irish members and ministers, it also provided Parnell with a useful political weapon for the future. The loose talk of Parnell and others, moreover, rapidly withdrew the veil of secrecy from the

[28] This version of the meeting is based on the memorandum written by Carnarvon after the event. See Hardinge, *Carnarvon*, III, pp. 178-181.

[29] Cecil, *Salisbury*, III, pp. 157-58.

interview; and those members of Parliament who were privy to the secret, including Gladstone, had fresh cause for speculating about Conservative intentions.[30]

Lord Carnarvon stayed in England over the weekend in order to attend the cabinet on Monday, August 3. Curiously enough, Ireland was never discussed at the meeting. The cabinet concentrated their attention instead on Burma and Afghanistan; and Carnarvon returned to Ireland unrelieved of his information and somewhat offended. As he explained to Lord Cranbrook: "But I did not desire to moot the subject and after the fashion of many cabinets we dawdled over some matters and galloped over others and broke up for the House of Commons before Ireland came up for consideration. I also *rather* regret that they did not hear what I had to say; for the position is a *very peculiar* one—in some respects wonderfully favourable, in others threatening."[31]

If the viceroy was diffident about raising the Irish Question in cabinet, he was indefatigable in the work of conciliation. Despite recurrent ill-health, Carnarvon set off in mid-August on a tour of the west, visiting remote districts such as Achill and the Aran islands, where no viceroy had ever been. Appalled by the poverty and squalor, which were permanent features of this coastal terrain, he discovered that nationalist sentiment did not interfere with expressions of loyalty toward the Queen. In the eyes of his colleagues, however, Carnarvon became something of a bore owing to his chronic anxiety about indiscretions concerning Ireland. In September he wrote both to Churchill and Salisbury, expressing his alarm lest ministerial statements about Irish affairs contradict each other. A number of "hot-headed" Conservatives, he contended, wanted to behave like Radicals by forcing the Government to declare a bold Irish policy; and he asked Salisbury to silence these "bitter and unscrupulous critics waiting for one small slip."[32] But Carnarvon's appeals for discretion regarding the Irish Question did not please every minister. Lord Iddesleigh,

[30] Gladstone presumably learned from Mrs. O'Shea that Parnell had been in touch with the Conservatives. See Hammond, *Gladstone and the Irish Nation*, pp. 421, 429-30.

[31] Carnarvon to Cranbrook, 5 Aug. 1885, Carnarvon MSS.

[32] See Carnarvon's notes and memoranda on his western tour, 17-19 Aug. 1885, *ibid.*; *Times*, 17-24 Aug. 1885; Hardinge, *Carnarvon*, III, pp. 182-85.

in whom scruples were a political failing, insisted that Dublin Castle issue a formal statement repudiating any Home Rule solution. Appreciating the ambiguity of that phrase, which could be interpreted as either a generous local government bill or complete separation, he feared the effects of the so-called Irish alliance upon the loyalty of Conservatives throughout the country.[33] In view of the approaching election, however, neither Carnarvon nor the majority of the cabinet wished to clarify their intentions toward Ireland beyond the limit made necessary by the political situation.

III. IRISH AGRARIAN CRIME

As the autumn progressed, the effects of Carnarvon's regime and of Parnell's restraining influence were reflected in the decline of serious crime. But there was no lull in boycotting, much of which was inspired by private feuds among tenants and shopkeepers. The agricultural depression showed no signs of abating, and the mounting number of evictions also gave cause for alarm. Magistrates could not prosecute boycotters for want of witnesses, evidence was scarce, and convictions few. According to one divisional magistrate, boycotting had increased to an "alarming" extent in September; and tenants often joined the league against their will in order to insure themselves against its punitive measures. The intensity of the agitation varied widely from one county to another. Large areas in Mayo and Galway remained relatively quiet: while the Castleisland and Kanturk districts in Kerry and Cork boasted some of the worst moonlighting in the country. Scarcity of cash led to evictions, which in turn precipitated outrages, and district inspectors warned that failure to reduce rents might touch off a full-scale land war.[34]

By the end of September Salisbury was growing uneasy about the increase in boycotting. Unlike Carnarvon, he feared that a "large mass of English opinion" would turn against the Government if nothing was done to reduce the evil.[35] Reports from Dublin Castle showed that outrages and lesser offenses had increased

[33] Carnarvon to Salisbury, 18 Sept. 1885; Iddesleigh to Carnarvon, 7 Sept. 1885, Carnarvon MSS.

[34] Carnarvon to Salisbury, 10 Aug. 1885, Salisbury MSS; Carnarvon to Queen Victoria, 31 Oct. 1885, Carnarvon MSS.

[35] Salisbury to Churchill, 29 Sept. 1885, Salisbury MSS.

during July; and the number of individuals requiring police protection had risen to absurd proportions. Since renewal of coercion was out of the question, Salisbury was forced to defend the policy of inaction by arguing that even special legislation had failed to discourage boycotting in the past. At the same time, he admitted that the refusal of witnesses to testify in court had taken the "mainspring out of the watch" of justice.[36] The situation was summed up by an Irish wit, who attributed the paucity of convictions to "jury's prudence."

Lord Randolph Churchill, who suspected that Carnarvon was furnishing unrealistic reports, decided to survey the scene himself. Crossing the Irish Sea at the end of September, he talked with leading Castle officials and with his close friend Lord Justice Fitzgibbon. He found Carnarvon frail and uncommunicative: "I have not had much conversation with him beyond a short walk on the sunny side of the kitchen garden: for he is 'très frileux' and only pops out now and again when the sun shines, like a bluebottle in autumn."[37] Having questioned Holmes, the attorney general, Churchill reported to Salisbury that, apart from boycotting, there was no cause for alarm. Holmes attributed most of the boycotting to the insolvency of the National League, which hoped to supplement its income by forcing the wealthier tradesmen and farmers to join.

The prime minister received such reports with satisfaction. The news that the Irish peasant was learning self-restraint without the scourge of coercion went far, he thought, to justify the decision to drop the Crimes Act; but such wishful thinking prevented ministers from appreciating the extent of demoralization in Ireland. In England prejudice or complacency led many people to treat boycotting as an innocuous and typically Irish expression of discontent. Carnarvon himself was ready to dismiss many acts of intimidation as mere inventions or the result of a native penchant for exaggeration. Churchill confidently declared: "Boycotting will in time cure itself, no law can deal with it; but everybody . . . will in time get so bored with the practice that it will disappear."[38]

[36] Salisbury to J. G. Lawson, 17 Oct. 1885, *ibid.*
[37] Churchill to Salisbury, 1 Oct. 1885, *ibid.*
[38] Churchill to Carnarvon, 27 Sept. 1885, Carnarvon MSS.

Unfortunately, boredom did not kill the boycott. Instead, the practice steadily increased in a climate of apathy. Irish patriots in America rejoiced in this fact and boasted: "We've got them where the wool is short." In the meantime, Ashbourne was growing more nostalgic about the Crimes Act and began to urge Salisbury to adopt a stronger line against the league. Preferring coercion to the kind of charity preached by Carnarvon, he insisted that remedial works alone could not restore order.[39]

The month of October began ominously with a request from Galway to send a gunboat, a magistrate, a sheriff, and forty police to the Aran islands in order to carry out evictions there. On October 5 the viceroy learned that boycotting had increased fourfold since June, but this news did not disturb him. Ashbourne, on the other hand, complained that so few boycotters had been convicted. Fearing lest the increase in intimidation lead to more violent crimes, he described the situation as "very serious."[40] With Carnarvon determined to play down the extent of agrarian unrest, the discrepancy in the reports reaching the cabinet from Ireland grew ever larger.

To the Irish landlord, Carnarvon's policy, however benign and well-intentioned, seemed destined to leave him at the mercy of the local league branch. In order to break up boycotting at fairs, plain-clothes policemen circulated at markets and in towns where the worst intimidation prevailed, and their presence often served to deter boycotters. But the majority of tenants obeyed the league at the mere threat of boycotting. As one of them remarked, it was less painful to subscribe a pound or ten shillings to the league than to have one's cattle mutilated, one's house burned, and oneself ostracized from the community.[41] As a class the landlords were slow to defend themselves against the National League, preferring instead to look to Dublin Castle for help. In county Cork, however, a group of landlords led by the enterprising Arthur Smith-Barry, M.P.,[42] formed the Cork Defence Union.

[39] Ashbourne to Salisbury, 8 Nov. 1885, Salisbury MSS.

[40] Boycotting had increased from 227 cases in June to 741 in October. Carnarvon's reaction was: "This seems to be a very small number considering the outcry"; Carnarvon to Ashbourne, 3 Oct. 1885; Ashbourne to Carnarvon, 5 Oct. 1885, Carnarvon MSS.

[41] C. P. Coote to Carnarvon, 13 Sept. 1885, *ibid.*

[42] 1843-1925; M.P. 1867-1874, 1886-1900; Vice-President of Irish

By pooling threshing machines, portable forges, provisions, and labor, the union managed to counteract the worst effects of the boycott in various parts of the county. The idea of similar land-lords' associations caught on subsequently in Kerry, Clare, and Waterford; but the resources of these county defense unions proved too limited to challenge the supremacy of the league in the south and west of Ireland.

Next to organized intimidation, widespread economic distress caused the administration the most anxiety. The harvest of 1885 approached complete failure in some districts of the country; and the depression in trade and agriculture prevented thousands of tenants from paying their rents. One landlord with a reputa-tion for honesty declared that his tenants were in no position to pay more than half their rents, so bad was the season: the only trouble was that he himself could not afford the reduction. While many tenants tried hard to meet their obligations, relatively few landlords showed a lenient spirit in the emergency. In times of famine, money lenders, better known as "gombeen men," charged interest rates as high as fifty-eight per cent. Impoverished by distress and threatened with eviction, the tenant often had no choice but to seek the protection of the league.[43]

There were several ministers who worried incessantly about the damaging effects of Liberal attacks on the working alliance between the Government and the Parnellites. They wished to avoid any further signs of fraternization with the Irish members. Lord Cranbrook, in particular, feared the maneuvers of Churchill. "I am afraid of our intriguing colleague," he confessed, "com-mitting us or destroying us by the supposition that we are com-mitted."[44] But it was Carnarvon, not Churchill, who began to promote a solution by Home Rule.

Unionist Alliance; Vice-President of Irish Landowners' Convention; Irish privy councillor 1896; created Baron Barrymore 1902. The Cork Defence Union was a subsidiary of the Irish Defence Union founded in 1885 under the direction of Lord Bandon. See *Times*, 6, 10 Sept., 23, 26 Oct. 1886.

[43] Report of Inspector General, RIC, 20 Dec. 1885, 6 Jan. 1886, Car-narvon MSS. The number of evictions in 1885 amounted to 3,127 families, or 15,423 persons of whom 8,614 were allowed to re-enter their houses as caretakers.

[44] Cranbrook to Carnarvon, 4 Aug. 1885, *ibid.*

CHAPTER IV

Stalemate

THE AUTUMN cabinets began early in October; and Carnarvon, after preliminary talks with Salisbury, raised the question of an Irish policy for the election. No agreement on this issue was reached; and three days later the cabinet met again to discuss the merits of Irish local government reform. Carnarvon described the state of the country "in the gloomiest colors," and proceeded to advocate a large concession to the nationalists. Citing the influence of the National League and the depression in agriculture as well as in trade, he insisted that the present state of suspended hostilities could not last forever. His solution to the problem consisted of an Irish parliament with sufficient powers to satisfy moderate nationalists. A central authority was more desirable, he argued, because local bodies would attract only third-rate Irish politicians; while a parliament would draw the most responsible and talented men in the country. Although he made no reference to his talk with Parnell, he intimated that of all the alternatives his plan would be most acceptable to the Irish leader. It was possible, he believed, to give Ireland the symbols of Home Rule without the substance; but if the Conservatives won the election, he could not endorse a policy that treated Ireland like a crown colony.[1]

After delivering this confession of faith, Carnarvon found to his dismay that none of his colleagues had been converted to Home Rule. They considered the problem far too hazardous to solve before the election. Salisbury preferred procrastination; Ashbourne and Cranbrook pressed the claims of coercion; while Churchill and Hicks Beach favored a program of remedial legislation. Appreciating the dangers inherent in any Home Rule solution, they had no wish to disrupt the party for the sake of

[1] Hardinge, *Carnarvon*, III, pp. 192-95; Gathorne Hardy, *Cranbrook*, II, p. 226.

appeasing Parnell. The cabinet's negative response, however, did not materially dampen Carnarvon's optimism.[2]

I. THE NEWPORT SPEECH

On October 7 Lord Salisbury delivered an address on foreign and domestic affairs at Newport before a gathering of the National Union of Conservative and Constitutional Associations. This famous speech only increased the confusion surrounding the Government's Irish policy. The passages dealing with Ireland were a masterpiece of ambiguity and left almost all sections of opinion hopeful. What the Parnellites interpreted as an invitation to revive Grattan's parliament was taken by the Conservatives as a pledge that any concessions depended entirely upon the results of the general election. Lord Randolph, grateful for what he thought were Tory democratic ingredients in the speech, praised Salisbury for "a truly great" performance.[3]

The address ranged from reforms in local government and the poor law to Sunday closing. Salisbury, in short, announced the party's intention to compete with the Liberals for the votes of the rural as well as the urban laborers. When he arrived at the Irish Question, however, his technique changed. From lucid and forceful phrasing he took refuge in the language of the diplomat. "To maintain the integrity of the Empire," he announced, "must undoubtedly be our first policy with respect to Ireland." As to local government reform, he insisted upon protection of minorities from the tyranny of the Catholic majority. Since he expected the nationalists to dominate any elective county or borough councils, he urged as a hypothesis the creation of a "large central authority" to prevent inequities. The central authority he had in mind was closer to a supreme court—as his previous letter to Carnarvon testified—than to an elective body. But Gladstone and Irish Home Rulers thought otherwise. They were convinced that Salisbury was talking about an Irish parliament. What these remarks implied but did not specifically state was that the Irish people were not politically mature enough to assume the responsibilities of self-government in any unadulterated form.

Salisbury passed as quickly as possible over the subject of boy-

[2] Hicks Beach, *St. Aldwyn*, II, p. 258.
[3] Churchill to Salisbury, 8 Oct. 1885, Salisbury MSS.

cotting: the administration were doing their best to combat what he described as a "passing humour." The practice, in his opinion, contained within itself the seeds of its own destruction; and he predicted that the league would start to discourage boycotting once it realized the nature of the Frankenstein it had created. For electoral reasons Salisbury deliberately minimized the extent and nature of agrarian crime. He was later accused of making a "philosophic defense" of boycotting, whereas his statement was simply an attempt to justify the decision to abandon coercion. Ireland occupied only a minor portion of the Newport speech; and Salisbury ended with a powerful defense of the established church, describing Radical threats of disestablishment as "Gladstone's last surrender."[4] Thus the prime minister carried off a major policy statement without committing the party to a specific Irish program. His equivocation preserved the Parnellite alliance and supported Carnarvon's goodwill campaign in Ireland. While Conservatives applauded the Newport speech, the Liberals gloated over the Irish paragraphs, confident that their opponents would become enmeshed in the question of Home Rule. Salisbury believed that he had said enough on the subject; and after Newport he tried to avoid further allusion to Irish self-government.[5]

Gladstone, too, avoided any binding statements on this issue, hoping that the Conservatives would relieve him of his compunctions toward Irish nationalism. In a speech at Edinburgh he deplored the reliance of both British parties on the Parnellite vote. Wishing to give his opponents ample room to maneuver, he refused to commit himself on the subject of autonomy for Ireland. In between his cryptic statements on the question he looked to Carnarvon, whose sentiments he knew, and to Salisbury, whose ability he admired, to educate the rest of their party about Home Rule.

The Newport speech failed to satisfy Carnarvon's demands for a specific policy. The continued reluctance of his colleagues to consider even a limited form of Home Rule moved him to draft

[4] For the complete text of the speech see H. W. Lucy, *Speeches of the Marquis of Salisbury*, London, 1885, pp. 171-204.

[5] Speaking at the Guildhall on November 9, Salisbury tried to atone for his previous ambiguity by a strong condemnation of boycotting; *Times*, 10 Nov. 1885.

a long memorandum advocating an Irish constitution. On October 31 he informed the cabinet that Ireland was passing through a great social revolution. The Protestant ascendancy had gone with the disestablishment; the landlords' ascendancy was gradually vanishing with the land purchase acts; and the Government had made no effort to replace these two stabilizing elements in society. Into the vacuum had rushed a violent and articulate form of nationalism supported by the vast majority of Irishmen. In view of the economic distress in Ireland it was no longer a question of never granting concessions, but of when and how. Carnarvon recommended that after the election a joint committee of both houses of Parliament, representing all parties, be appointed to draft an Irish constitution. If this proposal failed, he declared, coercion remained the only alternative.[6] After a brief discussion, the cabinet unanimously rejected his plea.

By November the breach between the cabinet and the Irish administration had become irreparable. Hart Dyke in London tried in vain to console the viceroy. Referring to Salisbury, he wrote: "I think that he is opposed, and thinks the great mass of the party in both Houses would be opposed, to any bold move. As regards the party, I fear he is right. . . . I find the same hopeless indifference and ignorance in every quarter, plus an amount of prejudice, which would drive John Bright wild with envy."[7]

Late in the month Carnarvon delivered an ultimatum to the prime minister: the Government could choose between Home Rule and his resignation. He hoped that this mild form of blackmail would compel ministers to adopt his proposals rather than face the embarrassment of a resignation. If the Government wished to retain his services, they would have to accept either the joint constitutional committee or a large concession to Irish education. When Salisbury asked for more time to consider the matter, Carnarvon insisted upon an immediate reply. The premier then declared that he could not behave like Peel in 1846 and split the party: he would resign first rather than betray his supporters. At length, pending the cabinet's decision on his ultimatum, Carnarvon agreed to remain in the Government.

[6] See Carnarvon's memorandum on Ireland, 31 Oct. 1885, Carnarvon MSS.

[7] Hardinge, *Carnarvon*, III, p. 196.

For all his pains and mild threats Carnarvon received only evasive replies. Tending to consider him an eccentric on the subject of Irish nationalism, his colleagues shunned any new departure in the midst of the general election. No one in the cabinet appeared to heed his warning that a policy of inaction might revive systematic outrage and would certainly alienate Parnell. A growing sense of frustration was Carnarvon's only reward for his high-minded, if inexpedient, approach to the Irish Question.

II. THE ELECTION OF 1885

The general election was distinguished by a deliberate avoidance of the paramount issue of the day. Ireland was left in the background, a problem undefined and threatening, while such questions as fair trade, local government, and social reforms appropriated the limelight. Lord Harrowby, lord Privy Seal, reported that the working-class men in the Radical strongholds of Kidderminster and the Potteries cared more about tariffs and free education than about Ireland.[8] Lord Hartington and Chamberlain had already denounced Parnell's statement that the nationalist platform consisted of "one plank only—and that plank Home Rule." In Midlothian Gladstone appealed for a solution of the Irish Question, but offered no specific remedies. To Lord Hartington he confessed that he expected the Government and the nationalist vote in Ireland to decide the future of the Union. And Harcourt spoke for many Liberals when he declared at Lowestoft that the Conservatives deserved to "stew in their own Parnellite juice."[9]

On November 21 Parnell fulfilled his promise to Churchill by endorsing the manifesto that ordered all Irish voters in Great Britain to vote against Liberal and Radical candidates. Dublin Castle had been expecting this pronouncement for at least a month.[10] The Irish leader, vexed by Gladstone's refusal to commit himself, hoped that this move would make the Liberals equally dependent on his support in the Commons. Carnarvon's behavior, moreover, had led him to anticipate a major concession from the Conservatives if they received a majority at the election. Parnell

[8] Harrowby to Salisbury, 21 Nov. 1885, Salisbury MSS.

[9] Morley, *Gladstone*, III, pp. 240-41; Gardiner, *Harcourt*, I, p. 542; Holland, *Devonshire*, II, pp. 77-97.

[10] C. Howard Vincent to Carnarvon, 26 Oct. 1885, Carnarvon MSS.

confidently assumed that the 150,000 Irish voters involved would follow his bidding. The fact that a number of them disobeyed orders and voted, as their priests told them to do, for the candidate who upheld the equality of board and voluntary schools, shows that religious scruples could prevail over political exigencies. Estimates of the consequences of the manifesto varied from a Liberal loss of two seats to thirty or forty. The Conservatives naturally minimized the effects of the decree, while the Liberals magnified their losses. Whatever the number, the Parnellites undoubtedly prejudiced their own cause in the future by antagonizing Liberal opinion during the election.[11]

The election lasted three weeks; and Conservative elation over the results in the boroughs soon gave way to gloom after the majority of agricultural laborers had voted Liberal. Churchill, contesting Bright's seat at Birmingham, and his rival Chamberlain set the tone for their respective party appeals, although the "unauthorized programme" attracted more votes than did Churchill's elusive strains of Tory democracy. The Liberals won a majority of eighty-six votes over the Conservatives, which was precisely the number of the Irish party, all of whom were pledged to Home Rule. Parnell had achieved what Gladstone most dreaded: the Irish party now controlled the balance of power in the House of Commons.

The new franchise in Ireland added much momentum to the nationalist movement. Four-fifths of the electorate voted for Parnell's "one plank"; and the National League proved its formidable efficiency as an electoral machine. The inspector general of the Royal Irish Constabulary informed Carnarvon of the electoral expertise shown by the nationalists: "In some places they formed themselves into a police and watched and prevented the slightest misconduct on the part of their followers . . . they drilled their supporters as to the procedure for voting so that they should make no mistake. Their zeal and devotion to the national cause are most remarkable."[12]

[11] See C. H. D. Howard, "The Parnell Manifesto of 21 November 1885 and the Schools Question," in *English Historical Review*, Vol. 62, No. 242, January 1947, pp. 42-51; Cecil, *Salisbury*, III, p. 272; Garvin, *Chamberlain*, II, p. 189; C. C. O'Brien, *Parnell and His Party*, pp. 105-08.

[12] Report of the Inspector General, RIC, 10 Dec. 1885, Carnarvon MSS. See also C. C. O'Brien, *Parnell and His Party*, chaps. 4 and 5.

The Liberals in Ireland lost all the fourteen seats they had won in 1880; and apart from Ulster, where the nationalists polled in surprising strength, the Conservatives fared no better. Carnarvon had predicted the outcome of the elections in Ireland as early as September, owing to the refusal of Orangemen in the south to cooperate with Liberals in an antinationalist coalition. With characteristic vehemence Churchill blamed some of the Government's reverses in the north of Ireland on the "abominable . . . foul Ulster Tories," whom he accused of intriguing with Whigs for certain seats.[13] When Lord Randolph learned of the election results, he was reported to have said to Justin McCarthy: "We've done our best for you. Now we shall do our best against you!"

More important than personal recriminations, Parnell's electoral feat impressed Gladstone with the need to settle the Irish Question before it brought the two major parties into ruinous conflict. Both as a party leader and a dedicated "House of Commons man" Gladstone dreaded the parliamentary chaos that would result if Parnell chose to switch the Irish vote from one side to the other as expediency dictated. Such tactics might mean the end of a two-party system. Lord Salisbury, on the other hand, took a more limited view of the election. The fact that so many Irishmen had supported Parnell and his party did not impress him. Since the British electorate had not endorsed Home Rule, he automatically excluded any such concession. But Liberal successes in the counties depressed him and strengthened his conviction that the days of the Caretaker ministry were numbered.

Two alternatives, besides maintaining the *status quo*, suggested themselves. The Government could either resign or coalesce with the Whigs and moderate Liberals. Resignation, Carnarvon argued, would force the burden of decision onto the Liberals and save the Conservative party from possible schism. The difference between a minority of twenty votes in June and of more than eighty in December, he urged, made the retention of office unjustified if not dangerous. And he worried lest the Government, by staying in power and refusing Home Rule, be accused of having intrigued to obtain Irish support at the election and of having discarded the Parnellites as soon as they had attained that end: "If we say something evasive to gain time we shall before long be brought

[13] Churchill to Salisbury, 16 Nov. 1885, Salisbury MSS.

64

to book and be in a still worse plight. . . . Further, if we try to tide on with fair words in a minority of about 75, the plain inference will be that we are depending on the Irish, and it will be believed that there has been a bargain . . . we must govern by and through the Irish—and unless we are ready to come to some understanding with them they will play us off against the Liberals and reduce us to the sorest difficulties." Carnarvon thus anticipated the traditional charge of Home Rule sympathizers after 1886. The viceroy concluded by pleading that resignation would save the party from the awkwardness of his own departure. Rumors of a schism would disappear: "As I go out with the rest of the cabinet . . . there is nothing to indicate any difference of opinion."[14]

The argument failed to move Salisbury from his determination to continue in office until Parliament met and expressed a verdict. He answered that if they resigned before January, the Government would automatically forfeit their right to oppose the Liberals on the issue of Home Rule until another election had taken place.[15] Salisbury used this same plea in cabinet on December 20: the party would be sacrificing their flexibility in domestic affairs and political tactics by premature resignation. Carnarvon, however, was unimpressed by this partisan outlook and renewed his demand with such vigor that Salisbury asked a reluctant Cranbrook to take on the Irish viceroyship in the near future.[16]

The state of foreign affairs supplied another reason for Salisbury's reluctance to resign immediately after the election. As foreign secretary he had managed to restore some of Britain's lost prestige, but in December many negotiations with foreign powers were still in a formative stage and Salisbury did not wish to disrupt this work. The Queen not only shared this view but virtually insisted that the Conservatives remain in office.

The other alternative was coalition. On November 29, when the polls indicated a Liberal victory, Churchill wrote to his leader suggesting a coalition with the Whigs and moderate Liberals. To facilitate the plan he magnanimously placed his own office at the prime minister's disposal. The inclusion of Hartington,

[14] Carnarvon to Salisbury, 6 Dec. 1885, *ibid.*
[15] Salisbury to Carnarvon, 12 Dec. 1885, Carnarvon MSS.
[16] Hardinge, *Carnarvon,* III, p. 205; Hardy, *Cranbrook,* II, pp. 233-34.

Goschen, and Rosebery would, he hoped, keep the "Irish-Radical" combination out of power for many years to come. Salisbury, however, did not approve of such a coalition. He thanked Churchill for his "patriotic offer" and explained that the plan was premature. If the only alternative consisted of a Whig alliance, he confessed that he would resign along with his Indian secretary. This rebuff did not prevent Churchill from drafting a lengthy memorandum early in December in which he not only urged coalition but set forth a legislative program for the reconstructed ministry. Such concessions as local government reform and grants to Catholic education in Ireland would, he was confident, lead to the "disintegration" of the Irish party and to a corresponding dilution of the Home Rule movement. Salisbury's reply on December 9 contained a long list of objections to this course of action. The time for coalescing with the moderate Liberals had not yet arrived, and he added: "If we are too free with our cash now, we shall have no money to go to market with when the market is open." Churchill was left dismayed and hurt. In vain he protested against his leader's "rigidly orthodox Tory" program and warned that the party would never gain the necessary urban and county votes with policies based on "old, worn-out aristocratic and class garments."[17]

The Queen added her own weight to the cause of coalition. Anxious about foreign affairs, she worked diligently to foster opposition to Gladstone within his own party; and although her plan to lure Goschen and Hartington away from the Liberal camp failed, the way was prepared for a future alliance.[18] Salisbury on his part, made it clear to the Queen that he opposed any idea of a central parliament in Dublin. Fearing the effects of Carnarvon's talk with her on the subject of Irish autonomy, he informed Ponsonby that Home Rule would, in his opinion, lead directly to separation and to persecution of the loyalist minority. Any surrender to Parnell, he wrote, would repel English opinion, would split the party, and "could only be carried out, *now*, at the cost of a great disruption of parties, and an entire loss of honour among public men."[19]

[17] W. S. Churchill, *Churchill*, II, pp. 6-7, 16-20.
[18] *Letters of Queen Victoria*, 2d series, III, pp. 706-07, 712-16.
[19] A. Ponsonby, *Henry Ponsonby: Queen Victoria's Private Secretary:*

Salisbury thus ruled out coalition as a solution to the parliamentary stalemate. He chose instead to remain uncommitted, waiting for Gladstone's impatience to manifest itself in some form or other. Carnarvon's zeal for a constructive policy disturbed what little calm remained to the Government. In another long memorandum, dated December 7, he advocated the familiar plan of a joint committee to consider the Irish Question. Churchill, Hicks Beach, and W. H. Smith studied the new paper and decided that they preferred resignation to the equivalent of Home Rule. Churchill exclaimed: " . . . if that blessed man sets the signal for concession flying, our party will go to pieces, as it did on the Irish Land Act."[20]

While the Conservatives deferred judgment until the meeting of Parliament, Gladstone spent the month of December at Hawarden meditating on many subjects, the most recurrent of which was Ireland. Appreciating the difficult position of his opponents, he wished "to do nothing to hinder prosecution of the question by the Tory Government." In order to expedite the generous concession he expected from the latter, and to keep the issue out of the "category of party measures," he was willing to pledge Liberal support to the Government. The cooperation of moderate elements in both parties was, in his opinion, the only possible way to solve the now urgent Irish Question.[21]

Lord Salisbury would have been amused, had he known the degree of Gladstone's self-delusion about Conservative intentions. Salisbury had never trusted the Liberal leader, and as a young man had written in the *Quarterly Review*: "It is a strange perversity that the very structure of Mr. Gladstone's mind, the ill-adjusted balance of his many commanding qualities, should simulate the insincerity which genuinely taints the mass of those around him."[22] Twenty-five years of political activity had not appreciably changed this opinion. The truth was that he con-

---

His Life from His Letters (hereafter *Henry Ponsonby*), London, 1942, pp. 199-200.

[20] W. S. Churchill, *op.cit.*, ii, pp. 21-22.

[21] Morley, *Gladstone*, iii, p. 261. See also *The Political Correspondence of Mr. Gladstone and Lord Granville 1876-1886*, ed. A. Ramm, Oxford, 1962, ii, pp. 392 ff.

[22] *Quarterly Review*, July 1860, Vol. 108, No. 215, p. 280.

sidered Gladstone guilty of intellectual dishonesty and hypocrisy by pretending to care more about moral principles than political power. Salisbury's personal impressions of Gladstone were important if only because they were not reciprocated. The latter admired his adversary's intellect and tended to exaggerate his feelings of compassion toward Ireland.[23] While Gladstone was looking to Salisbury to take the initiative over Home Rule, the latter was writing to Churchill: "The fact that Gladstone is mad to take office will force him into some line of conduct which will be discreditable to him and disastrous, if we do not prematurely gratify his hunger."[24] Sooner or later, he was confident, the Liberal leader would make his bid for office through the Irish party. With the exception of Carnarvon, every cabinet minister in fact was convinced that Gladstone cared more about political power than Irish self-government. It was unfortunate for the future of Anglo-Irish relations that both British party leaders so thoroughly misunderstood each other's motives and intentions.

Two crucial meetings of the cabinet took place on December 14 and 15. On both occasions the viceroy pleaded for a joint committee to study the relations between England and Ireland. This time there was less equivocation. The cabinet formally rejected the plan and Carnarvon tendered his resignation. Once again, however, Salisbury succeeded in persuading him to stay in Dublin until the meeting of Parliament. Carnarvon returned to Ireland burdened with a sense of personal failure. At Christmas time he sent his chief the bleak salutation: "With best Christmas wishes —I believe the best is that you should soon be out of office."[25]

[23] Admittedly, Gladstone distrusted Salisbury's penchant for secret treaties and did not approve of his caustic language. In 1880 Salisbury wrote to Balfour apropos of Gladstone: ". . . there are marks of hurry which in so old a man are inexplicable. I suppose he still cherishes his belief in an early monastic retreat from this wicked world and is feverishly anxious to annihilate all his enemies before he takes it"; Salisbury to Balfour, 16 June 1880, Salisbury MSS.

[24] W. S. Churchill, *op.cit.*, II, p. 22.

[25] Carnarvon to Salisbury, 26 Dec. 1885, Salisbury MSS. Salisbury informed the viceroy that he was free to resign at any time after the meeting of Parliament, and ironically suggested January 26. Salisbury to Carnarvon, 3 Jan. 1886, Carnarvon MSS.

III. THE HAWARDEN KITE

The political stalemate did not last long. Acting out of fear lest the leadership of the Liberal party fall into the hands of Chamberlain and the Birmingham caucus, Herbert Gladstone on December 15 released the news of his father's "conversion" to Home Rule. The newspapers distorted the account, attributing to the father many of the son's opinions. But the fact remained that the public associated a radically new departure with Gladstone's name. Although he denied the accuracy of the press statements, he did not specifically renounce a solution by Home Rule. Hartington and Chamberlain hastened to explain in public that they did not share their leader's views; and the Birmingham Radical decided that it was almost time to stop rubbing "the Tories' noses well in the mess they have made."[26]

The Conservative reaction to the Hawarden Kite was notable for the acrimony directed against Gladstone. Government members suspected that he had deliberately engineered the news release in order to win Parnell's support before the approaching session. Ministers believed that they had proof at last of his evil intentions. Lord Cranbrook observed: "I am all for letting him try his hand if he will. All the world seems convinced of the insatiable eagerness of the old man for office and his is the hand which, having destroyed the principle of property sacred and profane, should attempt the parricidal task of putting an end to Imperial unity in the so-called United Kingdom."[27] Salisbury, more convinced than ever of Gladstone's iniquity, described the Kite as having transformed a "chimera into a burning issue."

To an equal extent the Kite stunned the Liberals. After Lord Hartington and Chamberlain had reassured their constituents of their opposition to Home Rule, the aged Granville, unwavering in his loyalty to Gladstone, could only call the situation "thoroughly appalling." Labouchere, who loved to distort the truth, asserted that Gladstone was willing to give up not only Ireland but Mrs. Gladstone and his son in order to take office. As for the Queen, she reveled in the execration that fell upon Gladstone after the Kite and described him as a "wild fanatical

[26] H. Gladstone, *After Thirty Years*, London, 1928, pp. 307-13; Morley, *Gladstone*, III, pp. 256-76; Garvin, *Chamberlain*, II, p. 132.
[27] Cranbrook to Carnarvon, 17 Dec. 1885, Carnarvon MSS.

old man of 76."[28] Nevertheless, the ill-timed move of his son determined Gladstone to make a direct approach to the Conservatives for a bipartisan solution of the question. Unaware of the cabinet's decision on December 15 not to touch any form of Irish self-government, he expected the Conservatives to accept his plan.

Gladstone was optimistic for several reasons. In the first place, he recalled the precedents of 1829, 1846, and 1867, when sections of the Opposition had assisted the Government in securing major reforms. The franchise conference of 1884 provided another example of a working compromise between Liberals and Conservatives. The Government's control of the Lords added another cogent excuse for his desire to see them espouse Home Rule. From Mrs. O'Shea he understood that Parnell was confidently awaiting some such concession; and he assumed that the secret interview with Carnarvon had the cabinet's full support. The Newport speech, moreover, deceived him into thinking that Salisbury was contemplating some form of parliament for Ireland; and the latter's acknowledged ability in foreign affairs also convinced him that the Irish Question would be settled with equal wisdom and care.

A more compelling reason for Gladstone's optimism was supplied by the ubiquitous Canon MacColl. This energetic clergyman and pamphleteer, who insinuated himself into high political society, persuaded Gladstone that the Conservatives were prepared to cooperate in a joint venture to give Ireland Home Rule. During the negotiations in November, 1884, over the Franchise Bill, MacColl had acted as liaison between the two party leaders, and he wished to continue serving in this capacity as peacemaker and confidant of prime ministers. A Home Ruler himself, he secured an interview with Salisbury, stressed Gladstone's sincerity in wishing to support a Conservative measure in this direction, and then, in his report to Gladstone, proceeded to distort, however unintentionally, the essence of Salisbury's remarks. Not only was MacColl in the habit of glossing over the essential differences of opinion between his two eminent "friends," but he was also ignorant of Gladstone's Home Rule intentions. Assuming that the latter also opposed a Dublin parliament, he informed him: "I

[28] Ponsonby, *Henry Ponsonby,* pp. 201-02; Garvin, *Chamberlain,* II, pp. 143-45.

found Lord Salisbury . . . prepared to go as far probably as yourself on the question of home rule, but he seemed hopeless as to the prospect of carrying his party with him."[29] Unaware of MacColl's misconception about his own "advanced" views, Gladstone concluded that Salisbury also favored an Irish parliament. This false assumption had its immediate significance, and long afterwards Gladstone's apologists would flaunt the MacColl report as conclusive proof of Salisbury's Home Rule proclivities.[30]

The fact that several high-ranking officials in Dublin Castle shared Carnarvon's views also impressed Gladstone. Jenkinson, the chief of criminal investigation, had written to him on December 12 arguing the merits of Home Rule; while Sir Robert Hamilton sent a memorandum to Spencer, advocating a similar concession.[31] For such reasons Gladstone completely misunderstood the Government's intentions and their reaction to the Kite. Much of this apparent blindness was the result of wishful thinking. Gladstone was far too shrewd a politician not to sense the potentially explosive material in Home Rule; and it required little imagination to wish the curse of the Irish Question upon one's opponents, especially when they appeared to be asking for this very fate.

IV. POLARIZATION

It was in mid-December, just before Herbert Gladstone released the Hawarden Kite, that his father made a direct bid for a bipartisan settlement of the Irish Question. The place was Eaton Hall, only a short distance from Hawarden Castle, and his intermediary was Balfour, who happened to be staying with the Duke

[29] See G. W. E. Russell, *Malcolm MacColl, Memoir and Correspondence* (hereafter *MacColl*), London, 1914, pp. 118-23.

[30] MacColl's letter to Gladstone on December 28 clarified this misunderstanding: "All I told Lord Salisbury—indeed all I knew—hardly went beyond your public utterances on the subject of Ireland. The impression you left on my mind was that you were *not* in favour of a Parliament in Dublin"; *ibid.*, p. 126. This important letter has been overlooked by virtually every student of the period. See, for example, Hammond, *Gladstone and the Irish Nation*, p. 434, and James, *Lord Randolph Churchill*, p. 210. There is no evidence of Salisbury's alleged plan for Home Rule. He opposed anything resembling an Irish parliament and knew that the concession of county councils would never satisfy the nationalists. See Salisbury to H. Howorth, 10 Sept. 1885, Salisbury MSS.

[31] Hammond, *Gladstone and the Irish Nation*, pp. 435-36.

and Duchess of Westminster. Gladstone appeared unexpectedly in the afternoon, drew Balfour aside, and began a long discourse on the gravity of the situation in Ireland. The time for concession, he urged, was at hand, and if the Government refused to meet any of Parnell's demands, then systematic outrage would ensue. "In other words," Balfour said, "we are to be blown up and stabbed if we do not grant Home Rule by the end of next session." To which Gladstone replied: "I understand that the time is shorter than that." This ominous warning was followed five days later by a letter to Balfour virtually promising Liberal support for a Conservative Home Rule bill.[32]

As intended, Balfour relayed all this information to his uncle and the question was discussed in cabinet. The coincidence of Gladstone's overtures and his son's deliberate leak to the press was naturally interpreted by ministers as further proof—if any were needed—of the Liberals' evil intentions. Salisbury was never moved by threats, and the appeal for collaboration struck him as an obvious trap designed to ensnare his party. When he saw Gladstone's communication of December 20, he informed Churchill: "Gladstone has written Arthur a marvellous letter saying he thinks 'it will be a public calamity if this great subject should fall into the lines of party conflict'—and saying that he desires the question should be settled by the present Government. His hypocrisy makes me sick."[33]

Churchill confided the news to Labouchere, adding the sentiment that Gladstone "be damned." On December 23 Gladstone wrote again to Balfour in the same vein; and Salisbury interpreted this letter as "practically announcing that if we don't bring forward a plan for the Government of Ireland, he will: which is as it should be." Ministers were convinced that Gladstone was trying to force a disastrous policy on his opponents in order to save the Liberal party from disruption. The Gladstone-Balfour correspondence, in fact, served to underline the futility of a joint effort at solving the Irish Question. The Liberal leader was hurt by the

[32] For an account of Gladstone's interview with Balfour at Eaton Hall on December 15 and their exchange of letters afterwards, see Dugdale, *Balfour*, I, pp. 93-95; Balfour, *Chapters of Autobiography*, pp. 209-13; and Hammond, *Gladstone and the Irish Nation*, chap. 23.

[33] Salisbury to Churchill, 24 Dec. 1885, Salisbury MSS.

brusque manner in which the Caretaker ministry dismissed his offer, and he held Balfour partially responsible for ruining the only chance of cooperation.

Early in January Lord Randolph Churchill wrote to his chief, informing him that Gladstone was "entirely monopolised by the Irish question, talks of nothing else, and writes a great deal about it to his friends. Mr. G. was pleased to express great admiration of you and your policy: he also intimated that I was an unprincipled young blackguard or something very analogous thereto, and then he confided . . . that he was very much annoyed with Arthur Balfour . . . but he seemed to be under the impression that the artful Arthur had misrepresented him and betrayed him, for he had only received a curt and barely courteous acknowledgment in answer to his advances."[34]

In the meantime Balfour had told his uncle that almost all the former Liberal ministers, excepting Spencer, opposed the extreme measure advocated by Herbert and his father. Without the support of Hartington, Goschen, Chamberlain, and Dilke, he declared, it would be impossible for Gladstone to form a government. He advised the immediate resignation of ministers in order to force the burden of Ireland onto the Liberals. The cabinet made no pretence about treating the Irish Question in a partisan manner. Since they reckoned that Home Rule would break up any party that touched it, they wished to reveal Gladstone as the enemy of the Union as soon as possible.[35]

While the Liberals struggled to repair the damage caused by the Kite, the Government faced troubles of their own. Lord Randolph Churchill threatened to resign over a question of domestic policy. The cabinet proposed to meet Parliament with a Queen's speech that offered no concessions to Ireland. Churchill tried to convince his colleagues that reform of parliamentary procedure ought to take precedence over all other matters. The cabinet thought otherwise. Piqued at their complacent attitude toward what he considered an issue of the greatest urgency, he poured out his grievances to Salisbury. He was already "pledged

[34] Churchill to Salisbury, 3 Jan. 1886, *ibid.*

[35] Dugdale, *Balfour*, I, pp. 94-95. See also Balfour to Salisbury, 23 Dec. 1885, Salisbury MSS. Salisbury predicted that only Granville and Rosebery among the ranking members of the Liberal party would join Gladstone in a Home Rule solution; Salisbury to Churchill, 24 Dec. 1885, *ibid.*

up to the neck" on the question, he declared. The cabinet meetings were "mort et martyre" to him; and the neglect of procedural reform meant that he would have to "eat more dirt than ever, before those holy men Iddesleigh, Cross, John Manners & Co." Beach's behavior in deserting him at the last moment he considered unpardonable.[36] The familiar signs of neurosis that lay so close to the surface in Lord Randolph had returned. That he should turn on his friend Hicks Beach with such asperity shows something of the strain under which he worked throughout his career and which he imposed so often upon his colleagues. With that singleminded sense of injury which distinguished him, he placed his office at Salisbury's disposal, and waited to be wooed back again by his chief. Salisbury answered Churchill the same day, December 16, in a letter full of understanding and solicitude. The original draft revealed his anxiety to soothe the ruffled pride of his minister: "If we have any more cabinets, I shall suggest our meeting in my room in the Foreign Office—and then when the holy men are too much for you, you can seek solace from a cigarette in the little room at the side. I am sure many cabinet difficulties are owing to that filthy, small, close room." And he ended on the sympathetic note: "Believe me, you cannot be more anxious to be 'free' than I am. But to do our duty to those behind us, we must go on in spite of many disagreeables for a few weeks longer."[37]

In itself the rift amounted to no more than a passing fit of distemper; but it was symptomatic of more serious differences between Churchill and his colleagues. Hating to be contradicted, especially by the "old gang," Churchill feared that his precarious state of health might terminate his career before he had realized his goal of modernizing the party's structure and program. His impetuous behavior added another burden for Salisbury, who found the combination of the Foreign Office and the premiership more exhausting than he had anticipated. The accumulation of difficulties led him to remark early in January: "I am feverishly anxious to be out. Internally as well as externally our position as a Government is intolerable."[38]

[36] Churchill to Salisbury, 16 Dec. 1885, *ibid.*
[37] Salisbury to Churchill, 16 Dec. 1885, *ibid.*
[38] Cecil, *Salisbury*, III, pp. 283-84.

Lord Randolph atoned somewhat for his moodiness by supplying the prime minister with the latest news. Despite occasional storms, these were the halcyon weeks and months of their relationship. With his myriad contacts in political society, Lord Randolph kept his leader up to date about movements in the Opposition ranks. He reported Chamberlain's fury over the Kite and the efforts of Gladstone to "mollify and reconcile" him. "Natty" Rothschild, whom he interrogated at length, asserted that Parnell "had got Gladstone tight and that the latter had committed himself." From Labouchere, whom he considered the "most perfect cynic" he had ever known, he learned that Gladstone "was in a state of absolute insanity on the subject of returning to office, and that though he [Labouchere] did not pretend to the possession of scruples himself, he had been startled at the amount of unscrupulousness, lying, and recklessness covered up under a mountain of casuistry which the G. O. M. had recently displayed to him."[39] All this information—much of it idle, if not malicious, gossip—Churchill faithfully passed on to Salisbury.

On January 1, while Carnarvon was absent in Dublin, ministers unanimously rejected Gladstone's offer of assistance, but they found it more difficult to agree on the most effective way of answering him. Salisbury recommended public repudiation in the hope that this would force Gladstone to declare his intentions toward Ireland. It was time, he thought, to end the seven-month truce and to take a definite stand against any form of Home Rule. Some ministers, on the other hand, were more reluctant to leave office. Churchill and Hicks Beach wished to prolong the Irish alliance as long as possible in order to give the country the benefit of Conservative leadership in domestic and foreign affairs. Lord Randolph advocated procedural reform as a diversion from the lethal issue of Ireland. At the same time there were members of the Government who wished to stay in office but "would not stand moves made by Hicks Beach and Randolph Churchill that appeared eccentric."[40] The Maamtrasna debate had cast a long shadow.

After a sharp argument, the cabinet decided not to make any official announcement about their hostility to Home Rule. Balfour replied to Gladstone on January 4, acknowledging the offer of

[39] Churchill to Salisbury, 22 Dec. 1885, Salisbury MSS.
[40] Cranbrook to Salisbury, 31 Dec. 1885, *ibid.*

cooperation and refusing to satisfy Gladstone's curiosity about Government intentions. The ministry had resolved to meet Parliament, to concede nothing to the nationalists, and to be, in Salisbury's words, "more than ordinarily sensitive" to any vote of censure. W. H. Smith expressed the feelings of most Conservatives when he declared with relief: "I am very glad indeed that we have not soiled our fingers with home rule. It would have been destructive to us to have touched it: and I think it must smash up Gladstone."[41] By shifting the burden of proof onto their opponents, the cabinet had in effect adopted the Liberal tactics of the previous June.

So long as a glimmer of hope remained that Salisbury would attempt some solution, Gladstone refrained from taking any step toward courting the Irish members. He reminded Parnell through Mrs. O'Shea that the nationalists were still committed to support the Government, and that he had no wish to invite the charge of bribery by premature pledges to Home Rule. His refusal to pry Parnell away from the Conservatives until the last minute, however, did not deter the Conservatives from accusing Gladstone of caring more about office than about Ireland. Parnell himself suspected that the Kite had hardened ministers against concession, and he turned toward Gladstone, albeit with the caution of one who had no intention of squandering eighty-six votes in Parliament. At the same time he did not sever all ties with the Government. If both parties rejected Home Rule, Parnell preferred to keep the Conservatives in office on the basis of their commitment to land purchase and their majority in the Lords.[42]

And so Gladstone's attempts to raise the Irish Question above the play of party politics failed. Lost in reveries about creating an Irish nation, he failed to reckon with the pragmatism of men like Churchill, who desired to "pin" the Liberals to Home Rule and then dissolve Parliament on the issue of "the Empire in danger." Having no independent majority in the Commons and

---

[41] Harrowby to Carnarvon, 3 Jan. 1886, Carnarvon MSS; Smith to Salisbury, 18 Dec. 1885, Salisbury MSS. On December 17 Salisbury asked Smith to succeed Hart Dyke as chief secretary in the event of the latter's resignation. See H. Maxwell, *Life and Times of the Rt. Hon. William Henry Smith, M.P.* (hereafter *W. H. Smith*), London, 1893, II, p. 163.

[42] Katherine O'Shea, *Charles Stewart Parnell: His Love Story and Political Life*, London, 1921, p. 192.

feeling no compunction toward Irish nationalism, Salisbury spurned the two most reasonable means of settling the issue. Carnarvon's plea for a joint committee to draft an Irish constitution and Gladstone's overtures through Balfour revealed the Caretaker ministry in their most unimaginative and partisan mood. Party unity and integrity of empire took precedence over Irish national aspirations. Salisbury, who did not admire the "transformation scenes of 1829, 1846, 1867," was unwilling to betray his party on a fourth occasion. Pledged to uphold the Union and eager to expose Gladstone's perfidy, the prime minister, as Scawen Blunt shrewdly remarked, was at last educating Churchill, "not he Lord Salisbury."[43]

[43] Cecil, *Salisbury*, III, p. 281; Blunt, *The Land War in Ireland*, 2d ed., London, 1913, p. 21.

CHAPTER V

The End of the Caretaker Ministry

JANUARY was a crucial month for the leaders of each party as the denouement of the Home Rule crisis rapidly approached. Wild rumors filled the air, ministers quarreled heatedly over the details of a moribund program, and members of the Opposition awaited with growing impatience some clarification from Hawarden. The political world was poised on the verge of an upheaval more profound than that of 1846. Old loyalties would soon be shattered, careers disrupted, and the Liberal party permanently scarred. And all the while Gladstone almost seemed to enjoy keeping his own supporters as well as opponents in a state of high suspense.

I. CARNARVON'S RESIGNATION

In cabinet serious conflicts of opinion emerged about the tactics to be adopted when Parliament reassembled. Apart from Carnarvon, ministers were groping instinctively and often by different routes toward a policy that would rally the forces of virtue, wisdom, and property around the banner of Conservatism. For those politicians anxious to expose the menace of the so-called "new radicalism," Ireland supplied an ideal issue. From a partisan point of view Irish nationalism could be easily construed as a movement dedicated to the abolition of private property, the subversion of the Protestant faith, and the disintegration of empire. Conservative strategy now consisted of maneuvering Gladstone into a position that would identify him in the eyes of the British electorate as the champion of this sinister cause. Reasons of expediency as well as principle thus determined Salisbury to resign at the first opportunity, firmly pledged to maintain the Act of Union.

The last weeks in office proved exasperating to Lord Carnarvon, who still hoped to leave behind some tangible sign of conciliation in Ireland. During the Christmas holidays he drafted an Irish university bill and a technical education bill, but both measures died in cabinet. The failure of two other projects heightened his frustration. Wishing to alert Pope Leo XIII about the "sinister alliance" between the nationalists and the clergy in Ireland, he asked leave to transmit the necessary information by secret channels to Rome. Salisbury, however, vetoed the plan as being "too dangerous."[1] The other abortive proposal concerned relief of distress on the western seaboard, where the potato crop had failed, leaving many peasants close to starvation. Carnarvon briefed the cabinet on the situation and requested a Treasury loan of £10,000 to purchase seed potatoes, citing the precedent of 1879 when government funds had helped to avert a major famine. His appeal, however, was opposed by Hicks Beach, who argued that the present distress was not as widespread as that of 1879. State aid to isolated cases of impoverishment, he contended, would "open the dam" to numerous applications for assistance every time the slightest sign of crop failure appeared. Carnarvon thus lost another item from his depleted store of conciliatory projects.[2]

Despite these setbacks, the viceroy did succeed in reorganizing the Royal Irish Constabulary, and he also took steps to improve the internal security of the country in the event of a nationalist uprising. Although the Special Crime Branch of the RIC assured him that the chances of a rebellion were remote, he worried about the absence of any plans to meet such an eventuality. After appealing to the War Office, he received from Sir Garnet Wolseley a detailed memorandum concerning the proper disposition of military forces in case of insurrection.[3] Carnarvon's growing sense

[1] Salisbury to Carnarvon, 3 Jan. 1886; Carnarvon to Salisbury, 6 Jan. 1886, Carnarvon MSS.

[2] Beach to Carnarvon, 5 Jan. 1886, *ibid.* See also Carnarvon's memorandum on distress in Ireland, 8 Jan. 1886, *ibid.*

[3] Speculating on the causes of Irish discontent, Wolseley ended his report: "Myself, I don't believe in Irish rebellion. Formerly, Irish discontent was led by gentlemen of fighting families: now it is led by pork butchers and green grocers who will murder the unwary, but will never endanger themselves by an appeal to arms. It will not *pay* them. They prefer drawing salaries from the funds subscribed by poor servant girls in America"; Wolseley to Carnarvon, 18 Jan. 1886, *ibid.*

of frustration pervaded other members of the cabinet. The silence that surrounded Gladstone's intentions unnerved ministers and moved Lord Iddesleigh to confess his fears to Carnarvon: "I wish I were well quit of my Patronage! And, indeed, I go with you in wishing I were well quit of Downing Street. But I think it is our duty to make an effort to rally the loyal party before it is quite too late."[4]

On January 9 a schism developed in cabinet between ministers who inclined toward coercion and those who hoped to prolong their stay in office by avoiding Irish affairs altogether. Churchill, the chief opponent of resignation, chose this occasion to revile Ashbourne, whom he unjustly blamed for Carnarvon's "conversion" to Home Rule. The Irish lord chancellor had delivered a report on the condition of Ireland, emphasizing the widespread disregard for law and order. Lord Randolph considered the statement vague and, on the whole, "extremely unsatisfactory." After the meeting he took Ashbourne aside and fulminated against his "imprudent" speech. Later that day Churchill wrote to Carnarvon, complaining that Ashbourne's performance was "most delightful of course to Lord Cranbrook and others who always appear to me most happy when there is a prospect of strong coercion."[5] Such personal recriminations did not exactly help ministers in their search for a way out of the political impasse.

Four days later Carnarvon was en route to London when he read with astonishment in the *Standard* the news of his impending resignation. The leak, whether deliberate or not, embarrassed both the viceroy and his colleagues. By mutual agreement the announcement had been postponed until the end of the month, when a formal explanation could be made in Parliament. To forestall talk of serious dissension in the cabinet, Salisbury immediately authorized the publication of his June correspondence with Carnarvon on the conditions governing the latter's appointment.[6] But the damage had already been done; and many Liberals re-

[4] Iddesleigh to Carnarvon, 1 Jan. 1886, *ibid.*
[5] Churchill to Carnarvon, 9 Jan. 1886, *ibid.*
[6] To make matters worse, the newspapers intimated that differences of opinion had led to the resignation. Carnarvon to Salisbury, 15 Jan. 1886; Salisbury to Carnarvon, 15 Jan. 1886, Salisbury MSS. See also Hardinge, *Carnarvon*, III, pp. 210-11.

joiced at this sign of ministerial turmoil, little aware of its implications for their own party.

Carnarvon returned to Dublin for another fortnight in order to wind up his affairs, while controversy broke out over the choice of his successor. Basically, the dispute concerned the old dilemma of coercion or conciliation. Lord John Manners and Cranbrook recommended someone like General Wolseley, who would "demonstrate to Ireland our resolve to employ the whole force of the Empire to restore and maintain order in that country."[7] Churchill also campaigned actively for Wolseley in the hope that this choice would provide a sharp contrast with the Carnarvon regime. Lord Salisbury, on the other hand, preferred a more innocuous appointment in the person of his friend Lord Cadogan, who had some knowledge of Irish affairs.[8] Carnarvon desired a man closer to his own sympathies and, with the Queen's approval, nominated Lord Brownlow.[9] Anxious to find someone willing to continue his policy of "faith and good works," he objected strongly to Wolseley, whose military record in Egypt and Zululand would convince the Irish people that the Government wished to make a "declaration of war." So sharp was the division of opinion that the appointment was never determined. Churchill considered Cadogan unsuitable. "No extra laws," he informed Salisbury, "could make that good or stable."[10] And Carnarvon's colleagues deplored his presumption in seeking to name a successor. Wishing to avoid another source of contention, Salisbury decided not to appoint a new viceroy but to place the office in a commission of lords justices. The simultaneous resignation of Hart Dyke proved that Carnarvon had at least one supporter within the Government; but this act of protest did not deter ministers from their course.

[7] Manners to Salisbury, 28 Dec. 1885, Salisbury MSS.

[8] George Henry, 5th Earl Cadogan, 1840-1915; M.P. 1873; Under Secretary for War 1875-1878, for Colonies 1878-1880; Lord Privy Seal 1886-1892; Lord Lieutenant of Ireland 1895-1902.

[9] Adelbert Wellington, 3rd Earl Brownlow, 1844-1921; M.P. 1866-1867; Paymaster General 1887-1889; Under Secretary for War 1889-1892.

[10] Churchill to Salisbury, 16 Jan. 1886, *ibid.*

II. AN ELEVENTH-HOUR POLICY

Three critical cabinet councils followed the announcement of Carnarvon's resignation, and from these meetings the main features of an Irish policy slowly emerged. Lord Salisbury had made up his mind to challenge Gladstone directly on the question of the Union, even though ignorance of Gladstone's intentions still confused the issue. From Churchill, who had just talked with Chamberlain, Salisbury gathered that the Liberal leader might abandon Home Rule altogether and retire to Hawarden. "Joe" had also hinted that the Liberals would try to defeat the Government on an amendment to the address concerning the agricultural laborer. Although he himself preferred to keep the Conservatives in office, he knew that the bulk of the Liberals "thirsted" for the Government's blood. Lord Randolph had replied to Chamberlain that ministers would resign on the "first creditable opportunity."[11]

Armed with this information, Salisbury, at the cabinet on January 15, denounced both the league and Gladstone's tergiversations. The ensuing discussion showed that ministers were split into three schools of thought representing inaction, a moderate coercion bill, and outright suppression of the National League. Churchill aggravated the dissension among ministers by opposing both coercion and any formal measure outlawing the league. If the National League required suppression, he favored issuing a writ to this effect on the authority of the lord lieutenant, trusting to Parliament for an act of indemnity. The immediate object of his scorn was the coercion bill, which the prime minister had asked Ashbourne to draft without consulting the secretary for India.

Salisbury's evident failure to take Churchill into his confidence heightened the latter's irritability. After the cabinet Lord Randolph wrote a pained letter to his chief imploring him not to rely upon the inept advice of Ashbourne and the "holy men." The political situation in the Commons, he believed, virtually precluded the success of any crimes bill; and the defeat of such a measure would ruin the case for strengthening the law in Ireland. He urged Salisbury to wait one month before deciding about

[11] Churchill to Salisbury, 13 Jan. 1886, *ibid.*

coercion—an interim that could be filled with procedural reform—and ended his letter with the threat that any insistence on repressive legislation would result in the resignation of his two "most faithful" supporters. Beach, for his part, opposed coercion because he believed that the Government lacked sufficient evidence to withstand Opposition attacks. He blamed the absence of data on agrarian crime on the Home Rule sympathies of Castle officials, and objected to throwing over the pledges of conciliation given in June. Fear of offending the "susceptibilities" of potential Liberal allies also influenced the stand taken by Churchill and Beach, who desired instead a program of remedial measures ranging from local government to relief of distress.[12]

After the cabinet meeting W. H. Smith urged the prime minister to resign as quickly as possible. Trying to overcome the stalemate in cabinet, he argued that only a matter of time separated Salisbury's views from those of Beach and Churchill. Almost every minister, he believed, admitted the necessity of coercion sooner or later: "Public opinion favors it; it is in the air, but evidence is yet wanting." In conclusion he recommended a strong declaration against Home Rule in order to reassure both the Conservative rank and file and the general public.[13]

Thus the second cabinet ended in a deadlock, with Beach and Lord Randolph threatening resignation. Cranbrook complained that a "drifting policy has weakened the springs of government" in Ireland; while Salisbury tried to convince Churchill that cabinet solidarity took precedence over all other issues: "We have no right to the luxury of divided councils in a crisis such as this." The prime minister believed that the vast majority of the party desired a firm stand against the disintegrating forces of Home Rule. Above all, he could not allow the public to brand the party as "timid." The ensuing correspondence between Salisbury and his two recalcitrant ministers in the Commons illustrated the consternation that Gladstone's silence was causing the Government. Beach, in an uncompromising mood, stood his ground and

[12] *Letters of Queen Victoria,* 3d series, I, pp. 9-10; W. S. Churchill, *Churchill,* II, pp. 34-36; Hicks Beach, *St. Aldwyn,* I, pp. 258-59; Cecil, *Salisbury,* III, pp. 286-87.

[13] Smith to Salisbury, 17 Jan. 1886, Salisbury MSS.

refused to be guided by the "ignorant wish of the 'great majority of the party.' "[14]

The cabinet impasse finally resolved itself on January 18. Carnarvon, attending his last council, helped to polish the Irish paragraph in the Queen's speech, which declared that special powers would be requested from Parliament if the ordinary law proved unable to cope with crime. Carnarvon then warned that Parnell would regard the statement as officially ending the seven months' alliance; and Lord Iddesleigh registered his protest by threatening to resign over the want of a firmer Irish policy. The latter news prompted Salisbury to exclaim: "What a shriek of delight would arise from the other side if they only knew it."[15] But wiser counsel prevailed and Iddesleigh backed down. The cabinet compromised by phrasing the Irish paragraphs of the speech so ambiguously as to commit the Government neither to a crimes bill nor to immediate local government reform. Two days later W. H. Smith was appointed chief secretary in place of Hart Dyke. The way was now clear for a change of policy.

On January 21 Parliament assembled to hear the Queen's speech. A local government bill for Great Britain and Ireland was promised some time in the future; but no details were mentioned. Coercion was kept well in the background. The Opposition wasted no time in denouncing the speech. Gladstone accused ministers of having deceived the Irish party with promises of conciliation in June, but he refused to commit himself to any alternative course. At the same time a series of meetings of the Liberal leaders moved Goschen to observe: "The fat is in the fire, and a split almost unavoidable."[16]

In the House of Lords Salisbury tried in vain to defend the ministerial statement. The Government, he declared, had a very clear policy, which was to maintain the Act of Union. Unfortunately, the Hawarden Kite or Gladstone's "pilot balloon" had exerted a "fatal" influence on the Parnellites, while it had seriously

[14] Gathorne Hardy, *Cranbrook*, II, p. 235; W. S. Churchill, *op.cit.*, II, pp. 37-40.

[15] Salisbury to Churchill, 19 Jan. 1886, Salisbury MSS.

[16] *Hansard*, 3d series, Vol. 302, pp. 32-36; A. R. D. Elliot, *The Life of George Joachim Goschen, First Viscount Goschen* (hereafter *Goschen*), London, 1911, II, p. 9.

damaged Irish securities and shaken the confidence of every loyalist in Ireland. Accusing Gladstone of "skulking behind ambiguous denials," he declared that Ireland needed above all "steady, consistent" government: "If you have instability of purpose, if you have a policy shifting from five years to five years with each change in the wheel of political fortune, or the humour of political parties in this country, you are drifting straight to a ruin which will engulf England and Ireland alike."[17]

The Opposition quite rightly demanded a more explicit statement than this about the Government's Irish intentions. Veiled hints about the deficiency of the ordinary law failed to satisfy even the Conservative backbenchers. Lord Randolph tried to stall for time by moving the adjournment, but the motion failed and only increased the hostility of Liberals and nationalists. And Ashbourne lamely summed up the Government's case by attributing the National League to Liberal complacency. The situation was grave, he admitted, but it did not justify panic.

In the Commons Hicks Beach emphasized Carnarvon's success in conciliating Ireland, but warned that so long as intimidation continued to increase, the possibility of special legislation could not be ignored. Gladstone replied in a most equivocal speech, praising the virtues of Irish self-government without pledging himself to Home Rule. As "an old parliamentary hand," he cautioned his followers against rushing impetuously into the Irish controversy.[18]

For four nights the Government endured the humiliations of the Opposition assault. Even the Queen criticized the address, and Salisbury was compelled to write an apologetic letter defending Conservative policy. To a more sympathetic woman, Lady John Manners, he confessed: "What with cabinets, openings of Parliaments, and journeys to Osborne, and many other things, I am more chivied than ever. Oh! for a good adverse division! It will not be long coming if all tales be true. We have had great troubles and our internal condition is unsatisfactory."[19]

If it achieved nothing else, the debate on the address at least

---

[17] *Hansard*, 3d series, Vol. 302, pp. 67-69.

[18] *Ibid.*, pp. 74-78, 112-30.

[19] Salisbury to Lady John Manners, 24 Jan. 1886, Salisbury MSS.

convinced Churchill and Hicks Beach that their tactics were impracticable. On January 24 Salisbury informed the Queen that his "recalcitrant" colleagues had changed their minds about coercion "under party pressure." The Government, he added, would propose special legislation as soon as they received word from Smith. After seven months of indecision, the cabinet had at last resorted to the only policy that would protect them against charges of Home Rule sympathies. Coercion, Lord George Hamilton hoped, would serve as a wedge, driven deep into the Liberal party, to split Gladstone's following in two. The truce was over; the game of playing down Irish disorder had ended; and salvation for the Conservatives lay in resisting Irish demands with all the partisan forces at their command. Rumors that Hartington, Goschen, and even Harcourt would support them on a vote of censure only strengthened the Government's resolve to fall back on coercion.[20]

In the meantime W. H. Smith reported from Dublin that evidence to justify a crimes bill was not lacking: "In many parts of the country the National League is the Government *de facto*, and the Government *de jure* is powerless." The only alternative to suppressing the league, he concluded, was surrender to its will. On January 26 Smith was informed that an announcement would shortly be made in Parliament about the introduction of a crimes bill and a land purchase scheme.[21] After Beach had asked leave to give precedence to the crimes bill, Jesse Collings moved his amendment calling for increased benefits to the agricultural laborer. Gladstone, unable to tolerate the prospect of coercion, was prepared to advance toward Home Rule without either wing of his party if necessary.

In Dublin, Smith was unaware of the rapidly approaching crisis and complained that Lord Salisbury was harassing him with requests for prompt action. While Churchill tactfully explained the reason for haste, the prime minister wrote to the Queen to prepare her for the shock of impending defeat. He apologized for the appearance of vacillation in Government policy, but assured her that ministers would try to redress their "grave error"

[20] Gathorne Hardy, *Cranbrook*, ii, pp. 238-39.

[21] Smith to Salisbury, 25 Jan. 1886; Salisbury to Smith, 26 Jan. 1886, Salisbury mss.

as soon as possible. Denouncing Gladstone's consuming ambition, he lamented his inability to keep the "G. O. M." out of office.[22]

The new chief secretary never had a chance to complete his assignment, for on the night of January 26 the division on Collings' amendment brought adverse results. Although some seventy-six Liberals abstained and eighteen others voted with the Government, Gladstonians and Parnellites combined to make a majority of seventy-nine. Salisbury immediately tendered his resignation, regretting only the manner of defeat. The Conservatives had planned to abandon office on the Irish Question; but Gladstone cunningly kept the issue beyond their reach with a diversionary motion about "three acres and a cow." Agricultural laborers, however, were soon forgotten in the excitement of Gladstone's return to power. Like their predecessors, the Caretaker ministry, described by Balfour as seven months of "eating dirt," had foundered on the Irish Question. Both Cranbrook and Salisbury rejoiced at the prospect of release from the intolerable position of a minority government and from the burden of cabinet disputes. But the prospect of a Liberal ministry bent on appeasing Parnell cast a pall of gloom over the Conservative party.

The Government's defeat seemed to depress the Queen far more than it did her ministers. Respecting Salisbury's character and achievements at the Foreign Office, she dreaded Gladstone's return on a Home Rule platform. To Salisbury she made an impassioned plea for a dissolution. But he quickly disabused her of this notion, holding that it was wiser to wait a year, "when the agricultural labourer has to some extent found out the hollowness of the promises made to him." When Salisbury arrived at Osborne, he discussed the choice of Liberal ministers with the Queen and promised that the House of Lords would throw out any Home Rule bill that Gladstone chose to introduce. At the same time he talked candidly about the failure of the Carnarvon experiment and referred to the shortcomings of Ashbourne and Beach in their respective offices.[23]

"Pity the Queen!", exclaimed Lord John Manners, who advised

[22] W. S. Churchill, *op.cit.*, II, pp. 44-46; *Letters of Queen Victoria*, 3d series, I, pp. 19-20.

[23] *Ibid.*, pp. 22-34.

his chief to accept a Hartington ministry based on Conservative and moderate Liberal support.[24] Both Salisbury and Goschen, however, disapproved of such a coalition, and the Queen was left with no alternative but to send for Gladstone. She learned on January 30 that the Irish members had accepted Gladstone's sketch plans for a parliament in Dublin. Meanwhile, outgoing ministers listened with dismay to Smith's report on the "awful state" of Ireland. Churchill had by now completely shifted his ground on reconciliation with nationalist Ireland and swore everlasting hostility to the Parnellites; while most of the cabinet indulged in vindictive remarks about Carnarvon's commitment to Home Rule.[25]

The fall of the Caretaker ministry left Carnarvon one of the most isolated figures in British politics. He had ventured into the quicksand that awaits all politicians who stray from the straight and narrow path of party interests, and, although acting out of the loftiest motives, his behavior earned him nothing but reproaches from his colleagues. A victim of the powerful prejudices engendered by the Irish Question, he left Dublin with a sense of "neglect and failure of duty." Fortunately he still had the courage of his convictions, and in spite of all the difficulties that lay ahead he could write to a friend: "I leave Ireland with extraordinarily mingled feelings, but not without great hope that amidst all the checks and balances which the wise Ruler of the world generally interposes in the affairs of men, there may come a brighter day than the present dark clouds threaten."[26]

For their folly in sending Carnarvon as a goodwill ambassador to Ireland the Conservatives earned the rebuke of Justin McCarthy, who accused them of having "dallied" with the Irish Question, "helplessly, aimlessly, inconsistently." The Caretaker ministry, moreover, had "promised in that delightfully indefinite way which is the joy of Conservative statesmen, all sorts of speedy blessings for Ireland," few of which had ever materialized.[27] Indecision had characterized their Irish policy ever since July, and only at the last minute was coercion adopted as a purely expediential measure.

[24] Manners to Salisbury, 27 Jan. 1886, Salisbury MSS.
[25] See Hardy, *Cranbrook*, II, p. 240.
[26] Carnarvon to Redington, 27 Jan. 1886, Carnarvon MSS.
[27] J. McCarthy, *Ireland Since the Union*, London, 1887, p. 345.

Convinced that Gladstone lusted after office for its own sake, they hoped that the announcement of a crimes bill would force him to reveal his hand. But this stratagem failed altogether. Rebuffed by his opponents, Gladstone had no intention of gratifying their curiosity about Home Rule before the time was ripe.

The Conservative leaders fell back upon coercion in order to rally the party around the Act of Union, to repudiate formally the Parnellite alliance, and to lure Hartington and his followers away from the Liberal camp. From a Unionist point of view the policy enunciated on January 26 was no disaster but a political triumph. It brought to Ireland the merits and demerits of English supremacy for another thirty-five years and won the Unionist coalition a monopoly of office for almost half that period. But the Conservatives' decision was not based on party considerations alone. With the exception of Carnarvon, ministers repudiated the very idea of a parliament in Dublin. The precise extent of their objections in principle, however, has been the subject of much dispute and misunderstanding ever since the memorable night of January 26.

III. POST-MORTEM

The recriminations of Liberals and Irish nationalists about the conduct of the Caretaker ministry persisted long after its defeat. Home Rule sympathizers, eager to justify their own position, produced numerous accounts of Conservative duplicity based on prejudice and factual error. The Government were accused of having deliberately deceived both Gladstone and Parnell about their Irish intentions; and their critics contended that the decision to renew coercion came as a result of the general election, which rendered the Irish alliance useless.[28]

Viscount Gladstone, author of both the Hawarden Kite and *After Thirty Years*, set out in the latter work to defend the Kite and to justify his father's espousal of Home Rule. He also sought to erase some of the stigma attached to the Liberals for their conversion to the cause of Parnell by proving that the Caretaker ministry shared many of the Gladstone family's Irish sentiments.

[28] Gladstone wrote more than ten years after these events: "Subsequently we had but too much evidence of a deliberate intention to deceive the Irish, with a view to their support at the election"; Morley, *Gladstone*, III, p. 284.

Herbert Gladstone argued in the first place that the prime minister and "about one half the cabinet" considered a Dublin parliament right in principle and "advisable for Ireland."[29] Of all the cabinet only Carnarvon, in fact, advocated such a policy before and after the election. If Scawen Blunt, hardly a disinterested witness, can be believed, Churchill indulged in loose talk about Home Rule in May and June, 1885. But the vigorous defenses of his loyalty to the Union, written by those who knew and admired him, serve to prove that Lord Randolph was never a Home Ruler by conviction.[30]

Only the leading officials in Dublin Castle, Hamilton and Jenkinson, not to mention Hart Dyke, were genuinely interested in Home Rule. Beach favored conciliation through education and local government reform; Ashbourne inclined toward coercive legislation; while the rest of the cabinet—Iddesleigh, Cranbrook, Lord George Hamilton, Harrowby, and Smith—never showed the slightest sympathy for Irish nationalism. No cabinet minister came forward to support Carnarvon's October memorandum or his joint committee scheme in November and December; and the viceroy himself remarked that his colleagues neither possessed a substitute for Home Rule nor desired to find one.[31]

As for the prime minister, the sins had been those of omission and equivocation. Salisbury never objected to the principle of colonial self-government, but he insisted that the populace concerned should have proved themselves sufficiently mature to manage their own affairs. Self-government within the empire was in his mind a privilege not a right, and this honor ought not to be distributed without regard to the condition of the country in question. To Salisbury the case of Ireland was as special as its condition was deplorable. The grievous history of the country, its proximity to England, its chronic poverty, the existence of a loyal or Protestant minority, and the ignorance of the majority all militated against any tampering with the Act of Union. Popular agitation, which invariably ended in violence, had convinced him that Irishmen were, at least for the present, incapable

[29] H. Gladstone, *After Thirty Years*, p. 413.
[30] Blunt, *The Land War in Ireland*, p. 21; W. S. Churchill, *op.cit.*, II, pp. 55-58; Hamilton, *Reminiscences*, II, p. 20.
[31] Hardinge, *Carnarvon*, III, p. 218.

of governing themselves. The ingredients he found in the Home Rule movement—lawlessness, a desire to expropriate the land-lords, and hatred of Protestantism—struck him as singularly unsuitable foundations for responsible government. Some time in the distant future Home Rule might be conferred upon Ireland, but even then the concession of a "native" legislature should be surrounded with safeguards so as to protect minority interests. In the meantime Irishmen would have to learn the rudiments of good behavior and self-help.

In Salisbury's mind, moreover, the moral obligation to the loyalist minority loomed large. He refused to abandon Protestants to the "inevitable" tyranny of the Catholic majority and assumed that only steady and unyielding government would reduce the threat of this tyranny to manageable proportions. Once that goal had been achieved, Ireland would then be ready to join the other members of the empire enjoying self-government. Given internal stability and a degree of prosperity, Ireland would also be eligible for elective county and borough councils. But the process of teaching the populace respect for the law required time. The methods, if not the memories, of rebellion could not be effaced in less than a generation, he believed, and at the end of that period he hoped to see Ireland receive a substantial measure of control over her own affairs.

Those Home Rulers like Herbert Gladstone who tried to depict Salisbury as nurturing similar sentiments deliberately overlooked the fact that Salisbury had long opposed any such concession. In an article entitled "Disintegration," written in 1883 for the *Quarterly Review*, he had warned against the illusion that Home Rule was compatible with imperial integrity. Although admitting the "humiliating failure" of the English occupation in Ireland, he deplored the continuous cycle of agitation and concession, which left the people increasingly embittered. Repeal of the Act of Union was tantamount to separation and offered no solution to the problem. Home Rule, as he understood that phrase, would be nothing less than a "sentence of exile or ruin" upon Ulster: "All that is Protestant—nay, all that is loyal —all who have land or money to lose . . . would be at the mercy of the adventurers who have led the Land League, if not of the darker counsellors by whom the Invincibles have been inspired. . . . It would be an act of political bankruptcy, an avowal that we were unable to satisfy even the most sacred obligations. . . . Any political power conceded to an Irish assembly will be made the fulcrum by which more will be exacted, until complete practical independence is secured." Salisbury also expressed anxiety about the threat to national security posed by an independent and hostile Ireland, which would be easy prey for any continental power with belligerent intentions. Did the British public, he asked, have the strength to resist gradual disintegration—Home Rule by installments? "Or will our bargaining politicians, when votes grow scarce, open their market once more for a final clearance sale of all that remains of English rule in Ireland?"[32]

These arguments had been aired three years before Gladstone's so-called conversion to Home Rule, and the Liberal leaders would have done well to study "Disintegration" before jumping to conclusions about Salisbury's views on Ireland. The connection between the Act of Union and integrity of empire was always intimate and vital in Salisbury's mind. To meddle with the act was to undermine the mutual confidence that held the delicate framework of empire together. Integrity of empire was not just a convenient political slogan. As a man inordinately concerned with threats to British prestige, Salisbury feared that any concession to separatist forces in Ireland would be interpreted by such powers as France and Russia as a sure sign of imperial decay. The great majority of Englishmen, Salisbury believed, would never accept Home Rule unless their political instincts suddenly changed, and only a violent upheaval could achieve that. Writing to Canon MacColl in 1889, he pursued this theme: "As to Home Rule in your sense—which is Federation—I do not see in it any elements of practicability. Nations do not change their political nature like that, except through blood. It would require a subordination of all ordinary motives, a renunciation of traditions and prepossessions, a far-reaching and disciplined resolve, which is never engendered by mere persuasion, and only comes after conflict and under the pressure of military force."[33]

After the events of 1885 Salisbury was censured for lacking "moral strength" in his Irish policy.[34] Judged by Gladstone's

[32] *Quarterly Review*, October, 1883, Vol. 156, No. 312, pp. 559-95.
[33] Russell, *MacColl*, p. 137.
[34] Hammond, *Gladstone and the Irish Nation*, p. 380.

standards, he could plead only guilty to this charge. The two leaders approached the problem from diametrically opposed points of view. A sense of responsibility both to the Protestant minority in Ireland and to his party moved Salisbury to care less than Gladstone about high moral precepts. For years he had objected to the fluctuations between two extremes of policy in Ireland, which canceled out the advantages inherent in either. Although preferring conciliatory legislation to coercion, he made a careful distinction between the two remedies. Coercion, in his opinion, repressed a country no matter what the internal conditions of the society. But conciliation depended for its success upon the attitude of the recipients, and if ever the Irish people became convinced that conciliation derived from English fears rather than from motives of justice, then they would intensify their agitation in order to extract ever-larger concessions. It was just this contingency that he sought to prevent.

Gladstone, on the other hand, placed Irish national aspirations above party considerations. He owed his conscience about Ireland to many different impulses. A mission to Corfu, Burke on the American colonies, Cobden's gospel, the ugly phenomenon of Fenianism, Cavendish's murder, the Parnellite threat to parliamentary government, an idealization of the *Ausgleich* in Austria-Hungary, and a sense of destiny all led Gladstone to espouse Home Rule. Ireland was a nation in fetters, and the Liberal party was God's chosen instrument to emancipate the Irish people. This much was clear to Gladstone. A more difficult question was that of right timing, but he considered himself better qualified than his opponents to judge the "ripeness or the unripeness" of the question. And in 1886 he took it upon himself to educate England, "in her soft arm-chair," about the need of Ireland, "in her leaky cabin . . . to stop out the weather."[35]

If Lord Salisbury's reaction to Irish nationalism contained some patrician elements, he respected individual liberty far too much to wish perpetual coercion upon that country.[36] Only the criminal activities of the National League justified repressive

[35] W. E. Gladstone, *The Irish Question*, London, 1886, pp. 20-22.

[36] Salisbury's reverence for the liberty of the individual, which he considered "the highest prerogative in human nature," is described in Lady G. Cecil, *Biographical Studies of the Life and Political Character of Robert, Third Marquis of Salisbury* (hereafter *Biographical Studies*), London, n.d., pp. 78-82.

measures, and once the agitation against landlords and the Act of Union had ceased, then Ireland would receive her due share of conciliation. Salisbury's most palpable error in 1885 was his tendency to underestimate the urgency of the Irish Question. Preoccupied with the duties of premier and foreign secretary, he had allowed Carnarvon too much freedom of action as lord lieutenant. After the Carnarvon fiasco he used to complain that Englishmen who went to Ireland in an official capacity too often "became corrupted by 'Irish ideas' "; and in the privacy of Hatfield he declared sometime in the summer of 1885: "I am not easy about Carnarvon,—he is getting so very 'green.' "[37] Part of the trouble stemmed from his preference for a "loose" cabinet in which ministers were left to their own devices unless they chose to seek his opinion. Hicks Beach once drew a sharp contrast between Beaconsfield, who often forced his will upon a protesting cabinet, and Salisbury, who sometimes allowed a group of his colleagues to prevail over his own wishes on important issues.

Carnarvon, little dreaming that his harangues about Home Rule often bored the prime minister, remarked on the latter's overriding concern with foreign affairs: "It was with very great difficulty that any other subject could be brought before him. It convinced me . . . how great a mistake it is for a Prime Minister in these days to undertake any other office. If a man can be found with the physical strength, he certainly wants the time."[38] Salisbury did not possess either the health or the temperament necessary for the dual burden, and the physical strain of leading the Caretaker ministry left him exhausted. But it was no easy matter to deprive him of the Foreign Office, as events in 1886 would prove.

More important than ignorance of Irish nationalism as an explanation of Conservative behavior in 1885-1886 was awareness of the "new radicalism" in England. Unknown to Gladstone, the Conservative leaders saw in Home Rule, as well as in the disestablishment question, the beginning of a Radical ascendancy in the Liberal party. They expected Chamberlain to succeed Gladstone as leader in the near future; and, in order to thwart a Radical onslaught on private property and the constitution, the

[37] Hicks Beach, *St. Aldwyn*, ii, p. 362; Cecil, *Salisbury*, iii, p. 155.
[38] Hardinge, *Carnarvon*, iii, p. 219.

Conservatives used the Irish Question as a magnet to attract the moderates of both parties. The Queen was not the only person to foresee the advantages of a coalition dedicated to combat disestablishment and the "unauthorized program." However different their motives, the Conservative hierarchy dared not object to the idea of a united front against the militant radicalism, which they believed was slowly poisoning the political system and jeopardizing their position in society. In the minds of most Conservatives and Whigs, the security of private property as well as the integrity of empire were inextricably bound up with the Act of Union. Irish nationalism thus provided a timely excuse for buttressing the propertied classes against the menace of the masses. The irony was that the Home Rule convulsion threw Chamberlain and his Birmingham claque into the Unionist camp, which had been prepared to fight them to the bitter end.

For the Conservatives Home Rule was very much a party question. Salisbury knew that the issue would split his party, and he never forgot the obligations of a leader to his followers. As Lord Randolph's son once wrote, Salisbury always used his power only through and by, rather than in spite of, the party.[39] Peel in 1846 and Disraeli in 1867 had, in Salisbury's opinion, violated the indispensable trust that exists between party and leader—and with disastrous results. Any leader, he believed, who would risk splitting the party over Ireland or any other issue was unworthy of his place. In the end it was the Hawarden Kite that forced the Caretaker ministry to realize they could not compete against the Liberals on the basis of granting concessions to Ireland. Gladstone had raised the stakes too high: subsidies to industrial schools, land purchase acts, and goodwill tours were mere trifles compared with the prospective Liberal offering. Moreover, Salisbury knew that Parnell, especially after the Kite, would settle for nothing less than Home Rule; and he sensed that the English electorate would lose all respect for a party that tried to bid against the Liberals for Irish support. The policy of January 26 was thus designed to save party unity at the cost of office. In view of the results it was a small price for the Conservatives to pay.

[39] W. S. Churchill, *op.cit.*, I, p. 449. See also Cecil, *Biographical Studies*, pp. 7-18, 32-42.

CHAPTER VI

Killing the Bill

DURING February those forces in England and Ireland sworn to uphold the Union began to prepare for the great struggle ahead. Many Irish Unionists surrendered to despair and made plans to leave the country in the event of a Gladstonian victory on the Home Rule issue. But the Conservative leaders were not so susceptible to panic, and W. H. Smith cited Sir Robert Hamilton as a crowning example of the mental legerdemain in which the Liberals were indulging: "In October he advocates Home Rule with fancy safeguards and in January he tells me the country is in a state of revolution. It is alarm—fright—loss of fibre and of nerve—terror at the consequences following on the responsibility of government."[1] As the day approached when Gladstone would reveal his Home Rule "propositions," the various organs of the press committed themselves for or against the Union. Joining the *Times* in militant opposition to Home Rule were such papers as the *Standard*, the *Morning Post*, and the *Daily Telegraph*; also opposed was the *St. Stephen's Gazette*, which specialized in lurid pictures of outrages in Ireland. The war of words against Home Rule was also fought in the monthly and quarterly reviews as well as in the *Spectator* and *Saturday Review*.

The techniques of mass political organization and propaganda were also affected by the Irish Question. In their efforts to convince the British voter that Home Rule meant an end to empire and prosperity, the Conservatives used not only their conventional party machinery but the new apparatus of the Primrose League —that product of the Fourth party's fertile imagination. Although nominally a nonpartisan association, the league soon became a vital part of the campaign against Home Rule; and men like Salisbury no longer scoffed at the feudal trappings and quasi-democratic complexion of this order. The Primrose League,

[1] Smith to Salisbury, 3 Feb. 1886, Salisbury MSS.

in fact, owed its remarkable growth in the years 1886-1891 almost exclusively to the Irish Question. During this period the number of knights, dames, and associate members jumped from some fifteen thousand to over one million; and no organization worked harder to publicize the Unionist cause. Habitations or local associations sprang up in Ireland attracting merchants, manufacturers, and members of the professional classes. In both countries the league sponsored lectures, lantern slides depicting agrarian crimes, posters, pamphlets, fetes, and amateur theatricals, in order to convert the rural and urban worker to the faith of Unionism and imperial integrity.[2] Thanks to the league and other Unionist associations, the British electorate acquired a greater awareness than it had ever had before of imperial as well as Irish problems.

I. PRELIMINARIES

The Conservatives and their erstwhile allies the Liberal secessionists wasted little time in mobilizing their resources. On February 17 Lord Salisbury delivered a rousing speech at Hertford, where he impugned Gladstone's motives in taking up Home Rule and predicted that the latter would award the "oyster" to the Parnellites, while conferring the shells, "properly decorated and illuminated," upon his own party. Because no Home Rule bill could ever guarantee the enforcement of legal contracts, Salisbury warned that any so-called safeguards would be as useless as paper barricades.[3]

Lord Randolph went much further than mere rhetorical devices in his oratory. Late in December, if not earlier, he had told Labouchere that if a Home Rule bill were forthcoming, "I should not hesitate, if other circumstances were favorable, to agitate Ulster even to resistance beyond constitutional limits . . . "; and he asked that Gladstone be informed of this fact. Churchill was too shrewd a politician to ignore the potential weapon that lay in Ulster, and he crossed the Irish Sea late in February in order to play the "Orange card" with a vengeance. Given a tumultuous welcome at Larne and elsewhere, he sensed the temper of the Protestant loyalists and did his best to stir them into action, legal or otherwise, on behalf of the Union. Ulster Hall in Belfast was packed with

---

[2] See J. H. Robb, *The Primrose League,* Columbia, 1942, pp. 57 ff.

[3] Cecil, *Salisbury,* III, pp. 293-94.

Ulstermen clamoring to hear words of exhortation from this Conservative spokesman. And the audience was not disappointed. In a succession of memorable phrases delivered in vibrant tones, Churchill warned his listeners to watch, to organize, and to prepare for the conflict that was imminent. He compared Gladstone to Macbeth, who hesitated before murdering Duncan: Gladstone, too, asked for time "before plunging the knife into the heart of the British Empire." And even though the Conservatives were "essentially a party of law and order," there might come a time when circumstances would justify violence. The whole mood of the speech was one of belligerence and defiance. Later, in a letter to a Liberal Unionist, Churchill coined the phrase "Ulster will fight, and Ulster will be right."[4] His appeal to the Calvinist instincts of the Orangemen proved an unqualified success from a party point of view. When Sir Stafford Northcote had visited Ulster in 1883, he had congratulated himself upon his role as a "lightning conductor" in providing a safe outlet for the "electric fluid with which the air was heavily charged."[5] But by February, 1886, the man, the mood, and the situation had changed. And Churchill, who had gone to Ireland to generate rather than to ground electricity, returned like Essex, "bringing rebellion broached on his sword."

After the famous Belfast speech on February 22, Salisbury publicly hailed Lord Randolph's war cry as a "brilliantly successful effort"; and Churchill returned to England confident that he had played the "ace of trumps and not the two." Back at Westminster, Churchill hoped to consolidate the Unionist alliance by enticing Lord Hartington and his followers into a formal coalition. But the Liberal Unionists stubbornly insisted upon preserving their independence and separate organization. Churchill's influence within the shadow cabinet grew steadily during this period of intensive and secret negotiation. Although he was "wild

[4] W. S. Churchill, *Churchill*, II, pp. 28-29, 58-66.

[5] A. Lang, *Life, Letters, and Diaries of Sir Stafford Northcote, First Earl of Iddesleigh* (hereafter *Iddesleigh*), London, 1920, II, p. 260. Lord Randolph wrote from Ulster: ". . . if I am put upon any trial for high treason I shall certainly rely upon your evidence that at any rate up to the 22nd of this month my action was constitutional"; Churchill to Salisbury, 24 Feb. 1886, Salisbury MSS.

for an Irish row," believing that the policy of delay was losing the Conservatives much support, he failed to move Salisbury from his determination to wait for Gladstone's measure before launching a counteroffensive.[6]

So confident was Salisbury of the Unionists' position that he left for the Riviera early in March in search of rest after the strains of leading the Caretaker ministry. He remained there for a month while his colleagues pleaded with him to return. Having no wish to leave the Mediterranean for the cold and controversy of London, he replied to such entreaties: "I shall come back as soon as he [Gladstone] graciously allows us to do business—but not till then."[7]

While the Conservative leader relaxed at Monte Carlo, Churchill supplied him with a steady flow of information about people and events at Westminster. Parnell, whom he met in the smoking room of the House of Commons, was very "amiable and gracious," but believed that he (Lord Randolph) was "awfully unscrupulous." The Irish leader had refrained from accusing the Conservatives of having pledged themselves to Home Rule in 1885, because he thought it might be necessary some day to deal with them again. Churchill also revealed his cautious approaches to the Liberal Unionists and continued to plead with his chief for a quick return: the want of "originality or resource" in both Beach and W. H. Smith, he argued, made such a move imperative. Chamberlain he described as becoming more vindictive than ever about Gladstone, Morley, and the Irish nation.[8] The latest news also reached Salisbury through Balfour, who sent him an account of a talk with Chamberlain about the prospects of a Tory-Radical alliance. To this revealing communication Salisbury jauntily replied: "The conversation gives me the impression of Chamberlain's character vigorously expressed by the 'Pall Mall,' that he is 'as touchy as a schoolgirl, and as implacable as Juno.' The personal element is very strong. He will never make a strong leader. He has not yet persuaded himself that he has any convictions, and therein lies Gladstone's infinite superiority." If only the majority for Home Rule could be reduced to eighty-six, the

[6] Beach to Salisbury, 1 March 1886, *ibid.*

[7] Cecil, *Salisbury*, III, p. 297.

[8] Churchill to Salisbury, 9, 24 March 1886, Salisbury MSS.

number of the Irish party, then, in Salisbury's opinion, "the moral force for innovating purposes . . . [would be] gone."[9]

Rumors, most of them misleading, about the Government's Irish intentions kept the Conservative leaders and whips constantly busy. Beach reported to Salisbury toward the end of March that Gladstone was struggling hard to hold the party together: since the radicals were growing restless, the prime minister could rely only upon the Irish party for support; and Beach advised his chief to persuade the Liberal dissentients to take the initiative against the bill in Parliament. Chamberlain's resignation toward the end of March at first tempted Salisbury to consider forcing a dissolution on the Liberals. Although he knew that such an expedient would magnify the schisms within the Government, he was too sceptical of sustained public interest in Home Rule to carry the idea into effect. It was essential, he felt, to wait until an election could take place exclusively on the Irish Question, when the Liberal Unionists would be compelled to give "some friendly guarantees" to their allies.[10]

Much speculation surrounded Lord Hartington's position in the realignment of political forces. Salisbury believed that the Queen would ask Hartington to form a government in the event of Gladstone's failure to carry his bill. But what tactics should the Conservatives adopt in this case? Few members of the party relished the prospect of a coalition government in which Hartington and Chamberlain were to assume prominent places; but, on the other hand, a repetition of the Caretaker government would open up dangerous gaps in the Unionist alliance, especially if the next election were fought on domestic issues rather than on the Irish Question. Only if the dissolution took place with Gladstone in office and on the question of Home Rule would the possibility of a reunion of the old Liberal party be removed. Such was Salisbury's line of reasoning, and he summarized the situation for Churchill in rather gloomy terms: "I see no hope of good Parliamentary Government in England unless the right wing of the Liberals can be fused with the Tories, on some basis which shall represent the average opinion of the whole mass. But I see little hope of it. The tendency of grouping—caused mainly by the

[9] Dugdale, *Balfour*, 1, pp. 97-102.
[10] Cecil, *Salisbury*, III, p. 298; W. S. Churchill, *op.cit.*, II, pp. 73-74.

existence of various cliques of supporters—is becoming irresistible."[11] But more cheering news came from Lord Cranbrook, who wrote: "I cannot help thinking that the agitation and gloom of Ministerial faces in our House does not speak of smooth sailing in the cabinet—some evidences of mal de mer."[12]

On April 3 Salisbury returned to England. Churchill had already briefed him on the outlines of the Home Rule Bill, as passed on by Chamberlain. "Can you imagine twelve men in their senses," he wrote on March 30, "silently swallowing such lunatic proposals?" The Conservatives thus had the enormous advantage of knowing the principal features of both the Home Rule and Land Purchase bills, which Gladstone considered "inseparable." In the weeks immediately preceding the introduction of the bill, private conferences filled the calendars of the leading politicians; and last-minute preparations for the ensuing debates stirred the wirepullers at Westminster into frenzied activity. Salisbury helped to re-enforce the Unionist alliance by cultivating the company of Lord Hartington, and early in April he accepted Churchill's invitation to meet the "great Joe" at the Turf Club.[13] This was the beginning of a long and incongruous association between the scion of Hatfield and the Birmingham manufacturer whose "unauthorized program" and caucus had been largely inspired by an aversion to aristocracy.

Even during the Home Rule crisis of 1886 the Liberal Unionists made uneasy allies and taxed to the limit the patience of the Conservative leaders. In order to advertise the solidarity of the alliance, Salisbury, Goschen, and other prominent Unionists arranged the famous "Opera House meeting" at which the Whigs condescended to share the stage with their new friends. Some 250 supporters of the Union gathered on April 14 under the chairmanship of Lord Cowper to denounce both Gladstone and Home Rule. Hartington's followers, however, showed a marked dislike for this type of publicity—many still hoped for a Liberal reunion in the future—and the experiment was not repeated. The political coyness of the Liberal Unionists moved Salisbury to comment some-

[11] Salisbury to Churchill, 29 March 1886, Salisbury MSS.

[12] Cranbrook to Salisbury, 2 April 1886, *ibid.*

[13] Churchill to Salisbury, 30 March, 2 April 1886; Salisbury to Hartington, 5, 10 April 1886, *ibid.*

what bitterly: "Their view seems to be that, in allying themselves with us, they are contracting a mésalliance; and though they are very affectionate in private, they don't like shewing us to their friends till they have had time to prepare them for the shock."[14] But the Liberal Unionists atoned somewhat for their modesty by fighting tenaciously against the bill in Parliament.

II. THE BILL

On April 8, before a packed House, Gladstone introduced the celebrated measure that Cranbrook called "a scheme for the further degradation of Ireland and the dishonour of England." The prime minister's mastery of subject and rhetoric did not soften the impact of his recommendations upon those sworn to uphold the Act of Union. The fact of Home Rule had burst upon a country engaged in one of the greatest imperial ventures in its history; and to the men of means and influence who had committed themselves both financially and emotionally to the acquisition of vast tracts of land and trading rights in Africa and the Far East, the appearance of a disintegrating force in Ireland, not to mention Gladstone's "conversion" to this cause, was calculated to arouse the most profound fears. What guarantees were there that Gladstone would stop at Home Rule? How safe was private property? Would the empire be dismembered by forces that Gladstone and Parnell had set in motion? Far more was at stake in the Home Rule debates than just the fate of Ireland.

In Ireland the Home Rule Bill cast a pall over Anglo-Irish society. The conventional air of gaiety and studied nonchalance about politics at Westminster gave way to brooding fears, and on the eve of the bill's introduction the bookings at the Shelbourne Hotel fell off sharply.[15] A sense of approaching doom penetrated Dublin Castle; and magistrates, judges, RIC officers and constables, as well as land agents, speculated on their fates under a Home Rule settlement.

The House of Commons was jammed with members and distinguished guests when Gladstone at last revealed the essentials of his plan to give Ireland Home Rule. The proposals, in brief, entailed a legislature of two voting "orders," the smaller

[14] Cecil, *Salisbury*, III, pp. 299-300.
[15] E. Bowen, *The Shelbourne Hotel*, New York, 1951, pp. 154-58.

one representing the loyalist minority through higher property qualifications and the inclusion of the elective Irish peers. Both "orders" would sit together, although each could vote separately when desired, and each could exercise a suspensory veto over the other's measures. The parliament would have power over all affairs not specifically reserved to the imperial Parliament; this latter category included matters connected with the Crown, imperial defense, war, foreign relations and treaties, commerce, customs and excise, and regulation of currency. What attracted the sharpest criticism was the provision barring the Irish representatives from Westminster. As to imperial dues, Ireland was to contribute one-fifteenth of the United Kingdom's expenditure. The problem of Ulster was virtually ignored. Accompanying the measure was a land purchase scheme that created a state authority to regulate sales and authorized credit amounting to £150,000,000 in order to buy out Irish landlords. When Gladstone had finished his epic speech, the Opposition served notice that they would give no quarter to those who advocated this "drastic" concession.[16]

Halfway through the debates on the bill, Lord Salisbury delivered a speech at St. James's Hall, the repercussions of which lasted many years and proved the advantages of the more diplomatic language he had used at Newport. In developing his argument Salisbury asserted that the Irish people were not sufficiently responsible to deserve the privilege of autonomy. Although this was not the first time he had expressed such a conviction, on this occasion he drew an unfortunate analogy with the self-governing capacities of other peoples. The racist overtones were unmistakable. Grading the Teutonic tribes as the most proficient in this sense, he worked down through the "racial scale" of political maturity until he arrived at the African savage. "You would not confide free representative institutions," he observed, "to the Hottentots, for instance." Even though he rated the Irishman well above the savage, few Home Rulers bothered to wait for qualifying remarks. The Parnellites considered this a national insult and their anger soon found outlets in Parliament and in the press. Whether or not the indiscretion was intentional—and Salisbury had a habit of blurting out his real feelings at inaus-

[16] *Hansard,* 3d series, Vol. 304, pp. 1036-82.

picious moments—the Hottentot allusion only raised the temperature of the debates in Parliament.

A second damaging phrase in the St. James speech concerned the Conservatives' alternative policy for Ireland, which was "government . . . honestly, consistently, and resolutely applied for twenty years." When that period had elapsed, Ireland would be ready to receive such benefits as county councils, educational endowments, and industrial subsidies. Only a government that did not yield to agitation or tremble before outrage, he contended, would restore prosperity and peace to the country. Resolute government was an old formula for English rule in Ireland, but Salisbury's remarks were quickly abbreviated to "twenty years of coercion," and this slogan became another rallying cry for the Parnellites and their Liberal allies.[17]

When Salisbury learned of the furor aroused by his speech, he flatly denied that his policy consisted only of repression: "I have never proposed to enforce new repressive laws for 20 years. The only occasion on which I have mentioned that period of time is in asking for honest, resolute, and consistent government. If the prevalence and character of crime should be such as to require repressive laws at any time, of course in the interest of the innocent population they must be made, but whether that necessity will exist, and at what time, is a question on which I have expressed no opinion whatever. It is much less likely to exist if the conduct of government is marked by the three qualities which I have named."[18]

Lord Salisbury always argued that coercion in his sense of the word had nothing whatever to do with Conservative policy in Ireland. What that country needed above all was legislation to protect the liberty of innocent people against the encroachments of criminally inspired organizations, and if this guarantee of basic rights was to be called coercion, then such a measure ought to be applied not just for twenty years but forever.

On the evening after his St. James speech the Conservative leader attended a dinner party given by Churchill in order to meet

[17] Cecil, *Salisbury*, III, pp. 302-03.
[18] Salisbury to T. Stevenson, 15 June 1886, Salisbury MSS.

Chamberlain, who, according to his host, was engaged in "playing a great part which goes far to obliterate former wickedness."[19] Chamberlain repaid such hospitality by sabotaging the Home Rule Bill at every opportunity. As Harcourt warned Gladstone, the Radical leader was bent on "war to the knife." At the end of May, Chamberlain presided over a meeting of more than fifty Radicals in Committee Room 15, and their decision to vote against the second reading, combined with Bright's announcement of his opposition to Home Rule, meant that the fate of the bill was virtually sealed. In the Commons, Opposition spokesmen concentrated their attacks on the weakest points in the measure. The exclusion of Irish members from Westminster, the questions of internal security and of safeguarding the loyalist minority, and the size of the imperial contribution raised irrefutable objections in the minds of Unionists. Gladstone's land purchase plan, which created an enormous British liability, inspired no enthusiasm among the authors of the Ashbourne act. Time and again the Opposition, with Chamberlain in the vanguard, pressed these points home, to the discomfort of Government supporters.

At length the combined forces of Unionism prepared to test the Government's strength on the second reading. Gladstone's last-minute attempt to postpone a division by adjournment failed to deter his opponents. Speakers for both sides rose impressively to the occasion, and even Hartington spoke with eloquence. The debate reached a climax as the leaders of the Unionist and Home Rule alliances wound up their arguments with perorations both moving and forceful. Hicks Beach sounded a Burkean note of prescriptive right and imperial solidarity in the hope of rallying waverers to the cause of the Union. Parnell based his appeal on the verdict of future generations who would some day be able to say with pride that "England and her Parliament, in this nineteenth century, was wise enough, brave enough, and generous enough to close the strife of centuries, and to give peace, prosperity, and happiness to suffering Ireland." And Gladstone, last and magnificent in the imminence of defeat, having excoriated Chamberlain as a man who "has trimmed his vessel and . . . touched his rudder in such a masterly way that in whichever di-

[19] Churchill to Salisbury, 6 May 1886, *ibid.*

rection the winds of Heaven may blow they must fill his sails,"
ended his speech by asking that Ireland's prayer for prosperity
and peace be granted. In the early hours of June 8, exactly one
year after the Liberals' defeat on the budget, the House divided
on the second reading of the Home Rule Bill; and in an atmosphere of almost unbelievable tension the tellers conveyed the news
that the bill had been defeated by thirty votes.[20]

When the numbers were announced, there ensued one of the
most tumultuous scenes ever witnessed in the Commons. With the
Speaker gesturing in vain for silence, the Opposition benches
echoed with cheer after cheer. Conservative members shouted
themselves hoarse, waved their hats wildly, and jumped up and
down on their seats. During this demonstration Chamberlain remained seated and impassive. Ministers stared glumly at the
antics of their opponents. When the commotion began to subside,
the Irish members rose en masse and at a given signal of "Three
cheers for the Grand Old Man" warmly applauded the prime
minister. Outside the chamber, in the central hall, a tense crowd
had gathered to await the news of the bill's fate. Upon hearing
the verdict most of those assembled burst into cheering and then
sang "God Save the Queen." At Balmoral the Queen passed a
fitful night and woke in the morning to receive word of the
Government's defeat. "Cannot help feeling relieved," she noted in
her journal, "and think it is the best for the interests of the
country." Lord Cranbrook was somewhat more outspoken: "God
speed the cause of loyalty and patriotism against one-man rule,
servility, and idolatry." And at Hatfield Lord Salisbury stayed
up until 3:00 A.M. in order to hear the news, which came by
telegram.[21]

From Dublin came reports of deep relief among the loyalists.
There was no popular excitement, no noisy procession by jubilant
Unionists. Instead an unexpected calm prevailed, while the nation-
alists hid their true feelings behind a mask of indifference. The
Freeman's Journal boldly declared that the principle of Home
Rule had triumphed, even if the bill had been destroyed. Reaction
to the news was strangely muted in almost every part of Ireland

[20] *Hansard*, 3d series, Vol. 306, pp. 1184-1240.
[21] *Times*, 8-10 June 1886; *Letters of Queen Victoria*, 3d series, I, p.
143; Hardy, *Cranbrook*, II, p. 251.

save in Ulster. In Belfast the Orangemen paraded their joy with such flamboyance as to goad Catholic workers into counterdemonstrations, and some five persons were killed by the police during riots in the poorer districts, where the rival factions needed only the slightest provocation to fly at one another's throats.[22]

In the wake of victory most Unionists found their sentiments mirrored in the *Times,* which devoted an editorial paean to the defeat of the so-called "Irish Separation Bill" by a "crushing" majority. Never again would the country be "hoodwinked by Mr. Gladstone's verbal legerdemain or led astray by inflated sentiment." The *Times* predicted an early dissolution and looked forward to the day when the electorate would be able to record their disapproval of a policy that had been forced upon them.[23] On June 10 Gladstone gratified this wish by announcing the imminent dissolution of Parliament.

III. THE GENERAL ELECTION OF 1886

The prospect of an election stirred some Unionists into thinking about an alternative to Home Rule. As Balfour wrote to his uncle, there was a growing demand within the party for an Irish program that was more positive than twenty years of resolute government. The Liberal Unionists were especially hostile to coercion pure and simple; but a section of Conservative opinion also wished to conciliate the Irish by means of local government reform, land purchase, and grants to Catholic education. One prominent Conservative in Manchester wrote to Balfour complaining about the absence of a viable policy for Ireland: "I wish Lord Salisbury would give us some indication of a *definite* policy—and not let Chamberlain make all the running. I fear Hartington will be too negative: Chamberlain is on the right track—viz., increased self-governing powers in local areas for England, Scotland, Ireland, and Wales. . . . Many who see all the evils of Gladstone's plan and deplore his action would rather that the issue at the coming election should not be limited to a choice between *leaving things as they are* and the Government Bill."[24]

[22] *Times,* 8-11 June 1886.   [23] *Ibid.,* 8 June 1886.
[24] W. H. Houldsworth to Balfour, 13 June 1886, Salisbury MSS. Houldsworth, M.P. for Manchester NW, 1883-1906, received a baronetcy in 1887 for his services to the Conservative party.

While Chamberlain was advocating county councils for the whole United Kingdom, Hartington admitted the necessity of an Irish local government bill, but only one that was "consistent with the Union of the two countries." The Conservative leaders, on the other hand, were in no hurry to define a specific policy. Referring to "that large and most tiresome class—the 'we must have an alternative' people," the young and still arrogant Balfour agreed with his uncle that the party ought not to pledge themselves prematurely to any program for Ireland.[25]

Three weeks of intensive electioneering followed the dissolution of Parliament. More confused than enlightened by the torrent of words that flowed from the leaders of both parties, the electorate received a long-deferred chance to pass judgment on Home Rule. The guest list for a house party given by the Rothschilds at Waddesdon, which included Lord Hartington and his mistress the Duchess of Manchester, as well as Chamberlain, Balfour, and Churchill, symbolized the disruption of parties and principles.[26] Home Rule, as Gladstone predicted, had indeed caused a "mighty heave in the body politic."

Lord Salisbury worked hard to keep his pledge to the Liberal dissentients that no Conservative would oppose a Liberal member who had voted against the bill. But there was much grumbling and discontent within the Unionist alliance when members of one faction were asked to support a "rival" candidate. In south Manchester the dispute between the Conservative and Liberal Unionist organizations flared into the open and almost caused a serious breach. Balfour, however, was able to report to his uncle that the electoral prospects in Manchester were on the whole favorable, although the final result depended on those "two uncertainties, the Liberal *conversions* and the Irish *perversions*."[27]

[25] Balfour to Salisbury, 15 June 1886, Salisbury MSS. Another supporter appealed to Balfour to oppose any coercive measures directed exclusively against Ireland: "I am convinced that the working classes believe that there are *artificial* crimes in Ireland which are not criminal elsewhere. That is what they believe they mean *injustice to Ireland* and that idea must be knocked on the head in as plain language as possible"; C. Ransome to Balfour, 14 June 1886, *ibid*.

[26] Balfour to Salisbury, 15 June 1886, *ibid*. For Balfour's talk with Chamberlain at Waddesdon, see Dugdale, *Balfour*, I, pp. 103-04.

[27] Balfour to Salisbury, 25 June 1886, Salisbury MSS. For details of the

Having supervised the electoral arrangements and helped to settle a number of complaints arising out of the electoral compact, Salisbury left for the continent on doctors' orders, confident that the Unionist coalition could win the election without his presence.

The campaign he left behind was bitterly contested. Gladstone called it a "suicidal conflict," because 114 out of 292 contests in England, Scotland, and Wales were fought between Liberal candidates. Despite the efforts of the Irish National League of Great Britain and the presence of Parnellite members on English platforms, the Irish vote in England disappointed Gladstone. Voters who had abstained in the previous election declared against Home Rule, thus counterbalancing the Conservatives' loss of the Irish vote. Speaking at Wrexham and Manchester, Parnell repeated his charges about a Tory commitment to Home Rule in 1885. But such talk did not prevent Chamberlain and Hartington from submerging their profound differences just long enough to help defeat their former leader.

The election in Ireland was marked once again by the efficiency of the Parnellite machine, which selected, pledged, and in some cases paid candidates in all parts of the country. Branches of the National League printed intimidating notices that warned the populace against voting for Unionists or "alien aristocrats." At the same time a trend toward violence appeared. Catholic and Protestant laborers rioted in Belfast; in Dublin egg-throwing Unionists broke up a nomination meeting for the two University seats; and a more serious clash occurred there between nationalists and Orangemen on July 5. Working-class demonstrations in Londonderry and Cardiff furnished evidence that the depression rather than nationalist fervor lay at the root of much popular unrest.

In England the Unionist alliance, despite much internal friction, justified its existence on the constituency level. Although Liberal candidates won the majority of seats in Scotland and Wales, the English electorate rejected Home Rule decisively. The popular vote, however, showed that Gladstone's strength was far

---

electoral disputes in south Manchester and elsewhere, see Balfour to Salisbury, 25, 26, 28 June, 2 July 1886; Salisbury to D. Clarke, 11 June 1886, *ibid.*

more substantial than the Unionist majority of 118 in Parliament indicated.[28] In general the classes representing property, whether landed, industrial, or financial, supported the Union. Theirs was the cause championed by the Primrose League, proselytized by the *Times*, and graced by the verses of Swinburne.[29] Chamberlain's Radical Union and the dislocation of the National Liberal Federation were also important elements in the Unionist triumph. Lord Salisbury, vacationing in the Auvergne, received the news of electoral successes with a satisfaction marred only by the prospect of an early return to England. He hoped that Gladstone would meet Parliament and face a vote of confidence. But a telegram from the Queen on July 21 cut short his stay: Gladstone had resigned, and the Queen was summoning Salisbury to form a government. The following day he left for England, confiding to his private secretary: "The waters have done me a great deal of good—but I wish the old sinner had put off his resignation for another fortnight."[30]

The political situation confronting Salisbury on his return presented a marked contrast to that of the previous December, when Parnell had held the balance of power in the Commons. The Liberals lost heavily in the counties where they had obtained support six months previously. Many voters did not forgive Parnell for his electoral manifesto of November; and Gladstone's party was reduced to 192. The Conservatives were dependent on Liberal Unionist support for a majority, even though they had increased their numbers from 250 to 316. But the solidarity of the Unionist coalition was deceptive: the talents and voting strength of the seventy-eight Liberal Unionists did not belong to the Conservatives free of charge. The Liberal Unionists were,

[28] In English constituencies the Unionists won 339 seats against 126 for their opponents; in Scotland, Ireland, and Wales the figures were 54 and 151 respectively. In Great Britain the plurality in favor of the Union was only 94,000. *Times*, 21 July 1886.

[29] "Thieves and murderers, hands yet red with blood/ and tongues yet black with lies,/ Clap and clamour—'God for Gladstone and Parnell!'/ Truth, unscared and undeluded by their praise/ or blame, replies—/ 'Is the goal of fraud and bloodshed heaven or hell?'" From "The Commonweal: A Song for the Unionists," by Swinburne, *Times*, 1 July 1886.

[30] Salisbury to Henry Manners, 16, 21 July 1886, Salisbury MSS.

after all, still Liberals on all issues exclusive of Home Rule; and
for the next six years their leaders continued to sit on the same
bench as Gladstone and his colleagues. The working alliance with
the Conservatives during the debates on the bill and the general
election had been only provisional. Preserving their own party
organization and political creed, the Liberal Unionists, who were
made up of Whigs, Radicals, and disillusioned Gladstonians, posed
a large question mark for the future. Whether the single link
joining their forces to the Conservatives could withstand the
strains of disagreement on Irish, domestic, or foreign affairs in
the future remained to be seen.

In order to perpetuate the Unionist alliance beyond the general
election, Salisbury turned to the expedient of a coalition government. Balfour, however, strongly demurred. Afraid of over-
loading the party with too many "waifs and strays from the Whig
wreck," he tried to dissuade his uncle from incurring the risks
of a coalition government: "The advantages are obvious of
having one. But a Tory Government aided by half the Liberal
party, and opposed by the other half, is a state of things that will
not conduce to immediate peace within the borders of Liberalism:
—and when they coalesce again, the sacrifice they will offer up to
the Goddess of Unity will probably be the property of the Church
and not the property of the Landlords. Whereas, if the Whigs
first joined, and then gradually got absorbed in us, leaving a
united radical party to enter into the heritage of all the historic
strength of Liberalism, I conceive that the attack on land would
precede, as being easier, the attack on the Church."[31]

Such arguments notwithstanding, Salisbury determined to
pursue his goal. Disregarding for once the protests of Beach and
all his senior colleagues, he promptly offered the first position in
the new ministry to Hartington.[32] Not only did Salisbury consider
the time ripe for coalition, but, in addition, the move suited his
own plans. Having had his fill of the premiership, he could think

[31] Balfour to Salisbury, 24 July 1886, *ibid.* Referring to critics who remarked at the "feebleness" of the party's front bench in the Commons,
Balfour added: ". . . it must be owned that we do not seem to have impressed the public with the superabundance of our genius!"

[32] See Beach to Salisbury, 15 July 1886; Cranbrook to Salisbury, 15
July 1886; Smith to Salisbury, 19 July 1886, *ibid.*

of no one so qualified to conduct the country's foreign affairs as himself: "On the other hand the Foreign Office is a very difficult office to fill out of the ranks of the party as they stand. Carnarvon is out of the question—Cranbrook would probably say he was too old—and Harrowby and Cadogan—well, you will understand my difficulties. They form one of the many reasons why it would be the best arrangement that Hartington should be Prime Minister."[33]

Recent experience had taught him the dangers inherent in combining both offices. The *Times* shared this view and recommended Hartington as premier in order to give the Conservatives more strength in the Commons. The advantages of a prime minister sitting in the lower House were also pressed as justification for this move. But Hartington ended all speculation by refusing the offer on the grounds that any such coalition would make him premier in name only, owing to the preponderance of Conservatives. And he worried lest such an arrangement drive Chamberlain back to the Liberals. The Liberal Unionist leaders, it was clear, preferred to support the Government at a respectable distance. The Queen, however, managed to extract an assurance from Hartington that he would cooperate with the Conservatives so long as the Liberal party remained divided.[34] Salisbury, in the end, was compelled to accept the premiership and to renounce the cherished Foreign Office. The whole operation had sorely tried his patience and he confessed to Lord Harrowby: "The formation of this Government has been to me a very painful as well as a very irksome task. It has involved many personal changes which I would have been gladly spared. . . . The newspapers speak of my offer of the first place to Hartington as an act of self-sacrifice. It was nothing of the kind. I was earnestly anxious he should take it—not only on public grounds—but my own private comfort as well. I like the Foreign Office: but this duty is quite intolerable."[35]

The magnanimous Hicks Beach insisted that the leadership of the House should go to the more popular and brilliant Churchill, and, showing a high sense of duty, he consented to take the second most troublesome post in the Government—the Irish Office. The

[33] Salisbury to H. Manners, 16 July 1886, *ibid.*
[34] *Letters of Queen Victoria*, 3d series, I, pp. 172-74.
[35] Salisbury to Harrowby, 1 Aug. 1886, Salisbury MSS.

stage was set for a bold departure toward Ireland; but cabinet dissension and the exigencies of the Unionist alliance prevented the new ministry from immediately fulfilling that cure which Lord Salisbury had prescribed at St. James's Hall.

IV. A CARNARVON POSTSCRIPT

The story of Carnarvon's career after January, 1886, reflected the suspicions that his Irish sojourn had aroused among his colleagues. In July the former viceroy was passed over for office because, as Salisbury explained in a letter of consolation, his views on the Irish Question were incompatible with those of the party. Salisbury deplored the end of their official connection, but the principle involved happened to be the chief issue of the day.[36]

Upon his return from Ireland, Carnarvon had met with a chilling reception from his former colleagues. The circumstances of his resignation annoyed many Conservatives, and his anomalous position as an ex-minister committed, so they assumed, to Gladstone's policies worried them. Aware that any disclosures about the Parnell interview would seriously embarrass the party, Salisbury decided that the interests of the Union necessitated silencing Carnarvon until the vote on the second reading of the Home Rule Bill had been taken. Overcoming any initial scruples about imposing on the liberty of a friend, he told Carnarvon that party considerations required his temporary abstention from the fray. Out of loyalty to his chief, Carnarvon submitted to this injunction; and in the middle of February he left with his family for Portofino, where he polished his translation of the *Odyssey*. He did not return to England until the end of April, and even then kept his vow of silence. Throughout the debates on Home Rule Carnarvon was thus effectively muzzled, much to the relief of his colleagues. Lord John Manners informed Salisbury in May that he greatly appreciated the "wisdom" of curbing Carnarvon's tongue as long as possible.[37]

In the long run the Conservatives paid an exorbitant price for the censorship imposed upon Carnarvon. Salisbury might be

[36] Cecil, *Salisbury*, III, pp. 311-12.

[37] "Between you and me I have lost all faith in him"; Manners to Salisbury, 8 May 1886, Salisbury MSS.

able to restrict the speeches of his colleagues, but he had no control over Parnell. And on June 7, several hours before the fateful division on the second reading of the Home Rule Bill, the Irish leader revealed with more cunning than accuracy that the Caretaker ministry, had they won the November election, would have given Ireland a "statutory legislature" with power to protect Irish industries. Not only that, but the Government would have accompanied this concession with a more generous land purchase bill than Gladstone's. This announcement caused quite a stir in the House. Hicks Beach, as leader of the Opposition, took it upon himself to deny the accusation "utterly and categorically." Parnell then interrupted and charged that the information had been communicated to him by a member of the late ministry. Amidst cries of "Name!" Hicks Beach continued to denounce the allegation as false. Challenged to reveal the name of his informant, Parnell remarked that he would be glad to do so once he had received permission from the gentleman in question. Members again shouted "Name!", but Parnell kept silent, and Hicks Beach, after retorting that such insinuations were easier made than proven, passed on to his indictment of the Home Rule Bill.[38]

The first man to be suspected as the mysterious Conservative minister was Lord Randolph Churchill, whose friendly relations with some of the Irish party were common knowledge. But the *Pall Mall Gazette* soon put an end to speculation by naming Carnarvon as the culprit. Parnell's accusation impugned the honor of not only Carnarvon but all the members of the Caretaker government. The ex-viceroy could not and would not allow these charges to go unanswered. Much pained by the disclosure, he told Salisbury that he wanted to make a clarifying statement as soon as possible, since he earnestly believed that the Conservatives had nothing damaging to hide. Salisbury, however, took an entirely different view: any revelations about the secret parley with Parnell were bound to injure the party. In principle he objected to breaches of cabinet security; and for obvious reasons he disliked the prospect of airing the Parnell interview. At the same time he rationalized his feelings by asserting that one such explanation involving an official secret would set a dangerous precedent for the future. Quite naturally, Carnarvon assumed that

[38] *Hansard,* 3d series, Vol. 306, pp. 1181-1200.

his chief's opposition to confession was based on his wish to avoid any personal involvement in the affair. After all, what would the other members of the Caretaker ministry think when they learned for the first time that their leader had authorized secret talks with Parnell behind their backs? But Salisbury's concern was not wholly selfish: he was also anxious lest the entire party be automatically incriminated by any statement from Carnarvon. Nevertheless, Carnarvon insisted upon his right to speak after months of waiting, and Salisbury reluctantly gave his consent, while cautioning him to exonerate the Caretaker ministry from any part in the secret talks. His letter ended with the terse note: "Pray make it as dry as possible and without any sentiment."

"I shall be very short and simple," Carnarvon replied, "but I always eat my bread with butter."[39] And the viceroy was true to his word. On June 10 in the House of Lords he admitted his role in the interview with Parnell but denied vehemently having pledged the late government to an Irish parliament. "Both of us left the room as free as when we entered it," he declared. There was no need to make apologies for the meeting, because he considered it the duty of a viceroy to obtain information from every available source. If he had refused to see the Irish leader, he would have been guilty of the "greatest moral and political cowardice"; and since he had told Parnell that he was speaking only for himself and not for the rest of the cabinet, Hicks Beach had been perfectly justified in disclaiming all knowledge of the interview. At no time during this explanation was Salisbury implicated in the meeting.

Carnarvon's one tactical mistake, however, was to give vent to his own views about Irish self-government, which had been distorted in the press and censored by his colleagues. He denied outright any approval of Gladstone's bill. Some limited form of self-government consistent with the supremacy of the imperial Parliament he would welcome; and he wished some day to see Ireland's "national aspirations" satisfied. At the mention of this phrase the Conservative peers shuddered. They felt that the ex-viceroy had gone too far: the butter was thicker than the bread. When Carnarvon sat down, no Conservative rose to express confidence in his conduct. The ominous silence from the Opposition benches created

[39] Hardinge, *Carnarvon*, III, pp. 223-31.

the impression—and it was not far wrong—that the former viceroy was virtually an outcast in his own party.[40]

The controversy over the interview was soon transferred to the press, where Parnell published a statement repudiating Carnarvon's version. He insisted that the viceroy had acted as the official representative of the Caretaker ministry, and that the interview had ended with both men in complete accord on such issues as Home Rule and protection for Irish industries. Subsequently, he was shocked to find the Conservatives reneging on their pledge when the Irish party had failed to provide them with a majority at the general election: " . . . history will not record a more disgraceful and unscrupulous *volte face* than that executed by the Tory party last January. . . . " Although Salisbury called these charges a string of baseless fabrications, he refrained from entering into any particulars.

In the meantime, criticism of Carnarvon's behavior was mounting on all sides. In Dublin loyalists called the meeting "well meant but indiscreet," and they hoped that the incident would serve as a warning to those who wished to deal with such scurrilous opponents. The *Times*, visibly hedging on the subject, accepted Carnarvon's version of the talk but regretted that greater precautions had not been taken. And the nationalist press declared that Carnarvon was shouldering all the blame, which ought rightly to fall on every member of the late government.[41] During the electoral campaign Gladstone added more fuel to the controversy by asserting that Salisbury had known all along about the interview. When Carnarvon asked for permission to answer this latest charge by revealing the truth, Salisbury replied that cabinet secrecy must not be violated. But on June 22 Gladstone renewed his accusation, and Carnarvon appealed again to Salisbury, this time reminding him that he had not "as the head of the Government interposed to prevent the meeting." If this latest challenge went unheeded, he argued, the public would have no choice but to believe all that Gladstone said and more.[42]

Salisbury made one last effort to struggle out of the impasse, but he eventually decided that party interests would best be

[40] *Hansard*, 3d series, Vol. 306, pp. 1256-60.
[41] *Times*, 12-19 June 1886.
[42] Hardinge, *Carnarvon*, III, pp. 227-29.

served by satisfying some fraction of public curiosity. The occasion he chose was the annual dinner of the Constitutional Union at St. James's Hall. On June 28, the day before his speech, he wrote to Carnarvon: "I still shrink from the statement of anything that has gone on in cabinet. In fact I could not do it without the Queen's permission. But avoiding that rock, I think I might safely say what I have enclosed. . . ."[43] What he said the following night was "safe" enough. Having labeled the Gladstone-Parnell allegations as "absolutely untrue," he admitted that Carnarvon had given him a detailed report immediately after the meeting of August 1. In addition, he declared that Carnarvon had known about his own strong objections to Home Rule as early as July, 1885. To suggest that Carnarvon had pledged the government to Irish autonomy in the light of this fact was nothing less than absurd.[44] What Salisbury did not divulge was his foreknowledge and tacit approval of the interview. But in the midst of a general election fought almost exclusively on the issue of Home Rule it would have been the height of folly to reveal any more details of this now notorious affair.

The whole imbroglio served only to widen the gap between Salisbury and his old friend. Recriminations about the interview kept cropping up year after year; and in February, 1888, while Carnarvon was absent in Australia, Balfour had to defend him against fresh aspersions cast by Parnell. Although in January, 1886, Salisbury had emphasized Carnarvon's virtues in explaining the latter's resignation to his fellow peers, in private his thoughts ran along different lines. When the Queen expressed her vexation over the meeting, Salisbury replied: " . . . it is impossible to disguise the fact that he [Carnarvon] has acted impulsively, and with little foresight." The ex-viceroy had failed to realize "the shifty character of the man with whom he was dealing." And he added that Carnarvon had taken "singularly little precaution to protect either himself or his colleagues from misunderstanding."[45] All this furor and subsequent rancor, needless to say, could have been prevented by a simple but firm veto from Salisbury when the idea of a meeting with Parnell was first broached.

[43] Salisbury to Carnarvon, 28 June 1886, Salisbury MSS. See also his memorandum on the Carnarvon-Parnell interview, *ibid.*

[44] *Times*, 30 June 1886.

[45] *Letters of Queen Victoria*, 3d series, I, pp. 146-47.

In the spring of 1890 Carnarvon, then a dying man, tried to remove some of the ill-feeling that still clouded his experiences in Ireland. Unfortunately, the appeal of an elder and disillusioned statesman failed to achieve the desired reconciliation. He wrote to Salisbury that he pleaded not guilty to all the charges preferred against him since 1885:

"My task, when sorely against my will I went to Ireland, was an almost hopelessly difficult one. You had given up the Peace Preservation Act, and left me no adequate criminal law on which to depend—it was in truth requiring me to make bricks without straw. When later you introduced the Crimes Act, I gave it a hearty concurrence. Having said this, I wish once more to say that my chief object in now writing is to express my satisfaction that there are no personal differences between us. The times are critical: the risks to what we both of us consider great and fundamental interests are serious. . . . "[46]

Nevertheless, the personal differences remained; and it must be admitted that Salisbury did not exert himself to repair the breach with Carnarvon. Perhaps he thought that by ignoring the ex-viceroy he could somehow lay the ghost of the Caretaker ministry, which the Home Rulers insisted upon summoning whenever they saw fit. Whatever the reason, Carnarvon, after his Irish experiment, lived in a political limbo, accepted by neither party. He took refuge in colonial questions and classical studies, as if, after all those years of service, he had come to realize that party politics were an unmitigated evil.

In spite of all that he knew about Carnarvon's federal leanings, Lord Salisbury had failed to anticipate the "rapid crystallization" of the viceroy's views once he had arrived in Dublin. The Conservative leader acknowledged his error: only when it was too late did he realize that Carnarvon had "gone green" in Dublin Castle. In December, 1890, several months after Carnarvon's death, Lord Salisbury, while addressing an audience at Rossendale, called the Parnell interview an act of "more generosity than prudence." In a characteristic aside he added, to the crowd's delight, that the viceroy had been right to talk with Parnell, "but I think he had

[46] Carnarvon to Salisbury, 2 April 1890, Salisbury MSS. See also Salisbury to Carnarvon, 27 March 1890, and Salisbury's memorandum on the interview, 8 July 1893, *ibid.*

better have had another person in the room." Viewed in this light, Carnarvon's observation made in July, 1886, that Salisbury "sometimes seems to be only the old Robert Cecil grown older," becomes more than apt.[47]

[47] Cecil, *Salisbury*, III, p. 163; Lucy, *Speeches of the Marquis of Salisbury*, II, p. 7; Hardinge, *Carnarvon*, III, p. 232.

CHAPTER VII

The Hicks Beach Interlude

HAVING failed in his bid to evade the premiership, Salisbury began to form the new ministry, with his usual feelings of distaste for placeseekers and wirepullers. Lord Iddesleigh, the least opinionated and most fluent in French of the available candidates, became foreign secretary. Churchill's promotion to leader of the House and chancellor of the Exchequer caused the greatest excitement and no little uneasiness among the elders of the party. But his undeniable popularity and ability had elevated him to a commanding position in the eyes of most Conservatives outside the Carlton Club, and Beach's act of abnegation was a response to the wishes of this majority. Whether he knew it or not, Churchill also owed his triumph to the Irish Question. The future of the new government, Salisbury believed, depended upon the Irish chief secretaryship, and once that position had been filled, the other appointments would fall into place. Such was his line of argument to Harrowby: "Ministries to a great extent make themselves: that is, one or two appointments, exacted by some external circumstance, have a long chain of quite inevitable consequences. It has so happened in this case. Beach was evidently the necessary Secretary for Ireland; but that involved Churchill having the lead in the Commons: and that made both Cross and Stanley think that a migration to the Lords would be more comfortable for them. . . . " Only Beach, he concluded, could cope with the Irish Office, which, in his opinion, required more endurance and perspicacity than any other post in the Government.[1]

I. "BLACK MICHAEL"

Sir Michael did not accept his appointment with enthusiasm. As chief secretary under Disraeli he had sponsored improvements in arterial drainage, the deep-sea fishing industry, and interme-

---

[1] Salisbury to Harrowby, 1 Aug. 1886, Salisbury MSS.

diate education. But these minor successes had not blinded him to the disadvantages of the post. As he wrote to Salisbury toward the end of July, he had no wish "to take such an office unless I saw my way to doing some *real* good in it. Without that I could not again take up the petty irksome details which constitute much of the work of the office. . . . "[2] The truth was that Beach had grave doubts about a purely negative policy for Ireland, especially after the consummation of the alliance between Parnellism and Gladstonian Liberalism. Resolute government unrelieved by conciliation did not fit his idea of a suitable alternative to Home Rule.

It was once said about Beach, who was familiarly known as "Black Michael," that he "thought angrily." But beneath the forbidding exterior he was a man of moderation. In Dublin Castle he had established a reputation for hard work, efficiency, and absolute integrity. His aversion to the squandering of Treasury funds had not made him popular among the numerous placeseekers and contractors in the country; and the nationalists liked him even less.[3] Beach's very appearance—tall, thin, and adorned with a large black beard—, his manner—"icy cold"—, and his temper—easily aroused and expressed in the language of "the bargee"—were not calculated to disarm either colleagues or political adversaries. Although emotionally thin-skinned, he was respected for his powers of lucid analysis and judgment. As to Ireland, he was anxious to "do good," advising Salisbury: "I have thought much on the subject of an Irish policy since we met. I have not, so far, been able to see my way to do any real good. I am not even at all sure that you would approve of my ideas as to the lines on which the humbler task of 'keeping things going' should be attempted."[4]

The problem of governing Ireland effectively troubled many Government supporters who automatically equated reforms with concession. Irish landlords and loyalists were notoriously suspicious of all reformers in Dublin Castle. They remembered

[2] Beach to Salisbury, 25 July 1886, *ibid.*

[3] "I thought him . . . the best official I ever met here, for he was death on jobbery and in earnest at his work, but he was on that account none the more popular"; Lord Justice Fitzgibbon to Churchill, 27 July 1886, St. Aldwyn MSS.

[4] Beach to Salisbury, 25 July 1886, Salisbury MSS.

Beach's sympathy for both the peasantry and Catholic education and questioned the wisdom of his appointment at this critical juncture. The *Times*, which had not forgotten the Maamtrasna debate, drew attention to Beach's shortcomings as leader of the House during the Caretaker ministry.[5] In spite of Beach's obvious qualifications, the auspices under which he arrived in Dublin could hardly be called favorable.

The remaining posts in the Irish administration were soon filled. Ashbourne returned as lord chancellor of Ireland, despite the unpopularity aroused by his methods and mannerisms. Lord Londonderry was appointed viceroy.[6] A man of more vanity and wealth than intelligence Londonderry accepted the office somewhat reluctantly and on the condition that he would be relieved of all administrative responsibility. Because Beach wished to keep Ashbourne in Dublin, he did not recommend the lord chancellor for cabinet rank. This omission immediately touched off a minor crisis. Much offended, Ashbourne refused to accept what he considered to be a demotion. At this point Beach appealed to his chief:

" . . . I think it may be necessary to squeeze Ashbourne. Londonderry (quite rightly) made a point of having no responsibility for government. It is necessary . . . that the Irish Chancellor should remain in Dublin through the Parliamentary session, while I and the Law officers are in London. Else there will be no one on the spot whom I can trust to tell Londonderry what to do in the event of any emergency. Ireland cannot be governed *entirely* from London. . . . He [Ashbourne] argues that no one *could*, especially under present conditions, join a Government outside the cabinet having sat in it six months before, without unendurable loss of position: he would not only infinitely sooner be outside altogether, but could not take the Chancellorship on such terms." But it was Ashbourne who squeezed the chief secretary, for he

[5] *Times,* 22 July 1886.

[6] Charles Stewart Vane-Tempest-Stewart, 6th Marquess of Londonderry, 1852-1915; M.P. 1878-1884; Viceroy of Ireland 1886-1889; Chairman London School Board 1895-1897; Postmaster General 1900-1902; President of Board of Education 1902-1905; Lord President of the Council 1903-1905.

won back his seat in the cabinet thanks largely to the intervention of the prime minister.[7]

At the end of July a meeting of the Conservative party was held at the Carlton Club, where Salisbury explained his approach to Hartington and also praised members for their forbearance at the election. He emphasized the need for cordial cooperation with the Liberal Unionists in spite of their uncompromising attitude to a coalition government. By unanimous vote it was decided to dispense with an autumn session. With the success of the election, and with the danger of a Hartington-led ministry safely behind them, party morale appeared at its zenith.

Such optimism was premature. The eight months' sojourn of Hicks Beach at the Irish Office exposed the most vacillating and unimaginative aspects of Conservative policy toward Ireland. Hoping to avoid an autumn session, and anxious to make no final pledges about Ireland until the new year, the Salisbury administration drifted aimlessly through a critical period in Anglo-Irish relations, disturbed by inner troubles and wanting both the conviction and the courage that had marked the party during the supreme trial of the Home Rule debates. In its dilatoriness and apathy the cabinet during Beach's tenure had much in common with the Caretaker ministry. Ministers naively assumed that Ireland could wait until February for legislative treatment; and the discord within the cabinet engendered by Beach's Irish views bore a striking resemblance to the ill-fated Carnarvon experiment.

II. IRELAND REVISITED

During the few weeks remaining before the meeting of Parliament, Beach studied the Irish situation and found that even maintaining the *status quo* presented difficulties. The year 1886 brought severe hardships to the British Isles. Financial collapses on the continent, added to increasing competition for markets at home and abroad, resulted in a serious recession for British commerce and industry. This year marked one of the nadirs of the great depression of the late nineteenth century. Unemployment

[7] Londonderry to Salisbury, 28 July 1886; Beach to Salisbury, 28 July 1886, Salisbury MSS.

rates rose as high as twenty-two per cent, and disturbances broke out in many industrial cities. The plight of agriculture was even more distressing. Real wages as well as prices continued to decline and some landlords were forced to lower their rents by fifty per cent. For most farmers the decade of the 1880's proved calamitous: agricultural distress could no longer be called a temporary phenomenon or dismissed as the result of bad harvests. The Irish economy, with its lopsided reliance on agriculture, was especially vulnerable to changes in the world market, and in 1886 the number of unemployed laborers and evictions soared. While the value of land steadily depreciated, Irish landlords tended to be less sensitive than their English counterparts to the need for rent reductions. And whereas in England the extent and nature of industrialization facilitated the gradual depopulation of rural areas, in Ireland the tenant farmer had little choice but to emigrate.[8]

The depression in trade and agriculture enormously complicated Beach's task. Governing Ireland in normal times was, he knew, hard enough. Now he had a full-scale economic crisis on his hands. In addition, the hybrid nature of the Unionist alliance meant that every decision he made was bound to arouse criticism in some quarter of the coalition. But the carping of selfish interests did not dismay him so long as he had the complete backing of his cabinet colleagues.

One of the urgent problems confronting Beach was that of morale. The Home Rule Bill had demoralized many permanent officials both in the Castle and among the constabulary and magistracy. Unless this mood of "general flabbiness and inaction" could be dispelled, any chance of restoring law and order was virtually doomed. The situation that greeted him upon his arrival in Dublin was not reassuring: "The officials of every grade were not only completely demoralised by the introduction of the bill, but had no belief that they would be supported, even at the time, in doing their duty against the nationalists, and were left without any sufficient guidance as to the wishes and policy of the late Government in matters of administration."[9]

[8] For details of the economic crisis of 1886, see J. H. Clapham, *An Economic History of Modern Britain*, II, pp. 453 ff.

[9] From Beach's memorandum on Ireland, 4 Nov. 1886, St. Aldwyn MSS.

Since the defeat of Gladstone's bill, the condition of the country had steadily deteriorated. The most immediate problem Beach inherited was the riotous state of Belfast, where street fighting between Protestants and Catholics had broken out on June 9. For opening fire on a mob the police were dubbed "Morley's murderers" by the Orangemen. Further rioting occurred after the anniversary of the Boyne, when workers took advantage of relaxed security measures to renew the fighting with pitchforks, stones, bottles, and a few rifles. This time three policemen were killed. The disorder coincided with the change of ministry, so effective countermeasures were delayed. Before leaving office, Morley appointed a commission to investigate the riots; but this inquiry was as ineffectual as it was premature. On July 22 martial law was proclaimed and public assemblies forbidden. Early in August the street fighting was renewed and the number of deaths rose to more than a score.[10]

On August 5 Beach left for Dublin, where, after the swearing-in ceremonies, he remained for a week, taking steps to restore order in the north. Having interviewed magistrates and the commander-in-chief of the military forces, he dispatched 1,200 soldiers to reenforce the police in Belfast. This display of firmness inspired subordinates with much-needed confidence and won the chief secretary praise. Beach blamed the disturbances on the unsettling effects of the Home Rule Bill and on Morley's blatant neglect of the condition of the country. The arrival of troops in Belfast heralded a lull in the civil strife, and Beach returned to London for cabinet discussions.[11]

Mindful of recent mistakes, Lord Salisbury was determined to explore every possible way to keep Ireland tranquil during the next few months. Although Russian activities in the Balkans and unrest in Burma demanded the cabinet's attention, Ireland was still the question of the hour. Proof of this fact was the creation of an Irish committee of the cabinet, composed of Salisbury,

[10] *Times,* 12 July-12 Aug. 1886. See also Report of the Belfast Riots Commissioners, *H.C. 1887,* Vol. 18.

[11] "They had got Belfast into a terrible mess. I hope I have started things on a better footing, and that as soon as the present outbreak of rioting is put down there will be no recurrence of it"; Beach to Churchill, 8 Aug. 1886, St. Aldwyn MSS.

Beach, Churchill, Home Secretary Matthews, and Secretary for War W. H. Smith. Designed to review policy and to prepare legislation, this committee reflected the Conservatives' desire not to neglect the Irish Question as they had in 1885.

The Government never lacked expert advice on the subject of Ireland. Recommendations for special measures came from many quarters, but Chamberlain was particularly persistent in advocating remedial legislation. He hoped that the administration would produce an Irish local government bill because he was certain that it would "break Gladstone's heart and render him completely impotent." In addition, he recommended two royal commissions to inquire into the working of the land acts and to report on the country's capacity for industrial development. As to evictions, he suggested that some legal distinction be made between tenants who were unable to pay rents and those who refused. Churchill feared that these ideas would be "impatiently dismissed" by the cabinet. But Chamberlain's proposals, in fact, anticipated the main lines of Conservative gestures at conciliation in the ensuing months.[12]

Of the many aspects of the Irish Question in need of solution, one of the most controversial concerned the land. From the time of the first conquests and confiscations, Irish leaders had relied upon the disaffection of the peasantry in order to achieve their ends. A noted patriot Fintan Lalor had written in 1848 that the land question was a railway engine to which the carriages of Home Rule could be conveniently attached, and that without this motive power the cause of independence would be permanently stalled. At times, however, the locomotive threatened to run away with the train. It had not been easy for Parnell to assert the primacy of the national movement over the land question, and the competition between these two related forces would continue. In 1886 Beach's overriding ambition was to reduce the tensions that had so long prevailed between tenant and landlord. He hoped thereby to deprive the nationalists of their largest source of energy. By persuading the landlords through private negotiations to avoid harsh evictions, and by encouraging the arbitration of rent dis-

---

[12] Garvin, *Chamberlain,* ii, p. 267; Churchill to Beach, 5 Aug. 1886, St. Aldwyn MSS.

putes, he aimed to reduce tenants' grievances and thereby eliminate the need for coercion. Since revision of the judicial rents
fixed under the Land Act of 1881 would involve long delay,
Beach sought some temporary means of reducing exorbitant rents,
pending a comprehensive reform of the land laws. In direct
intervention by Dublin Castle he believed that he had found a
way to transform the Irish landlord into a rational and charitable
creature during a time of crisis.

Unlike some of his colleagues, Beach did not put much faith in
repression. He was determined to govern as far as possible through
the ordinary law because he felt that coercive measures only
provoked the nationalists to greater lawlessness. While Salisbury
insisted that the Irish be taught respect for the law through
firm government, Beach always cared more about the causes than
the effects of Irish discontent. He sought to limit the appeal of
Irish nationalism by removing the source of disaffection from the
agrarian scene, and by promoting the material welfare of the
country through industrial subsidies. "To administer the law
without fear and without favour," to invigorate the officials of
Dublin Castle after the laxity of the Liberal regime, and to
prosecute agrarian crimes by means of the ordinary law: these
were the lines along which Beach's mind worked in preparing
his Irish policy.[13]

With regard to outrages and boycotting, Ireland represented
a patchwork pattern wherein relatively peaceful counties adjoined
areas of flagrant lawlessness. The condition of each parish or
district varied with the poverty and tenant-landlord relations
prevalent there. Throughout most of Ulster and in the midlands
the crime rate resembled that of an average English county.
But in the southwest, from Connemara to county Cork, the
National League was more powerful than the law. In Kerry, Clare,
and Cork alone the activities of Captain Moonlight accounted
for almost half the agrarian crimes recorded in Ireland. In Kerry
Justice O'Brien described a scene: " . . . such as could hardly be
found in any county that has passed the confines of natural
society and entered upon the duties and the relations and acknowledged obligations of civilized life. The law is defeated, perhaps
I should say, has ceased to exist, houses are attacked by night

[13] Hicks Beach, *St. Aldwyn*, I, p. 278.

and day, even the midnight terror yielding to the noonday audacity of crime, person and life are assailed, and a state of terror and lawlessness prevails everywhere."

In county Clare much the same language was used by the judiciary to depict local conditions; and the condition of county Mayo "approached as near to rebellion against the authority of the country as anything short of civil war could be."[14] The large number of peasants made idle through unemployment, eviction, or choice meant that there were always enough recruits to perform the league's dirty work. Cattle were mutilated with knives or sledge hammers, hay ricks were burned, arms seized, and jury members intimidated. In addition, "landgrabbers" or tenants who had taken evicted holdings, as well as land agents and those who defied the league, were shot at and occasionally killed. Fortunately, most moonlighters proved as inaccurate with firearms as the Fenians had been inept in handling explosives. In the Castleisland district of Kerry, one of the most lawless in the country, every night produced its victims of terrorism. Outrages also disturbed parts of Limerick, Donegal, Galway, and Roscommon; but the conditions rarely matched those in the southwest, where landlords required extensive police protection. Magistrates complained that the law was inadequate and that police garrisons were too small to patrol the large areas subject to intimidation. And many offenses, attributed to the league, were the product of private rather than national passion. The National League furnished an ideal shield behind which peasants could settle their personal feuds with impunity. It was no easy task to determine whether an outrage had been committed for motives of private malice or of public spirit.

Largely as a result of the Liberal alliance with Parnell, serious crimes had diminished since 1885. The Unionists explained the decrease as proof of the league's absolute supremacy: intimidation alone was sufficient to control the tenantry. But no guarantee existed in the minds of either landlords or Govern-

[14] These excerpts from the judges' charges to their respective grand juries during the summer assizes of 1886 are contained in a cabinet memorandum on Irish crime, 26 July 1901, Salisbury MSS. See also Report of the Divisional Magistrates on the condition of Ireland to the end of October 1886, 5 Nov. 1886, St. Aldwyn MSS.

ment officials that Parnell would continue to work through constitutional channels. The dependence of the nationalists upon funds subscribed by Irish emigrants abroad convinced most Unionists that the Parnellites would soon have to obey the dictates of dynamiters or "physical force" men.[15]

A large degree of complacency, nevertheless, marked the Conservative administration in Ireland during the next few months. Although reports from the southwest revealed that not only every parish, but often every two or three townlands, boasted a branch of the National League, the principal law officers in the Castle tended to rest satisfied with the fact that murder was on the decline. Ashbourne, having talked with officials in Dublin, informed Salisbury that Parnell's anxiety to please the Liberals would produce a general improvement. He saw, however, that trouble was likely during the winter months, and he warned that the situation required the utmost vigilance.[16]

At the same time Ashbourne saw no immediate need for coercive legislation. With the exception of Belfast and the southwest, he found the over-all scene as satisfactory as could be expected: "It is quite impossible to make any generalising statement about Ireland. Some parts are bad, others indifferent, and others again in a fairly good state. Kerry is the worst. Clare possibly is next in badness. Limerick is bad and in parts nearly bankrupt. Other counties are some degrees better. Rents in some districts will be paid fairly; in others with substantial reductions; in others not at all. I do not expect any large increase of outrages or open crime anywhere."[17]

Such intelligence reassured the cabinet; but the renewal of rioting in Belfast on August 14 had a sobering effect. Embittered by police brutality in suppressing the previous clashes, bands of Orangemen had opened fire on Catholic workers and several military patrols. Tension in the city was mounting. As a palliative to the public, the Government appointed a new Belfast commission to inquire into the civil strife with power to subpœna witnesses under oath.

[15] See Beach's notes on the organization of Irish secret societies in America contained in Secret Papers, Nov. 1886, *ibid.*

[16] Ashbourne to Salisbury, 18 July 1886, Salisbury MSS.

[17] Ashbourne to Salisbury, 16, 17 Aug. 1886, *ibid.*

It was the Government's fervent wish that Ireland would remain as tranquil as possible so as to avoid summoning Parliament before the new year. In Dublin, Ashbourne was strongly opposed to a November session. "What is most urgently needed here," he informed Salisbury, "is to let mens' minds settle down quickly; and this would be prevented if it was preordained that in three months' time the country would be again exposed to all the disturbing influences of parliamentary debate." By February, he expected, the Parnellites would have adopted new tactics in their agitation and the Government would then be armed with sufficient evidence to prescribe legislation. But for the time being a policy of "wait and see" was the most sensible course.[18]

Apart from matters of general policy, one special problem vexed Beach and his colleagues. Sir Robert Hamilton, an avowed Home Ruler, continued to hold the office of permanent under secretary. No one disputed Hamilton's ability or the extent of his influence in the Castle, but many Unionists questioned the wisdom of his remaining there. With the *Times* in the vanguard, a concerted campaign was launched by influential Unionists to transfer him elsewhere. Although Home Rulers and civil servants alike protested against this form of discrimination, Irish loyalists insisted that the under secretary had undermined the authority and morale of the constabulary throughout the country. Beach avoided any hasty action, especially because he appreciated Hamilton's experience and administrative talents; and Salisbury, who regarded "with some dismay the effect which his [Hamilton's] unfortunate proclivities have had upon the development of events in Ireland," did not dare antagonize public opinion to the extent of an outright dismissal.[19]

Instead of ousting Hamilton immediately, ministers decided

[18] Ashbourne to Salisbury, 12 Aug. 1886, *ibid.*

[19] The Duke of Abercorn called Hamilton " 'the fons et origo' of nearly all the mischief that has been instilled into the late Prime Minister's infantile brain. He is a bitter radical, a great hater . . . of anything connected with the Irish, and a bitter foe of the Union. He has done an immense amount of mischief since he has been in this country, and he has taken such an active, sub rosa part in politics as is really not consistent with his position as a Permanent Official. There will be no peace in this country so long as he remains. . . ." Abercorn to Salisbury, 23 July 1886, *ibid.* See also Salisbury to the Marquess of Waterford, 28 July 1886, *ibid.*

to appease Unionist feeling by recruiting a professional soldier whose mission would be to restore law and order in the southwest. As a result, Major General Sir Redvers Buller, V.C., was asked to take command of the civil and military forces in counties Kerry and Clare. In the middle of August W. H. Smith told Buller that a "special commissioner" was needed in Ireland to suppress moonlighting and boycotting. He warned that it would be an "unpleasant job" but assured him that he would be responsible only to Beach in matters of policy. Buller eventually accepted the post, after stipulating that he would be on temporary leave from the adjutant general's office. The news of his appointment caused an uproar among the Parnellites, who interpreted this move as a declaration of war and as an affront to the dignity of the Irish people—for Buller had won his decorations fighting against the equivalent of the Hottentots.[20]

III. PROCRASTINATION

At the lord mayor's banquet on August 11 Salisbury reminded his audience that Ireland still remained the "skeleton in our cupboard." The primary aim of the Government, he declared, was to free the loyal population from the tyranny of the league. Other governments, especially those on the continent, might be swayed by fear of popular feeling, but the ordinary Englishman, he contended, was not so easily cowed by the mob violence exhibited in Ireland. In the nationalist press Lord Salisbury's Irish policy was summarized as "twenty years of manacles and Manitoba."[21]

During the same month the cabinet decided to postpone legislative action on the Irish Question by appointing commissions to study the land problem and other aspects of the Irish economy. Apart from motives of political expediency, there was a genuine need for accurate information on the state of the country's finances and resources. The effects of the agricultural depression required analysis, while subsidies to native industries, arterial drainage, and light railways could not be administered without expert advice.

[20] C. H. Melville, *Life of General the Rt. Hon. Sir Redvers Buller* (hereafter *Buller*), London, 1923, I, pp. 302-03.

[21] *Times*, 12-13 Aug. 1886. By Manitoba was meant a scheme of forced emigration overseas.

Parliament assembled on August 19 for what ministers hoped would be a brief session designed to clear the agenda. The Queen's speech dealt mainly with the financial arrangements for the remainder of the budgetary year and omitted any specific references to Irish legislation. In the House of Lords Salisbury emphasized the Government's determination to maintain the Union by restoring law and order and by developing the country's natural resources. If the ordinary law failed to discourage intimidation, he warned that coercive measures might be necessary. Turning to the land question, he asserted that many landlords were receiving no rents whatsoever owing to "illegal combinations," and he refused to accept the excuse of tenant insolvency, arguing that the fall in prices applied mainly to wheat and barley, which were not widely grown in Ireland. For such reasons the Government had no intention of revising the judicial rents authorized by the Land Act of 1881. What Ireland required was stability, and no amount of tampering with the rents fixed by the land commissioners could achieve that goal. If some adjudicated rents turned out to be unfair, then the state rather than the landlords, he declared, ought to absorb the loss. Lord Salisbury ended his speech with a defense of land purchase. The system of dual ownership created by Gladstone was an unmitigated evil, and only the conversion of occupiers into owners would cure the country's basic ills.

In the Commons the Opposition greeted the Queen's speech with scorn and impatience. Gladstone approved the absence of a crimes bill but condemned the postponement of remedial legislation until February. With the gale rents due, the harvest uncertain, and prices falling, the Government were taking a grave risk, he warned, in refusing to offer immediate relief to the tenantry. Churchill promptly rose to attack Gladstone and his "close, intimate, and indissoluble connection" with Parnell. The Liberals, he asserted, had made a major error by compressing three aspects of the Irish Question—social order, the land question, and local government—into one great measure. The Conservatives planned to treat each of these problems separately. After affirming the inviolability of judicial rents, Lord Randolph announced the terms of reference for the Royal Commission on the land question; the commission was to be headed by Lord

132

Cowper. A smaller commission, consisting of three experts, would be created to advise the Government on financial assistance to Irish industries. As to local government reform, Churchill promised that the Government would examine several proposals during the recess and prepare a bill for the coming session.

The Parnellites accused the Government of procrastination, and much invective enlivened the debate as they joined issue with some of the Ulster members. Beach did not speak until August 23, when he defended the appointments of both the royal commissions and General Buller. The chief secretary explained how the Home Rule Bill had so demoralized the Irish populace that local government and land tenure reforms would have to wait until February for attention. In the meantime he hoped that landlords would avoid eviction wherever possible and that tenants would purchase their own holdings.[22] In content and expression Churchill's statement on Ireland far surpassed that of his colleague Hicks Beach. After Lord Randolph's lucid and powerful defense of procedure by royal commission, members concluded that the leader of the House had more to say about Irish policy, and said it better, than the chief secretary. There was, in fact, good reason for Beach's self-effacement.

IV. CABINET TROUBLES

During the week end that separated their two speeches, Lord Randolph discovered Beach "in a fuming state" at a country house near Maidenhead. To his trusted friend the chief secretary confessed his distaste for a policy of inaction. He hated the thought of having to "administer Ireland too much on a 'Landlords' Rights' basis." The time had arrived for some compromise with the tenantry, he declared. "Moreover," as Lord Randolph reported to Salisbury, Beach "dislikes and despises the Irish landlords and has no inclination to make much effort on their behalf." According to Churchill's account, Beach objected most of all to the Government's attitude about tampering with judicial rents. He insisted that he had originally agreed to accept a moratorium on rent revision for the present, but he had made no promises about the future. In addition, he strongly disapproved of Salisbury's contention that the Treasury ought to bear the

---

[22] *Hansard,* 3d series, Vol. 308, pp. 60-70, 107-32, 297-302.

expense of compensating landlords for any errors committed by the Land Court in adjudicating rents. At length Churchill managed to soothe Beach with the assurance that the cabinet had made no final decision. He advised the chief secretary to limit his speech in the House to a defense of the commissions and to avoid all semblance of discord. Such was the background to Beach's timid statement in the Commons.

Lord Randolph himself did not deny that Beach's criticisms had some foundation. Acting the unfamiliar role of peacemaker in the cabinet, he warned Salisbury against weighting the Cowper Commission too heavily in favor of the landlords: "It was just possible you were trying on Saturday to make the Commission too much a landlords' one, more so than the present situation would quite bear. We have promised the landlords strong executive action and we are their natural friends and they must be prepared for a little give and take."[23] Churchill wished to prevent at all costs another schism over Ireland; but the friction increased rather than diminished. Several weeks later he informed Lord Hartington of the conflict within the Government and confessed his fears about the future effects of this divergence of opinion:

" . . . it is right that you should know that Lord Salisbury and the Chief Secretary look at the Irish Land Question from very different aspects. The former takes up the high ground of the rights of property and the enforcement of the law, the latter occupies the rather lower ground of expediency. I, myself, incline to Lord Salisbury's views but knowing the value of Beach to the administration, have been mainly occupied with the assistance of Lord Hamilton and W. H. Smith in preventing too great or sharp a divergence between the P.M. and the Chief Secretary. So far with much success; but what may happen next year if legislation is required I cannot say and am very anxious about."[24]

In a manner reminiscent of the Caretaker ministry, a breach in the cabinet over Irish policy had appeared; only this time Churchill was working with two of his colleagues to bring round an old friend. The schism was no less serious because it involved the land

[23] Churchill to Salisbury, 22 Aug. 1886, Salisbury MSS.
[24] Churchill to Hartington, 13 Sept. 1886, St. Aldwyn MSS.

question and not Home Rule. To landlords and loyalists the rights of land tenure and the integrity of the judicial rent contracts were sacrosanct. Beach's original worries about the wisdom of his appointment had proved justified.

Public reaction to the address varied between Irish disappointment over the absence of remedial legislation and Unionist satisfaction with the cautious procedure that ministers had adopted. The *Times* welcomed the firmness of the declarations given by the prime minister and Churchill; while the nationalist press fulminated against Buller's nomination. At the same time rumors began to reach Dublin Castle of an impending conspiracy against rent. Churchill considered such talk mere gossip, but the rumors persisted.

In the House of Commons Parnell stressed the dangers of neglecting the land question during the winter. Attacking every aspect of the Government's Irish policy, he urged ministers to adjust rents in proportion to the fall in prices. Failure to concede the necessary abatement would result in a renewal of the land war, and in this event he advised the administration to "urge their fires, to sharpen their pincers, and prepare their scorpion whips" for the conflict that would follow. In the form of an amendment to the address Parnell proposed a number of remedies for the depression. He wished to simplify the method of revising rents, to reduce the term of judicial rents from fifteen to three years, and to admit leaseholders to the benefits of the Act of 1881. This motion set the tone for the remainder of the debate. Speakers on both sides used the available statistics on evictions and rents to fit their own predilections. Despite the reasonable nature of the amendment, ministers remained obdurate about concessions. Beach denied that tenants were unable to pay their rents, arguing that the equity of the judicial rent and the right of appeal against harsh eviction provided adequate safeguards against injustice. Although his private views on the rent question had not changed, he had decided to submit temporarily to the majority will in the cabinet. On August 27 Parnell's amendment was defeated by a majority of 123.[25]

When the House adjourned after the division, Lord George

[25] *Hansard,* 3d series, Vol. 308, pp. 341-42, 384-403, 761-66.

Hamilton walked home with Beach through St. James's Park and found him acutely depressed about public as well as private affairs. The chief secretary revealed that his differences with Salisbury had narrowed to a dispute over the state's guarantee of rent in favor of the landlords, and to his own profound contempt for the Irish landlord. Hamilton urged his friend to forget these differences and assured him that there was no need to discuss the revision of the statutory rents until the prime minister had set down his views in a draft bill. Although Beach's mind was somewhat eased by this counsel, Hamilton realized that the chief secretary would require close surveillance, and he wrote immediately to Churchill reporting the incident:

"He evidently dislikes his post the more he sees of it. His health, wife and money affairs all are against his long retention of his post. He is a very highly strung, nervous organization, and I am afraid that he may suddenly resign. If he were to do this in the present session, it would bust us up. As next to you he is the minister upon whom most of the House of Commons work now hinges, and he could not now be replaced. . . . You have managed with great tact and success the House; it is a minor difficulty to manage and soothe a colleague, and I am sure that if you could smooth down Beach a little, you could ease a tension, that may otherwise end in a rupture."[26]

Soon after Churchill received this letter, he asked Lord George Hamilton to his room in the House of Commons and there began to condemn Beach's attitude toward Irish landlords. In the midst of his harangue Beach entered the room, but Lord Randolph continued his scolding unperturbed. According to Hamilton the chief secretary took the tongue lashing calmly and did not reply in kind. The sound of the division bell broke up this curious scene. Churchill must have known what he was doing, for he reported to Hartington: "No doubt the Chief Secretary's first speech did not harmonize in tone and expression with mine, and it may be interesting to you to know that the difference led to an explanation between me and him of so extremely frank and candid a nature that for a short time the existence of the Government was in

[26] Hamilton to Churchill, 27 Aug. 1886, St. Aldwyn MSS.

much danger."[27] Evidently shock treatment was what Beach needed, for he began to show greater forbearance in cabinet when the land question came up for discussion. But his anxiety about the task confronting him in Ireland remained, and the possibility of more serious disputes in the future did not ease his mind.

With his usual insight Churchill described Beach as "one of the most honourable and upright men I have ever had to do with but he does not possess the amount of firmness and resolution which some suppose, and if your communications to him lead him to think that you are not definitely determined on cardinal points of policy, his frame of mind becomes very considerably weakened for the discharge of executive duties. . . . " Subsequent events more than once bore out this analysis. But the chief secretary was not the only cause of concern. "The position of this Government must always be most precarious," Churchill concluded; "it may have a long life but it is a ricketty infant. . . . "[28]

[27] Hamilton, *Reminiscences*, II, pp. 38-39; Churchill to Hartington, 13 Sept. 1886, St. Aldwyn MSS.
[28] *Ibid.*

CHAPTER VIII

Tenants' Relief versus Landlords' Rights

I. THE BULLER MISSION

FOR THE MOMENT the Government had forestalled Parnell's attempt to split the Unionist party on the question of rents. While the debate dragged on, Irish officials were growing nervous about the perennial problem of eviction. As the last resort of landlords, eviction had many disadvantages. The execution of a decree took time and only aggravated the ill-feeling between owners and occupiers. Owing to the league's vigilance, the tenants imported by landlords to occupy evicted holdings were intimidated and boycotted without mercy. When tenants resisted eviction, the cost of their removal often exceeded the amount of arrears in dispute. And eviction, with its emotional overtones and physical suffering, made the highest grade of propaganda for the nationalists. Over fifty per cent of all evictions in Ireland, however, did not involve actual dispossession. The law permitted tenants to re-enter their dwellings, either as caretakers or as leasees, for a period up to six months, during which time they could redeem themselves. Although the Parnellites talked in terms of many thousands of evictions each year, the actual number of tenants dispossessed was much lower.[1]

When Buller arrived in Ireland at the end of August, the league had already organized resistance to eviction on a large scale. Assisted by members of the local league branch, tenants facing eviction barred their doors and windows with logs and bundles of thorns, and prepared hot liquid to be squirted through syringes and various projectiles with which to greet the sheriff's

---

[1] Until 1887 the first eviction was a reminder that the tenants' arrears could no longer be tolerated. If the tenant failed to redeem during the period of grace, a second and final eviction was the result. In 1885 out of 3,127 applications for eviction decrees 1,540 involved no permanent disturbance of the tenant. *Hansard*, 3d series, Vol. 308, p. 408.

party. Besides the protection of their homesteads and families, resistance to eviction had two main objects. The first was to make the work of the evicting party difficult and, indeed, painful enough to render the cost of further evictions prohibitive. So elaborate were the fortifications of some houses that not even the combined forces of bailiffs, emergency men hired by the Property Defence Association,[2] and the police could effect an entry. The tenants thus pursued delaying tactics, but were careful not to inflict mortal injuries on their assailants. The other purpose of resistance was publicity. Defiance of the law in this manner won sympathy not only in England but abroad. English Home Rulers as well as newspaper correspondents flocked to those estates where evictions were scheduled; and every detail of the more notorious evictions was carefully reported in the English and Irish presses.

On the Woodford estate of Lord Clanricarde in the eastern part of county Galway the policy of resistance proved successful in both these respects. The eviction of several tenants in August, 1886, required the presence of two resident magistrates, more than five hundred officers and men of the RIC, and an assortment of bailiffs and emergency men. The league branch had made special preparations for resistance in order to focus attention on the most famous example of absentee landlordism. The resultant operation, which in design and execution resembled a medieval siege, cost the authorities some £3,000 and gave Dublin Castle formal notice of what difficulties lay ahead.[3]

Not all evictions matched those at Woodford for size and intensity of feeling. But the psychological effects of such scenes on tenants in other parts of the country upset the officials in Dublin Castle: if similar tactics were adopted elsewhere, an army would be needed to uphold the rights of landlords. Hicks Beach decided that the only remedy against such defiance of the law lay in eliminating the evictions themselves. If landlords could be made more reasonable about arrears, he knew that evictions would

[2] The PDA was founded in the winter of 1881-1882 by a group of prominent Irish landlords, including the 1st Duke of Abercorn and his sons. The Earl of Courtown was president and Captain Edward Hamilton honorary director. See Lord Claud Hamilton to Salisbury, 11 Dec. 1881, Salisbury MSS.

[3] For details of these evictions see *Times*, 23 Aug. 1886, and *Freeman's Journal*, 23-25 Aug. 1886.

rapidly decline: legislation on this subject was out of the question. Having no love for the Irish landlords, Beach felt no remorse about asking them to desist from eviction; and, like Carnarvon, he soon discovered that some of his subordinates shared the same point of view.

Buller was the first to succumb to Beach's prejudices. The "generalissimo" had already made a tour of inspection through Kerry and Clare, familiarizing himself with the terrain and the officials under his command, and briefing district inspectors and magistrates about necessary security measures. Unfortunately, Buller's appointment seemed to goad the nationalists into increasing their nightly ration of shootings, arms raids, and cattle maiming. He wasted little time in making up his mind as to the causes of Irish discontent and their cure. From the outset the general asked for special powers with which to prosecute agrarian criminals, and he even suggested suppressing the National League.[4] Beach had to remind him constantly that the parliamentary situation precluded such a move and that he would have to rely upon the ordinary law in coping with outrages in the southwest.[5] Buller's somewhat pachydermatous nature did not take kindly to these admonitions. He was certain that a firm hand would win through against the forces of disorder. But the initiative had to come from above, and the state of morale in Dublin Castle gave him no reassurance on this score. One sign of weakness from the Government at Westminster, and these officials would, in his opinion, become more "shakingly weak-kneed" than ever. The Home Rule Bill, he reported, had put "all Irish officials into the attitude described by the Yankees as 'sitting on the fence.' The questionable future that that bill disclosed to them set them all thinking of the parable of the unjust steward. In short they were all preparing to trim. . . . "[6]

[4] Buller to Beach, 30 Aug., 4 Sept. 1886, St. Aldwyn MSS.

[5] Beach argued that the League could not be proclaimed a dangerous association because it posed as a "political organisation working in a constitutional way: they compare themselves e.g. to the Primrose League. Even if the whole of the Conservative Party would vote for suppressing an organisation so representing itself (which I doubt), I feel sure the Liberal Unionists would not"; Beach to Buller, 3 Sept. 1886, ibid.

[6] Buller to Beach, 26 Oct. 1886, ibid.

For Buller the only solution lay in the land question. Like many Unionists, he argued that if the agrarian problem were settled, " . . . the question of Home Rule [would] sink . . . forever into oblivion, and . . . it would be exceedingly difficult to induce the Irish masses to agitate in favour of any measure which would be calculated to withdraw them from the protection of England, either as regards domestic legislation or otherwise."[7]

The General aspired to greater things than the supervision of police patrols in the southwest. He wished to remove the causes of agrarian discontent by a novel procedure. Landlords, he believed, required a special type of coercion just as much as did the tenants: "You must combine a species of coercive land settlement with a coercive crime settlement . . . , " he wrote to Beach.[8] Deeply impressed by the size of tenants' arrears in his district, and loathing the grim scenes at evictions, Buller found himself in harmony with his chief on the subject of the Irish landlord.

In September Beach sent his new deputy in the southwest an important memorandum in which he asserted that the safest way to eliminate evictions was through "personal representations and advice privately given" to the landlords. In cases where many eviction decrees were pending on one estate, he advised Buller to approve the eviction of only the most intransigent tenants. As a last resort, he suggested that the local authorities might even refuse police protection to the sheriff and his evicting party. But Beach hoped that such an extreme course would not be necessary. Although there was also the possibility of discouraging evictions by forcing harsh landlords to bear the costs of police protection, he decided that the plan of personal intercession in rent disputes would suffice for the present.[9]

Acting on this advice, Buller issued an order requiring every landlord intent on eviction to state on an official form the time, place, and reason for the proceeding. Failure to comply with the regulation, it was made clear, would mean the absence of a protecting force at the eviction. If police inquiries failed to convince Buller that the eviction was justified, then he reserved the right

[7] From Buller's memorandum on Irish crime, 30 Oct. 1886, *ibid.*
[8] Buller to Beach, 4, 5 Sept. 1886, *ibid.*
[9] Hicks Beach, *St. Aldwyn*, I, pp. 289-90; Beach to Salisbury, 15 Dec. 1886, Salisbury MSS.

to withhold the sheriff's escort on some pretext or other. Unfortunately for both the Irish executive and tenantry, the idea of refusing landlords full recourse to the law shocked more than one Conservative. Sir Richard Webster, the attorney general, vigorously opposed this policy and advised Beach to drop his plan to introduce Government counsel as a third party in eviction cases reaching the law courts. He also argued that Beach's wish to guarantee every insolvent tenant against eviction was tantamount to accepting Parnell's demands. The great majority of Government supporters shared these views.

II. TENANTS' RELIEF REJECTED

In the House of Commons the Irish members continued their obstructionist tactics and accused Churchill of inciting the Belfast riots. More important, Parnell gave notice of a bill to deal with the "desperate situation" of the tenantry. A delay of five months, he warned, would cause serious hardship and might result in spontaneous uprisings all over the country. Hoping to secure Irish cooperation in bringing the session to an end, Churchill agreed to allow time for Parnell's motion. But the Parnellites were not in a bargaining mood and they continued to obstruct debate on the estimates. The prospect of reopening the land controversy caused Churchill some anxiety, and he impressed upon Salisbury the "vital importance . . . that no encouragement should be given to Parnell to think that by any plausible speeches and proposals he can divide the Unionist party."[10] Later, he explained to Hartington his reasons for granting time for the Irish motion, and warned him about the wedge that Parnell sought to drive between the Conservatives and Liberal Unionists on the rent question.[11]

Parnell designed the Tenants' Relief Bill to lure as many Liberal Unionists as possible away from their support of the Government. Although both Beach and Hartington agreed in principle with some of the provisions relating to the protection of the tenantry against eviction, they considered the bill as a whole

[10] *Hansard*, 3d series, Vol. 308, p. 1224. "Another desperate night in the House of Commons. You may imagine how bad was the Irish conduct when Beach's last words to me were: 'I am now all for a strong cloture. . . .'" Churchill to Salisbury, 4, 15 Sept. 1886, Salisbury MSS.

[11] Churchill to Hartington, 13 Sept. 1886, St. Aldwyn MSS.

a form of coercion against landlords. The nationalists, according to many Government supporters, actually wanted the bill to be rejected so that they might have an excuse for launching a new land agitation. Beach wished to limit evictions by using the discretionary powers of the courts and Dublin Castle, and he suspected Parnell's motives in producing a bill certain to be defeated. The *Times* went further by calling Parnell's scheme "irrelevant, futile, iniquitous."[12]

On September 20 Parnell introduced his bill, which he described as a temporary expedient to relieve the tenantry during an emergency. The main clause empowered tenants, whose rents had been fixed before December 31, 1884, to apply to the Land Court for an abatement provided that they had paid one-half of the rent due in 1886 and one-half of any antecedent arrears. The bill also admitted all leaseholders to the benefits of the Land Act of 1881 and suspended evictions where genuine insolvency could be proved. If the Government waited until February to act, Parnell contended that the tenants would receive no relief until the following November. Having stressed the relationship between famine, evictions, and crime, he concluded with a plea to suspend all evictions in Ireland. If the bill was rejected, then even his authority, he warned, could not prevent the peasants from organizing an agitation to secure their aims.[13]

During the ensuing debate ministers blandly disputed the existence of abnormal poverty. The Irish solicitor general, who was Ashbourne's brother, accused Parnell of inventing a system of "compulsory credit" for tenants whose rents had been adjudicated before 1884.[14] It was argued that this bill made no provision for those 76,000 tenants whose rents had been revised since the end of 1884. In short, Unionist spokesmen denied that the current distress justified any tampering with the judicial rents. Lord Hartington challenged the accuracy of Parnell's statistics and urged members to postpone the issue until the Cowper Commis-

---

[12] *Times*, 9 Sept. 1886.

[13] *Hansard*, 3d series, Vol. 309, pp. 984-86. See also the Irish solicitor general's memorandum on the deficiencies of the bill, Sept. 1886, Salisbury MSS.

[14] John George Gibson, 1846-1923; M.P. 1885-1888; Serjeant 1885; Irish Solicitor General 1885, 1886-1887; Irish Attorney General 1887-1888; Judge, Queen's Bench, High Court of Justice, Ireland 1888-1921.

sion had reported their findings. He accused the nationalists of having deliberately contrived the measure for ulterior purposes and demanded its rejection. Hicks Beach, concealing his real feelings on the land question, denied that rents needed immediate revision. The administration, he declared, would not succumb to extortion: "We will not attempt to govern Ireland by a policy of blackmail." The resultant division gave the Government a majority of ninety-five. Parnell lost his bill but won a good excuse to revive the land war in Ireland.[15]

The Government's refusal to entertain Parnell's bill has been much criticized in the past, and with some justice. The fact that in 1887 the same ministers enacted portions of the bill as recommended by the Cowper Commission has not enhanced their reputation for consistency. But the Conservatives in September, 1886, held fast to the belief that any concession to Parnell would in effect contravene all their pledges to the landowning class in Ireland. Few Unionists could approve the surrender of a landlord's right to evict a defaulting tenant; and the cabinet refused to compromise on the question of judicial rents. The Government had conveniently pledged themselves to uphold the Land Act of 1881 (of which they had never approved), fearing any concessions to the tenantry so soon after the crisis of Home Rule.

As Parnell had predicted, the rejection of his bill led to a deterioration in the state of Ireland. Outrages began to increase and Buller's reorganization of the security forces in the southwest proved less effective than the commander had supposed. The transfer of numerous policemen from protection duty to regular assignments had produced some minor successes against moonlighters; and Buller's bluff, jocular manner, combined with his courage in refusing to carry arms, favorably impressed his adjutants and members of the RIC. But such factors failed to discourage local ruffians from indulging their instinct to do violence, as if in protest against the omnipresent poverty. One resident magistrate reported from the notoriously disaffected Millstreet and Kanturk districts of Cork: "I view the financial condition of this country with great gloom and cannot see what is to avert the collapse which is now pending and which I believe cannot be

[15] *Hansard*, 3d series, Vol. 309, pp. 1032-1247.

staved off for many months." Boycotting persisted, and jurors were warned to vote for acquittal in the interests of their own health. John Dillon, whose influence gained steadily as Parnell retired further into the background provided by Mrs. O'Shea, predicted that the Government would evict two thousand families during the winter and urged the tenantry to unite against landlord oppression.[16]

Such forebodings did not prevent Ashbourne from informing the prime minister in September that the general tone of the country had improved, although he suspected that tenants might refuse to pay their rents during the winter. More sympathetic than Beach to Irish landlords, the lord chancellor praised their "thoroughly reasonable spirit" in granting rent abatements. A month later he proudly stated that his Land Purchase Act was making steady progress. Not only were tenants buying their holdings at a rate much lower than their rents, but an additional grant of ten million pounds would probably be needed in the following year.[17] The Irish committee of the cabinet met on September 23 to discuss the possibilities of a renewal of the land war, and decided that they had little choice but to continue governing the country without special powers.

At the end of the month Beach arrived in Dublin to take personal charge of the administration. Although in poor health and feeling the strain of the session just past, he was determined to invigorate the Castle's personnel and the magistracy. While in England he had received a complete briefing on the activities of the Irish Republican Brotherhood both in America and Ireland. Although reports indicated that the IRB were preparing to launch a campaign against "landlords, bailiffs, and landgrabbers" during the winter, and were importing arms from England hidden in tea chests, there was no evident cause for alarm: the organization had been instructed to "do all in their power to prevent" outrages.[18] The New Departure had once again as-

[16] For a description of conditions in the southwestern counties, see Buller to Beach; 4, 5, 9, 12, 17, 24, 29 Sept. and 2, 11, 16, 24 Oct. 1886, St. Aldwyn MSS.

[17] Ashbourne to Salisbury, 10 Sept., 26 Oct. 1886, Salisbury MSS.

[18] Beach also warned Buller that he had received reports from several informers of threats to Buller's life if he adopted a landlord's attitude and

serted its authority. After interviewing various officials in Dublin, Beach instructed all units of the RIC to obtain complete lists of the league's members and to record the activities of each local branch. Despite rumors to the contrary he did not intend to suppress the league: the object of the order was purely exploratory. In addition, the chief secretary increased the Castle's detective force, some of whom were assigned to guard his own children.

Beach's presence in Dublin may have accounted to some extent for the marked improvement in the general state of the country during October. Since September, outrages and serious crimes had diminished by half. Prospects for the harvest appeared good, with satisfactory prices for potatoes and oats. Against the boycott, however, the administration failed to make headway. At Woodford in county Galway a special store had to be opened in order to supply boycotted police with provisions sent from Dublin. The most effective defense against boycotting in the south continued to be the Cork Defence Union, which was directed by the resourceful A. H. Smith-Barry. Crops were harvested and provisions stocked by employees of the Defence Union in an attempt to remove the worst effects of the league's tyranny. During his stay in Ireland, however, Hicks Beach refused to despair about the boycott. He saw no need for special measures to curb the practice: "As to boycotting, I may of course be wrong, and there is doubtless a good deal of suffering while we wait; but I think I see that it is beginning to work its own cure; and if people learnt to give it up for their own sake, the lesson would be well worth the waiting and suffering."[19]

Even though many landlords were granting voluntary abatements of rent, evictions were steadily increasing along with the tenants' determination to resist them. The pitched battles fought between policemen and defiant tenants in their fortified houses made mockery of the landlords' insistence that their motto was really "live and let live." The lull in more serious crime, however, cheered Beach, and reports reached him from all over the country

encouraged evictions. See report on IRB, 18 Sept. 1886, and memorandum on the IRB in Ireland by E. G. Jenkinson, 6 Oct. 1886, St. Aldwyn MSS.

[19] Beach to Salisbury, 20 Oct. 1886, Salisbury MSS; Beach to Buller, 22 Oct. 1886, St. Aldwyn MSS.

that both tenants and landlords were beginning to behave. Any new rash of evictions, he feared, might provoke the league to commit serious outrage. Buller suggested that harsh landlords be publicly scolded by the administration in order to "gain the sympathies of the masses." But Beach was forced to veto this plan, even though he agreed in private that such a practice might have a salutary effect on landlords like Lord Clanricarde who flatly refused to grant abatements.[20]

In a more optimistic mood Beach reported to Salisbury late in October: "There are signs that the people are getting sick of the tyranny of the National League, which, in the worst places, is becoming an instrument of private malice, e.g., of one shopkeeper against another. If they could but be brought to throw it over for themselves, it would do more for Ireland than anything that has happened in my time."

Although he feared the reaction of Irish extremists against Parnell's constitutional policy, Beach hoped to survive the winter without special legislation. The fact that the administration could in an emergency always apply to Parliament for coercive powers had, he believed, helped to restrain the nationalists: " . . . I think the rod in pickle has done good service already, and I want to keep it there as long as I can."[21]

III. THE PLAN OF CAMPAIGN

Such optimism was short lived. As Beach informed Buller: "There is something about the present quiet . . . which is like the lull before the storm."[22] As it turned out, this premonition had substance, for the nationalists had decided to inaugurate a new phase in the land war. On October 23 *United Ireland* published the Plan of Campaign. A partial substitute for the Tenants' Relief Bill, the Plan gave the tenantry a more efficient form of collective

[20] Beach to Salisbury, 20 Oct. 1886, Salisbury MSS. Hubert George de Burgh Canning, 2nd Marquess of Clanricarde, 1832-1916; M.P. 1867-1871; owned some 57,000 acres in Galway and was the most famous absentee landlord of his generation. For details of the dispute with Clanricarde, see Beach's memorandum on the subject, 5 Nov. 1886, St. Aldwyn MSS; and Hicks Beach, *St. Aldwyn*, I, pp. 289-95.

[21] Beach to Salisbury, 20 Oct. 1886; Beach to Churchill, 22 Oct. 1886, Salisbury MSS.

[22] Beach to Buller, 14 Oct. 1886, St. Aldwyn MSS.

bargaining than they had ever known in the past. Fintan Lalor, while crusading for a "moral insurrection" in 1848, had suggested a roughly similar combination against rents. But the chief credit for the Plan belonged to Timothy Harrington, the National League's secretary, who was indebted for advice to Dillon and William O'Brien. The new scheme was impressively simple: tenants demanded an abatement from their landlord; if the latter refused to cooperate, the tenants paid their rent, less the desired reduction, to a committee of trustees appointed by the Plan's organizers. The funds thus collected would be spent on promoting the scheme and subsidizing evicted tenants. It was a bold and cunning stratagem, sufficiently legal to cause both landlords and the law officers endless trouble. The time had arrived, the nationalist press proclaimed, for the tenant to defend himself against "the crowbar brigade" and the vested interests of the Unionist party.[23]

Those tenants who subscribed to the Plan welcomed any excuse to reduce their rents. Although Parnell had given ample warning about the dangers of rejecting his bill, he took no active part in the Plan. Owing to his bad health and the attractions of Mrs. O'Shea, much of the initiative for policy-making within the Irish party had passed temporarily to two of his most talented lieutenants, Dillon and O'Brien, who had championed the cause of a rent war during their American tour. For the next few years the Plan of Campaign was shrewdly directed by a small clique within the Irish party.[24] It became the dominant weapon on the agrarian front and caused Dublin Castle untold anxiety. In promoting the Plan the Parnellites had successfully adapted their tactics to the conditions imposed upon them by their alliance with the Liberal party; and the new agitation against landlords served as an effective means of reminding legislators and the British public alike of the existence of serious grievances in Ireland.

After the Plan's publication Hicks Beach redoubled his efforts

---

[23] For details of the Plan's origins and aims, see C. C. O'Brien, *Parnell and His Party*, pp. 201-06; M. Davitt, *The Fall of Feudalism*, London, 1904, pp. 516 ff.; and Beach's cabinet memorandum on the Plan of Campaign, 13 Jan. 1887, St. Aldwyn MSS.

[24] See F. S. L. Lyons, *The Fall of Parnell 1890-1891*, London, 1960, pp. 17-30.

to reconcile landlords and their tenants before it was too late. Those landlords who sensed the serious nature of the threat posed by the Plan responded to the chief secretary's appeal in the hopes of saving something of their shrinking incomes. Almost every day the English press contained reports of voluntary abatements ranging from ten per cent on judicial rents to as much as forty per cent on nonjudicial rents. Where a landlord insisted on his right to evict, Buller prevaricated by requiring him to answer the Castle's special questionnaire ten days before the date of eviction. More cautious than Beach when it came to withholding an eviction force, Buller continued to fret about the inadequacy of the administration's powers. As he wrote to Beach:

"You are asking the District Magistrates and County Inspectors to take a small risk, and a good deal of obloquy by refusing protection, and you are further asking them to take a good deal of responsibility by squeezing the landlords about evictions. I believe they are doing this but I know privately from all of them that they none of them think they have the sort of authority they would like for it."[25]

When tales of interference with evictions reached Dublin, the nationalist leaders promptly accused the Government of using a "dispensing power." Buller, rather than Beach, received the main brunt of the nationalists' attack. He was derided as a convert to the cause of the National League—to the acute discomfort of many Unionists, who were hypersensitive on the subject of property rights. Beach was forced to deny the statement outright, while privately wishing he had a "dispensing power" at his command.[26]

The threat of a new campaign against rents did not seem to disturb the complacency of Dublin Castle. Ashbourne informed Lord Salisbury that conditions had improved noticeably during the last few months: landlords were behaving more generously, tenants were eager to purchase their holdings, and Buller had raised morale in Kerry and Clare. Parnell's absence from the country, moreover, appeared to have calmed even the extreme nationalists. The Irish lord chancellor reported that affairs were "*steadily* settling down," and that with some luck and dili-

[25] Buller to Beach, 26 Oct. 1886, St. Aldwyn MSS.
[26] Beach to Buller, 5, 14 Nov. 1886, *ibid.*; *Times*, 5-9 Nov. 1886.

gence on the part of officials the situation ought to be under control during the winter. The omission of any reference to the Plan of Campaign reflected the Castle's tendency to underestimate the resourcefulness of their opponents.[27]

During November, Dillon and O'Brien held numerous meetings to promote the Plan on individual estates. Other leading Irish members, such as T. D. Sullivan, the two Redmonds, Thomas Sexton, and David Sheehy, also stepped up the campaign against landlords in various parts of the country. The Parnellites were determined to carry into effect their leader's threats about the consequences of neglecting the land question. But the Irish administration was slow to recognize the potential strength of the Plan; and the cabinet did not give serious attention to the agitation until almost a month after its announcement in the press. Buller, writing his monthly report at the end of October, gave notice that the Government ought to be prepared for a relapse in the patient's condition at any moment:

"While the general tone of my Report is good, it must be recollected that this goodness is only skin deep. The elements of disorder are still in force . . . the bulk of the landlords have not yet commenced to appreciate the significance of past events, and are holding their hands rather than mending their ways; and the tenants, who are a body of serfs just emancipated, have as yet no leaders but men of the party of disorder. . . . The wound in the body politic between the governors and the governed still gapes as wide as ever."[28]

IV. A LOCAL GOVERNMENT FEUD

In mid-October the *Daily News* published a story alleging that the Government were drafting a bill to establish provincial councils in Ireland. Beach thought it wiser to leave the charge unanswered on the ground that a denial would lead to further mis-

[27] Ashbourne to Salisbury, 26 Oct. 1886, Salisbury MSS.

[28] "The country, deeply wounded, is recovering from the fever of the wound, but its circulation is at the lowest point. Credit has been withdrawn all round, the pressure of debt is very heavy. A judicious expenditure in public works, and a systematic fair coercion of the sheriff's action in distraints etc. would do more to quiet this part of Ireland than anything else"; Buller memorandum on the state of the southwest, 30 Oct. 1886, St. Aldwyn MSS.

representations. The report in fact was not altogether false: the cabinet had already started discussing a bill to provide county councils for the United Kingdom. For the majority of cabinet ministers local government reform was an unwanted child forced upon them by the exigencies of party politics; and the question provoked fierce disagreement in a ministry that was beginning to resent the lectures of Lord Randolph Churchill.

Local government reform took precedence over all other domestic problems during the November cabinets and produced a first-class ministerial crisis. The chief protagonists were the prime minister, Churchill, and Hicks Beach; and the dispute brought to the surface all the discontent that emanated from the want of an Irish policy and the presence of Churchill in the Government. At the general election of 1885 the Conservatives had pledged themselves to deal with local government throughout the United Kingdom. The Liberal Unionists were known to favor such a reform, especially in Ireland. During the August debate on the Queen's speech Churchill had announced that the signposts of Conservative policy in this field would be equality, similarity, and simultaneity of treatment. Anticipating some trouble over the question, Salisbury asked Hartington not to leave on his proposed trip to India before advising the cabinet about his views on county councils. This request put the Liberal Unionist leader in something of a quandary, and Balfour mischievously commented: "Hartington, as I understand it, is standing (like Garrick between Tragedy and Comedy) with the Liberal Unionists pulling him one way, and Her Grace of Manchester pulling him the other. Victory yet hangs in the balance. . . . "[29] Thanks in part to the Queen's entreaties, Hartington remained in England; but even his proximity did not prevent a sharp conflict of opinion from developing in cabinet.

The crux of the problem concerned Churchill's three signposts. None of them aroused much enthusiasm among ministers. Lord Salisbury objected to all three; but he disapproved most strongly of the arrangements for administering Poor Law relief, which abolished the old boards of guardians and entrusted outdoor relief to the representatives of the rural working classes. The prospect of such a change appalled him: the result would be a "lavish and

[29] Balfour to Salisbury, 19 Oct. 1886, Salisbury MSS.

demoralizing administration of outdoor relief." To Lord Cranbrook he confessed that the proposal was "rather like leaving the cat in charge of the cream jug"; and he informed the Queen that all his cabinet ministers, excepting Churchill, shared this view.[30]

Lord Randolph, grown more domineering with time and authority, occupied the pivotal position in the dispute. His famous Dartford speech on October 2 had committed him to a more Liberal, if not Radical, position in domestic affairs; and having just finished with distinction his first tour of duty as leader of the House, he felt that he deserved better of his colleagues on the question of elective councils. Churchill, in fact, cared nothing about simultaneity: Ireland could wait for local government reform as far as he was concerned. What really mattered was the English voter's conversion to Tory democracy. With hopes of outbidding the Liberals for the allegiance of the new electorate, Churchill wanted a county councils bill that included Poor Law reform as a sop to the English agricultural laborer.

Hicks Beach, on the other hand, not only cared more about the principle of equal representation and taxation of owner and occupier in the new county councils, but insisted that Ireland should receive this concession at the same time as England and Scotland. During November the rift in the cabinet steadily widened and tempers grew short. Once again Churchill became disenchanted with Beach, supposedly his closest political associate, and confessed to Salisbury: "I think Beach is going to be very nasty, sometimes indecently radical, sometimes disgustingly reactionary. I believe Gladstone to be the fated governor of this country."[31]

All attempts to reason with Churchill failed. Salisbury tried to convince him that a policy balanced between the "classes and the masses" contained the only hope for the party. Such conciliatory efforts met with no success. Churchill, it seemed, was set on behaving like "a whip trying to keep the slugs up to the collar." Salisbury, who was criticized for showing too much self-effacement, explained that he was making "a vain attempt to pour oil upon the creaking and groaning machinery."[32] And he was not

[30] Cecil, *Salisbury*, III, p. 327; *Letters of Queen Victoria*, 3d series, I, pp. 226-27.

[31] Churchill to Salisbury, 6 Nov. 1886, Salisbury MSS.

[32] Cecil, *Salisbury*, III, pp. 326-27.

blind to the implications of Churchill's latest campaign, for he wrote to his private secretary: "The problem is a difficult one—for the state of the Union question makes it unusually difficult for us to resign: and the fact that (Beach having refused) there seems no possible leader in the Commons but Randolph: these two facts taken together involve the consequence that Randolph can always put before us the dilemma of accepting his views or endangering the Union with Ireland: and this gives him a strong position."[33]

Lord Hartington, whose counsel Salisbury valued, suggested a compromise in the form of an Irish county councils bill. Convinced of the need for constructive measures, he argued that further neglect of Irish distress would dishearten many Liberal Unionists. Salisbury agreed that an Irish bill had the added advantage of postponing Poor Law reform, but this attempt at compromise was short lived. Churchill still insisted that an English bill should come first; and through the agency of Ferdinand de Rothschild he persuaded Hartington to withdraw his plan. Having achieved this minor victory, he proved more accommodating on the Poor Law question. With some misgivings Salisbury drafted a proposal that excluded local government reform in Ireland and postponed any changes in the system of outdoor relief.[34]

Now it was Beach's turn to object. He deplored this new compromise because it neglected Ireland and lacked equitable representation of owners. Further attempts at reconciliation were deemed hopeless; Salisbury lamented the failure of his "eirenicon"; and the cabinet relapsed into the dissensions that culminated in Lord Randolph's resignation.[35] In view of the strife engendered by this issue it was small wonder that Salisbury grumbled: "I wish there was no such thing as Local Government." And Churchill, who felt increasingly estranged in a cabinet dominated by the "Old Gang," was moved to exclaim that Ireland, like France, ought to be told to "go to the devil."[36]

[33] Salisbury to H. Manners, 28 Nov. 1886, Salisbury MSS.

[34] Salisbury to Cranbrook, 28 Nov. 1886, *ibid.*

[35] Among those ministers who approved of Salisbury's compromise were Smith, Churchill, Cranbrook, Lord George Hamilton, and Stanhope. Salisbury to Beach, 1 Dec. 1886; Salisbury to Churchill, 30 Nov. 1886, *ibid.*

[36] Churchill to Salisbury, 29 Nov. 1886, *ibid.*

CHAPTER IX

Deterioration

I. IRISH TRIALS AND TRIBULATIONS

ALTHOUGH by the end of November the Plan of Campaign had come into operation on a dozen estates, the Irish judiciary still withheld judgment on its legality. Large rallies were held by Plan organizers to enlist tenant support, and the nationalist leaders taunted ministers with charges that they were afraid to coerce the Irish people. In the meantime Beach consulted his advisers in Dublin Castle as to how the ordinary law could deal effectively with the conspiracy against rent. The law officers, however, pleaded for more time to construct a case against the Plan's methods and promoters. The impetuous Buller wished to suppress the National League as the first step toward prosecuting the Plan. But Beach objected to any course that required summoning Parliament and replied that the offenses of the league rather than the league itself ought to be punished.[1]

Home Rulers in both countries accused the Government of being too obsessed with the facts and figures of agrarian outrage. Convinced that there was nothing illegal about the boycott, they asserted that the Unionists were merely trying to fabricate a case for coercion. It was true that the agrarian crime rate from 1879-1882 made the agitation of 1886 look tame by comparison. But Beach and his colleagues were not worried so much about the statistics of crime as they were about the general attitude of the Irish people toward the law. Intimidation or widespread boycotting was as pernicious in its way as more violent outrages, and its effect upon the country's economy, the resultant paralysis of trade in some areas, loomed large in the minds of men like Beach. To most Unionists boycotting was all the more dangerous because it lacked the dramatic and tangible qualities of other

[1] Hicks Beach, *St. Aldwyn*, I, p. 287.

crimes, and because witnesses were afraid to testify for fear of being boycotted themselves.

In the meantime General Buller was growing ever more sympathetic toward the tenants' plight. He drew a grim picture of the situation in Kerry, where he found landlords determined to mulct tenants of their hard-earned capital:

"The fact is the bulk of the landlords do nothing for their tenants but extract as much rent as they can by every means in their power, and the law helps them: and the tenant, even if an industrious, hardworking man, has no defence. Landlords are not evicting now in Kerry but they are distraining cattle where they can: and a distraint punishes a tenant really more than a process of eviction, if the latter is not pressed home. The leases in Kerry, the customs and traditions are all those of rackrenters. There are only two resident landlords in Kerry who are not bankrupt and most of the large absentee landlords are not much better. What chance has a tenant under the present law? No, you must alter the law if you are to have peace. Of that I feel convinced."[2]

Unfortunately for Buller and the tenantry, the political situation at Westminster precluded the kind of legislation he envisaged. The only alternative was to exert clandestine pressure on landlords who ignored the realities of the agricultural depression. Colonel O'Callaghan, for example, a landlord who had earned a name for harsh treatment of his tenants, insisted upon wholesale evictions on his Bodyke estate in county Clare after refusing to lower the judicial rents fixed in 1882. Buller intervened and in a private letter bluntly asked: " . . . is the game worth the candle?" Evidently O'Callaghan thought that it was, because the Castle was forced to postpone the evictions on the grounds that they were "indefensible." According to Buller, the administration's action had put O'Callaghan, who was a "driveller" anyway, into a "blue funk."[3]

[2] "For 120 years British bayonets have backed up landlords in extracting excessive rents, and have supported them in grossly neglecting their tenantry. What is the result of these 120 years—the tenants have combined against the injustice and persecutions; and where are the landlords? Nowhere. Bankrupt in money, in political, and in moral power. Is there not a lesson in this?" Buller to Beach, 15 Nov. 1886, St. Aldwyn MSS. See also Melville, *Buller*, I, pp. 314-15.

[3] Buller to Beach, 15, 25, 26 Jan. and 11 Feb. 1887, St. Aldwyn MSS.

Another example of Buller's use of arbitrary powers was his handling of Captain Edward Hamilton, who was not only the agent for the Brooke estate at Coolgreaney in county Wexford, but was also honorary head of the Property Defence Association. In December Hamilton called on the new under secretary in order to appeal for help in fighting the Plan at Coolgreaney. Buller refused his request for wholesale evictions and advised him to evict several of the wealthiest tenants before making a settlement with the other tenants through the parish priest. Hamilton scorned this suggestion, asserting that the priest was "at the bottom of the whole business"; and the interview became somewhat tense when the agent threatened to send for a thousand Orangemen in order to evict every Plan subscriber on the estate. Buller remained obdurate. For the last 120 years, he retorted, the landlords had collected their rents with the help of "British bayonets." But times had changed, landlords' rights had been pruned, and mass evictions such as those at Woodford, which had cost the administration several thousand pounds, settled nothing. Hamilton left the Castle in a bitter mood. There was no settlement through the priest at Coolgreaney; and the long contest between landlord and tenants began with the first in a series of "piecemeal" evictions.[4]

In England ministers bravely kept up the pretense of resolute government. At the Mansion House on November 9 Lord Salisbury declared that the relations between landlord and tenant had definitely improved. While denying that Buller had used a dispensing power, he admitted that the Castle had urged landlords to treat defaulting tenants with leniency. In steady and honest government, he remarked somewhat tritely, lay the key to Ireland's future prosperity. Four days later Hicks Beach, speaking at Bristol, called an Irish crimes bill unnecessary, yet warned that the Government would not hesitate to ask Parliament for special powers if the law proved unable to cope with the Plan of Campaign. On the subject of Irish landlords the chief secretary asserted that no greater enemy of property existed than the man "who at-

---

[4] Transcript of interview contained in George Brooke to Balfour, 23 June 1892, Salisbury MSS. Buller's comment was: "As for my contretemps with Hamilton it has done no harm; and I have been able to explain to his friends what a blackguard he is"; Buller to Beach, 15 Jan. 1887, St. Aldwyn MSS.

tempted harshly to exact its rights and failed to perform its duties." And he added for good measure that it would take Ireland many years to recover from the demoralizing effects of Gladstone's Home Rule Bill.[5]

The first hint of a change in Government policy appeared with the news that Sir Robert Hamilton was to leave his post in Dublin.[6] The *Times* expressed regret that the under secretary had not been transferred sooner. But more than a shake-up in personnel was required to salvage the Government's rapidly declining prestige. From the southwest came reports of Buller's strenuous efforts to save tenants from eviction. The failure of the police to protect several eviction parties moved landlords to protest vehemently. If the Government really believed in the supremacy of landlords' rights, the Irish landowning class was at a loss to find proof of this policy. On November 22 the cabinet debated the merits of prohibiting all rallies sponsored by the league. Because ministers failed to agree, action was postponed; but they did decide to make an example of at least one prominent Parnellite. Two days later Beach left for Ireland and instituted proceedings against Dillon for the use of violent language in a recent speech. The chief secretary also prohibited a meeting scheduled at Sligo to intimidate jurors at the assizes. The nationalist press hailed the action against Dillon as "a declaration of war." At last the Government appeared to be redeeming their pledges about firm rule in Ireland. But when Beach consulted the Castle's law officers about the Plan article in *United Ireland*, they strongly advised against prosecuting either the paper or any of its readers. The Law Room naively assumed that tenants would not surrender their money to unknown trustees on whom they had no legal hold. They implied that the new agitation would come to nothing. No action was taken to forestall the Plan until Beach's return to Dublin late in November, when he suggested prosecuting the ringleaders of the Plan on each estate in the Court of Bankruptcy. By this means he hoped to recover the funds subscribed and to obtain enough evidence to prosecute the Plan's original authors.

[5] *Times*, 10, 15 Nov. 1886.

[6] Hamilton became Governor of Tasmania at a salary of £5,000. Beach was instrumental in finding him this post. See Sir R. Hamilton to Beach, 2, 19 Nov. 1886, St. Aldwyn MSS.

He assured Salisbury that the law officers would soon declare the Plan illegal, but worried lest too stringent a policy provoke the nationalists to retaliate with systematic outrage.[7]

At Beach's suggestion Lord Salisbury asked Churchill's advice about the safest way of combating the Plan. Churchill recommended patience: prohibiting Plan rallies might force the conspirators into more violent action. Salisbury himself agreed with the argument of expediency and counseled Beach not to commit himself prematurely: "I think you had better let the flames spread because you won't get the parish engine to come out till you have a good conflagration." The prime minister also warned Beach about the impending prosecution: " . . . if your powers are not strong enough you will be in trouble. A game of bluff is dangerous with a man like Dillon."[8] Neither Salisbury nor Churchill wished to engage the Parnellites in open conflict before the meeting of Parliament; but their tactics did not coincide with the ideas of many Unionists about resolute government. Beach had no choice but to accept the policy of inaction, and he contented himself for the time being with banning meetings called for the specific purpose of intimidation.

In November the gale rents fell due, and the Castle carefully watched the response of tenants throughout the country. On Plan estates the great majority of tenants obediently paid their rents to the designated trustees. Elsewhere, according to official reports, rents were being paid except in those areas dominated by the league. Many landlords had forestalled the Plan by granting abatements. Where the league exercised less influence and better relations between landlord and tenant prevailed, the tenantry paid their rents as usual. Like the incidence of agrarian crime, the resistance to rent depended largely upon the poverty of the local population, their susceptibility to nationalist propaganda, and their fear of the league's authority.

At the end of the month Buller was named to succeed Sir Robert Hamilton. Although only a provisional appointment, the general's promotion was calculated to appease Irish loyalists who had decried Home Rule sentiments in the Castle. For some time Beach

---

[7] Beach to Salisbury, 30 Nov. 1886, Salisbury MSS.
[8] Salisbury to Beach, 1 Dec. 1886, *ibid.*

had contemplated reforms in the Irish administration, such as making the under secretaryship a political rather than a civil-service appointment. He also desired to give parliamentary representation to various Irish departments, such as local government, fisheries, and education, thereby relieving the chief secretary of numerous responsibilities. But these projects never went beyond the planning stage because more urgent problems took precedence.[9]

If Irish officials hesitated to call the Plan illegal, Lord Salisbury did not. Addressing the City Conservative Club on December 8, he described it as a fraudulent form of patriotism that imperiled all obligations between owner and occupier. Such a system of "organized embezzlement" was bound to destroy any remaining hope of peace and prosperity in the country. The English people, he was confident, could never be misled about the character of the Plan, as they had been on the question of Home Rule.[10]

At Dillon's trial, which began on December 13 in the Queen's Bench division, Justice O'Brien took an important step by declaring the Plan "an absolutely illegal organization." The court found the defendant guilty, but he was bound over on good behavior and released after giving securities for £2,000 bail. As a test case the prosecution was hardly a success: Dillon continued to make inflammatory speeches; and the nationalist press paradoxically considered the Plan vindicated. But the fact remained that a leading judge had pronounced the Plan illegal.

As a result of this verdict Beach prepared to take immediate action. On December 15 he informed Salisbury that he intended to strike his first direct blow against the Plan. Although he felt nothing but contempt for those Irish landlords who "prefer to lie on their backs and howl to the Government," he decided that the time for action had come. Orders were drafted for a surprise raid on a Plan rent collection at Loughrea in county Galway,

[9] With Buller's help Beach made one important change in the administration of justice by reorganizing the Special Crime Branch of the RIC. This department, which pursued its inquiries under conditions of the utmost secrecy, was given special status and proved its value in succeeding years. See Buller to Beach, 14, 26 Nov. 1886, and Beach to Buller, 26 Nov. 1886, St. Aldwyn MSS.

[10] *Times*, 9 Dec. 1886.

which was a center of tenant disaffection. If the venture succeeded, Beach hoped that tenants would be less prone to join the
conspiracy against rents. "I hope you won't think this plan too
Irish!", he wrote to Lord Salisbury the day before the scheduled
raid.[11] The first phase of Beach's operation went smoothly enough.
Although the element of surprise was lost, the police invaded
the site and seized four Irish M. P.'s, a cashbox, and the books of
the Plan's trustees. While the nationalists belittled the raid, they
also feared the adoption of a stringent policy in Dublin Castle,
for the Plan was simultaneously proclaimed "an unlawful and
criminal conspiracy" by decree of the lord lieutenant. After several months of hesitation and compromise, the Irish administration
appeared to have found some of the resolution that Salisbury
had promised earlier.[12]

effect of Loughrea

Unfortunately, the Loughrea seizure not only failed to deter
tenants from joining the Plan, but it also raised the stock of Campaigners in the eyes of the tenantry. As a precaution against
further raids, the Plan organizers immediately ordered all rent
collections to be conducted in secret; and the Castle was thereby
deprived of an important advantage in the land war. By this
time even the chief secretary admitted the necessity of strengthening the criminal law. The intimidation of jurors and estate agents,
as well as fierce resistance to eviction, had exposed the weaknesses
of the Irish executive; and the Plan of Campaign threatened the
entire legal basis of land tenure. Every day the newspapers carried
accounts of some new act of defiance or infraction of the law in
Ireland perpetrated in the name of the National League. As Lord
Salisbury once complained bitterly, "The cumbrous processes
and precautions of English law are an unwieldy armoury
against modern forms of lawlessness."[13] In mid-December Hicks
Beach began work on the drafts of a land bill to deal with judicial
rents and a crimes bill that would become a permanent part of the
legal code. Apart from extending summary jurisdiction and introducing change of venue for serious crimes, the measure contained no drastic alterations in the law.

[11] Beach to Salisbury, 15 Dec. 1886, Salisbury MSS.

[12] Dillon, O'Brien, M. Harris, and D. Sheehy were remanded on bail.
Times, 17 Dec. 1886.

[13] Salisbury to Alfred Austin, 27 Oct. 1887, Salisbury MSS.

II. CHURCHILL'S SMASH

Beach's work on these bills was interrupted by a more urgent matter. On December 18 the cabinet met to consider Churchill's daring proposals for the budget. W. H. Smith, who for several months had been pestered with requests from Churchill to effect economies in the War Office, called the budget "a brilliant effort of genius." But the provisions therein, he was convinced, would never pass in the House of Commons. "It has found out so many corns on which it jumps," he wrote to Salisbury, "that there is great danger it may be beaten in detail."[14] The prime minister needed no such strictures to confirm his own suspicions about the budget. The consensus within the cabinet was that certain provisions would have to be revised; but Lord Randolph's tactless behavior at this suggestion served only to crystallize the opposition mounting against him. The fact was that by December the cumulative strains and tensions engendered by the clash between two conflicting temperaments and ideologies had reached a breaking point. Salisbury and Churchill were backing themselves into emplacements from which there was no escape through compromise. The cabinet—indeed the party—was too small to contain both men in positions of authority; and the budget happened to afford the most convenient site for their final duel. The sequence of tactical moves on both sides, which led up to Churchill's ultimatum of December 20, is too well known to bear repetition here. Lord Randolph's request that he be allowed to resign brought his adversary face to face with the dilemma he had anticipated in November.[15]

Thus Churchill's budget precipitated the most serious ministerial crisis of the entire administration. With mixed feelings of relief and anxiety for the safety of the Union, Salisbury appealed to Beach for advice. Isolated as he was in Ireland, out of touch with the swiftly moving events in London, Beach occupied a key position in the controversy if any compromise was to be achieved. Torn between loyalty to a friend and disapproval of his cause, the chief secretary was confident that he could reason with Church-

[14] Smith to Salisbury, 18 Dec. 1886, *ibid.*
[15] A full account of the ministerial crisis may be found in W. S. Churchill, *Churchill*, ii, chaps. 15-17.

ill when the latter arrived in Dublin for the Christmas holidays. Having no idea of the speed with which the climax was approaching, he informed his chief: "It may do no harm to let him see that I think so little of it as to go away the day before he comes. . . . By that time he may have thought better of it: and at any rate, will be separated from Wolff!"[16]

But on the very day Beach wrote, December 22, Salisbury sent an uncompromising reply to the chancellor of the Exchequer in which he refused to accept his version of what the military estimates ought to be. Implicit in the letter was his acceptance of Churchill's request. The latter now burned his last bridge. Seeing no hope of conciliation, blocked at every turn, he acknowledged this decision from Hatfield, and later that night authorized the editor of the *Times* to publish the news of his resignation on the following morning. When Hicks Beach learned this, he gave in to despair and urged Salisbury to resign at once: a coalition government including Lord Hartington was, in his opinion, the only alternative. But the prime minister was determined to preserve his ministry as well as the Act of Union, and he set about trying to repair the extensive damage caused by the resignation.[17]

Lord Randolph, several days later, tried to explain away his dedication to economy in the budget and to more liberal policies in general as merely an attempt to "concentrate popular support for the Government on the Irish question": but this lame excuse did not impress Salisbury, who had no second thoughts about removing what he described as a painful "boil." To a friend the prime minister revealed the deep gulf that separated him from Lord Randolph: "His character, moreover, is quite unrestrained: both in impulsiveness and variability, and in a tendency which can only be described by the scholastic word 'bully,' he presents

[16] Beach to Salisbury, 22 Dec. 1886, Salisbury MSS.
[17] Beach to Salisbury, 25 Dec. 1886, *ibid.* On this occasion Beach revealed that his own health was deteriorating, and he disqualified himself on this score among others from taking the lead in the Commons. See Hicks Beach, *St. Aldwyn*, I, pp. 301-02. Balfour, who played an important role in these events, advised his uncle to ensure that Churchill resigned on some issue about which the majority of the party had no strong opinions. Balfour to Salisbury, 21, 23 Dec. 1886, Salisbury MSS.

the characteristics of extreme youth. Whether there is any growth left in him I do not know. . . . "[18]

There are always two sides to a fight, and the intense struggle for political power between Hatfield House and Blenheim, reminiscent at times of the Cecils' classic feud with Essex and his faction (although Churchill himself never qualified as the Queen's favorite), proved no exception to the rule. It would be as unjust to blame Salisbury for accepting Churchill's offer of resignation on the face of his past conduct as it would be absurd to deny that the cabinet would have been wise to dilute their "rigidly orthodox" policies with an infusion of so-called Tory democracy.

Hicks Beach and Ashbourne arrived from Dublin for the critical cabinet on December 28, when overtures to Hartington and Goschen were considered. The chief secretary refused to accept the leadership of the House, on the grounds that he lacked the requisite strength and popularity. Throughout the ensuing parleys between ministers and the Liberal Unionists, Salisbury never forgot that the "first consideration" was Ireland. In the Government reshuffle Beach remained chief secretary, because, in his own words, he knew "the ropes better than anyone else." In spite of the overwhelming difficulties facing him, he promised to "keep things going patiently and firmly without much regard to abuse from either side."[19] Goschen, the man whom Churchill was commonly supposed to have forgotten, became chancellor of the Exchequer. Although a difficult man to work with, almost too clever at times, he was an important catch for the Unionist party. No Conservative or Liberal Unionist was a more dedicated opponent of Irish nationalism. T. P. O'Connor once compared Goschen's "raucous" voice to the croakings of frogs he had heard in California; and the ex-Liberal was not a popular figure on either side of the House.[20] But his tenacity as a debater and

[18] Sir James Stephen to Salisbury, 28 Dec. 1886; Salisbury to Sir James Stephen, 30 Dec. 1886, *ibid*.

[19] Salisbury to Beach, 24 Dec. 1886, 3 Jan. 1887; and Beach to Salisbury, 25 Dec. 1886, 1 Jan. 1887, *ibid*.

[20] T. P. O'Connor, *Memoirs of an Old Parliamentarian*, II, p. 117. W. H. Smith wrote: "Goschen is difficult to get on with—politically he is suspicious—distrustful in administration, and believes in no one so entirely as in himself, but he has weight in the country if not in the House. . . ." Smith to Iddesleigh, 22 Feb. 1886, Iddesleigh MSS.

his remarkable acumen as a financier placed him among the ranking politicians of his day. W. H. Smith, the "plain, honest, businessman," was promoted to leader of the House. The Government survived a supreme crisis and, as it turned out, gained considerably in terms of Liberal Unionist support and cabinet harmony. Churchill was left to roam the political scene: in Dilke's words, like a "rogue elephant."[21]

From Ireland came word of nationalist delight over the cabinet turmoil. The Duke of Abercorn reported that the Parnellites regarded Churchill's action as a sign of the disintegration of the Unionist forces. Some Ulster loyalists, on the other hand, were not sorry to see Lord Randolph go.[22] The resignation even moved Chamberlain, who called Goschen the Whig "skeleton at the feast," to consider reunion with the Gladstonian Liberals out of fear of a Tory reaction within the Government.[23]

III. A "LICKING" FOR IRELAND

With the ministerial crisis resolved, Beach returned to the second phase of his campaign against the Plan. On January 4 the conspiracy trial of the leading Plan agents arrested at Loughrea began in Dublin. Buller, testifying along with Beach and the Irish attorney general, denied any interference with the landlords' right to evict. His work in Kerry and Clare, he readily assured the court, had been confined to organizing security measures against moonlighters. Under cross-examination Beach refused to answer any questions about his role in making the landlords amenable to rent reductions. The nationalists had succeeded in embarrassing the administration and in bringing the under secretary to the point of perjury. After long delays, re-

[21] The Government sustained another blow when Lord Iddesleigh dropped dead of a heart attack in the anteroom of 10 Downing Street on January 12. He died in Salisbury's presence, shortly after learning from the newspapers that in the ministerial reshuffle he was to be replaced as foreign secretary by Salisbury. See Cecil, *Salisbury*, III, pp. 339-45.

[22] Abercorn reported that Churchill "has always been looked upon by the Loyalists in Ulster with suspicion—so perhaps in the end his removal may have a beneficial effect upon the Government." The Duke also urged that Beach remain in Ireland. Abercorn to Salisbury, 26 Dec. 1886, Salisbury MSS.

[23] Garvin, *Chamberlain*, II, pp. 276-84.

peated violations of their bonds by the defendants, and much fanfare from the nationalist press, the conspiracy trial ended with an acquittal, due to lack of evidence. It took the administration many weeks to recover from this severe blow.

January was a month marked by the notorious evictions at Glenbeigh, county Kerry, on the estate of the Hon. Rowland Winn (later Lord Headley), where several cottages were deliberately destroyed. The evictions, which even some Unionists called cruel and unnecessary, dragged on for over a week and provided the nationalists with ideal publicity.[24] Glenbeigh was one of the first estates to become the playground of English Radicals, who used the Irish Question to promote their own political ends as well as the cause of humanity. Home Rulers from England visited eviction sites and exhorted the tenantry to resist the emergency men and bailiffs. Occasionally these Radical missionaries would join the tenants in repulsing the forces of the law. The Dublin regime suffered another setback when Buller's correspondence with the Glenbeigh land agents over rent reductions was published in the press. Few landlords welcomed the news that the under secretary had strained his powers in an attempt to prevent the evictions.[25] The *Times* condemned the Castle's policy as "a masquerade of power . . . a hollow and unsightly sham"; and Irish loyalists accused Beach and Buller of strengthening the tenants' position at the expense of the landlords. To militant Unionists the signs of appeasement were unmistakable.[26]

The cabinet met on January 15 to hear Beach report on the condition of Ireland. Describing the Plan as a variation on an old theme, he pointed out that under ordinary law the courts could not convict the promoters on a charge of either sedition or conspiracy.

[24] Winn owned some 14,000 acres between Killorglin and Glenbeigh with a total valuation in 1878 of only £1,382. The estate was heavily mortgaged and the tenants' arrears exceeded £6,000. See *Times*, 13-20 Jan. 1887.

[25] "My view throughout was that Glenbeigh would be made a battleground of the Nationalist party—that if I could get a sufficiently large abatement made I might beat the Nationalists there and then they would fall all over Kerry"; Buller to Beach, 27 Jan. 1887, St. Aldwyn MSS. See also Melville, *Buller*, I, pp. 323-26.

[26] *Times*, 27 Jan. 1887; W. H. Smith to Salisbury, 13 Jan. 1887; Beach to Salisbury, 4 Feb. 1887, Salisbury MSS.

Then, too, there were many obstacles involved in bringing the Campaigners to justice: "Unless evidence of a provincial offence be forthcoming before the middle of November, the trial cannot take place until the following March, and even then in the local venue the result is almost sure to be abortive." Some alteration of the law Beach considered essential. In conclusion he denied that the Castle had used a dispensing power in impeding or prohibiting evictions.[27] After submitting the drafts of a crimes bill and a land bill to the cabinet, the chief secretary urged Salisbury to avoid the word "coercion" in the Queen's speech and to promise remedial measures for relief of the tenantry. Several days later the cabinet listened to a report written by Buller about the dangerous activity of the National League and the need for prompt action. After Beach had confirmed that the situation was "unquestionably grave," the cabinet gave their unanimous assent to the Crimes Bill.[28]

As to remedial legislation, Beach postponed action pending the reports of the Cowper Commission and of the Royal Commission appointed to inquire into improvement of the fishing industry, harbors, arterial drainage, and railways. Without expert advice he could not move ahead with his plans for constructive measures. Beach was also actively engaged in seeking a concession to Catholic higher education. A number of letters passed between the chief secretary's office and Archbishop Walsh on the question of a Catholic college or university; and on January 6 Beach, who owed some of his ideas to Carnarvon's draft bill of the previous January, had a private talk with Walsh, who insisted that the new institution have an endowment equal to that of Trinity College. The negotiations lasted well into February, and their cordial tone gave promise of some solution in the near future.[29]

Late in January legislators returned to London for the open-

[27] From Beach's memorandum on the Plan of Campaign, 13 Jan. 1887, St. Aldwyn MSS.

[28] Salisbury to Queen Victoria, 15 Jan. 1887; Beach to Salisbury, 18, 26 Jan. 1887, Salisbury MSS. For Beach's ideas on the subject of promoting drainage, harbor construction, and light railways, see his memorandum on remedial legislation, Aug. 1886, St. Aldwyn MSS.

[29] See Walsh to Beach, 9, 16, 19 Dec. 1886 and 16, 19, 20 Feb. 1887; Beach's notes on talk with Walsh, 6 Jan. 1887; and copy of a draft bill for university education in Ireland, 16 Jan. 1886, *ibid.*

ing of Parliament. The Queen's speech announced that, despite a decrease in serious crime, the organized resistance to rents made some changes in the criminal law imperative. An early report from the two commissions investigating the land question and Irish industries was promised, and the possibility of Irish local government reform was not ruled out. In the House of Lords Salisbury chided the Liberals for their alliance with the authors of an illegal agitation, namely the Plan, to which the Government would never surrender. A re-enforcement of the criminal law would, he hoped, eliminate the delays and weaknesses of the present system. Ashbourne denied that Buller had used a dispensing power: what Dublin Castle had done was merely to supply "friendly advice" to the landlords. But such euphemisms did not impress the Opposition. In the House of Commons Gladstone blamed the Plan of Campaign on the rejection of the Tenants' Relief Bill, and admonished ministers for having publicly denied the tenants' inability to pay rent while secretly promoting arbitration in rent disputes. The Irish members accused the Castle of having exerted pressure on judges, landlords, and tenants alike. Beach brusquely dismissed these charges, but the Parnellites were out for ministerial blood and proceeded to obstruct debate for the next seventeen nights.[30]

While the debate on the address continued, the nationalist leaders held protest meetings in the south and warned tenants that the Government planned to turn the country into "one vast Glenbeigh, one vast scene of misery, poverty and desolation." With evictions meeting ever-stouter resistance, the Castle had some cause for anxiety; and Buller delivered a disturbing report to his chief:

"I am coming to the conclusion that Ireland never was in a worse state. There is not much outrage because the League is so firmly established, but the people are rapidly losing any regard for the law, and unless you can get the full act you are proposing passed soon, the whole country will join in the Plan of Campaign against the payment of the March Rents. My deliberate opinion is that unless you can introduce *very shortly* a summary method of procedure for the prosecution of crime and also take some powers which will enable you to coerce bad landlords such as

[30] *Hansard*, 3d series, Vol. 310, pp. 4-48.

Colonel O'Callaghan, that so far as governing Ireland is concerned, you may as well chuck up the sponge. What is wanted is to show the people that the law is the strongest. . . . I honestly think that matters are getting serious. If Paddy once gets regularly to no rent you will require to kill a good many before you get him back again."[31]

Only one cheering item of news reached the Irish Office in London during the debates: Lord Londonderry reported that his levees in Dublin had attracted the largest gathering of society in twenty years.[32]

When news of the verdict in the conspiracy trial reached London, the cabinet determined to compensate for this defeat by prosecuting the bellicose Archbishop Croke of Cashel, who had encouraged a no-rent movement. Ashbourne, Buller, and the law officers, however, were nervous about Irish public opinion and managed to scuttle this proposal, even though Salisbury vigorously opposed any sign of appeasement lest Unionists accuse the ministry of having "thrown up the sponge."[33] Soon new anxieties supervened. Obstruction in Parliament forced ministers to consider strengthening the closure. At a party meeting on February 21 Lord Salisbury explained the urgency of procedural reform and asked his supporters to forget their differences over the merits of closure by an absolute or relative majority in the interests of unity during a crisis. A crimes bill would be introduced, he announced, as soon as parliamentary circumstances permitted.

At the end of February the prime minister enlightened Beach about his real intentions toward Ireland. Commenting on Buller's plea for a mixture of repression and conciliation in equal parts, Salisbury made the following significant point: "I agree with Buller that you cannot govern the Irish, or anybody else, by severity alone; but I think he is fundamentally wrong in believing

[31] Buller to Beach, 2 Feb. 1887, St. Aldwyn MSS.

[32] "I do not wish to appear to boast, but I cannot conceal from myself a feeling of satisfaction that I have been able to awaken feelings of loyalty and respect to the Sovereign which . . . must have been long dormant; and which I do not think anyone else could have aroused"; Londonderry to Salisbury, 7 Feb. 1887, Salisbury MSS.

[33] Beach to Salisbury, 28 Feb., 1 March 1887; Salisbury to Beach, 28 Feb. 1887, *ibid.*

that conciliation and severity must go together. The severity must come first. They must 'take a licking' before conciliation will do them any good."[34] Translated into legislative terms, this declaration meant a stringent crimes bill that would be relentlessly enforced. This principle underlay Conservative policy not only in Ireland but in other parts of the empire where the indigenous population showed any distaste for British rule. Only after the Irish people had learned respect for the law, Salisbury implied, would they deserve the bounty of remedial legislation.

IV. BEACH'S COLLAPSE

In the midst of the debate on procedural reform the Cowper Commission presented their findings. The majority report asserted that the problem of crime took precedence over any relief legislation for the tenantry. The commissioners admitted the existence of a fall in the value of land and agricultural produce, and recommended a quinquennial revision of judicial rents. In direct contradiction of Ashbourne's reports, they also noted a general reluctance among tenants in the south to buy their holdings under the act of 1885. Hopes of extorting further concessions from the Government and fear of offending the league, they surmised, kept the tenantry away from purchase. By recommending both the admission of leaseholders to the Land Act of 1881 and the revision of judicial rents every five years, the Cowper Commission substantially vindicated Parnell's bill of September.[35]

In the Commons the Government experienced another setback when Irish obstruction forced them to suspend work on procedural reform and to take supply instead. The decision to postpone the new closure rules exasperated both Conservative and Liberal Unionists, who wondered what had happened to Salisbury's promises of resolute government. Churchill's loss was keenly felt; and Lord Hartington expressed a widespread pessimism within the Unionist coalition when he told the Queen that a deadlock in Ireland was unavoidable. The Parnellites appeared to have scored a major success in their campaign to discredit the Government.

[34] Salisbury to Beach, 28 Feb. 1887, *ibid.*
[35] See Report of the Royal Commission on the Land Law (Ireland) Act, 1881, and the Purchase of Land (Ireland) Act, 1885, *HC 1887*, Vol. 26.

What with the failure of the Dublin trial, the findings of the Cowper Commission, the temporary reversal over the closure, and the many allusions to Beach's use of a dispensing power, ministers had lost considerable prestige in the span of a fortnight. And police reports from Ireland about fresh outbreaks of boycotting and the Plan of Campaign did not provide much encouragement.

An even graver crisis awaited the Government. In the midst of these misfortunes Beach informed the prime minister that he could not continue in office on the grounds of bad health. His doctors had discovered cataracts in his eyes and found him in a state of general exhaustion: they offered him a choice between retiring or risking blindness. Beach explained the medical report to Salisbury and implored him to put a successor "into harness before grave mischief . . . [breaks] out."[36] Although considerably shaken by the loss of so important a minister, Salisbury had no choice but to begin looking for a new chief secretary. He did not have to search far. Without much hesitation he chose his nephew Arthur Balfour, then secretary for Scotland. But when Beach was told of this decision, he immediately expressed concern about Balfour's apparent fragility. He warned Salisbury: "Physique is, in this office, quite as important as ability—perhaps more. . . . If he breaks down, after me, how much does that strengthen the Home Rule argument. Forster and Trevelyan suffered very heavily in health: I have failed altogether: a fourth failure would almost prove that no man could do the work." If Balfour decided to accept the appointment, Beach would advise him to transfer the burden of the Crimes Bill to the home secretary, so that he could devote all his energies to the new Land Bill; and he insisted that Balfour avoid overexertion in his first session as chief secretary.[37]

On March 3 Hicks Beach denounced the Plan of Campaign in Parliament as an "organized system of robbery." A combination of severe physical pain and Parnellite interruptions drove him to

[36] Beach to Salisbury, 5 March 1887, Salisbury MSS. See also Hicks Beach, *St. Aldwyn*, I, pp. 312-13.

[37] Beach to Salisbury, 1, 5 March 1887, Salisbury MSS. Smith, Goschen, and Cranbrook endorsed Balfour's appointment even before Balfour had been approached; Salisbury to Smith, 3 March 1887, *ibid.*

remark in angry tones that Irishmen would soon feel something harder than batons if they did not mend their ways. It was Beach's last speech as chief secretary, and this threat did not enhance his reputation among the Parnellites. Two days later Balfour, having passed a medical examination, left for Dublin in order to be sworn into office. The news of Beach's resignation caused surprise and consternation in both countries. The *Freeman's Journal* rejoiced at the inability of the "'Tories' strongest man" to cope with the Irish Question, and it attributed Beach's retirement not only to ill-health but also to the fact that he was "at the end of his tether" after the failure of all his policies, from government by "pressure" to cabin burning and state prosecutions.[38]

From all sections of the Unionist party, on the other hand, came tributes to Beach's courage and integrity. The blow had come so soon after Churchill's resignation that many Government supporters despaired of the ministry's ability to survive the crisis. Chamberlain was kind enough to inform Beach: " . . . you have paid the penalty for your devotion, but you have earned the respect and gratitude of every loyal subject."[39] And in a speech at the National Conservative Club Salisbury declared that Beach's loss was as great a disaster for the country as it was for the party. He defended the Government's Irish record, arguing that the farce of trial by jury in Ireland left the administrative machine without a vital cog, and that until this part was repaired, social order could never be re-established. The prime minister went on to emphasize that larger issues than rent disputes were at stake. The Government was engaged in a struggle that would determine the future of the British empire. What Ireland required was self-confidence and the means to achieve prosperity, while England needed both patience and tenacity: "Our national fault is that too much softness has crept into our councils; and we imagine that great national dangers can be conjured by a plentiful administration of platitudes and rose-water."[40]

[38] *Freeman's Journal*, 7 March 1887.

[39] Chamberlain to Beach, 10 March 1887, St. Aldwyn MSS. Churchill wrote to Beach: "Indeed, you are a great loss to Ireland and to the party and to me. Now that you are gone, there is no one in the Government I care a rap about. . . ." W. S. Churchill, *Churchill*, II, p. 343.

[40] *Times*, 7 March 1887.

The allusion to "softness" clearly referred to Beach's regime in Dublin. Irish loyalists used more extreme language to describe the shortcomings of the administration. For this group Beach's resignation may have been untimely but it turned out to be no calamity. As the instrument of resolute government, Beach, with his antilandlord bias, lacked most of the qualities demanded by Salisbury and the bulk of the Irish Unionists. To the nationalists, who were accustomed to extracting concessions by force, such goodwill as Carnarvon and Beach brought to Ireland was interpreted as an inherent sign of weakness. Whatever Balfour's views on the Irish Question might be, his uncle knew that "platitudes and rose-water" were not among them.[41]

After seven months in office the Government had little to boast about in Ireland. The Cowper Commission had virtually vindicated Parnell's bill; the inauguration of the Plan and the influence of the National League pointed up other deficiencies of the administration. Against the somber background of the Belfast riots and the Woodford and Glenbeigh evictions, Beach and Buller had worked in vain to keep Ireland quiet. The general's efforts to reduce rents and evictions as well as crime, not to mention his assertion before the Cowper Commission that bad landlords ought to be coerced just as firmly as bad tenants, naturally dismayed many Unionists.[42] Buller himself subsequently admitted to Beach: "I have all my life got into most of my troubles by an inconvenient habit of saying too much and I fear I am too old to mend—but I will try."[43] On the question of tenants' relief the Government paid a heavy price for their obstinate attitude to concession. Had ministers anticipated Parnell's motion with a measure designed to aid leaseholders and to reduce exorbitant rents,

[41] For Salisbury's reservations about Beach, especially as a colonial secretary, see Salisbury to Smith, 19 Sept. 1887, Hambleden MSS.

[42] Buller insisted that the law had never been fair to the tenantry; the result of this injustice had been disorder, which in turn had led to concessions. But these concessions had never sufficed to allay the discontent, "and so Ireland has drifted into its present state, and no concealment of facts and no drivel of pigheaded Lord Milltowns [one of the Cowper Commissioners] with their talk about 'an ignorant and excitable peasantry' will alter that fact"; Buller to Beach, 27 Nov. 1886, St. Aldwyn MSS.

[43] Buller to Beach, 15 Jan. 1887, *ibid.*

both the Plan and the private representations of Beach and Buller might have been avoided.

In spite of Salisbury's absence from the Foreign Office until January, 1887, and the creation of the Irish committee of the cabinet, the firm policy expected by Unionists had failed to materialize. Worried by the ineptitude of Iddesleigh at the Foreign Office and by the bullying tactics of Churchill, the prime minister had allowed Beach, like Carnarvon before him, too much freedom of action. Always hesitant to impose his will upon his colleagues, Salisbury discovered too late that Beach had also "gone green" in Dublin. Balfour later remarked upon Beach's proclivity for indecision: "He was always like that, always he would and he wouldn't."[44] Beach, for his part, had relied too much on the advice of Buller, whose reputation for committing indiscretions grew almost daily. Lord Salisbury's shrewd verdict left no margin of doubt about the under secretary's abilities: "Buller had reached that pitch of eminence at which men become indocile."[45] The combination of Beach and Buller, added to Salisbury's other responsibilities, meant that Ireland had to wait several months for the "licking" that had been prescribed.

[44] A. Chamberlain, *Politics from Inside*, pp. 262-63.
[45] Salisbury to Balfour, 3 Oct. 1887, Add. MS 49688.

CHAPTER X

Coercion

I. "NIMINY-PIMINY"

BALFOUR's appointment as chief secretary marked a turning point both in his own career and in Anglo-Irish relations. After 1887 the whole tenor of Government policy in Ireland changed, and for the first time the Parnellites faced an adversary willing to fight fire with fire. The abortive attempts at conciliation under Carnarvon and Beach had convinced the nationalists that the Conservatives feared coercion more than concession. Except for the Ashbourne act, Ireland had received no substantial relief from Parliament since the Land Act of 1881; and land purchase had not reduced the crushing poverty of the tenantry. While the Irish members insisted upon fair rents and the abolition of arrears, and while Liberal and Radical Unionists urged conciliation, the Conservatives were agreed that the problem of crime overshadowed all other aspects of the Irish Question. Twenty years of resolute government, in short, could not begin without a crimes bill. In the south two laws competed for the allegiance of the people; and at night the law of the league usually prevailed. The Plan of Campaign was aggravating the relations between landlord and tenant; convictions of moonlighters were rare when compared with the number of crimes committed; and thanks to Beach's policies as well as to Irish contumacy, the entire legal machine appeared on the verge of collapse.[1]

Against such a background, Balfour's appointment as chief secretary startled the political world. The news was greeted with

---

[1] For the statistics and character of agrarian crime during this period, see monthly reports of Crime Department, Special Branch; Return of Outrages (1879-1893) prepared for the RIC; and cabinet memorandum, "The Working of the National League," 17 Aug. 1887, in State Paper Office, Dublin Castle, hereafter SPO. From 1 Jan. 1886 to 31 March 1887 there were 72 convictions out of 1,310 agrarian crimes recorded.

"a scream of mocking laughter." Nationalists and their Liberal allies laughed loudest; but Conservatives too, especially the back-benchers, sneered at the choice and called it nepotism. According to the *Freeman's Journal*, Balfour had only three qualifications to commend him: he was the prime minister's nephew, he had no statesmanlike reputation to injure, and he was totally ignorant of Ireland. The paper's London correspondent wrote in a more trenchant vein: "It seems like breaking a butterfly to extend Mr. Arthur Balfour on the rack of Irish politics. He is an elegant, fragile creature, a prey to an aristocratic languor, which prevents him from ever assuming any but the limpest attitude. He is also noteworthy for a sublime affectation of intellectual culture, which has proved singularly useless to him in making a mark as a politician. . . . Mr. Balfour's whole life seems to be a protest against being called upon to do anything but sniff a heavily perfumed handkerchief while he sprawls in poses of studied carelessness on the benches of the House of Commons."[2]

Since he had first entered Parliament in 1874, Balfour had been one of the more obscure members, contributing to debates only when he could overcome his seemingly incurable indolence. Two years had passed before he delivered his maiden speech. During the early phase of the Fourth party he had shown flashes of ability and a talent for baiting Gladstone. But more often he appeared to be suffering from—or perhaps enjoying—an extreme lassitude. The stiletto build, the drooping posture, and the absence of any robust or gregarious qualities inspired English and Irish wits to invent nicknames with the relish of schoolboys. At Cambridge his collection of blue china and fondness of repose had won him the title "Pretty Fanny." And after his election to Parliament he attracted a host of epithets from the seemingly more virile members of the House. The implications of these names were clear enough: "Clara," "Niminy-piminy," "Tiger Lily," "Daddy Long Legs," and "lisping Hawthorn bird." The news of his appointment as chief secretary stirred the Irish nationalists to new heights of invention. This "palsied masher," this "silk skinned sybarite whose rest a crumpled rose leaf would disturb," they taunted, could never last long in the Irish Office. One Parnellite who had heard the news was reported to have said:

[2] *Freeman's Journal,* 7 March 1887.

"We have killed Forster, blinded Beach, and smashed up Tre-velyan,—what shall we do with this weakling?"[3] For Parnell and his party the nomination of Balfour was the last gasp of a moribund government. Of all offices that of chief secretary ap-peared the least suitable for a man of Balfour's constitution, temperament, and relative inexperience. Even in the eighteenth century the Irish Office had carried a reputation for discouraging, if not actually injuring, men of delicate health as well as tastes. "That office," one of Burke's friends wrote to his wife, "requires nerves and bad taste, as Windham proved by flying from it."[4] And a century later, after the rise of Parnell and the Liberals' conversion to Home Rule, that stricture was all the more ap-plicable.

In March, 1887, only a few men credited Balfour with strength of any kind. Most of his contemporaries found something slightly reprehensible in his past behavior. For years he had dallied with politics, while appearing to prefer week ends at Hatfield and golf or estate management in Scotland. In a political sense he had sheltered in the ample shadow of his uncle, except for a brief flirtation with Lord Randolph Churchill's "ginger group" after 1880. The more rough-hewn Parnellites, and indeed many of his own party, found in the "young" Balfour—he was thirty-eight at the time of his new appointment—a touch of Bunthorne. Here was another apostle of the "high aesthetic band," a man who enjoyed standing in "stained glass attitudes," an intellectual sufficiently aloof and eccentric to be a university don. All agreed, friends, foes, and family alike, that he suffered from excessive languor; his physical appearance and a studied air of indifference to all earthly cares heightened this impression. Sir Winston Churchill later noted the feline qualities in Balfour; but until 1887 the sharpness of the claws and the power and speed of the intellect were hidden behind the velvety exterior.[5]

Balfour was, of course, much more than "an ultrapoetical, superaesthetical, out of the way young man." Possessing more

[3] B. Alderson, *Arthur James Balfour* (hereafter *Balfour*), London, 1903, pp. 62-64; Cecil, *Salisbury*, III, p. 347.

[4] T. H. D. Mahoney, *Edmund Burke and Ireland*, Cambridge, Mass., 1960, p. 389 n. 24.

[5] See W. S. Churchill, *Great Contemporaries*, New York, 1937, p. 214.

than an uncle in Lord Salisbury, he grew up in a privileged world embellished by Hatfield and Whittingehame.[6] At Cambridge in the 1860's he indulged his speculative instincts in laboratory research and in attempts to reconcile the facts of science with the beliefs of religion. The upshot of this pursuit was a book, *The Defence of Philosophic Doubt*, published in 1878, which caused some stir among theologians. In spite of the title, beyond which the general public did not venture, Balfour was no agnostic seeking to undermine faith. Rather, he wished to restore a note of moderation and reason to the great debate then raging around the concept of evolution. In his conclusion Balfour denied any basic incompatibility between religion and science: each depended upon a different system of revelation or methodology; and the rational man, he argued, felt "a practical need for both."[7]

While at Cambridge Balfour had also acquired a taste for that state of social and intellectual grace known as *sprezzatura*. In everything he attempted and at which he excelled, whether philosophical inquiry, politics, parlor games, tennis, or golf, he studiously remained the amateur. At all costs the preparation, the hours or years of hard work indispensable to success, had to be concealed in order to preserve the ideal of the gentleman. This late Victorian courtier had to prove himself in each field of endeavor, while maintaining all the time a casual, nonchalant pose. By early manhood Balfour had managed to acquire what has been so deftly described as the "tranquil consciousness of effortless superiority."

Scawen Blunt, that perennial romantic, once scolded the Balfour brothers for their "scientific inhumanity."[8] Detachment would have been a more appropriate word. Arthur Balfour's metaphysical instincts allowed him to see both sides of a case and he was capable of defending either with equal skill. This superior perspective, the very ambidexterity of his mind, was often mistaken for arrogance or interpreted by his enemies as pure meanness of spirit. In politics the legendary charm known to friends

---

[6] Balfour was only eight when his father died, and he was raised by his mother Lady Blanche, who was Salisbury's sister; see Dugdale, *Balfour*, I, pp. 14-24.

[7] *Ibid.*, I, pp. 28-29, 49-51; II, pp. 413-34.

[8] Blunt, *My Diaries, 1888-1914*, London, 1919-1920, I, p. 85.

and relatives gave way to ruthless, if brilliant, sallies against opponents. Sarcasm in all its forms came naturally to him, and his gift of deflating adversaries was reminiscent of the young Lord Robert Cecil. There was no doubt about Balfour's status as the favorite nephew of Lord Salisbury; but even so, the young man's talents were too individualistic to permit domination by any single person. The role of "a Great Man's Great Man," Balfour once declared, did not suit him; and yet for more than twenty years he was the intimate confidant and adviser of his uncle.

As secretary for Scotland since July, 1886, Balfour received his baptism in agrarian agitation, when crofters in the highlands and the Hebrides launched a no-rent campaign. Evictions led to open revolt; and Balfour called in the military to restore order and to enforce migration or what he termed a "benevolent act of transportation." Tenants who expressed their grievances by defying the law, whether in Scotland or Ireland, never aroused his sympathy. Neither did Lord Randolph Churchill, whose influence in the party Balfour had tried to curb for several years. Churchill's resignation had restored a Cecilian equilibrium to the Government, and Balfour was safe at last from the threat of having to compete against Lord Randolph's prestige at Westminster and his popularity in the provinces.[9]

Within a few weeks of his promotion to the Irish Office Balfour entered upon the first, or parliamentary, phase of his campaign. The second phase followed six months later, when he had carried two important measures and was ready to apply the provisions contained therein to Ireland. For his new assignment Balfour had in mind more than repression. Diagnosing England's failure in Ireland as the result of oscillation between two extreme policies, he decided to try a different approach. Ireland, in his opinion, deserved not only "a licking" but also some form of relief. The essence of his policy lay in the simultaneous treatment of the land question and social disorder. Cromwell, he declared, had failed in Ireland because he had relied on coercion alone:

[9] Dugdale, *Balfour*, I, pp. 107-18; *Hansard*, 3d series, Vol. 308, pp. 942-50; Balfour to Salisbury, 19 Oct. 1886, Salisbury MSS. Upon his promotion to cabinet rank in November, 1886, Balfour expressed his hopes that he might serve "as a counterpoise even though a feeble one, to Randolph."

"That mistake I shall not imitate. I shall be as relentless as Cromwell in enforcing obedience to the law, but, at the same time, I shall be as radical as any reformer in redressing grievances, and especially in removing every cause of complaint in regard to the land. It is on the twofold aspect of my policy that I rely for success. Hitherto English Governments . . . have either been all for repression or all for reform. I am for both: repression as stern as Cromwell; reform as thorough as Mr. Parnell or anyone else can desire."[10]

Owing to Irish obstruction, the relief program took several years to complete; but if conciliation lagged behind coercion, it came nevertheless, bringing work and wages to many destitute tenants. Contrary to popular belief, the process of "killing Home Rule with kindness" began with Arthur, not Gerald, Balfour.

II. THE CRIMINAL LAW AMENDMENT BILL

The Irish people, according to Balfour, would never appreciate remedial measures so long as they could commit crime with impunity; and for this reason he was determined to give precedence to a stringent crimes bill. During March the Irish committee of the cabinet revised Beach's draft measure so as to make a number of offenses liable to summary justice. The new bill was based on past coercion acts, and yet some ministers insisted that it was too mild. Lord Cranbrook, for example, argued that a more drastic measure could be carried just as easily as a moderate one. "The dismal thing," he complained, "is that English people seem as little moved as if all these horrors were taking place in China or Peru." Salisbury agreed with him that the clauses relating to change of venue, to special juries, and to summary procedure needed strengthening in order to cope with conditions in the southwest, where society appeared to be "in pieces."[11] In a cabinet deserted by Carnarvon, Churchill, and Beach, these more Draconian provisions found no opponents.

Opposition was not missing in Parliament, however. Parnell described Conservative policy in Ireland as "stumbling, shifting, broken-kneed"; and his party helped to prolong the debate on

[10] Alderson, *Balfour*, p. 71.

[11] Cranbrook to Salisbury, 8 March 1887; Salisbury to Cranbrook, 9 March 1887; Balfour to Salisbury, 9 March 1887, Salisbury mss.

the address for sixteen nights. So intense was the obstruction that ministers were forced to introduce new rules of procedure. After another fortnight of acrimonious debate, a closure resolution was carried that permitted the Speaker to apply the guillotine more frequently; and the House then turned to face the next ordeal—Balfour's crimes bill.[12] Determined to show his contempt for obstructionist tactics, Balfour appointed a wealthy Irish landlord, Colonel King-Harman, as assistant parliamentary under secretary for Ireland. King-Harman's chief function was to answer the questions of Irish members in the House of Commons. The new post was designed to save Balfour from the vexatious chore of listening to Irish harangues and barbs during question time. No appointment could have been more irksome to the Parnellites. It was well known that they heartily detested King-Harman because he had once been a member of Butt's Home Rule party. And the fact that he had consented to act as the chief secretary's "mouthpiece" hardly endeared him to the nationalists, who regarded him as nothing less than a traitor.[13]

In the beginning Balfour hoped that the Criminal Law Amendment Bill would excite as little controversy as possible in Parliament. It did not take him long to realize how seriously he had underestimated the determination of the Opposition not to swallow this bitter legislative pill. The latest effort of an English government "to make better provision for the prevention and punishment of crime" in Ireland was aimed at speeding up the process of apprehending moonlighters, boycotters, and other agents of the land war. The bill was divided into six main parts, relating to preliminary inquiry, summary jurisdiction, special juries and removal of trials, proclamation of districts, dangerous associations, and legal procedure. Under section one, resident magistrates were authorized to examine on oath and in private any persons considered capable of giving material evidence. Section two relegated the following offenses to prosecution before a court of summary jurisdiction: criminal conspiracies against rent, boycotting, in-

[12] *Hansard*, 3d series, Vol. 310, pp. 774 ff.
[13] Edward Robert King-Harman, 1838-1888; M.P. 1877-1888. See H. W. Lucy, *A Diary of the Salisbury Parliament, 1886-1892*, London, 1892, p. 75; Salisbury to Smith, 30 Oct. 1887; Londonderry to Salisbury, 18 June 1888, Salisbury MSS.

timidation, rioting, unlawful assembly, resistance to eviction, and the inciting of others to commit any of the above crimes. Sections three and four allowed the attorney general to transfer cases involving trial by jury from an agitated district to one where, in his opinion, a "fair and impartial" trial could be guaranteed. The bill also empowered the lord lieutenant, in conjunction with the Irish Privy Council, to declare by proclamation that the provisions of the act were in force in any specified part of the country. Such areas were officially known as proclaimed districts. Any proclamation by the lord lieutenant would expire, however, if either house of Parliament should present a hostile address to the Queen. Parliament could thereby keep a restraining hand on the machinery of coercion. In addition, the lord lieutenant in council could declare any association that indulged in criminal activities to be dangerous, and by naming that association in a "special proclamation" he could subject all its members to prosecution. Once again Parliament was given the power of review in such instances. The maximum sentence handed down by a court of summary jurisdiction was to be six months' imprisonment with hard labor; and every prisoner received the right of appeal. Whenever he saw fit, the lord lieutenant could revoke wholly or in part any proclamation under the act. Lastly and most significantly, the measure was to become a permanent part of the Irish legal code. In sum, the clauses pertaining to the proclamation of districts and dangerous associations gave to the act an elasticity that was intended to make it more effective in Ireland and more palatable at Westminster.[14]

When Balfour introduced the bill in the House of Commons on March 28, he followed the example set by Gladstone in 1881 by emphasizing not only the quantity but also the character of agrarian crime in Ireland. The extent of intimidation and other crimes, he asserted, could be found, not merely in the official reports that lay upon the table, but in the widespread demoralization of the populace. Any postponement of coercion would render "absolutely nugatory" the effects of remedial legislation in the future. And he went on to quote extracts from judges' charges to the

[14] See *HC 1887*, Vol. 2, pp. 1-46. Section five empowered the lord lieutenant to proclaim specified parts of the country, and section six pertained to dangerous associations.

grand juries in the most lawless counties as proof of the "existing paralysis of the law." Just as in nature certain "diseased parasitic growths" mimicked the shape and nutritional laws of the organisms to which they were attached, so the National League imitated "with terrible fidelity" the processes of the common law.[15]

To several observers, apart from the Home Rulers, Balfour's speech appeared weak and lackluster. Lord Randolph Churchill, who was hardly a disinterested party, found fault in almost every detail of Balfour's debut; and he wrote to Beach: "Arthur Balfour fills your place very badly. He made a terrible fiasco introducing the Bill on Monday—want of knowledge the most elementary, want of tact and judgment coupled with an excited manner and a raised voice. Of course the Irish interrupted brutally and he was quite unable to cope with them. . . . I think the Bill itself first rate and only hope the Government have sufficient resolution and authority to carry it through." Beach, in reply, proved more tolerant and argued that Balfour had had only a short time in which to "digest" the facts about Ireland. Although Beach blamed any deficiencies in the speech on his own sudden retirement, the fact remained that set speeches were not Balfour's forte.[16]

Defying the new closure, the Home Rule coalition dissected the measure phrase by phrase. Opposition leaders retorted that the crime rate was not high enough to justify coercion; and Gladstone excused the boycott as a "legitimate weapon" in the war against rack rents. Crime records extending back to 1832 were used to support opposing arguments; and protest meetings, banquets, and addresses for and against the bill heightened the political tension within Parliament and outside. The *Times* materially assisted the Government's case by publishing a series of "authoritative" articles entitled "Parnellism and Crime," which alleged collusion between the physical force party in America and the Parnellites. On April 18, the day of the bill's second reading, the paper printed a facsimile letter linking Parnell, by implication, with the Phoenix Park murders. This dramatic document, supplemented by other equally damaging letters, caused a furor; and in Parliament irate Unionists challenged the Irish leader to

[15] *Hansard*, 3d series, Vol. 312, pp. 1181-1658.
[16] Churchill to Beach, 30 March 1887; Beach to Churchill, 9 April 1887, St. Aldwyn MSS.

disprove the charges in a court of law. Although refusing to commit himself to the authenticity of the facsimile letter, Balfour did assert that a formal inquiry was essential.[17]

When the Opposition unleashed a torrent of amendments against the bill in committee, Lord Salisbury complained at the Royal Academy dinner about the "dreary drip of dilatory declamation." The machinery of government had attained such perfection, he declared, that it no longer served the will of the majority, but existed merely to test the patience of its members. Salisbury's only consolation was that cabinet harmony had been restored and that Balfour's health had "not yet sprung any leak." But he estimated that the committee stage of the bill would last well into July. The degree of obstruction gave him the impression that the Commons was "performing some mysterious penance for some obscure offence." The only solution he could find—the English people being a practical race—lay in the replacement of members of Parliament by "a steam Irish party, an electric ministry, and a clockwork Speaker." At length the Government decided to move amendments in groups rather than individually. On June 17 the Speaker moved all remaining amendments; and after repeated use of the guillotine, the bill passed its third reading on July 8, becoming law ten days later.[18]

On July 22 Balfour left for Dublin to brief the Castle's law officers and divisional magistrates on the new Crimes Act. The Irish Privy Council immediately proclaimed eighteen counties under the first four sections of the act and partially proclaimed thirteen others. Protest meetings all over Ireland revealed the defiant mood of the nationalists; and in Parliament the Irish members made mockery of the proclaiming orders. Despite Unionist boasts, the Castle was slow to enforce the Crimes Act. No trials for serious crimes took place for over a month, largely because Balfour was afraid to risk prosecution before a jury unless conviction seemed certain. The law officers, he knew, required not only a strong case but that rarity—an unintimidated

[17] For the *Times*'s other articles on the "criminal" content of Parnellism, see *ibid.*, 7, 10, 13 March; 12, 18 April; 2, 13, 20 May; and 1, 7 June 1887.

[18] Salisbury to Beach, 15 April 1887, Salisbury MSS; *Times*, 2, 21 May 1887; *Hansard*, 3d series, Vol. 315, pp. 1594-1609.

SALISBURY SISYPHUS

Lord Salisbury struggling with the "Irish Difficulty" in the spring of 1887.

jury; and he did not want to see the Government's prestige tarnished by an acquittal at the outset. Aware of the hazards involved, he advised Buller: "The nerves of our Resident Magistrates will very likely play us the same tricks as the partiality of the local jurist. I further agree with you that the leading agitators are the most important people to catch. But I do not understand this principle . . . as implying that the smaller fry are to be allowed to break the law with impunity."[19]

More important than individual prosecutions, however, was the question of when and where to proclaim the National League under section six of the Crimes Act. Balfour had made up his mind to suppress the league as early as June, but he failed to anticipate Liberal Unionist objections and minimized the diffi-

[19] Balfour to Buller, 2 Aug. 1887, Add. MS 49826.

culty of justifying such a move in Parliament. Ministers soon discovered that the decision to proclaim the league a dangerous association imposed a serious strain on the Unionist coalition. Chamberlain, a poor coercionist at best, called the scheme "suicidal" and argued that it would drive the agitators underground, where they would be twice as dangerous. The Land Bill would, in his opinion, restore order much more effectively: besides, he was already publicly pledged to conciliation.[20] As a result, Salisbury glumly admitted that ministers were in a "state of decided pout" with their allies, and he told the well-known publicist Alfred Austin: "The sensitiveness of the Unionists is very remarkable: the high price which some of them charge for their 'unparalleled sacrifices' provokes a feeling of resistance: and has a bad effect on our men." Irish loyalists felt that suppressing the league had become a question of "now or never." "The rabble are boasting that Government dare not do it," the Duke of Abercorn wrote to Salisbury. At length, on August 12, the cabinet assented to Balfour's demand; and the Liberal Unionists, as well as Churchill and Beach, were left to ruminate about the folly of a purely negative policy for Ireland.[21]

Balfour hoped that the suppression of the most active branches of the league in Kerry and Clare would discourage other branches from perpetrating outrages. To prosecute every member of the league was out of the question; but he calculated that partial proscription would drastically reduce agrarian crime. The Government, moreover, was under considerable pressure from Irish Unionists, who insisted on suppression as a prerequisite to pacifying the country. One of their spokesmen reminded Balfour: " . . . if you do not beat the National League they will defeat you. It is a distinct and defined struggle, and the Irish populace will lean to whichever side proves itself strongest. They are sick and tired of Land League tyranny but they will not cut themselves away from it until they are convinced that the Government is stronger and more certain in its action than the League."[22]

[20] "Joe is much given to self-justification"; Salisbury to Balfour, 20 Oct. 1887, Salisbury MSS; Dugdale, *Balfour*, I, p. 148; Garvin, *Chamberlain*, II, pp. 309-14.

[21] Salisbury to Lady John Manners, 31 July 1887; Salisbury to A. Austin, 3 Aug. 1887; Abercorn to Salisbury, 12 Aug. 1887, Salisbury MSS.

[22] Lord Castletown to Balfour, 17 July 1887, Add. MS 49826.

The debate on the proclaiming order lasted two nights in the Commons and gave the Opposition a chance to condemn Government policy as the last resort of tyrants. In the division Chamberlain and five of his followers voted against the Government for the first time since the Liberal schism. This show of independence caused the ministry much embarrassment and supplied the prime minister with a cogent excuse for naming Chamberlain as chief of the Fishery Commission to discuss fishing rights with American representatives in Washington.[23] Combined with several Government reverses in by-elections, the dissensions over the Crimes and Land bills caused much anxiety in Unionist circles; but the mass protest rallies in Trafalgar Square and in the Dublin rotunda, which followed the news of the league's proclamation, did not mar Conservative and loyalist enthusiasm over this sign of firmness in the Government's Irish policy.

III. DUBLIN CASTLE REVIVED

In August Balfour began to look for a new permanent under secretary: Buller's appointment was due to expire in the autumn, and the prospect of prolonging his stay appealed to few Unionists. The cabinet discussed various alternatives and eventually agreed on Sir Joseph West Ridgeway, a soldier who had distinguished himself as commander of the Indian contingent of the Afghan Frontier Commission during the difficult negotiations over the boundary dispute in 1884-1885.[24] As Balfour informed Buller, the candidate was "an Irishman by birth which is a good thing but has never lived in Ireland, which is not a bad thing."[25] Ridgeway later described the circumstances of his appointment and his first meeting with the man under whom he would serve for the next four years: "I pointed out to Mr. Balfour that though Irish blood ran through my veins, I knew little of Ireland, that I had few friends and no correspondents there, and did not

[23] Salisbury had first thought of sending Carnarvon or Morley, and as an afterthought he suggested Hartington or Chamberlain; Salisbury to Smith, 26 Aug. 1887, Salisbury mss. The Queen heartily approved of the decision to send Chamberlain: "It is a wise measure in many ways"; Queen Victoria to Salisbury, 28 Aug. 1887, *ibid*.

[24] 1844-1930; Under Secretary for Ireland 1887-1892; Governor of Ceylon 1896-1903; K.C.S.I. 1886; K.C.B. 1891.

[25] Balfour to Buller, 6 Aug. 1887, Add. ms 49826.

even know what the postage was. Mr. Balfour smiled cynically and replied, 'Then that is a great qualification for the post, for you will not be besieged by your friends in search of employment.' "[26]

Ridgeway also made it a condition of his acceptance that the National League be proclaimed at once; and he expressed a wish to tour the disturbed areas of Ireland before taking up his new duties. Balfour immediately sensed that Ridgeway's way of thinking closely corresponded with his own, and he sent him on a reconnaissance trip to Ireland incognito.[27] The undersecretary-designate toured counties Kerry, Clare, and Cork, and interviewed divisional magistrates as well as various departmental heads in Dublin Castle. He reported to Balfour that the situation bore "a resemblance, almost absurd, to certain districts in India and Afghanistan." In the middle of October Ridgeway formally succeeded Buller, and it was not long before a new spirit of vigor began to pervade Dublin Castle. Shrewd, resourceful, and a sworn enemy of appeasement, he proved the ideal deputy for Balfour. Salisbury called Ridgeway's appointment a "great venture"; but then anything was better, he reckoned, than Buller.[28] During the next four and a half years Balfour served as architect and Ridgeway as engineer of Unionist policy in Ireland, and Ridgeway's contribution to the success of the regime deserves a recognition that has too long been withheld.

The passing of the Crimes Act ended the era of abortive state trials. In place of the unwieldy legal methods of the past, the stipendiary magistrates dispensed summary justice for lesser crimes in the proclaimed parts of Ireland. Drab and informal, the tribunals over which they presided resembled police courts, and after the first few months the trials attracted little notice. When, in October, reports of successful prosecutions began to come in

[26] Ridgeway memorandum, n.d., Ridgeway MSS.

[27] "The more people you see of all sorts—official and unofficial—and the more independent the survey which you take of their various opinions, wishes, and prejudices, the more safely will you be able to steer your course among the difficult shoals of Irish politics"; Balfour to Ridgeway, 12 Aug. 1887, Add. MS 49826.

[28] Ridgeway to Balfour, 28 Aug. 1887, ibid., 49808; Salisbury to Balfour, 3 Oct. 1887, Salisbury MSS.

from the provinces, the nationalists realized that Balfour was not the "fragile butterfly" they had supposed.

The success of coercion depended almost entirely on the personnel who administered the Crimes Act. Balfour, though often absent from Ireland, instilled confidence into his subordinates by not flinching in the face of Home Rule attacks. All was not harmony in the Castle, however. In that small, bureaucratic world personal animosities were bound to assume exaggerated significance. Balfour's temperament and mannerisms could make enemies as well as admirers, and a case in point was that of the Irish lord chancellor. Ashbourne had been the Conservatives' acknowledged expert on Irish affairs for a number of years, and he considered Balfour an upstart who knew next to nothing about Ireland and was lucky enough to have Salisbury as an uncle. Balfour, on the other hand, never cared for loud men—Ashbourne was known for his booming voice—and was unimpressed by his intellect and blatant ambition. Throughout their association in Ireland Balfour did his best to prevent Ashbourne from interfering in matters of policy. By 1889 relations had reached such a nadir that he tried to persuade Ashbourne to accept the vacant lord chief justiceship, the highest legal office in the country. But Ashbourne, who guarded his cabinet rank jealously, knew that acceptance meant automatic exclusion from that honor. He was not one to be outmaneuvered, and the price he asked in return for this sacrifice proved so exorbitant as to imply a refusal. Balfour was left fuming, and this incident hardly improved the relations between the two men.[29]

Fortunately, Balfour's other associates in the Irish administration were more compatible. By his express orders the viceroy, Lord Londonderry, was excluded from responsibility for political affairs

[29] "I enclose Ashbourne's reply. It has afforded me an infinite entertainment as a study of human nature:—from other points of view it is annoying. It only remains for him to ask for the garter and a perpetual pension and he will then perhaps feel that his incalculable services to his country have been adequately rewarded! The joke is that this man, who wants an earldom in order to sweeten the bitter pill of receiving . . . £6,000 a year, had the face to tell me that Lady Ashbourne would have preferred to remain plain (to be sure that she is bound to remain!) to remain, I say, 'plain Mrs Gibson'!" Balfour to Salisbury, 16 Nov. 1889, *ibid.*

and was left to supervise patronage and official receptions. Although Londonderry chafed at being deprived of a role in policy matters, he managed to avoid antagonizing Balfour, who tolerated him as a well-meaning but rather unimaginative man. One of Balfour's most devoted aides was George Wyndham, whose honeymoon in Italy was interrupted with a request to serve as his private secretary. Wyndham accepted, resigned his commission in the Coldstream Guards, and reported to the Irish Office in Great Queen Street, Westminster, to begin his new assignment.

Wyndham was much more than an aspirant politician. In spite of his youth—he was only twenty-four at the time—he was a soldier who had seen action in Egypt, a poet, and a keen horseman. Moreover, he was highly sensitive, charged with an abundance of nervous energy, and strikingly handsome. One of his closest friends once described him as "an artist by nature and a politician by accident." The new private secretary spent most of his working hours, whether in London or Dublin, preparing material for Balfour's speeches or answering the endless accusations and inquiries about Government policy in Ireland. The job soon lost its initial glamor: he complained to his friend and cousin Scawen Blunt, "I long for a pure breath of poetry to clear my lungs of the poisonous dust of Political controversy." At times the number of letters issued by Dublin Castle averaged seventy a day, and most of these were either written or edited by Wyndham, whose literary skill could be discerned even though the subject might be land purchase or prison uniforms. Balfour left him a free hand in this sphere of public information and rarely bothered to read those letters that were published in the *Times* and elsewhere; Home Rulers rewarded Wyndham for his activities by calling him "Mr. Balfour's devil" and "Miss Arthur," much to his own amusement. For Wyndham the dreary routine of paper work in the Castle was relieved only by dinner parties or family gatherings in the chief secretary's lodge, and by hard, fast fox hunts on the week ends. During the parliamentary recess he escaped to his family, his books, and verses at Saighton Grange in Cheshire. He was destined to put his Irish experiences to good use when he became chief secretary in 1900; and however unhappy the circumstances of his resignation five years later, the appointment proved the remarkable continuity of Conservative policy in Ireland from 1887 to 1905.[30]

With Ridgeway Balfour's relations were always cordial. The abilities and the temperaments of each man complemented those of the other, and on many questions their minds functioned as one. In return for Ridgeway's unswerving loyalty Balfour protected his interests whenever they were threatened. And in November, 1887, when the treasury tried to reduce the under secretary's salary, Balfour sent a letter of protest to Goschen and reassured Ridgeway: "The piddling economy of the Treasury with regard to Ireland at this moment is extremely annoying. I think it quite possible that if Ireland were as easily governed as Yorkshire, the general scale of salaries might be too high and the number of officials too great. But it is really intolerable that they should choose a period of revolution in order to effect economies in a system which has been going on unchecked for fifty years."[31] The Treasury meekly retreated. In the Castle Ridgeway occupied a pivotal position between his chief and the congeries of departments that were responsible for the actual execution of policy. From the point of view of efficiency, the Castle bureaucracy left much to be desired and Ridgeway could never afford to relax his vigilance.

From the beginning Balfour believed that the coercive machine could not function properly without a marked improvement in morale. Irish officials had recently undergone the traumatic experience of Gladstone's Home Rule ministry, and this ordeal had been followed by the vagaries and indecision of the Hicks Beach regime. Too many of the Castle personnel had lost their nerve, if not their faith in the ability of either British party to restore order in the country. The urgent need to raise morale was constantly on Balfour's mind, and he wrote to his uncle in the autumn of 1887: "If I had not to go to Balmoral tomorrow I think . . . that I would move on to Dublin at once; not because I or anyone else can prevent Irish officials from blundering, or English newspapers from magnifying their blunders, but simply in order to keep up

[30] See J. Biggs-Davison, *George Wyndham: A Study in Toryism*, London, 1951, p. 80; and Wyndham and Mackail, *Wyndham*, I, p. 230.

[31] Balfour to Ridgeway, 10 Nov. 1887, Add. MS 49826.

their spirits."[32] Blunders there were in every department. Virtually everyone wished to shirk responsibility, to avoid decisions, and to refer the matter to the chief secretary, who never stopped wondering when the next lapse in discipline or judgment would occur.

Three indigenous factors hampered the administration of the Crimes Act during these years: the timidity of the Irish law officers, the shortcomings of the judiciary, and the negligence of certain magistrates combined to save Ireland from what might have been a more drastic "licking." In the first place, the members of the Law Room never entirely satisfied either Ridgeway or Balfour. Buller had once pointed out this weak spot in Dublin Castle: " . . . as per usual the Irish Executive is terribly hampered by the Irish Law Officers: who mean well, but who will advise when they ought to act, and who are so . . . vain, that they are always looking at prosecutions and so on as personal matters instead of as abstract propositions."[33] In Ireland it was a rare occasion when the attorney general, the solicitor general, the lord chancellor, and the lord chief justice agreed on any prosecution of importance. Salisbury used more vigorous language when he wrote to his nephew: "It is borne in upon me—as I suppose it is on most people—, that you have the stupidest lot of lawyers in Ireland any Govt was ever cursed with. There is nothing for it but for you to form your own judgment upon every question of procedure, of law, of drafting etc. etc."[34]

Legal officers who could both prosecute in an aggressive spirit and excel at administrative or parliamentary duties were rare. The most able or effective law officer was Peter O'Brien, a man of forceful personality who had learned much of his law when deviling for Chief Baron Palles of the Court of Exchequer. O'Brien had been raised in the Burren country of Clare, where the slate-grey sheets of limestone rise imposingly from the sea, and his

[32] Balfour to Salisbury, 10 Oct. 1887, Salisbury MSS.
[33] Buller to Beach, 19 Oct. 1887, St. Aldwyn MSS.
[34] Salisbury to Balfour, 3, 14 Oct. 1887, Add. MS 49688. Churchill had written in 1886: "The unreliability of the Irish people is shown in its most concentrated form in the Irish Bench. I have carefully gone over the list of judges and there is only one in whom the Gov't could confidently rely for law and courage. That is Fitzgibbon"; Churchill to Salisbury, 13 Jan. 1886, Salisbury MSS.

ebullient and courageous qualities, added to an instinctive under-standing of the Irish people, impressed even his bitterest political foes. Although he lacked erudition and was a second-rate ad-ministrator, he had built up a reputation for winning cases by the simple if controversial expedient of challenging all jurors whom he considered unreliable. Owing to his success in securing "safe" juries, O'Brien was known all over Ireland as "Peter the Packer," and his indifference to abuse as well as his devotion to the Union made him an ideal Crown lawyer from Balfour's point of view.[35]

Apart from O'Brien, the Law Room in Dublin Castle did not contain men of outstanding ability. John Gibson, the brother of Lord Ashbourne, proved a feeble attorney general, and Balfour was not sorry to see him replaced in 1888 by O'Brien. In general, the law officers feared that any display of zeal in prosecuting of-fenders under the Crimes Act would provoke the nationalists into retaliating with organized outrage. In other words, as Balfour informed his uncle: "The Law Officers show much greater in-genuity in picking holes in their own act than they ever did in passing it. At every turn I find myself hampered by what may perhaps be good law but is certainly not good sense." To counter-act this tendency, the legal officers were ordered to stop their "eternal *minuting*" of cases so that local magistrates would no longer see their discouraging comments about the inadvisability of prosecution.[36]

Time and again the Crown lawyers balked at an important prosecution. Occasionally they had sound legal reasons for in-action, but more often they were ruled by motives of expediency. Nothing frightened them more than the prosecution of priests and members of Parliament. The evidence had to be overwhelming and the jury guaranteed to return a verdict of guilty before they would consent to proceed. In order to ensure the conviction of

[35] 1842-1914; created Baron O'Brien of Kilfenora 1900; Q.C. 1880; Irish Solicitor General 1887-1888; Irish Attorney General 1888-1889; Lord Chief Justice of Ireland 1889-1913. Balfour wrote of him: "No man is perfect, but he certainly is most remarkably endowed with the knowl-edge, the experience, and the judgment which we particularly need in dealing with a certain class of our difficulties"; Balfour to Ridgeway, 23 July 1889, Add. MS 49828.

[36] Balfour to Salisbury, 22 Oct., 28 Nov. 1887, Salisbury MSS.

prominent nationalists, Ridgeway usually had to spend much of his time "gingering up" the law officers, whose constant want of nerve made his task all the more difficult. Exasperated by the weakness of his legal advisers, Ridgeway attributed the vindication of the law entirely to Balfour. "These lawyers," he wrote, "dislike any innovation. All our material successes—e.g. Section I enquiries, boycotting prosecution, proclamation of meetings—have been forced on them by you."[37] At times Ridgeway indulged in personalities: the solicitor general, John Atkinson, was a "deadly upas tree," whose "sterilizing influence" was "most baneful." And he had a special grievance to nurse because he thought he had uncovered a plot by the lord chancellor and his leading advisers to limit his own jurisdiction in the Castle to matters of crime and internal security. So long as Balfour was in command, however, there was no need to worry about Ashbourne's attempts to extend his own powers.[38]

The Irish law courts constituted Balfour's second problem in administering the Crimes Act. He described them as "cowardly and corrupt" and complained that they impeded the advance against crime. The Dublin magistrates were so completely ineffectual that to proclaim the city under the Crimes Act would have been a waste of time. Like judges, they enjoyed security of tenure and could not be removed by executive order. The coroners' juries were "corrupt" and the county magistracy was "packed" with nationalists. Against these latter bodies he was prepared to take a "somewhat high hand," but there was little chance of his applying effective measures in the case of the Dublin magistracy.[39] Several county magistrates, however, were removed to districts where their shortcomings would be less noticeable. According to Balfour the quality of the Irish judicature was equally deplorable. Whenever William O'Brien, Dillon, and other nationalists appealed their sentences, the judges usually granted bail, knowing full well that the defendants would repeat their offenses as soon as they had left court. At such time the Irish executive longed to

[37] Ridgeway to Balfour, 27, 29 Nov. 1887, 27 July 1888, 8 Feb. 1889, Add. ms 49808-809.

[38] Ridgeway to Balfour, 29 Aug. 1889, 20 Feb., 11 July 1891, *ibid.*, 49810-812.

[39] Balfour to Salisbury, 16 Oct. 1887, Salisbury mss.

restrict the process of appeal but dared not. In 1889 Ridgeway caught some county court judges reducing sentences without the Castle's permission, and exclaimed: "Of all that is contemptible in this country the Irish judge is not the least contemptible. There is scarcely one who does not fear the newspapers more than he fears God."[40] It soon became obvious to Balfour that Irish judges required as much supervision as his own legal advisers in the Castle.

One man in particular often frustrated the Irish executive in the pursuit of Crimes Act offenders. This was Christopher Palles, lord chief baron of the Court of Exchequer.[41] Many important cases came before Palles, who was a devout Catholic, and his judgments did not always tally with the Castle's interpretation of the evidence. He tried to save Blunt and later Dillon from conviction, and in a much-publicized boycotting case he gave the administration "a bad fall" by acquitting the defendants. Most of the Law Room either respected or feared this champion of the common law, whose long career was devoted to preserving the independence of the Irish Bench. Ridgeway never trusted Palles and had to exhort the attorney general to challenge his decisions. "These trimmers," he noted, "should be beaten not conciliated, and I would go for the Chief Baron and expose him whenever there is an opportunity." Although Balfour considered him "the chief obstacle to the proper government in Ireland," he was powerless to curb his authority. Early in 1888, however, a county court judge credited Palles with having done much to pacify the country. "Priests and people believe in him," he reported, "and as with the former, law when they believe in it is as binding as Theology, those judgments must have the effect of taking the priests out of the agitation—a consummation devoutly to be wished for." Throughout the land war the bluster of officials in the Castle did not ruffle Palles, who continued to deliver judgments in his impartial, fearless way. And it was in part a tribute to his qualities and legal stature that Palles, the last of the chief barons,

[40] Ridgeway to Balfour, 31 May 1889, Add. MS 49809.

[41] 1831-1920; Q.C. 1865; Irish Solicitor General 1872; Irish Attorney General 1872-1874; Chief Baron of the Exchequer 1874-1916. See V.T.H. Delany, *Christopher Palles: His Life and Times*, Dublin, 1960, chaps. 4-10.

received the honor of an English privy councillorship from the outgoing Government in 1892.[42]

For its ultimate success the Crimes Act relied upon the stipendiary magistrates, better known as "removables," who dispensed summary justice in the proclaimed districts. The country was divided into five sections—the northern, midland, southeastern, southwestern, and western divisions—each of which was supervised by a divisional magistrate. These officers were responsible for the maintenance of law and order, and the function of the resident magistrates was to suppress illegal combinations, meetings, and newspapers as directed. To the Parnellites there was scarcely a single magistrate fit to exercise his powers, and although Balfour scoffed at their charges of incompetence, he often worried about the effects of such attacks on the morale of the magistracy.[43] Instances of disloyalty on the part of the magistrates were fortunately rare. One such case occurred in the southeast division, where a man with the appropriate name of Captain Owen Slacke neglected his duties to an extent that verged on actual cooperation with the nationalists. This apathetic official concealed his shortcomings for several years; but in 1889 Ridgeway decided to investigate why Slacke's division lagged so far behind in terms of improvement. The inquiry revealed that Slacke had winked at the activities of the league, while allowing the morale of the RIC to reach a "very low ebb." Ridgeway took personal charge of the case and informed Balfour that the police had lapsed into "something very like disloyalty." "They have been shutting their eyes to boycotting etc.," he reported, "—if they have not been actually conniving at it. The evil is widespread and will have to be very cautiously touched."[44] Balfour acted quickly. Ignoring Slacke's professions of innocence, he transferred the offending magistrate to the northern division. Ridgeway, who should have known more about Slacke's activities in the first place, still insisted that most magistrates were reliable men, but he had to admit that "contin-

[42] Ridgeway to Balfour, 6, 22 Feb. 1888; Balfour to Ridgeway, 28 July 1888; P. O'Brien to Balfour, 25 Feb. 1888, Add. MS 49808, 49827, 49689.

[43] Balfour to P. O'Brien, 25 April 1888, *ibid.*, 49826. In 1860 there were seventy-two resident magistrates; in 1912, sixty-four.

[44] Ridgeway to Balfour, 1 June, 5 Oct. 1890, *ibid.*, 49811. See also Balfour to Ridgeway, 8 July 1890, *ibid.*, 49829.

ued fagging" was essential in order to keep them up to the mark.[45]

In general, the Royal Irish Constabulary, which was composed of both Catholics and Protestants, behaved in an exemplary manner during the years of coercion. If presence of mind occasionally deserted district inspectors and other officers, the succession of riots and boycotting conspiracies would have strained the patience of even the best men. The Police were never sparing in their use of batons, but much worse damage could have been done. In Tipperary, for example, a county inspector almost caused a massacre when he twice ordered his men to load and fire at a menacing crowd. The order was countermanded just in time; and Ridgeway was able to inform his chief: "I have the fellow carefully chained up here . . . a fine specimen of an overfed Bull —most of the C.I.'s are cows—fine pluck and physique but *no* brains." In the southeastern division some county inspectors were reported as being both "impotent and nerveless."[46] But these cases were the exceptions, and the majority of police officers behaved commendably in the face of constant provocation. It was always a source of frustration to Balfour, however, that the Irish executive had no power to interfere in disciplinary matters within the RIC; these were the sole purview of the Inspector General Andrew Reed, of whom Balfour had a low opinion because he kept the worst cases of insubordination secret.

By the spring of 1887 the morale and efficiency of the RIC were in a state of disrepair, and when Balfour arrived in Dublin, his first official act was to call a meeting of the divisional magistrates and ranking RIC officers in order to discuss appropriate measures for meeting any defiance of the Crimes Act. One of the fruits of this conference was a special order sent by telegram to the district inspector at Youghal in county Cork, the contents of which were allowed to leak out to the public. A riotous assembly was expected at Youghal, and the local inspector received the following instructions from his superior, Captain Plunkett, D.M.: "Deal very summarily if any organised resistance to lawful authority. If

[45] "Slacke's policy has always been to let things slide and take optimistic views, and this spirit has pervaded all ranks in his Division. There has undoubtedly been an inclination to regard the battle as won and the spurt to be over"; Ridgeway to Balfour, 3 June 1888, *ibid.*, 49827.

[46] Ridgeway to Balfour, 27 May, 6 June 1890, *ibid.*, 49811.

necessary do not hesitate to shoot them." The nationalists promptly accused the Castle of planning a "wholesale butchery."[47] As a warning to National League members, however, this order had a sobering effect. No one was killed at Youghal; and Balfour had served notice that the law would be enforced even at the cost of lives.

This new note of stringency did not ease the task of the police. On eviction sites the constabulary were reviled and attacked with stones; and in some of the most disaffected areas the natives did not dare to speak to a policeman without incurring the censure of the league. The baton and bayonet charges against rioters in the provinces made them no more popular. Sooner or later, as Balfour half suspected, a serious collision between the police and the people was bound to occur.

IV. "BLOODY BALFOUR"

The spark was struck at Mitchelstown in county Cork, on September 9, 1887. The occasion was the trial of William O'Brien and a local farmer John Mandeville on the charge of inflammatory speechmaking. The curious and idle had come to Mitchelstown from the outlying villages to watch one of the most famous Parnellites challenge the Crimes Act for the first time. To mark the event the National League called a protest meeting in the market square to which several members of Parliament, including Dillon and Labouchere, were invited. Although O'Brien failed to appear, the rally was well attended by men carrying blackthorns. When the speeches began, the magistrate in command ordered the police to clear a way through the dense crowd so that the police reporter could take note of what was said. Instinctively the audience resisted the passage of the reporter with his escort. Threats, curses, and blows followed in quick succession. Outnumbered by 100 to 1, the police withdrew, some of them badly wounded, and took up defensive positions in their barracks. In the confusion and panic that followed, the police opened fire on the advancing mob, and their volleys killed two and wounded several others. News of the clash spread rapidly, shocking public opinion in both countries. Labouchere accused the police of behaving like "wild beasts"; and Gladstone's terse comment,

[47] *Freeman's Journal,* 14-16 March 1887.

"Remember Mitchelstown," became a battle cry during the land war.[48]

Among the spectators at the Mitchelstown "massacre" was a tall, young lawyer with angular features named Edward Carson. As a legal officer of the Crown, he had been assigned to conduct the first prosecution under the Crimes Act. In the early stages of the riot Carson, who was well on the way to becoming the devil's advocate from the nationalist point of view, left the court house and walked with remarkable composure through the milling crowd. No one dared to assault him, although the purpose of his visit was common knowledge. The sights and sounds of the street fighting and the vicious temper of the local "blackthorn brigade" left a deep impression on Carson; and he assisted the secret inquiry into the causes of the riot with little compassion for the nationalist victims. Balfour had spotted this "provincial Irish lawyer" soon after his arrival in Dublin, and the two men took an instant liking to one another. In spite of his traditional contempt for lawyers, Balfour "made" Carson, teaching him something of the lore of politics and shaping his early career, so that London inevitably became the next world to conquer for this ambitious crusader. Carson repaid Balfour with unwavering loyalty and with a long series of prosecutions against the leading Parnellites. Under the titles of "Coercion Carson" and "Balfour Junior," he became the most respected and feared Crown counsel in the country.

As Carson once remarked, Mitchelstown also "made" Balfour, by showing that he had no intention of deviating from his policy of "kicks and ha'pence." Although aware that bloodshed might easily have been avoided, Balfour vigorously defended the conduct of the police, while infuriated Home Rulers clamored for an official investigation and for disciplinary action against the constables involved. Balfour's support of the RIC not only boosted morale but paid handsome dividends during the era of coercion when police cooperation was essential.

Immediately after the riot, the Irish Privy Council met in Dublin and the cabinet assembled in London to discuss the crisis. In Parliament the debate on Mitchelstown lasted two days; and Balfour's calm demeanor incited bitter retorts from the Opposition

---

[48] *Ibid.*, 10-11 Sept. 1887; Dugdale, *Balfour*, I, pp. 140-47.

benches. The Government's case rested on two points: the nationalists had provoked the riot and the police had fired in self-defense. Although Balfour regretted the fatalities, he insisted that the vindication of the law was involved and that all other considerations were subordinate to the law of public safety. After a coroner's jury in Ireland had returned a verdict of willful murder against five constables, the Government announced the appointment of a sworn inquiry.[49]

Balfour arrived in Dublin on September 14 and soon learned the depressing facts of the case. The real trouble, he found, stemmed from the chronic "helplessness of the ordinary Irish official in the face of an emergency." Lord Salisbury advised his nephew that the evidence indicated "not merely Irish blundering, which is of course perennial, but a want of definite rules." And Buller, who had been absent from the Castle during the riot, wrote to his chief somewhat pompously: "You can take a decision . . . and I can take a decision; nobody else in Ireland can." In the end, Balfour attributed the calamity to loss of nerve by the county inspector in charge and to the incompetence of Ashbourne and his legal advisers in Dublin.[50]

The Mitchelstown affair prompted Balfour to start rewriting the instructions for members of the RIC present at proclaimed meetings. After a brief stay in Dublin he left for Scotland, where he completed a memorandum for police procedure based on the errors made at Mitchelstown. The new operational orders left no room for misinterpretation: if the baton-carrying police failed to subdue a defiant mob, then a detachment armed with rifles were to open fire or use their bayonets according to the circumstances. "Both humanity and efficiency," he informed Salisbury, "seem to require this strategy." In addition, the Castle received instructions to improve their security arrangements whenever prominent nationalists faced trial under the Crimes Act.[51] For several months the Castle's secret inquiry into the Mitchelstown affair dragged on, exposing much conflicting evidence and a general desire to evade

[49] Smith to Salisbury, 10 Sept. 1887, Salisbury mss; *Hansard,* 3d series, Vol. 321, pp. 229-336.

[50] Balfour to Salisbury, 21 Sept. 1887; Salisbury to Balfour, 15 Sept. 1887, Salisbury mss.

[51] For the rest of this memorandum, see Appendix i.

all blame. The RIC officers in the area were found suffering from a "very bad state of discipline and morale."[52] Balfour's memorandum, however, went far to rectify some of the major defects in police tactics. And if from Mitchelstown the chief secretary earned the popular sobriquet "Bloody Balfour," he may well have saved many lives in the future by reducing the chances of another Irish "Peterloo." Irishmen did not forget Mitchelstown, but neither did the administration, and for that reason both sides profited from the costly lesson.

The proper administration of the Crimes Act thus depended on firm leadership from above and on loyalty from the ranks. And Balfour, by defending the action of the Mitchelstown police, managed to inspire confidence among the constabulary and the officials in the Castle. Here was a man upon whom they could rely even in times of adversity. This confidence, as Wyndham was quick to perceive, had long been absent from the administration in Ireland. And the reasons for Balfour's popularity among the loyalists in the country were not hard to divine. "Arthur is by no means Alexander," Wyndham wrote to his father in January, 1888, "but having for his battleground a field from which all have run away, he creates a very great impression upon men who have been used to tremble at every threat, and to truckle with the most contemptible of their opponents upon every occasion. They can hardly believe that he does not care 2d for anything which 'United Ireland' here, and the 'Pall Mall' over the way may say of him."[53]

To Ridgeway the question of efficient administration was one of loyalty pure and simple. Either a man gave his allegiance to the Castle or he belonged to the large group of Irishmen who were merely the dupes of the league: "I came to this country absolutely devoid of religious prejudices, but I have been forced to the conclusion that it is not safe to place an Irish Roman Catholic in a position where he will have unpleasant duties to perform. His connections, his women, his Priests are all at him and it requires a very strong man, or an Irishman whose connections are English, to withstand the influence thus brought to bear."[54]

Not only the quirks of Irish officials, but public opinion, too,

[52] Ridgeway to Balfour, 23 Feb. 1888, Add. ms 49808.
[53] Wyndham and Mackail, *Wyndham*, I, p. 216.
[54] Ridgeway to Balfour, 5 May 1888, Add. ms 49808.

influenced the policy of resolute government. The cabinet always worried more than Balfour about the reaction at home to prosecutions and convictions in Ireland, and colleagues often tried to soften his attitude toward the nationalist agitation. There was no doubt in their minds that tales of repression in Ireland, carefully distorted by Home Rulers, were having an adverse effect upon the electorate in England. In addition, the Government faced a steady stream of criticism from Liberal Unionists, who insisted that the constituencies would not put up with unrelieved coercion in Ireland. The loss of several by-elections at the end of the year showed that ministerial fears on this score were not groundless.

A more vivid warning to ministers occurred in November, 1887, when a demonstration led by members of the Social Democratic Federation and other radical workingman associations erupted into an ugly riot. Although the meeting in Trafalgar Square was held ostensibly to protest the imprisonment of William O'Brien, the size and vehemence of the crowd showed that the workingmen of London were more troubled by "hard times" than by coercion in Ireland. The prolonged depression meant that social disorder was a phenomenon by no means confined to Ireland. Sporadic outbreaks of violence throughout the autumn culminated on November 13 in a protest march of over fifty thousand persons, many of whom were jobless and hungry, as well as irked by O'Brien's harsh treatment in jail. When the police were ordered to disperse the crowd, they applied their truncheons with sufficient force to mark the occasion "Bloody Sunday" for posterity. Two of the most prominent agitators, John Burns and R. B. Cunninghame-Graham, M.P., were arrested and received prison terms. The immediate outcry against police brutality did not enhance the Government's cause in the eyes of the working classes and many "moderates." General Buller blamed the riot on Irish machinations; and the socialists were accused of trying to destroy parliamentary government by violent means. Too few observers interpreted the battle of Trafalgar Square as but another symptom of the endemic disease that was affecting the whole British economy, not to mention that of Europe.[55]

Against such a background of popular unrest it was only

[55] Buller to Ridgeway, 15 Nov. 1887, Ridgeway MSS; Ensor, *England: 1870-1914*, pp. 180-81.

natural that Salisbury should advise his nephew to use moderation in enforcing the Crimes Act. "The only course," Salisbury wrote, "is to go on 'pegging away.' You will soon by experience learn the precise limit of your powers,—and then within those limits you will be able, without ever, or often, incurring a defeat, to inflict an intolerable amount of annoyance."[56]

To Balfour the success of his undertaking also depended upon the cooperation he received from his colleagues in London. With his uncle there was no problem. But for his purposes a cabinet that was ignorant of conditions in Ireland was virtually useless and, even worse, inclined to be timid. It was vital, he believed, to keep ministers well informed about the scale of the nationalist agitation; and to achieve this end he suggested in October that a cabinet memorandum on Irish affairs be circulated from time to time. Salisbury took up this proposal with enthusiasm. Such a report would, he hoped, relieve ministers of their chronic anxieties about Ireland: "They are very apt to imagine that when they hear nothing, nothing is being done." The first such brief on Ireland was being read by ministers within a week. On that occasion Balfour specially requested that the memorandum be kept out of the Irish lord chancellor's hands. "How they all hate Ashbourne!" was Salisbury's pained remark to W. H. Smith. The cabinet circulars proved valuable, for they educated ministers about the difficulties facing the Irish administration, and they spared members much needless argument on points of fact. At the same time the Irish committee of the cabinet received a new stimulus under the more dynamic lead provided by Balfour. With the passing of the Crimes Act and the scheduling of legislation to relieve distress, the committee found its burdens and responsibilities enormously increased. But by expediting decisions on matters relating to Ireland the committee more than justified its existence.[57]

V. PROSECUTIONS

Balfour's conception of Parnellism was clearly reflected in his administration of the Crimes Act. Regarding the agitation for Home Rule as nothing more than insurrection in disguise, he

[56] Dugdale, *Balfour*, I, p. 147.
[57] Balfour to Salisbury, 17 Oct. 1887; Salisbury to Balfour, 20 Oct. 1887; Salisbury to Smith, 30 Oct. 1887, Salisbury MSS.

treated the participants as rebels. Under the Crimes Act no distinction was made between political and nonpolitical prisoners. The moonlighter or boycotter was, in his opinion, no more guilty than the man who incited him to perform the act. In other words, the Dillons and O'Briens, the parish priests, and league organizers who exhorted the peasantry to defy the law deserved just as harsh treatment as those who obeyed their orders. The category of political crimes as distinct from common misdemeanors simply did not exist for the Irish executive; and the sooner the agitators entered prison, the better for Ireland and the Unionist party. In laying down this policy Balfour not only made little allowance for public opinion, but grossly underestimated the ease with which nationalist prisoners became martyrs to the cause of liberty.

In their campaign against coercion the Parnellites and their Liberal allies fixed upon prison treatment and the arbitrary powers of Irish judges as the two most effective weapons in their arsenal. In the war of words that filled *Hansard*, the newspapers, and the public platforms of Great Britain during these years, Home Rulers spared few aspects of Balfour's administration. The chief secretary answered his critics with irony, contempt, and a wealth of statistics; but he did not always succeed in exonerating his subordinates, and the tedious repetition of such words as "tyranny" and "atrocity" convinced many people that Dublin Castle was inhabited by sadists.

The stream of invective directed against the administration did not, however, deter Balfour and his aides from implementing the clauses of the Crimes Act. The Castle made it quite clear that priests and members of Parliament were just as eligible for prison as the humblest moonlighter. As of August, 1888, some twenty-one members of Parnell's party had received prison terms ranging up to six months with hard labor, and by the end of the year eleven more were facing prosecution.[58] Parnell himself refrained from participating in the land agitation and thereby escaped prosecution. But his more industrious lieutenants—men like Dillon, O'Brien, Sheehy, Crilly, and others —received the brunt of coercion.

Dillon and O'Brien spent a large part of this period either

[58] *Annual Register: 1888*, p. 155; Balfour to Salisbury, 28 Dec. 1888, Salisbury MSS.

evading arrest or in gaol; and their many brushes with the law would make an epic tale, full of excitement, hardship, and not a little humor. The truth was that these two men caused the administration almost as much trouble in prison as they did when free. The Irish law officers never enjoyed the prospect of prosecuting them; yet they were so prominent that the Government could not afford an acquittal under any circumstances. Balfour, on the other hand, urged the Law Room to proceed against the pair whenever possible, because he believed that their imprisonment would take the heart out of the land agitation. Lord Salisbury did not always agree. Anxious about English public opinion, he cautioned his nephew against overdoing coercion. Too many prosecutions of O'Brien would, he feared, do more harm than good, if only because the electorate expected some leniency from the Government: " . . . the scare being over, the English public are getting good natured again. Both on this question and on the Educational question your very success will have an embarrassing effect. The public is no longer compelled by fear to concede what it naturally dislikes."[59]

Ridgeway shared these sentiments: "We are winning," he wrote to Balfour, "and can afford to be generous, if we can do so without injury to the public interests. A semblance of generosity would have a good effect and somewhat disarm our opponents in England." On this occasion Balfour gave way, but only temporarily, for in April, 1888, Dillon and O'Brien were arrested again on charges of promoting the Plan, and a month later they were sentenced to six months in jail.[60] The outcry raised by Home Rulers in both countries confirmed Salisbury's worst fears; and the second exposure to Balfour's prison rules did not stop either of the two from defying the Crimes Act after release. Too late the administration learned that incarceration only hardened the resolve of men like Dillon and O'Brien.

In Ireland, where concessions were always associated with weakness, the Castle's officials worried about the best method of relaxing coercion. Balfour at first opposed any move in the direction of leniency. The Government, in his opinion, owed all

[59] Salisbury to Balfour, 18 Jan. 1888, *ibid.*
[60] Ridgeway to Balfour, 10 Nov. 1887; Balfour to Ridgeway, 9 April, 12 May 1888, Add. MS 49808, 49826.

their success to the nationalists' awareness that "neither Parliamentary clamour nor any other instrument of political intimidation" could interfere with the cause of law and order. Any show of softness, he maintained, would be hailed by the nationalists as an act of surrender; and the Government could not afford to alienate Unionist supporters at home, let alone to lose control over the agitation in Ireland. When, in October, 1888, O'Brien and his "satellites" delivered a number of inflammatory speeches, the chief secretary rebuked the Law Room for treating these offenses too tolerantly. The time had not yet arrived, he wrote, "for in any way relaxing the policy which has hitherto proved successful: and which, I firmly believe, has gained instead of lost in the estimation of the whole Unionist Party in England." And he urged the attorney general to prosecute the offenders "without troubling ourselves as to whether they will have to be released long before their term of imprisonment has expired, either by the action of the *Times* commission, or on grounds of health. . . ."[61]

Irishmen were not the only members of Parliament to receive first-hand experience of the Crimes Act during these years. English radicals in search of excitement and a cause frequently interfered with bailiffs at evictions and participated in Plan rallies. One of the most inveterate enemies of coercion in any country was Wilfrid Scawen Blunt, who in 1885 claimed the distinction of being a Tory Home Ruler. Few Englishmen were better equipped for martyrdom than this impassioned traveller and man of letters who loved to dress like an Arab sheikh. Having just been a guest along with Balfour at the Wyndhams' family seat, Clouds in Wiltshire, this champion of the "backward nations of the world" went to Ireland in October, 1887, with the express purpose of defying the Crimes Act. His destination was the Clanricarde estate at Woodford, and his first act upon arrival was to attend a midnight rally at which O'Brien burned a copy of the lord lieutenant's order proclaiming all political meetings in the district. On October 23 the local inhabitants gathered to hear the eccentric delegate of the English Home Rule Union, and the police moved in to break up the meeting. In the melee that followed Blunt was twice dragged from the platform, and his wife Lady Anne was knocked down. Eventually, he was ar-

[61] Balfour to P. O'Brien, 13 Oct. 1888, *ibid.*, 49827.

rested and taken off to Loughrea where he spent the night in jail. The news caused a mild sensation in England; and Salisbury wrote to his nephew: "I was delighted to see you had run Wilfred Blunt in. The only unfavourable symptom in the present situation to my eyes is that Randolph is supporting us so zealously. The archfiend is getting lightheaded."[62]

At his trial Blunt delivered a discourse on the right of free speech and threatened to bring suit against the police for assault. After the magistrates had found him guilty of defying the law, Blunt lodged an appeal to Quarter Sessions and was released on bail. Although Ridgeway doubted the strength of the case, Lord Salisbury heartily approved of the prosecution. An exemplary sentence was needed, and on this occasion the premier did not fear public opinion: "The great heart of the people always chuckles when a gentleman gets into the clutches of the law."[63] Early in January the appeal was heard at Portumna where Carson, acting as Crown counsel, made certain that the judge confirmed the original sentence. Blunt received two months' hard labor for what Balfour called a crime "directly levelled against society." The Blunt episode proved that the chief secretary did not intend to spare either gentlemen or friends—George Wyndham's cousin included —from the Crimes Act. And the rigors of prison served to discourage this poet-adventurer from further defiance of the law in Ireland.[64]

Blunt's Irish saga, however, was not quite finished. While in Galway jail he unraveled strands of old rope and composed sonnets during nights made sleepless by the plank bed. He also committed a serious indiscretion. In the presence of the visiting prison justices he accused Balfour of having boasted during the house party at Clouds of his intention to imprison some six of the leading and least robust Parnellites in the hope that the experience would kill them. The newspapers took up this story with alacrity. Home Rulers now had all the proof they needed to convict Balfour of premeditated murder. Balfour himself labeled the charge a "ridiculous lie" and refused to believe that Blunt had ever made such

[62] Salisbury to Balfour, 26 Oct. 1887, *ibid.*, 49688.

[63] Dugdale, *Balfour*, I, pp. 155-56. Cranbrook called Blunt a "conceited ass"; Cranbrook to Salisbury, 24 Oct. 1887, Salisbury MSS.

[64] Blunt, *The Land War in Ireland*, pp. 355-67.

a statement. George Wyndham thought that Blunt must be "temporarily out of his senses." But the prisoner stuck to his tale and repeated his charge in a letter to the *Times* after his release. Balfour was forced to declare his innocence in a public address wherein he stated that, apart from the absurdity of the accusation, his begrudging respect, if not liking, for the Parnellites was too profound to wish for their absence from the House of Commons. The charge, nevertheless, remained to haunt Balfour's administration, especially during the subsequent prison crises. But the real victim was Blunt himself, whose breach of good taste, if not of a gentleman's honor, lost him several friends and numerous invitations. Balfour subsequently forgave him but others did not.[65]

Another English "martyr" to coercion was C. A. V. Conybeare, M.P. for Cornwall NW., one of the most pugnacious crusaders ever to arrive in Ireland under the auspices of the English Home Rule association. Conybeare not only advocated but practiced active resistance to eviction. He also proved adept at publicizing the use of battering rams to capture fortified cottages scheduled for eviction in Donegal and elsewhere. His behavior finally exhausted the patience of the authorities. In July, 1889, he was convicted on charges of conspiracy and incitement and sentenced to three months' imprisonment in Londonderry jail.[66] The punishments meted out to men like Conybeare and Blunt undoubtedly tended to reduce the number of English Home Rulers who were willing to try their luck by defying the forces of the law in Ireland.

The prosecution of members of Parliament raised several important questions about parliamentary immunity. Despite Liberal and Irish protests on the subject, Balfour contended that Parnellite members facing prosecution in Ireland ought not to be allowed to attend debates on the Irish estimates. Some confusion arose, however, when W. H. Smith practically pledged the Government to accept the presence of such offenders at these debates. Although this blunder vexed Balfour, he had no choice but to accept the ruling in the hope that the Irish members in question would behave so badly as to convince the English public that they were abusing

[65] *Ibid.*, pp. 383-94; see also Blunt, *My Diaries*, I, pp. 27, 66.

[66] Ridgeway reported that Conybeare had been "insufferably insolent" by breaking into the room of the divisional magistrate at 1:00 A.M. in order to make "some preposterous demand"; Ridgeway to Balfour, 20 April 1889, Add. MS 49809.

the immunity allowed them.[67] Ultimately Balfour succeeded in imprisoning most of the active members of Parnell's party except for the leader himself. But the Government paid a high price for this achievement in terms of mounting public resentment and parliamentary obstruction.

One of the high points in the tragicomic opera of coercion was the law suit that William O'Brien brought against Salisbury in the summer of 1889. The case arose from a speech delivered by the prime minister at Watford in which he accused O'Brien of inciting the Plan tenants at Tipperary to boycott, rob, and even murder all "landgrabbers" in the area. Determined to publicize the struggle at Tipperary and to test the partiality of English courts, the Irish member instituted legal proceedings against Salisbury for slander and claimed £10,000 in damages. The trial was held at Manchester; and Salisbury, on the advice of his chief counsel Sir Edward Clarke, Q.C., decided to waive privilege and appear in court in person. A large crowd greeted the premier on his arrival in Manchester on July 19, and the reports of the trial were eagerly read by the public. The defense paraded a number of witnesses who testified about the "appalling" conditions in and around Tipperary; while the prosecution rested its case on the plea that O'Brien had incited the tenantry to boycott only, and not to commit graver offenses. But as Clarke was quick to point out, O'Brien must have known that his inflammatory speeches—for which he had already been jailed—would lead inevitably to violence. The jury took only six minutes to return a verdict in favor of the defendant. Unionists were jubilant; while O'Brien made a futile attempt to reverse the decision in the Court of Appeal. After the trial had finished, Salisbury thanked Clarke warmly for his "skill and eloquence"; Balfour wrote to Ridgeway that the verdict was very "useful" and ought to be "rubbed in"; and the hapless O'Brien never repeated the experiment of prosecuting an English prime minister in his own country.[68]

[67] Balfour to Ridgeway, 29 Nov. 1888, *ibid.*, 49827. See also Balfour's memorandum on the prosecution of M.P.'s, 6 Dec. 1888, *ibid.*

[68] Balfour to P. O'Brien, 16 May 1889, *ibid.*; Balfour to Ridgeway, 23 July 1889, *ibid.*, 49828; D. Walker-Smith and E. Clarke, *The Life of Sir Edward Clarke* (hereafter *Clarke*), London, 1939, pp. 202-06.

VI. PROCLAIMED MEETINGS

The Crimes Act also empowered the Castle to ban all meetings calculated to incite violence or intimidation. But to Balfour's annoyance, the Law Room failed to adopt an aggressive attitude in this matter. The lawyers spent much of their time worrying lest the proclaiming of speeches give rise to a host of civil actions against the Government for violating the right of free speech. At the same time Balfour himself was not above tolerating nationalist rallies on the grounds of political expediency. Because freedom of speech was so precious a right to Englishmen and Irishmen alike, the administration behaved in a most equivocal manner on the subject; and, since every proclaimed meeting raised loud outcries from the Liberal Unionists as well as Home Rulers, the Castle shied away from using the powers contained in section five of the Crimes Act. Public opinion thus forced the Castle to compromise by banning only those meetings specifically intended to intimidate persons or to promote the Plan. Rallies in support of Home Rule were classified as "political" and invariably escaped proclamation.

Owing to the timidity of the Law Room, Ridgeway assumed full responsibility for proclaiming speeches. In deciding not to ban a meeting he always ran the risk that an ostensibly political speech would turn into an harangue against a particular landlord or "landgrabber." Whenever the Castle received advance notice of a violent speech, the resident magistrate was ordered to disperse the meeting. Sometimes the nationalists were considerate enough to circulate an abstract of their speech several days before the meeting; and in April, 1888, the Castle proclaimed a meeting called by O'Brien on the basis of his own publicity notice.

At first the Castle's proclamations were constantly disobeyed. Blunt arrived in Ireland with the express purpose of challenging the Government's right to prohibit free speech. Those nationalists who wished to avoid arrest relied upon "hit and run" tactics. By laying false scents, the "proclaimed" speakers would elude the police and hold their meetings near the original site. At times they addressed crowds from hotel windows, from moving wagons, and from boats anchored off a lake shore. Deficient in both transportation and reliable information, the police often gave up the pursuit in despair; and Balfour's suggestion that they use tricycles to capture offenders aroused no interest in RIC headquarters. Both the Government and the nationalists attached considerable importance to the success or failure of these banned meetings; and the extravagant countermeasures adopted by the Castle attested to the fact. After several years of practice Dillon and O'Brien had become masters of the art of evasion, holding illegal meetings all over the countryside, to the chagrin of the authorities. In the spring of 1888 Ridgeway informed his chief that the nationalists were planning an extensive series of rallies in the south of Ireland: "I have no doubt that there will be the usual cut and run programme with 'hole in the corner' meetings. I have warned the D.M.'s confidentially against *arresting* the promoters and thus giving them an excuse for following Blunt's example. But of course it is quite possible that in a melee one or two M.P.'s may get their heads broken."[69]

Such defiance, however, gradually diminished, and by the spring of 1889, after a number of prosecutions under section five, the nationalists began to obey the proclaiming orders. With improved intelligence work and with the constabulary's greater knowledge of nationalist ruses, the number of illegal meetings declined rapidly. The defiant mood of the league organizers was gradually succumbing to the attrition of the Crimes Act.

VII. PRESS PROSECUTIONS

One of the administration's most vexing problems concerned freedom of the press. Balfour regarded press prosecutions as essential to the maintenance of law and order; but he did not underestimate the difficulties involved. English public opinion, as he well knew, was more articulate and sensitive on this subject than on any other; and fear of offending this force affected Government policy to a large degree. Balfour, while personally immune to nationalist insults, strongly objected to what he considered incessant lies about Unionist policy in the Irish or English Home Rule press. Some of these "lies," needless to say, came uncomfortably close to the truth. But he soon discovered that there was little he could do to stop the flow. In Ireland, moreover, the press served another purpose besides abusing the Castle. Newspapers, especially in the provinces, actively assisted the National League by printing

[69] Ridgeway to Balfour, 8, 14 April 1888, Add. MS 49808.

boycott resolutions of local branches. Balfour realized that the Government had a much stronger case for prosecution in this instance. Although he wished to punish editors for their polemical articles as well, he knew the strength of English prejudice on the subject: "Public opinion," he lamented, "is sensitive about phrases though callous about things. I am afraid of the freedom of the press." Originally he had envisaged press prosecutions as a "necessary element" in his campaign against the league. When drafting the Crimes Bill, he had paid special attention to the press clauses contained in section two, which were designed to "hit the papers" hard and with lasting effect.[70]

In December, 1887, Balfour discussed press prosecutions with his uncle, and together they worked out a plan for dealing with the most abusive papers. Having more experience of English opinion, Salisbury cautioned his nephew against alienating the English press by excessive measures in Ireland. To date, the administration had prosecuted only those papers that published illegal notices; and Salisbury wished to confine prosecutions to this offense. Balfour, on the other hand, argued that only the prosecution of such papers as the *Kerry Sentinel* or *United Ireland* would deter other editors from publishing diatribes against the Government. One way to discourage the sale of offending newspapers, he suggested, was to prosecute the news vendors.[71] But the public outcry that followed several such arrests convinced many Unionists that the procedure was inopportune. In a memorandum dealing with "the tenderest part of our policy" Balfour set down his ideas on the subject of press prosecutions. Failure to attack both the league and its journalistic organs within the near future would, he asserted, only aggravate disorder throughout the country. The most reprehensible papers were those that published the proceedings of suppressed branches of the National League and thereby kept the local association alive. Up to the end of the year no newspaper had been prosecuted for "expression of opinion" even of the most virulent kind; and news vendors who had out of ignorance sold copies of suppressed papers, or who had promised not to repeat their offense, had been spared prosecution.

[70] Balfour to Buller, 15 March, 8 Aug., 27 Dec. 1887, *ibid.*, 49826.
[71] Ridgeway to Balfour, 10 Dec. 1887, *ibid.*, 49808.

To Balfour these facts added up to extreme leniency. What troubled him most was the widespread misunderstanding about the Castle's strategy. He reminded his uncle: "The general public regard this press prosecution as a separate department of our policy. This is not so. It is an element, and, I fear, in some shape or another a *necessary* element, in the policy of suppressing the League in Clare and Kerry. . . . It must be judged therefore not by itself, but in connection with the general question of dealing with the League."[72]

Salisbury replied that the electorate ought to be the final judge of the matter, and that the prosecution of news vendors would be impossible to defend in England. Popular sympathy for the victims of coercion was steadily mounting and ought not to be aggravated by a new dose of severity. Salisbury thus advised his nephew to relax coercion "as unobtrusively as possible—simply abstaining from this or that prosecution without giving any reason. Do not avow a change of policy—even to your pillow, for pillows chatter in Ireland." In vain Balfour retorted that it was never "good policy" to let the press win, especially in Ireland, where editors so often had the last and most offensive word. Any sign of leniency, he feared, would spur newspapers to publish illegal notices. "Dangerous shoals" surrounded the problem, and unless the Government acted swiftly, the nationalist press would seize the initiative. Unmoved by these arguments, Salisbury insisted that the public demanded a milder policy. After February, 1888, the prosecution of news vendors ceased. Balfour had bowed to the private wish of Hatfield and, indirectly, to English public opinion. Realizing that press prosecution was "the weakest point in our line of defence," he conceded that "to hold our hand: to watch events carefully: to take careful note of any illegal publication" offered the safest approach to the problem. He hoped thereby to avoid any actions that would be difficult to defend either in Parliament or in the provinces. "I think, if we went at anybody," he wrote to Salisbury, "we should be obliged to go at *United Ireland,* and there would come to be a life and death struggle between that newspaper

[72] Balfour memorandum on press prosecutions, 22 Dec. 1887, Salisbury MSS.

and the Government, having among its incidents repeated prosecutions, and, possibly, imprisonment of William O'Brien."[73]

As the Irish executive learned by experience, it was virtually impossible to draw up any hard and fast rules about press prosecutions. When the cabinet reviewed press policy in March, 1888, Balfour stipulated that proof of "local injury" to an individual or to the cause of law and order ought to be the deciding factor in prosecuting a paper. But even this criterion opened up a wide field of interpretation. In September of that year both Ridgeway and Balfour wished to prosecute *United Ireland* for publishing an article that compared the administration to "devils citing Scripture." The Irish law officers, on the other hand, opposed any such move on the grounds of what Ridgeway contemptuously called their usual "hollow opinions." In the end the cabinet decided that a prosecution would be too dangerous, and no legal action was taken.[74] Ministers and Crown lawyers alike, heavily influenced by electoral considerations, thus combined to frustrate Balfour's intentions and to reduce the number of press prosecutions to a bare minimum. In the heat of political controversy, needless to say, it was all too easy for Home Rulers to forget that a Liberal government had suppressed *United Ireland* late in 1881 and had ordered the arrest of the editor O'Brien, along with most of his staff, while the type and stereoplates were systematically broken up.

Apart from the tribulations of press prosecutions, the Irish administration also faced the problem of keeping the public properly informed about events in the country. Balfour was most anxious to refute the "daily flood of misrepresentation" that appeared in the nationalist press. In a cabinet memorandum on press relations he urged the need to match Parnellite propaganda word for word, declaring that "we can hardly live in an atmosphere of chronic commissions of Enquiry." Failing any contradictions from Dublin Castle, the English public, he feared, had no choice but to believe the myths invented by Irishmen. During

[73] Dugdale, *Balfour*, I, pp. 150-52. For rest of the letter, see Balfour to Salisbury, 27 Dec. 1887, Salisbury MSS. Balfour to Ridgeway, 13 March 1888, Add. MS 49826.

[74] Balfour memorandum on press prosecutions, n.d. March 1888; Ridgeway to Balfour, 29 Sept. 1888, Add. MS 49826, 49808.

parliamentary recesses, and when Balfour himself was not making speeches in public, the Castle lacked any formal means of circulating their version of events. To remedy this deficiency Ridgeway suggested the use of some respectable newspaper, preferably in London, as a vehicle for exposing nationalist "lies."[75] Balfour thought the proposal a sound one, and after making some preliminary inquiries he received promises of cooperation from none other than the *Times*. Owing to sympathies of a personal as well as political nature, the editor George Buckle welcomed Balfour's request for news space; and after February, 1889—that crucial month in the history of the *Times* and the Special Commission—the administration had an official outlet for statements about Ireland.[76]

Thwarted in his press policy by the cabinet, by the Law Room in the Castle, and indirectly by English public opinion, Balfour derived little consolation from prosecuting provincial papers for publishing the names of boycotted persons. By 1888 he had learned most of the limits to which a coercive regime could go in a society based upon constitutional procedure and common law. Even though he experienced moments of acute discouragement, he could still offer words of comfort to Ridgeway, who despaired of ever taming the nationalist press:

"Your feelings about the Press . . . have been shared by everyone who has held your office. . . . It is clear that any idea of muzzling the Press in Ireland is absolutely chimerical and must be abandoned. The English people never will submit to Ireland being deprived of what they regard as one of the elementary privileges of free citizens. And therefore if we cannot govern Ireland with an unshackled press, we must give up hope of governing it at all."[77]

Proof of the invigorating effects of Balfour's work was not long in coming. By the end of the parliamentary session in September, 1887, praise for the new chief secretary was pouring in from his

[75] Balfour memorandum on press relations, n.d. Jan. 1889; Balfour to Ridgeway, 31 July 1888; Ridgeway to Balfour, 14 Feb. 1889, Add. MS 49827, 49809.

[76] Balfour to Buckle, 24 May 1888; Balfour to Ridgeway, 11 Feb. 1889, Add. MS 49826, 49809.

[77] Balfour to Ridgeway, 19 May 1888, *ibid.*, 49826.

fellow ministers. Lord Cranbrook delighted in the failure of the Parnellites to scare or embarrass Balfour: "They cannot make much of Balfour," he wrote to Salisbury, "who foils them by his skill and coolness and indeed leaves no just opening for their rancour." W. H. Smith, equally pleased, informed the prime minister that Balfour's performance in the House of Commons "could not have been done better." And in December Salisbury himself boasted to Lady John Manners: "The Treasury Bench is infected with the spirit of Arthur Balfour and very much disposed to vigorous measures."[78] No higher praise could have been forthcoming.

[78] Cranbrook to Salisbury, 1 Sept. 1887; Smith to Salisbury, 14 Sept. 1887; Salisbury to Lady John Manners, 21 Dec. 1887, Salisbury MSS.

CHAPTER XI

Suppressed Ireland

COERCION under Balfour cut two ways. Not only Parnellism but Unionist policy as a whole was on trial before the electorate in both countries. The fortunes of the Conservative party, not to mention the fate of the Union, depended on the degree of resolute government actually achieved in Ireland. For this reason Home Rulers did their best to publicize and exaggerate Government setbacks while dismissing their own reverses as inventions of Balfour's propaganda machine. In essence, the land war was as much a contest of wits as of endurance; the stakes were high, and defeat for either side might mean the loss of countless votes in British constituencies. In view of the enormous outlay of energy and money on both sides, the fact that more Irish heads were not broken attests to the restraint generally shown by the RIC and the military. The Irish Question had not yet reached the stage when terrorism was met by retaliation in kind.

I. THE NATIONAL LEAGUE

Balfour's primary object in proclaiming the league an unlawful and dangerous association was to destroy the headquarters of both Parnell's political machine and the land agitation. What he failed to foresee was that any large-scale operation against the league would alienate some of the Government's most influential supporters. Many Liberal Unionists questioned the wisdom of suppressing the organization, and Chamberlain had already voted against the proclaiming order on the grounds that it would create new grievances and would also drive the agitators underground. Afraid of public opinion and convinced that suppression could never succeed in practice, these moderate Unionists preferred positive relief to negative repression.

The majority of ministers were unmoved by such arguments. For them the choice lay between prosecuting or condoning an

216

association that used the old methods of Ribbonmen, Whiteboys, and Fenians. For Balfour the league was the nerve center of the Home Rule movement; and not until the machinery that propelled Irish nationalism was dismantled would the country ever know stability. Moreover, suppression of the league might drive the agitators into rebellion. And Balfour infinitely preferred to deal with "disloyalty under the disguise of Fenianism" than with disloyalty concealed behind a "so-called constitutional agitation."[1] What he objected to vehemently was the air of legality that the nationalists affected. Like most of his party, Balfour deliberately referred to the National League as the Land League, being convinced that Davitt's association had changed only its name under Parnell.

Those Unionists who denied the constitutional ingredients of Parnellism mistakenly assumed that the methods, not to mention the objectives, of the new league had remained unchanged. Admittedly, on the local level the National League continued to reflect the ancient antagonisms between tenant and landlord; but on the national plane Home Rule had effectively supplanted the agrarian inspiration of the Land League. Considering the amount of information compiled by Dublin Castle on the manifold activities of the National League, ministers had no excuse for misinterpreting the significance of this organization as an integral part of the New Departure.[2] Balfour, at least, realized that he could expect no help in the coming struggle from the Irish landlords. Like Beach, the chief secretary soon discovered the nuisance value of this class; and to his uncle he complained: "What fools the Irish landlords are! They always cry out before they are hurt when the Government is concerned:—but when the National League is concerned, they fold their hands and do nothing."[3]

In September the chief secretary assembled the leading law officers and divisional magistrates in the Castle in order to work out the details of the orders proclaiming the league a dangerous association. County Clare came first on the list of branches marked

[1] Balfour to Ridgeway, 1 Dec. 1887, Add. ms 49826.

[2] See "The Working of the National League as depicted in the published Resolutions and Reports of Proceedings of its Local Branches," RIC, Crime Ordinary, SPO.

[3] Balfour to Salisbury, 2 Nov. 1889, Salisbury mss.

for suppression, while Cork and Kerry followed close behind. The orders signed by the Irish Privy Council on September 17 empowered the authorities to disperse all meetings of the branches named, to arrest the ringleaders, and to stop the publication of league notices in the papers that served these communities. Anticipating the proclaiming decree, numerous branches published resolutions of defiance. The Knocknagashel branch vowed to continue meetings in secret; and at Annaduff, league members boasted in public that they would "cheerfully accept the privations of the prison and its plank bed, sooner than be sworn under the inquisition clauses of the Jubilee Coercion Act." But Balfour was confident that the proclaiming orders would suffice "either to root out or to render impotent and contemptible any branch against whom they are employed." For the two hundred branches thus affected proscription meant that their meetings would be dispersed and their books and ledgers seized. Nevertheless, the machinery of justice moved slowly. A lull followed the proclamation; and the nationalists began to suspect that Balfour was only bluffing and dared not risk a setback now that public opinion was thoroughly aroused in both countries.[4]

Once again the Parnellites underestimated their opponent. Three weeks later the actual enforcement began; and the majority of suppressed branches ceased criminal operations within six months. The Castle owed this success to close cooperation between the police and the magistracy. Although proclaimed branches devised elaborate systems of secret communication, such tactics failed in the end against the vigilance of the Special Branch. Some suppressed associations continued to hold regular meetings, but the new order greatly reduced their potential to do harm. In November "slow progress" was reported. According to the Castle's sources, nationalist funds were dropping off, suppressed branches were meeting at irregular intervals, and their resolutions lacked the defiant tones of the past. In December Ridgeway reported that the league was "decidedly dissolving." Special Branch officers in the southwest exuded confidence: all that was needed to defeat the league were good lawyers and numerous

[4] See Balfour's memorandum on proclaiming the League, 21 Sept. 1887, *ibid.; Times,* 6-21 Sept. 1887. See also report of District Inspector Bourchier of Crime Department, Special Branch, 5 Sept. 1887, SPO.

convictions. By the summer of 1889 want of funds had become a serious problem because Irish patriots overseas were growing less enthusiastic about Parnellism, and Irish farmers at home were tired of donating funds to a losing cause. Most of the suppressed branches were dormant. Prosecution awaited members who strayed above ground; ineffectiveness plagued those who remained in hiding.[5]

Clare remained one of the weak points in the Castle's offensive. In 1890, when the league was rapidly disintegrating elsewhere, bands of moonlighters still roamed the county. Compared with the rest of the country, the law had made only small advance there. Too many partisan priests and too much poverty bound the people together in a fierce loyalty that often rendered the Crimes Act impotent; and Buller's successor in the southwest, Colonel Turner, appealed to the Castle for special powers in order to uproot agrarian crime.[6] In parts of Kerry, notably around Castleisland, progress was equally slow. Even Carnarvon had considered the use of emergency measures against the notorious outlaws of this region. Moonlighting there continued well into 1889, largely because witnesses who talked were rare. These districts, however, were the exceptions; and by 1889 the authorities had disarmed most of the active branches in the southwestern counties.[7]

As Balfour expected, the suppressed branches made strenuous efforts to convince the public that the Crimes Act had failed to impair their work. The boycotting resolutions of these branches continued to appear in the provincial press, much to the embarrassment of the administration. Upon investigation, however, some ninety per cent of these notices were found to be "absolutely bogus." The alleged meetings had never taken place: the branch president or secretary had merely asked the newspaper in question

[5] DICS, Bourchier, 12 Nov., 13 Dec. 1887, *ibid.*; Ridgeway to Balfour, 1 Dec. 1887, Add. MS 49808.

[6] Afterward Maj. Gen. Sir Alfred Edward Turner, 1842-1918; A.D.C. and private secretary to the Lord Lieutenant of Ireland 1882-1884, 1886; Special Commissioner of RIC in counties Cork, Clare, Kerry, Limerick 1886-1892; Inspector General Auxiliary Forces 1900-1904; K.C.B. 1902. See Turner's report, 4 June 1888, Crime Special, SPO.

[7] DICS, Shannon, 4 April 1888; DICS, Gambell, 12 May 1888; DICS, Jones, 22 Feb., 3 May 1889, *ibid.*

to publish the names of landgrabbers or other "obnoxious persons" on his own authority.[8]

One of the most successful techniques used by the Castle against the league was a system of official warnings. Wherever agrarian crime broke out anew, magistrates would threaten the branches concerned with immediate suppression if they continued to defy the law. In most cases one such warning sufficed. The branches usually modified their behavior, and the police were thus spared much work. Between 1889 and 1891 twelve out of thirteen branches responded successfully to this treatment. The warning method proved a cheap but effective way of disarming the league without resorting to the more laborious legal procedure.[9]

Another tactic used by the police against the league was known as "shadowing." Balfour borrowed this practice from the league agents who dogged the footsteps of men marked for boycotting and who denounced their victims at fairs and even in church. Dublin Castle adopted the same technique and used it successfully against prominent nationalists as well as against the boycotting rings that plagued cattle markets in the south. To facilitate shadowing, the Special Branch divided nationalist agitators into three categories, according to their importance. When in Ireland, all the members of Parnell's party, as well as the paid organizers of the Plan and the league, and the heads of secret societies, were shadowed.[10] The Parnellites, needless to say, did not welcome the attention of plainclothesmen. In Parliament they protested vigorously against police shadowing and thus gave Balfour a chance to mock their concern over a practice perfected by themselves. Shadowing was also used effectively against the boycott. Policemen disguised as cattle dealers broke up a number of boycotting rings at local fairs in counties Waterford, Tipperary, and Wexford. By shadowing the "shadowers of the League," the police collected sufficient evidence to convict the offenders, and thereby removed

---

[8] Out of twenty-seven meetings of suppressed branches in Kerry, reported in the nationalist press during February and March 1888, twenty-two were considered "bogus" by the authorities. See DICS, Shannon, 6 Feb., 4 April 1888, *ibid.*

[9] See Vol. 25 of the "Fenian Papers," *ibid.*

[10] See Appendix II.

many of the obstacles to the sale of livestock in these counties.[11]

After the split in the Irish party, the National League fought its last and most embittered campaign—not against the Castle, but against equally patriotic Irishmen. Although much embarrassed by want of funds, the league competed fiercely against its new rival, the National Federation, and for several months the outcome remained in the balance. But by Christmas, 1890, Special Branch officers were reporting the steady breakup of the league's branches, many of which simply changed their name and began working for the federation.[12] At Parnell's death the league had ceased to exist as an effective political force over large areas of the country. In addition, the Government's relief works exerted a calming influence upon the tenantry. What Balfour and the Crimes Act had begun in winning the land war Gladstone and the nonconformist conscience helped to finish.

The suppression of the National League also meant that a traditional outlet for agrarian discontent had been abruptly shut off. Combined with the events taking place inside the Irish party, the removal of this safety valve had serious implications for the future. For the moment the Government had won a decisive victory. If, however, coercion had severely damaged the machinery of the nationalist agitation, beneath the superstructure there still remained the motive power of Home Rule—the grievances of a "garrisoned" people. And no amount of summary justice could exorcize that.

II. PRISON ANTICS

The stories circulated by the nationalists about the excesses of coercion invariably found sympathetic audiences in England, where distinctions between fact and fiction were blurred by passion. In addition, the Liberals' determination to win the marginal vote in English constituencies on the issue of coercion meant that the

---

[11] For the activities of police shadowers and the county defence unions in fighting the boycott at fairs, see Ridgeway to Balfour, 18 Dec. 1888, Add. ms 49809; DICS, Bourchier, 7 May 1889; DICS, Crane, 5 Sept., 23 Oct., 1889, 9 April, 2 Sept., 1890, SPO.

[12] DICS, Crane, 5 March, 5 May 1891, *ibid.* For details of the league's reaction to the Parnellite split, see DICS, Crane, 5 Jan., 2 Feb., 4 July, 5 Aug., 5 Sept. 1891, *ibid.*

country was soon deluged with tales of barbarous acts committed by the Irish constabulary and prison warders. Balfour's prison rules, in particular, made effective propaganda for the Home Rule press. What the chief secretary considered an exemplary punishment, the nationalists called retributive. The plank bed and hard labor were intended, they charged, to eliminate the prisoner as well as agrarian crime. Balfour, on the other hand, always insisted with sublime assurance that prison rules in Ireland were more lenient than those in England. More to the point, he worried about the propaganda value of prison conditions and confessed to his uncle in the autumn of 1887 that he expected some "prison scandals" in the winter. "The smallest failure," he wrote, "would be made the most of and I am afraid the Prison Board is even more incompetent than the rest of the Irish Departments."[13]

Such fears were not misplaced. The classification of criminals under the Crimes Act excited the fiercest controversy during these years. Balfour saw no reason why lawbreakers who happened to be men of education or position should be treated any better than the "humbler classes of the community"; and he published a letter to this effect in the *Times* in order to silence further criticism:

"An offence does not become political because it is committed by a politician; and neither in law nor in reason is there the slightest ground for punishing with greater severity the man who resists the officers of the law and pours boiling water on the police than the yet more guilty individual who incites the people to commit these offences."[14]

Moreover, as he answered one critic of his policy, Irish prisons offered far more sanitary conditions than did the slums of Dublin or the towns and villages of the southwest. Only public opinion and the stubbornness of men like William O'Brien prevented him from carrying all his ideas on the subject into effect.

What embarrassed the administration most during these years was the chronic sickness of the leading nationalists. Balfour realized that the death of any prisoner would be disastrous, and he often complained in private about the existence of "some mys-

[13] Balfour to Salisbury, 21 Sept. 1887, Salisbury MSS.
[14] Balfour to B. Armitage, *Times*, 26 Nov. 1887.

terious connection between diseased lungs and Irish patriotism."[15] Bad health was, indeed, as much a feature of Parnell and his party as the Home Rule pledge. Both Parnell and O'Brien had delicate constitutions and suffered from chronic physical disorders. Dillon was consumptive, with a long family history of tuberculosis.[16] Moreover, the grueling pace set by the promoters of the Plan during these years would have drained the reserves of the strongest man, especially in a country where meetings were not called off owing to inclement weather.

Of the many prison crises that plagued the administration, the saga of John Mandeville was perhaps the most dramatic and damaging in its effects. Mandeville, a relatively prosperous tenant farmer on the Kingston estate at Mitchelstown, had earned the Castle's attention by promoting the Plan of Campaign in the distinguished company of William O'Brien. Both men had received summons under the Crimes Act for their activities, and the day set for their trial had ended in the Mitchelstown massacre. The two were subsequently tried and found guilty of using seditious language. O'Brien received a three months' sentence and Mandeville two. From the Cork county jail they were secretly transferred in November to Tullamore, where the governor of the prison had a reputation for enforcing the rules without flinching. Having agreed beforehand to resist all attempts to deprive them of their status as political prisoners, they refused to wear prison uniforms, to clean out their cells, and to associate with common criminals. Mandeville's protests resulted in the use of force. Five warders were required to strip off his clothes, and he spent an entire day wrapped only in a blanket before succumbing to the insult of a uniform. For his persistent defiance of the rules Mandeville was placed in solitary confinement, with its plank bed and diet of bread and water, and he was denied all exercise. Although he complained of a bad throat and diarrhea, the prison doctor, named

[15] "It is a singular piece of of ill-luck that so many of these so-called Irish patriots have such very bad constitutions. Possibly there may be some physiological connection between criminal agitation and weak lungs"; Balfour to Ridgeway, 30 Aug. 1888, Add. MS 49827.

[16] Dillon also suffered from dyspepsia or what was known at the time as "intestinal catarrh"; Balfour to Salisbury, 17 Sept. 1888, Salisbury MSS. See also C. C. O'Brien, *Parnell and His Party*, p. 211 n. 2.

Ridley, pronounced him physically fit to bear such treatment. Mandeville was released on Christmas eve. Seven months later, on July 8, 1888, he died of a throat infection, or what was called a "diffused septic inflammation."[17]

The Home Rule party lost no time in holding Mandeville up as a martyr of Balfour's coercion. Questions about Mandeville were asked in the House of Commons; the nationalist press accused the prison officials of criminal negligence, if not murder; and the "victim" was given a hero's funeral attended by a crowd of six thousand. The nationalists charged that this "courageous" man had died of an infection contracted during his ordeal in Tullamore. What better proof could there be, they asked, that Balfour really did intend to exterminate his opponents one by one in Irish prisons. The chief secretary treated all these accusations with contempt. Mandeville, he insisted, had died of a throat infection that had no connection whatsoever with his incarceration. And the *Times* supported this stand by ridiculing the notion that the Government should be held responsible because a prisoner "justly convicted of a grave offence" might suffer in health during his confinement.

On July 17 the formal inquest on Mandeville's death began at Mitchelstown. Three days later the case won even greater scandal value when it was announced that Dr. Ridley had committed suicide with a razor. Although a number of personal reasons drove the Tullamore doctor to this desperate act, the public naturally interpreted it as a clear admission of guilt.[18] Meanwhile, the coroner's inquiry exposed in lurid detail all the privations under which Mandeville had suffered while in jail. When Dr. Barr, the medical consultant for the Irish Prisons Board who had seen Mandeville on several occasions in Tullamore,

[17] *Times*, 10-18 July 1888; *Freeman's Journal*, 9-31 July 1888. See also S. Hallifax, *John Mandeville, Martyr*, London, 1888. Balfour believed that Mandeville's letters in this pamphlet were forgeries.

[18] Of Ridley's suicide in a Fermoy hotel, Ridgeway wrote: "I hear that he was in great pecuniary trouble—partly if not chiefly owing to his having lost his Tullamore private practice. Yet I distinctly told his father that the question of compensation would be considered if he proved his assertions: also his throat . . . had become bad and an operation was probable"; Ridgeway to Balfour, 23 July 1888, Add. MS 49808.

called the evidence of the latter's wife and personal doctors entirely false, there was no longer any doubt in the jury's mind that the Government were trying to whitewash the whole affair. The verdict was unanimous that Mandeville had died from the effects of his "brutal and unjustifiable" treatment in jail.

In Parliament Balfour dismissed the verdict as partisan; and in private he complained about the perjury of witnesses and the "notoriously corrupt" jurors at the inquest. The time had come, he felt, "to expose the system of organized mendacity by which politics are at present being carried on." Earlier he had suggested to Ridgeway that criminal proceedings be brought against a Home Rule newspaper, the *Star*, for calling Mandeville's death murder. A libel action in England, he believed, would at least bring out the "facts" in the case for the benefit of the British public. Moreover, as he explained, " . . . we cannot hope that everybody sent to an Irish prison will prove immortal; and if this kind of agitation is to be repeated every time that some ex-prisoner goes the way of all flesh, it may have a bad effect; whereas if we can show the first time the howl is raised how utterly unreasonable it is . . . it may save us trouble in the future." Such was his intention. But when Balfour broached the idea to some of his colleagues, he received a cool response, and the criminal action against the *Star* was dropped. As usual the cabinet behaved with extreme discretion when it came to newspaper prosecutions; and the Government lost the opportunity to present their version of the Mandeville affair in an English court of law.[19]

At the end of September Balfour told an audience in Glasgow that the officials in Tullamore jail were in no way to blame for Mandeville's demise. The infection that killed him, he contended, had set in long after his release. Several weeks later he accused the Opposition leaders of creating a "sham tragedy" out of the case. Many moderates in his own party were disappointed, and Home Rulers were infuriated because Balfour never expressed his regret over the death. Ridgeway erred when he assured his chief that thanks to the Glasgow speech Mandeville was "dead and

[19] Balfour to Ridgeway, 13, 28 July 1888; Ridgeway to Balfour, 27, 29 July 1888, *ibid.*, 49827, 49808.

buried at last."[20] The truth was that nationalist efforts to turn his death into a "minor Mitchelstown" had a sobering effect upon both the Castle and the cabinet, and eventually bore fruit in the commission appointed to investigate prison conditions. There was no doubt that prison rigors had gravely weakened Mandeville's powers of resistance to infection; and the Castle could not afford another such calamity.

On the other hand, neither Balfour nor Ridgeway intended to let considerations of health impair the working of the Crimes Act. They ordered prison officials to show no leniency except in cases where a prisoner's health "absolutely required" special treatment. In order to prevent any fatalities in prison, Balfour assigned an English doctor to examine the more prominent inmates. Dillon's frail physique gave rise to medical bulletins twice a week, and the slightest changes in weight were recorded with scrupulous care. Balfour himself admitted that any breakdown in Dillon's health would amount to "almost a national calamity."[21] Eventually the administration became so sensitive to prison scandals that many Crimes Act prisoners managed by systematic malingering to spend most of their time in prison hospital. After 1889 some were classified as first-class misdemeanants and thus received certain privileges of dress and of prison routine. Those who had the easiest time in jail were priests and members of Parliament. According to the Castle's records, some sixty per cent of the offenders in these two categories enjoyed "special indulgences" while behind bars.[22]

There were moments when the Irish administration wondered whether it would not have been wiser to keep the leading Parnellites out of jail. William O'Brien agitated against coercion almost as effectively inside prison as outside. In November, 1887, he amused the Unionist world by refusing to wear prison underclothes; and he made a show of spurning the extra food prescribed by the prison doctor at Tullamore while eating sandwiches that

[20] "I have lately been feeling vindictive, but after reading your remarks regarding O'Brien and Gladstone, I felt like a thirsty man who has had a good drink"; Ridgeway to Balfour, 10 Oct. 1888, *ibid.*, 49809.

[21] Balfour to Ridgeway, 28 June, 21 Aug. 1888, *ibid.*, 49827.

[22] Balfour to Ridgeway, 11, 23 Feb. 1889, *ibid.*

had been smuggled into his cell.[23] In Parliament the Parnellites accused the administration of torturing both O'Brien and Mandeville; and Balfour found himself in the awkward position of having to defend the ineptitude of his subordinates. The full story could be revealed only to his uncle:

"The whole Prison episode, though a storm in a tea cup, is amusingly characteristic of Irish administration. The Prison doctor depends largely on his independent practice. The Magistrate who has been chiefly concerned in misusing the visitatorial powers, is also a Doctor, and the prison doctor's professional rival. So that he has enjoyed the double luxury of injuring his competitor, and annoying the Gov't by the same set of proceedings. He should I think be kicked out of the Magistracy. But whether Ashbourne will rise to the occasion I do not know: I admit there are difficulties. Meanwhile the Prison Officials are frightened out of their wits: the Prison Board, who ought to manage the whole thing without coming to me, are so much terrified at the idea of taking the smallest responsibility that at last I had to write all the telegrams to the Governor myself! I have got over an English Doctor to protect the Irish Officials in the future: and to stop any illegitimate attempt to shorten O'Brien's term on the grounds of health. This step I took against the strongly expressed advice of every one of my Irish advisers: & it may fail. But I think I was bound to try it.—I fear O'Brien is very delicate."[24]

O'Brien's prison sojourn, however, ended on an ignoble note. In September, 1889, he decided to protest his confinement by an act of voluntary constipation. The ordeal lasted nine days, while the prison doctor tried in vain to conceal the necessary pills in his food. Balfour regarded O'Brien's gesture of defiance with sardonic

[23] Ridgeway blamed the suicide of Dr. Ridley directly on O'Brien, and described O'Brien as "the meanest and most malignant reptile crawling" because he had victimized the prison doctor. Ridgeway to Balfour, 29 Sept. 1888, *ibid.*, 49808. During his second term in prison O'Brien refused to eat mutton chops as part of his special diet, and Ridgeway wrote: ". . . I fancy that in Galway prison, where there is no one to advertise his abstinence (or perhaps to feed him with sandwiches), his appetite will overcome his principles"; Ridgeway to Balfour, 3 Sept. 1889, *ibid.*, 49810.

[24] Balfour to Salisbury, 27 Nov. 1887, Salisbury MSS.

amusement; Ridgeway felt nothing but disgust. The Castle received daily bulletins on the case from the Prisons Board and finally in desperation sent for a consultant physician. Fortunately for the frayed nerves of the officials concerned, the martyrdom ended on the tenth day; and Ridgeway, obviously much relieved, sent this jubilant message to Balfour: "William O'Brien has had a motion!! This last heroic act of the self-sacrificing martyr has been telegraphed all over the world and has sent a thrill of joy into every Irish heart—checked alas! by the reflection that you will not be hung. Pye's [the consultant physician] was the hand that administered the pill to Ireland's darling."[25]

Fair play, as Balfour sadly admitted, was not the nationalists' strongpoint.[26]

If Dillon's behavior in gaol was less spectacular, his health caused greater alarm. Prison officials treated him as an "honored guest"; and Chamberlain, upset by an article in the *Freeman's Journal* about Dillon's emaciation, asked the chief secretary to show some leniency in his case. In 1888 the doctors recommended Dillon's early release before the damp of winter affected his health. Reluctantly Balfour consented; and Salisbury approved the decision on the grounds that Dillon would be "far more formidable dead than alive." The same stricture applied in varying degrees to all the nationalists, whether members of Parliament or not; and so long as the Crimes Act was in force, the Government exposed themselves to charges of maltreatment in prison.[27]

The number of Home Rule sympathizers employed in Irish prisons meant that the administration could never afford to let up on their vigilance. The governor of Richmond jail, for instance, tried to convert the premises into a hotel for prominent nationalists; and when the authorities discovered this fact and transferred Dillon to Tullamore prison, the visiting prison justices there approved unlimited visitors, and he was offered the freedom of the city. At times Ridgeway despaired of ever finding a loyal prison official in Ireland: "The fact is that *no one* here is sound on that

[25] Ridgeway to Balfour, 5 Sept. 1889, Add. MS 49810.

[26] "It is curious how few of these fellows seem able to fight like gentlemen"; Balfour to Ridgeway, 4 Sept. 1889, *ibid.*, 49828.

[27] Balfour to Ridgeway, 28 July 1888; Ridgeway to Balfour, 24 Aug. 1888, *ibid.*, 49827, 49808; Salisbury to Balfour, 20 Sept. 1888, Salisbury MSS.

subject—there is such a variety of underground influence at work."[28]

Under Balfour's regime Englishmen proved just as adept as the Parnellites at performing stunts in prison. Conybeare, the indefatigable member for Cornwall, achieved further notoriety during his prison term by alleging that he had become infested with crab lice. At the same time he refused to undergo medical examination. When Ridgeway learned that the prison officials suspected Conybeare of having imported the "parasites" into his cell in a pill box, he described the affair as the "last sordid detail of the Irish administration," and vented his feelings to Balfour: "Never have we had such a mean, dirty, little cur in our prisons before." The Conybeare case gained widespread publicity, and the Parnellites besieged the chief secretary in the House with questions about prison hygiene. Balfour persistently denied the charges of inadequate sanitation; while Ridgeway complained in bitter tones: "Really, between O'Brien and Conybeare the Irish administration is becoming unfit for gentlemen to engage in. . . . What scoundrels—and dirty scoundrels—these fellows are!"[29]

After Mandeville's death, prison policy was increasingly dictated by expediency. Ridgeway, for example, was prepared to assuage public opinion by relaxing the rules about prison uniforms and hair clipping. Such concessions, he believed, would exhaust the "sentimental grievances" of the British public. But the plank bed, the bread and water diet, and other "désagréments" ought to be retained and used whenever the need arose. In the end it was public opinion, thoroughly aroused by the ordeals of Mandeville, Dillon, O'Brien, and other prisoners, that forced the administration to adopt more lenient measures. Balfour himself continued to deny in speech and writing that there was any injustice involved in treating Crimes Act prisoners like common criminals.[30]

In February, 1889, fresh stories of prison mistreatment reached the press. A Parnellite member who refused to wear prison garb had been forcibly undressed, his moustache and hair had been clipped, and he had spent the next few days virtually naked on

[28] Ridgeway to Balfour, 3, 6 Dec. 1887, Add. MS 49808.

[29] Ridgeway to Balfour, 3, 20 Sept. 1889, *ibid.*, 49810.

[30] Ridgeway to Balfour, 25 Feb., 2, 6, 7, 10, 16 March 1889, *ibid.*, 49809.

a plank bed.[31] Once again overzealous officials had put the Government in an awkward position. Ridgeway immediately rebuked the offending warders; but the damage had already been done. Challenged in Parliament by Parnell and Liberal spokesmen, Balfour coolly explained that all prisoners were subject to the same regulations, and that the prisoner in question deserved no sympathy because a clean set of prison clothes had been provided. Crimes Act offenders, he insisted, received far more "medical" privileges than any other category of prisoner in Ireland. Such excuses did not impress the Home Rule party, and Morley, in a speech bristling with indignation, indicted the whole range of Unionist policy in Ireland.[32]

Early in March Chamberlain wrote to Balfour protesting what he called the "convict treatment" of Crimes Act prisoners. This note came on the heels of Pigott's exposure in the Special Commission; and popular feeling against the Government was reaching dangerous proportions. Although the chief secretary had no use for "weak-kneed Unionists" who ran to Chamberlain with their complaints, he did agree to certain concessions pertaining to uniforms and hair cutting. Like Ridgeway, he was willing to leave the enforcement of such regulations to the individual judgment of the prison governors. But he steadfastly refused to segregate political prisoners from the other inmates of Irish jails, and he told his colleagues quite bluntly that he was making these concessions not from an Irish but from an English point of view, and as a member of the Government rather than as chief secretary.[33]

The upshot of much embittered debate on the subject was the appointment of a sworn inquiry into Irish prison conditions. The investigation was hampered throughout by the obfuscation of prison officials. Because of a careful selection of test cases by Dublin Castle the commission unearthed no new scandals, and as a result no sweeping reforms ensued. Nevertheless, the inquiry

[31] The prisoner was J. L. Carew, M.P. for Kildare N., who had been sentenced to four months without hard labor for using intimidating language. He was released on grounds of bad health in May 1889.

[32] *Hansard*, 3d series, Vol. 333, pp. 212-17, 270-319.

[33] See Balfour to Ridgeway, 4, 8, 9, 12 March 1889, Add. MS 49827; Salisbury to Queen Victoria, 9 March 1889, Salisbury MSS.

served to remind the Irish executive that closer supervision of the Prisons Board was essential in order to reduce the chances of further blunders. In their report the prison commissioners recommended greater leniency as well as consistency in the application of rules about dress and personal hygiene; and the somewhat chastened officials in the Castle instructed prison governors and warders to use greater discretion in handling Crimes Act prisoners.[34] The consideration, amounting at times to deference, shown to Dillon and O'Brien by police and prison officials upon their arrest following the Boulogne negotiations illustrates the degree to which the rules had been relaxed by 1891. No doubt the prison antics of the Parnellites had served their purpose in spite of Buller's contention that "the Irish will not follow long, leaders who cry like children in prison, or who play at hide and seek to escape penalties which they have declared they will have. . . . "[35] Needless to say, none of the Parnellites jailed under the Crimes Act ever suffered as much, let alone as silently, as had Michael Davitt during his long confinement in Dartmoor in the previous decade. But then times had changed, and with them the tactics of effective agitation.

III. PRIEST PROSECUTIONS

One of the most elusive targets of the Crimes Act was the parish priest, that ubiquitous figure in Irish life and fiction. In Ireland, where the clergy had first reached political maturity under the tutelage of O'Connell, no administration could afford to neglect the servants of the Catholic Church without exposing itself to grave dangers. The working alliance between Parnellism and the Irish hierarchy left the priesthood, with but a few exceptions, a wide field of endeavor in secular matters. For the great majority of parish priests, who neither could nor would draw a line of distinction between secular and spiritual matters, the land war provided an ideal opportunity to exert their authority in a worthy cause. In many districts the main prop of the agitation was the resident priest or canon: wherever the league

[34] Lord Aberdare presided over this commission. See Report of the Committee of Inquiry as to the Rules concerning the Wearing of Prison Dress etc., in *HC 1889*, Vol. 61.

[35] Buller to Ridgeway, 15 Nov. 1887, Ridgeway MSS.

was most active or the Plan of Campaign most deeply entrenched, a priest often commanded the local garrison of nationalists. Traditionally jealous of any outside meddling in the affairs of his parish, the priest more often than not believed that Home Rule would end both Protestant influence and landlordism in the country. His background—most of the priesthood were recruited from the tenant class, and almost all had been educated in Irish seminaries—made him an integral part of the community as well as its spiritual leader. He understood his parishioners, knew their histories, their lands, and their problems only too well; and nothing was more natural than his concern when they suffered at the hands of land agents, evicting parties, or Dublin Castle.

Distinguished by a hearty appetite for polemics of any kind, the clergy were ideally equipped to participate in the land war because their frock gave them relative immunity from the law (or so they thought), and because they had an intimate knowledge of their parishioners' affairs. Neither the league nor the Plan could ever have attained its hold on the population without the clergy's active support. The ties that bound the tenantry to their sacerdotal leaders were numerous and inviolable. There were Irishmen who dared to denounce the league, even at the risk of being boycotted; but to defy the parish priest's command was another matter altogether. In a country where many inhabitants believed that disobeying their priest would bring not only excommunication but death to their livestock and ruin to their crops, clerical influence was not to be treated lightly. True, many of the league's branches were wholly free of priestly domination; and those priests or canons who repeatedly challenged the Crimes Act formed only a small minority of the whole. But as one district inspector reported in 1891, the parish priest was " . . . the most potent element in Irish politics, when the influence of the moonlighter and the boycotter has been removed or reduced to a minimum by firm government."[36]

In view of their commitment to the land war, Balfour felt no compunction about prosecuting priests who condoned or incited agrarian outrage. To achieve this end, however, he was forced to rely upon the Irish hierarchy and the Vatican as well as the Crimes Act, because the Law Room showed the utmost reluctance

[36] DICS, Crane, 30 Oct. 1891, SPO.

to prosecute members of the clergy. By November, 1887, no priest had been tried under the Crimes Act, and Irish Unionists were growing impatient. Ridgeway worried lest the Government be accused of cowardice for ignoring clerical offenders. The prosecution of the "worst" priests, he informed his chief, was a matter of "urgent necessity."[37] As a result, the Law Room received a strongly worded note from Balfour directing them to proceed against any priests who defied the law.

Balfour fully realized that priest prosecutions were risky: too many legal actions of this type might well drive the hierarchy to encourage open resistance to the Crimes Act. After consulting his uncle, he decided that one or two test prosecutions of militant priests could do no harm and would serve to gauge the reaction of the church leaders. But there was another string to his bow. To cope with less severe clerical offenses Balfour recommended that the local bishop be notified, in the hope that an episcopal reprimand would chasten the wayward priest. Balfour was not blind to the disadvantages of appealing to the hierarchy: " . . . 1) you cannot be quite sure where a correspondence will land you. 2) it may be interpreted as indicating that we are *afraid* to prosecute priests." But he argued that notification "puts the bishop very much in the wrong if he does nothing . . . it shows also that we desire no insult to the Roman Catholic Church:—and it might be appreciated at *Rome*."[38] Not every cabinet minister approved this procedure. Lord Salisbury had to convince a sceptical W. H. Smith that a mixture of hierarchical warning and prosecution would achieve the best results against offending priests. Notifying the bishop, if not "theoretically correct," at least strengthened the Government's case in the eyes of the Holy See. And to clinch his argument, he added that it also provided a better excuse for "putting the priest on a plank bed" if he continued to defy the law.[39]

The activities of some priests in Clare, Kerry, Donegal, and

[37] Ridgeway to Balfour, 8 Nov. 1887, Add. ms 49808.

[38] Balfour to Ridgeway, 9 Nov. 1887, *ibid.*, 49826. According to Balfour, the Protestants whom he met in Dublin were far more afraid of prosecuting priests than were Catholic loyalists. See also Balfour to Salisbury, 22, 28 Oct., 27 Nov. 1887, Salisbury mss.

[39] Salisbury to Smith, 24, 30 Oct. 1887; Smith to Salisbury, n.d. Oct. 1887, *ibid.*

elsewhere made such an excuse unnecessary. These clerical recruits to the Plan and the league were not cowed by threats of prosecution, and the faintheartedness of the Law Room only increased their zeal, to the profound annoyance of Ridgeway. Those priests who behaved like "thorough scoundrels" deserved, in his opinion, all the punishment the Crimes Act could inflict. Unfortunately, his legal advisers stood in the way. "Indeed I think," he wrote to Balfour, "that *la haute politique* obtains a great deal too much attention in the Law Room and that until you change the policy laid down as regards priests, we need not allow it in this instance to hamper us." Balfour, on the other hand, worried lest an excessive number of priest prosecutions "seal the existing breach between the clerical and the Fenian element." But it was an unavoidable risk; and, as it turned out, his fears proved groundless.[40]

A more distinguished candidate for the Crimes Act than any parish priest was Archbishop Croke of Cashel, who ranked high on Balfour's list of desirable prosecutions. Whenever Croke made a speech or wrote an open letter to the press, he pronounced his contempt for the Castle in unmistakable terms. Several times the cabinet considered taking legal action against him, but their fear of public opinion in England and of the Vatican's reaction —not to mention the chronic pessimism of the Law Room—saved the Archbishop from having to stand trial. In February, 1887, and again in January, 1889, when Croke defied the Papal Rescript forbidding clerical participation in the Plan of Campaign, the cabinet discussed and then retreated from his prosecution. On the latter occasion Balfour wrote to his uncle: "The best thing would be that Rome should act decisively. Croke's action is a direct defiance to the Pope: for the tenants had joined the Plan, and the Archbishop condemns, in language verging on impiety, the only method by which the Plan can be met. In the event of Rome's declining to act or postponing action, ought we to remain quiescent? We shall have a good many evictions soon on 'Campaign' estates: it is with a view to these no doubt that Croke has written this letter."[41] Croke, who sensed the Govern-

[40] Ridgeway to Balfour, 16 April, 28 June, Add. MS 49808; Balfour to Salisbury, 27 Nov. 1887, Salisbury MSS.

[41] Balfour to Salisbury, 15, 18 Jan. 1889, *ibid.*

ment's quandary, continued to flaunt his nationalist sympathies, supremely confident that he would never see the inside of a court room. And he was right.

Catholic priests and prelates were not the only ecclesiastics to misbehave in Ireland. In November, 1887, Ridgeway reported somewhat wryly to his chief: "The Lord has delivered into our hands a Mr. Ellis, a Yorkshire Parson, who has made a very violent speech in Clare. I think it will be politic to prosecute a Parson and a Priest simultaneously. They will of course go to the same prison."[42] But the symmetry of the plan was spoiled because the parson never went to jail: the law officers decided to abandon the case on the grounds of insufficient evidence. By arresting Ellis, the administration had, nevertheless, given warning to those Protestant divines who thought themselves above the law. Not all of them took the hint. The Reverend Richard Hallowes of Arklow earned the distinction of being the most troublesome Protestant minister in the country. A devout Unionist and a fanatic anti-Catholic, Hallowes became an *agent provocateur* by holding large rallies in the Catholic quarter of the town, where he delivered sermons of a fire and brimstone order at the expense of nationalism and Rome. The result was usually a riot between the local Catholics and his own congregation. Hallowes also insisted upon halting his processions outside the houses of the parish priest and his curate while he vilified both men. When the case was brought to his attention, Balfour recommended prosecution either for obstructing traffic in a thoroughfare or for unlawful assembly. But he suspected that the trial would offend a good many Irish loyalists: "All rational Protestant opinion is no doubt against Hallowes; all Protestant opinion, however, is not rational." In January, 1891, Hallowes was tried by the petty sessions court of the district and found guilty of traffic obstruction. Being a good Christian, he chose prison instead of the payment of a one pound fine. After his discharge he promptly resumed his open-air preaching; and Balfour had to send him a long, admonitory letter explaining the magistrate's position and warning him against further defiance of the law. Eventually, Hallowes began to mend his ways. But as Balfour knew, similar offenses might break out elsewhere; and he expressed the irony

[42] Ridgeway to Balfour, 27, 29 Nov. 1887, Add. MS 49808.

of the situation to Ridgeway, when he wrote: "If the Roman Catholics knew their business, they would set to work preaching in the Orange quarters of Belfast. Under such circumstances the Orangemen would probably take a very different view of freedom of speech."[43]

Over a period of three years some twenty-three priests were prosecuted under the Crimes Act. Although only a minority of these found their way to prison, the passions aroused by these proceedings, not only in Ireland but among Catholics the world over, placed the Government in an awkward position. Irishmen in America and elsewhere earnestly believed that English ministers were trying to revive the religious persecutions of the past; and the series of priest prosecutions severely strained the already delicate relations between the Government and the Vatican. In spite of his impersonal administration of the Crimes Act, Balfour never succeeded in taming the clergy. As in the case of the Parnellites, coercion only hardened the resolve of its victims; and the militant core of the Irish priesthood, men like Canon Keller of Youghal, Father M'Fadden of Gweedore, Father Ryan of Kilballyowen, Canon Maher of Luggacurren, Father Humphreys of Tipperary, and Father White, the hero of all Clare—to name but a few—continued to defy the criminal, as well as canon, law, whenever their consciences so dictated.

[43] Balfour to Ashbourne, 4, 24 Feb. 1891; Balfour to Ridgeway, 24 Feb., 2 April 1891; Balfour to Hallowes, 7 Feb. 1891. Balfour described Hallowes as "a mad attorney turned parson—a horrible combination"; *ibid.*, 49829.

CHAPTER XII

Balfour and the Plan of Campaign

As THE Parnellites devoutly hoped, the Plan of Campaign caused the administration more anxiety and frustration during these years than any other form of agitation. Much of the difficulty stemmed from the judiciary's reluctance to prosecute tenants for combining together in order to reduce unfair rents. Balfour, however, saw nothing ambiguous about the Plan. O'Brien, Dillon, and company, he maintained, had invented a "grossly illegal conspiracy" in order to strengthen the tenants' bargaining position at a heavy cost to the landlords. Not only did he expect the law courts to prosecute the Plan as a criminal conspiracy, but he insisted that the Irish landlords were morally obligated to form a countercombination in order to protect their interests as a class. Only through such cooperation could social anarchy be avoided. From the outset Balfour thus looked to the landlords *N B .* to bear half the burden in the struggle against the Plan. If this class proved unwilling to combine for the purpose of self-protection, then it would have to suffer the consequences.[1]

While the Home Rule party blamed the Plan on the rejection of the Tenants' Relief Bill in 1886, Balfour always contended that this antirent conspiracy was merely another step in the "Irish revolutionary movement," which had been launched in 1879. The Tenants' Relief Bill was a convenient "stalking-horse" for the Plan, and those tenants who joined were not acting spontaneously: they had been either bribed or terrorized. While Balfour was willing to admit the existence of "some stupid, some criminal, and many injudicious" landlords in Ireland, he had no sympathy for solvent tenants who refused to pay their rents. "If I were an Irish landlord," he declared in Parliament, "I would beg my bread before I gave in to the Plan of Campaign."[2]

[1] Balfour to J. Bullough, 24 June 1889, Add. MS 49828.
[2] *Hansard*, 3d series, Vol. 349, pp. 1485-96.

The success of the Plan depended on the hostile relations that prevailed between owner and occupier on many estates. Fear, ignorance, or hatred led the tenantry to adopt the Plan, and threats of intimidation often kept them in a cooperative mood. Many tenants were promised generous compensation for eviction, and they could hardly be blamed for finding the prospect of pay without work or responsibility attractive. Not all tenants, however, welcomed the Plan. Some wished to remain on good terms with their landlord, others distrusted the Plan's trustees, and many resented agitation for its own sake.[3]

Parnell himself had mixed feelings about the Plan. Caught in the conflict between Irish and Liberal opinion about the importance of the land question, he resorted to equivocation. He was shrewd enough to realize that any overt hostility to the Plan on his part would endanger the effectiveness of the Home Rule movement, and for this reason, among other personal ones, he approved the Plan in principle while eschewing any direct role in its operation. When the sudden success of the Plan began to make the Liberal leaders uneasy, Parnell was placed in an awkward position. First he asked William O'Brien to limit its scope, and then, in a speech at the Eighty Club in London, he expressed regret that this form of combination had alienated public opinion in England. By stressing his own role in trying to curb the Plan, he managed to chastise both the agrarian and clerical sections of the New Departure while affirming the paramountcy of Home Rule.[4] The Eighty Club address naturally caused much resentment among the Plan's promoters; but in Dublin Castle it had the opposite effect, for Ridgeway wrote elatedly to Balfour that Parnell's speech had been "another blow at the P. of C." According to the under secretary, the final defeat of the Plan was not far distant. Only time would prove him wrong.[5]

[3] John Dillon, testifying in 1893 before the Evicted Tenants Commission, declared that the Plan had operated on 116 estates of which sixty had given in to the tenants' demands without a struggle. On the remaining fifty-six estates, the landlords in twenty-four cases had eventually submitted to the Plan; fifteen had held out until the tenants had abandoned the Plan; and seventeen estates were still unsettled in 1893. See Evicted Tenants Commission Report in *HC 1893-1894,* Vol. 31.

[4] For this account of Parnell's motives I am indebted to C. C. O'Brien, *Parnell and His Party,* pp. 202-06, 218-20.

[5] Ridgeway to Balfour, 10 May 1888, Add. MS 49808. For further de-

Dillon, O'Brien, and the other organizers of the Plan chose their victims with care. They looked for those estates where the worst relations between landlord and tenant prevailed and where the owner's resources were not large enough to sustain a long siege. The Plan had far less chance of success against a wealthy landlord; and as Balfour observed, the nationalists invariably selected encumbered estates in the hope that the landlord's creditors would force him to surrender to the Plan. By the autumn of 1887 many landlords were granting abatements at the mere mention of the Plan, and Balfour knew that only prompt action could prevent surrender all along the line. Since any direct intervention by the administration was bound to raise a hue and cry in both countries, Balfour had no choice but to adopt clandestine methods. The great majority of landlords, it was clear, either would not or could not save themselves.

I. THE TEST ESTATES

It was ironic that Balfour should arrive at some of Beach's conclusions about the Irish landlord. He once described them as "maddening clients," and Ridgeway exclaimed in exasperation: "What wonderful people these Irish landlords are! Do not they, as a class, deserve annihilation?"[6] When a landlord in county Galway not only surrendered to the Plan but refunded the cost of maintaining his evicted tenants, Balfour exploded in a letter to his uncle: "It is utterly useless to try and help the Irish landlords by trifling grants from the Treasury—when they show themselves so utterly incapable of the simplest combination to be destroyed piecemeal in this fashion." But it was his job to defeat the Plan, and he was determined to help those landlords against whom the Plan had been launched "without the shadow of an excuse."[7]

At first Balfour considered the possibility of proclaiming the Plan a dangerous association so as to enable magistrates to prose-

---

tails of "Balfourian Coercion" written by a Home Ruler, see Lord Eversley, *Gladstone and Ireland*, London, 1912, pp. 337-51.

[6] Ridgeway to Balfour, 1 Oct. 1890, Add. MS 49811; Balfour to Salisbury, 29 Feb. 1888, Salisbury MSS.

[7] The landlord was Sir Henry Burke, 5th Bart., who owned some 25,000 acres around Woodford. Balfour to Ridgeway, 13 March 1888, Add. MS 49826.

cute its members with ease. But public opinion and other practical difficulties ruled out this solution and forced him instead to adopt a more laborious procedure. Wherever evidence could be found, the Plan's organizers were arrested and sent to trial for conspiracy under the Crimes Act. By such means he hoped to remove the men responsible for the agitation. These prosecutions, however, achieved only limited success. The Plan's agents were elusive and the tenants proved capable of carrying on the scheme by themselves. A bolder and more imaginative course was required.

Balfour soon discovered a viable alternative. Since the Government could not hope to fight the Plan everywhere, he decided to choose some half-dozen estates where the landlords had been "reasonable" about abatements in the past and where the Plan was deeply entrenched. On these so-called "test estates" the Castle would commit all its resources to defeat the combination.[8] Balfour was confident that the landlords, with the Government's help, could win in every case. Just how far the administration went to assist the owners of the test estates directly is not known. But what is certain is that the resources of the leading landlords' associations were concentrated and applied to the estates in question. Not only the Irish Defence Union and the Property Defence Association, but also the Land Corporation, came to the rescue of the hard-pressed landlords. The latter group was the inspiration of a wealthy landowner, Arthur MacMorrough Kavanagh, M.P.,[9] and its chief function was to protect "landgrabbers" from intimidation and to help in the cultivation of evicted holdings. On all the test estates such forms of aid were essential in order to

[8] The test estates belonged to Lord Lansdowne at Luggacurren, Queen's co.; George Brooke at Coolgreaney, co. Wexford; Wybrants Olphert at Falcarragh, co. Donegal; Capt. Hector S. Vandeleur at Kilrush, co. Clare; Col. Charles G. Tottenham at Ballycurry, Ashford, co. Wicklow; and C. Talbot Ponsonby at Youghal, co. Cork. In each case the assistance furnished by the Castle varied considerably.

[9] Kavanagh, M.P. 1868-1880, was born with only stumps for arms and legs and yet became a proficient horseman and fisherman besides pursuing a public career. Another director of the Land Corporation, which was founded in July, 1882, was the English philanthropist Walter Morrison, M.P. 1861-1874, 1886-1892, 1895-1900.

keep the land productive, and without these landlords' combinations resistance to the Plan would have been doomed to failure.

A defeat on any of these estates, Dublin Castle was well aware, would gravely injure both the landlords' and the Government's position in Ireland. The nationalists also recognized the crucial *Parnellites & anti* nature of the test estates; and as late as 1891 both factions of the Irish party were determined to continue the fight on these properties. As one anti-Parnellite member remarked to a prominent Irish-American in July of that year, only ten of the remaining twenty-four Plan estates were really "important"; and the tenant combinations on those estates could not be abandoned merely for want of funds from America.[10]

In Balfour's mind the only guarantee of success against the Plan was active cooperation among the Irish landlords, and he *III N B.* devoted much thought to the best way of educating this class to their responsibilities in the land war. As he reminded Lord Courtown: "Every landlord in Ireland is interested in the issue of the test estates, and it is madness on their part to leave it to be fought out by the owner and his immediate neighbours. The Government can, of course, do something to vindicate the law by prosecuting offenders, and by stopping meetings which are clearly illegal, but it is by combination that the tenants have been successful; and in my opinion it is only by combination that they can be adequately met. . . . I do not mean that combination to ask the Government for this or that special kind of relief. . . . I mean legal combination to fight the illegal combination which Dillon and Co. have persuaded the tenants to adopt."[11]

If the test estates were to be saved, prompt action was essential. Through loss of income and large arrears of rates and county cess, most of the landlords concerned hovered close to insolvency; the Exchequer was pressing them for payment; and the other landlords in their vicinity refused to help them. To ease their situation Balfour secretly offered the test landlords temporary relief by asking Goschen to exempt them from estate duties until the Plan had been defeated. He persuaded the chancellor of the Exchequer that the victims of the Plan deserved "the very tenderest treatment from the Government." By 1888 the Irish

[10] J. F. X. O'Brien to T. A. Emmet, 13 July 1891, Emmet mss AIHS.
[11] Balfour to Lord Courtown, 2 May 1888, Add. ms 49826.

Office had compiled lists of defaulting landlords, with particulars as to the causes of arrears in each case; and the Treasury also made a confidential study of the finances of the Campaigned landlords in order to decide what justification there might be for temporary exemptions. The outcome of these private inquiries was that the nationalists began to suspect Government machinations, and ministers were accused of caring far more about landlords' than about tenants' arrears. For several years the Treasury had been lax about collecting landlords' debts; and if the size of these arrears ever became known, Balfour feared that the Opposition would make a "great parliamentary row." With Goschen's cooperation, however, he managed to win special deferments for the owners of the test estates. In addition, on some of the Campaign estates the Irish Board of Works, acting on Ridgeway's orders, postponed the collection of drainage charges.[12]

On the principal Plan estates Dublin Castle pursued two courses. The first involved arbitration. Contrary to nationalist propaganda, Balfour never ruled out the possibility of settling disputes over rents and arrears by responsible negotiation between owner and occupier. But because the nationalists always hailed arbitration as a victory for the Plan, the Castle approached this expedient with caution. In certain cases, especially when the tenants appeared more reasonable, Balfour recommended its use, provided the negotiations were "delicately handled." In general, the only advantage he could see in arbitration was its "plausible sound" to the public ear. The Government might lose many votes in England if they steadfastly refused any form of negotiation. Arbitration thus had its electoral uses, but Balfour still insisted that tenants renounce the Plan altogether and make "reasonable proposals" before he encouraged landlords to accept this solution.[13]

If arbitration failed, the second weapon against the Plan was eviction. English public opinion, as Balfour knew, would not tolerate any repetition of the Woodford or Glenbeigh scenes; and under his regime the Castle tried, with varying success, to supervise all evictions on Plan estates. Whenever landlords cooperated with the local magistrates and police, the evictions went

[12] Balfour to Goschen, 31 Jan., 20 Dec. 1889; Balfour's memorandum on landlords' arrears, 23 March 1888, *ibid.*, 49826-828.
[13] Balfour to Ridgeway, 15 May 1889, *ibid.*, 49827.

off smoothly. But there were times when a magistrate or inspector would show too much zeal and authorize wholesale clearances of an estate, and Ridgeway would have to intervene to avoid further damage both to the tenants' cottages and to the Unionist cause.

The Castle's eviction policy was, in fact, dictated by pure expediency. Because the Home Rule press followed scrupulously the course of the Plan on the larger estates, the administration could not risk too many evictions that might be considered "harsh and unnecessary."[14] As a result, Balfour arrived at an effective compromise that combined eviction with arbitration. Having ordered the sheriff to turn the Plan ringleaders out of their holdings on an estate, he then allowed the remaining tenants to negotiate on terms as satisfactory to both parties as possible. Eviction, nevertheless, provided no final solution to the land question. Rather, it produced a host of new troubles. Tenants reoccupied their houses illegally, the land lay fallow, and intimidation made the reletting of evicted holdings both difficult and dangerous. At Coolgreaney, for instance, on the test estate of George Brooke, the intensive persecution of landgrabbers served to deter other "imported" tenants from taking the evicted holdings. Where tenants could prove genuine insolvency Balfour usually shunned eviction in favor of arbitration. Parliamentary exigencies, too, influenced eviction policy. When the Land Bill reached the Commons in June, 1887, the Government wished to avoid as many evictions as possible during the debates. The chief secretary therefore asked the Castle to restrain the evicting parties on several important estates (including that of Colonel O'Callaghan, where "reasons of humanity" made such a course necessary). In cases where harsh landlords had greatly aggravated the poverty of their tenants, it was as well, thought Balfour, to temper justice with mercy.[15]

From the Castle's point of view eviction was a costly and painful process, made all the uglier by the resistance of tenants and the severity of the weather. Long experience of land agents, bailiffs, and emergency men had taught the Irishman something

[14] See Balfour's memorandum on the Clanricarde estate, 30 Jan. 1889, *ibid.* Balfour wished to save "the energies of the Government" in order to deal with the test estates where drastic evictions were necessary.

[15] Balfour to Buller, 11, 23 June 1887, *ibid.*, 49826.

about siege warfare, and he used to good effect such expedients as boiling liquid and stones. Balfour tried to discourage resistance to eviction with heavy sentences for tenants found guilty of this offense, but the fortifying of houses continued nevertheless. The undefined role of the protecting force at evictions resulted in a marked loss of efficiency by the bailiffs and emergency men. While the police and military stood by impassively, the sheriff's party received the brunt of the tenants' resistance. As an aid to eviction the protecting force had proved worthless, and Balfour never approved of wasting manpower. In January, 1889, therefore, he completely reorganized the tactics of the protecting force. Henceforth the armed detachments would do more than merely watch the "elaborate" defense put up by prospective evictees. In a recent eviction, he reminded the Castle officials, only the threat of firing had convinced the tenants inside their small, improvised fortress of the futility of resistance. In future the soldiery were to be used, Balfour stated, not just to "overawe the crowd," but to aid the police and bailiffs whenever they stood in danger of violence either from the besieged or from the throngs of spectators. Implicit in the new orders was the doctrine that rifles were not to be regarded as mere ornaments worn by the militia: the prospect of another Mitchelstown did not seem to frighten the chief secretary as much as it did his colleagues and subordinates. In order to prevent bloodshed—if at all possible—he proposed to equip the bailiffs and emergency men with suitable "appliances" designed to overcome the defensive weapons of the tenantry. What Balfour had in mind was, among other tools, a battering ram complete with "testudo arrangement" to protect its users against projectiles.[16]

These recommendations for eviction procedure were sent for approval to Salisbury, who raised some important questions: "I quite concur in your view. The necessity of firing would be lamentable: but not so lamentable as leaving the Police to be mutilated. It seems a pity that the precise period of eviction should be so loudly announced. Cannot more be done by way of surprise? The provision of apparatus is of course quite right— but how do you mean to pay for it? Shall you put it on the

[16] Balfour to Salisbury, 8 Jan. 1889, Salisbury MSS. For complete text of this memorandum, see Appendix III.

Estimates?—or will you let it out to landlords at so much an hour?"[17]

As a matter of fact, one enterprising magistrate in the south had already authorized the construction of a battering ram on his own initiative and had used it effectively in several evictions where its mere presence on the scene was enough to discourage resistance. But the ram caused a furor among Home Rulers, who refused to let the Government include this item in the Irish estimates. Eventually the apparatus was paid for out of Secret Service funds, although the transaction was concealed under the name of the Property Defence Association.[18] As to the element of surprise in carrying out evictions, the difficulties were almost insuperable. There were far too many security leaks, from Dublin Castle down to the smallest police station, to keep the time of an eviction secret; and by ringing the local church bells, the parish priest could give warning of the bailiff's approach and assemble a crowd in a matter of minutes.

The science of fortifying houses against eviction reached a new level of sophistication at Coolroe, near Burkestown, in county Wexford. In August, 1888, a tenant named Somers who was due for eviction turned his homestead into a fort by throwing up earthworks twenty feet high around his house. Beyond this barrier was a deep trench; iron bars were fastened to the windows by chains; and the road of approach was blocked with felled trees. The siege of Somers' fort was significant because for the first time the battering ram was defeated. Not only did the earthworks protect the walls from demolition, but they also stymied the efforts of the emergency men to set up the huge tripod from which the ram was suspended. After repeated assaults with scaling ladders, crowbars, and finally with fixed bayonets, the defenses remained intact and the bruised and battered police were forced to retreat. At length the inspector in charge threatened to open fire, and after the intercession of the parish priest, Somers and his cohorts surrendered. Among those who witnessed this scene were several foreign visitors, whose impressions of British justice could only have been jaundiced by the experience.[19]

[17] Salisbury to Balfour, 10 Jan. 1889, Add. MS 49689.
[18] Ridgeway to Balfour, 18, 20 April 1889, *ibid.*, 49809.
[19] *Freeman's Journal*, 17-18 Aug. 1888.

Such flagrant defiance of the law could not continue without serious damage to the Castle's prestige. Balfour had studied the statistics and methods of eviction in New York; and he was much impressed by the severity of eviction laws in France, where defiance of the bailiffs by more than twenty persons could mean penal servitude.[20] The era of leniency was at an end; and armed with two battering rams, crowbars, and with the revised order of battle, the bailiffs, emergency men, and police returned to their work with new vigor. Balfour soon found that it was not easy to justify these harsh measures in Parliament, especially when his information was "*necessarily* imperfect." But Dublin Castle, he realized, had the far more difficult task of governing a country "parts of which are practically in a condition of revolution," and of striving for success "when everything they do is lied about and where they have not only to keep an eye on the proceedings of rebels in Ireland, but on those of their parliamentary allies in England." The most effective way for a landlord to fight the Plan, Balfour maintained, was not to "clear the countryside," but to select the chief conspirators who could well afford to pay their rents, to evict them, and, if necessary, to destroy their houses. The latter course, he admitted, was an extreme one; but the league's insistence upon reinstatement of evicted tenants might make it unavoidable.[21]

At one time the Irish executive planned a wholesale and simultaneous clearance of the test estates. The scheme commended itself to Balfour because Parliament could then debate all the evictions at once rather than separately: "You do not provoke more row by having eviction scenes simultaneously in five places than by having them in one:—but if you have five acts in your tragedy, you will move your audience five times, have five adjournments of the House etc. etc. . . . " The scheme went well beyond the planning stage. After consulting the local authorities, Ridgeway scheduled the operation for the first week in April, 1889, when the weather would be more favorable, the tenants unprepared, and the protecting force well drilled. The evictions,

[20] "The French stand no nonsense in the way of resisting eviction. If the bailiff is assaulted, the punishment is very severe. . . ." Balfour to Salisbury, 31 Oct. 1888, Add. MS 49827.
[21] Balfour to Ridgeway, 13 March 1888, 18 April 1889, *ibid.*, 49826-827.

however, never took place. At the last minute several of the landlords succumbed to fright and backed out of the arrangement; and the cabinet disapproved on the grounds that it would alienate public opinion at home. "What a pity . . . ," Balfour exclaimed, "now we shall have a separate debate on each one of them."[22] In the end both the Government and the Plan tenants were spared much inconvenience by the decision to drop the project.

Evictions in Ireland invariably attracted contingents of English Home Rulers, who swarmed across St. George's Channel like angry wasps, causing extreme discomfort to Irish officials. Whether they were members of Parliament, journalists, free-lance writers, or Oxford dons and undergraduates, these groups headed straight for the Plan estates where resistance to eviction was expected to be most severe. Although Dublin Castle resented the intruders, nothing could be done to stop them or to prevent their distorting the facts thereafter. The presence of these partisan spectators often forced the magistrate or sheriff to change his evictions plans. Even Balfour recognized the need for moderation on such occasions, and when a group of Liberal and Radical M.P.'s journeyed to Donegal in the spring of 1889 to study evictions "from the life," he warned the divisional magistrate in charge to make sure that the local police officers did not "allow zeal to outstrip discretion."[23]

As the Irish executive expected, the Home Rule party made much political capital out of evictions. Admittedly, the Parnellites lost more money than they could well afford in granting relief to evicted tenants. But it cannot be denied that tales of harsh evictions left an indelible impression upon many voters in Great Britain. In the House of Commons and in English constituencies the Parnellites accused the Castle of conniving with the landlords to clear the "test estates"; and many Englishmen were led to believe that bailiffs were evicting thousands of insolvent tenants from their holdings each month. While Balfour tried to

[22] Balfour to Ridgeway, n.d. April 1889, Ridgeway MSS; Balfour to Ridgeway, 5 March, 30 May 1889, Add. MS 49827-828.

[23] Balfour to Ridgeway, 18 April 1889, *ibid.*, 49827. On this occasion Henry Harrison was arrested, along with his Balliol tutor Benson, for supplying besieged tenants with provisions. The charge was eventually dropped.

refute these charges by arguing that more evictions took place each year in London or New York than in all of Ireland, the fact remained that the current of English public opinion, as recorded at by-elections, was running against the Government.

II. THE SYNDICATE

During the land war some of the test estates came very close to defeat, and there was widespread fear in the Castle lest victory for the Plan on one or two such estates influence the outcome of the whole agitation. A more detailed study of several crucial estates shows how much importance both sides attached to the struggle.

One of the most famous clashes between the Castle and the Plan took place on a test estate belonging to Charles Talbot Ponsonby at Youghal, county Cork.[24] The property had been chosen as a likely Plan site, owing to the owner's heavy arrears, his semi-absentee status, and the unreasonable attitude of his agents. Ponsonby owed money to the Department of Woods and Forests, to the Crown (in the form of quit rents), to the Board of Public Works for drainage and road repairs, and to the local tithe collector. When the Plan organizers first struck, Ponsonby decided to resist their demands for abatement, and he held out against the Campaigners for several months. By the end of 1888, however, he was on the verge of bankruptcy; indeed Balfour informed his uncle early in the new year: "Ponsonby is completely '*broke*,' and has lost all nerve. He has no money to pay his charges and none to provide himself with bread and butter. I must try and get him some by hook or by crook: on condition he fights on. But I am doubtful of success. I am working the thing to the best of my ability. But of course I have to keep in the background: and the want of funds hampers me seriously." More was involved at Youghal, he urged, than the surrender of one Irish landlord to the Plan. "If Ponsonby gives in," he commented, "it will be the worst thing that has happened to us for sometime past."[25]

[24] For details of the struggle on this estate see the article in *Irish Loyal and Patriotic Union 1890* (hereafter *ILPU*), pp. 249-56; and W. H. Hurlbert, *Ireland Under Coercion: The Diary of an American* (hereafter *Coercion*), 2d ed., Edinburgh, 1888, II, pp. 60-76, 353-60.

[25] Balfour to Salisbury, 18 Jan. 1889, Salisbury MSS.

After more than a year's exposure to the Plan, Ponsonby's finances and morale were in sad condition, and his spirit of defiance was rapidly waning. Relief from arrears alone could not save him from surrender; it was clear that more drastic measures were required. The Castle tried to promote arbitration between Ponsonby and the Plan trustees. But Canon Keller, the parish priest who had been imprisoned in 1887 for refusing to give evidence about the Plan of Campaign, rejected the landlord's terms outright. Ridgeway next suggested bringing pressure to bear on Keller from Rome: "All that is required is an injunction to him and other priests in a similar position to act the part of peace makers."[26]

Balfour had other ideas. He turned for help not to the Vatican but to the Carlton Club. His stratagem involved rescuing the estate by means of a secret syndicate composed of the wealthiest landlords he could find. Ponsonby would then be persuaded to sell his property to the group, which would manage it as a joint stock company. Evictions would follow at the Castle's dictation. The success of this venture, Balfour knew, depended upon absolute secrecy. If the news ever leaked out that the Government had contrived to defeat the Plan in this fashion, the nationalists would raise an uproar that might be heard all over the British Isles. But Ponsonby's surrender, as far as he was concerned, would mean that the Plan remained "master of the field"; and in that event, the Castle could not guarantee the safety of any property in Ireland. Originally, he had thought in terms of raising a special fund—"a kind of secret service money"—in order to relieve landlords on the test estates. The reluctance of Irish landlords to cooperate with each other in fighting the Plan had driven him to suggest this course. None of Ponsonby's neighbors had offered any material assistance, though all had exhorted him to hold out. Such selfish behavior exasperated Balfour and moved him to favor the use of a floating fund about which the landlords' associations would be kept ignorant, "as this would dry up at once the shallow stream of their generosity. . . ."[27] But this expedient did not commend itself either to the cabinet or the Treasury; and with his uncle's approval he turned to the syndicate.

[26] Ridgeway to Balfour, 11 Dec. 1888, Add. MS 49809.
[27] Balfour to Lord Northbrook, 21 Jan. 1889, *ibid.*, 49827.

In the first weeks of February, 1889, Balfour completed his arrangements for the Youghal syndicate. Using Lord de Vesci as his "contact man," and relying on the organizational ability of A. H. Smith-Barry, the chief secretary managed to persuade some of the richest landlords in both countries to join the enterprise. Among those approached directly or indirectly were the Dukes of Norfolk, Bedford, Devonshire, and Westminster, as well as Lords Ardilaun, Brownlow, Fitzwilliam, Pembroke, Derby, and Revelstoke, and the wealthy philanthropist Walter Morrison, M.P. Most of those who joined subscribed £10,000 each, and Balfour assured them that the risks involved would amount to only a few hundred pounds' loss per man. Balfour informed Lord de Vesci: "It is very much out of the line of my proper duties, I am afraid: and I beg that you will keep the fact that I am mixing you up in it absolutely confidential."[28] By mid-February the dozen members of the syndicate had appointed a committee to manage the estate headed by Smith-Barry, and Ponsonby was left as "the lay figure" or nominal landlord. Ridgeway confidently expected an early victory over the Plan and wrote to his chief: "We shall never again have such an opportunity of smashing the League or of fighting them under such favourable conditions as on the Ponsonby estate." Defeat for the Campaigners there, he asserted, would have a striking effect on all other Plan estates.[29]

The initial optimism of the Irish executive was soon dashed, for within a week of the transaction the *Freeman's Journal* reported the sale of the estate to a London company of which A. H. Smith-Barry was reputed to be a director. Although no connection between the Government and the syndicate was made at the time, the object of the purchase was alleged to be the clearance of every Plan tenant off the notorious Youghal estate. Once Smith-Barry's name had leaked out, it was not long before the nationalists were demanding the names of the other company directors. Ridgeway called the disclosure a "great blow" and advised Balfour that every precaution would have to be taken in order to conceal his own role in the formation of the syndicate,

[28] Balfour to De Vesci, 25 Jan. 1889; Balfour to Lord Pembroke, 8 Feb. 1889; Balfour to Abercorn, 26 Jan. 1889; and Balfour to Ridgeway, 14 Feb. 1889, *ibid.*

[29] Ridgeway to Balfour, 15 July 1889, *ibid.*, 49810.

as well as to protect the remaining subscribers.[30] When Parnellite members asked pointed questions in Parliament about the Ponsonby sale, Balfour flatly denied any knowledge of the syndicate on two occasions. And the leading officials in the Castle were warned that the nationalists must on no account learn any further details about the syndicate. Balfour did not mince his words in writing to Peter O'Brien about the grave consequences of exposure:

"It will do great harm on the Ponsonby Estate. It will make it absolutely impossible, under any circumstances, to get together another Syndicate. It will be most unfair upon the gentlemen who have joined the existing Syndicate, and I cannot doubt that it will give a stimulus to the, so-called, 'new departure' in Ireland, and, what is much worse, in England which will be serious. To this last consideration I attach the very greatest importance. I feel perfectly certain that if the names are known, it will be easy for English Agitators, not merely to raise public feeling in a manner which will be productive of permanent injury to us, but also that they will be enabled to collect large subscriptions on this side of St. George's Channel for the purpose of meeting what they will misrepresent as being a conspiracy of English landlords against Irish tenants. . . . I can assure you that I am not exaggerating the effect of disclosures, should disclosures be made."[31]

Unfortunately, the revelations about the Ponsonby estate prolonged the hardships for both landlord and tenants; and Smith-Barry, the exposed investor, paid a heavy price for his complicity. In cooperation with Dublin Castle the syndicate ordered the eviction of several dozen tenants, after the Plan's ringleaders had rejected their terms for arbitration. Although Balfour considered these evictions "melancholy and pitiable," he insisted that those tenants who continued to support the Plan had to be taught a lesson. The dispute on this estate dragged on for more than four years, and in 1892 some tenants had still not settled with Ponsonby, who had by then received his property back from the syndicate. Parts of the estate were worked by agents of the Land Corporation. Unlike the emergency men of the Property Defence Association, who were once described as "enfants

---

[30] Ridgeway to Balfour, 21, 25 Feb. 1889, *ibid.*, 49809.
[31] Balfour to P. O'Brien, 3 Aug. 1889, *ibid.*, 49828.

perdus," the employees of the Land Corporation were chiefly experienced farmers, many of them Protestant and Ulstermen.
The corporation also operated farms on other test estates where
local intimidation had prevented the landlord from letting evicted
holdings.

If the landlords' syndicate on the Ponsonby estate failed to
uproot the Plan, it did save the owner from certain defeat, and
his replacement by a group with unlimited resources caused the
land agitators serious inconvenience.[32] The contest at Youghal
revealed Balfour in his most determined and imaginative mood.
Like Hicks Beach, he had been forced to stretch his powers beyond
the limits prescribed by the Law Room; but this time the landlords,
not the tenantry, had received the benefits of these emergency
measures. Balfour had at last succeeded in turning the nationalists' own weapon of combination against them; and on most of the
other test estates he applied the syndicate method, or some version
thereof, in order to save the owners from surrender.

III. "MAD TIPPERARY"

The second critical estate belonged to Smith-Barry, whose role
in the Ponsonby syndicate earned him the full attention of the
Plan's organizers.[33] Dillon and O'Brien had waited a long time
for an excuse to launch the Plan against the guiding spirit of
the Cork Defence Union. The enterprise and resolution shown by
Smith-Barry in the past made him almost unique among Irish
landlords. And the bitter struggle fought on his estate in the town
of Tipperary is prominent in the annals of the land war. For over
two years the once-prosperous community became the center of

---

[32] "It naturally has irritated the campaigners to be thwarted by the
syndicate stepping in between their victory over the landlord at the
eleventh hour"; DICS, Jones, 1 July 1889, SPO. The defiant tone of the
Plan organizers about the syndicate was echoed in the *Freeman's Journal*,
8 Oct. 1890: "Even if it were a mere question of purse against purse, the
purse of the plutocratic Syndicate against the purse of the poor Irish
people, we believe in our soul that the people would conquer and break
down the richest Syndicate that was ever formed, backed up by the basest
Government that was ever in power."

[33] For details of the Plan on Smith-Barry's estate, see "Mad Tipperary,"
in *ILPU 1890*, pp. 257-88; and "the Reign of Terror in Tipperary," *ibid.*,
pp. 441-48. These accounts were, of course, written by and for Unionists.

an intensive agitation by nationalists, who reveled in boycotting, intimidation, and vigilance committees. Under the spell of nationalist tirades against the landlord, which included references to his illegitimate ancestry, the local inhabitants indulged in sporadic rioting; and long-festering rivalries among shopkeepers flared into the open. Those tenants who remained loyal to Smith-Barry underwent a stifling boycott; and the market town became a place of deserted streets and lingering fears. The nationalists committed all their resources to the struggle. William O'Brien organized the construction of a special mart with two streets of houses and shops, costing some £50,000, for those tenants evicted by the obdurate landlord. The result, "New Tipperary," was the crowning achievement of O'Brien's work and a symbol of the fierce loyalty that he inspired among some of the local tenantry.[34]

"New Tipperary" could not have been built without the help of the Tenants' Defence League, which Parnell, aided by O'Brien and his colleagues, founded in the autumn of 1889 in retaliation against the Ponsonby syndicate. This league financed the Plan in its last years and saved the funds of the Irish party from being exhausted by the land war. Heralded with much fanfare by the nationalist press, the Tenants' Defence League bore out Balfour's prediction about the consequences of publicizing the existence of the Ponsonby syndicate. Ridgeway, however, treated the new league lightly, calling it "dust to cover a retreat" and a tacit admission of the Plan's failure.[35] The nationalists, on the other hand, hailed the organization as the weapon that would "make the last breach in the last ramparts of landlordism." In the Castle the impression prevailed that the league would have only a limited appeal to the tenantry. But the initial response to the fund drive launched by the league exceeded the hopes of even the Plan promoters. In their first appeal the association collected an estimated £60,000, and a special campaign in Australia netted a further £40,000. The resentments of Irishmen the world over toward landlords' syndicates and the Crimes Act accounted for the generous contributions. But in Ireland the more prosperous farmers and tradesmen grumbled about the latest demand for

[34] See monthly reports of DICS, Crane, and DICS, Jones, from Aug. 1889 to Dec. 1890, SPO.

[35] Ridgeway to Balfour, 11 July 1889, Add. MS 49810.

funds to support the land agitation. They wished to be left alone to manage their businesses without the incessant appeals of politicians for money. As one farmer, a staunch member of the National League, exclaimed: "To Hell with the National League, Tenants' League and every other d—n League: what are we doing but supporting as gentlemen a pack of b----y cut-throats and ruining ourselves and families?" The initial enthusiasm about the Tenants' League gradually gave way to indifference and apathy. The O'Shea divorce and the party split diverted not only attention but also money from the land agitation; and the league, which had given a new lease of life to the Plan, succumbed in turn to superior pressures after 1890.[36]

The Tipperary contest ran its course of riotous assemblies, baton charges by the police and relentless boycotting. Officers of the Special Branch shadowed the vigilance men, who were employed by the Campaigners to spy on those tenants suspected of sympathizing with Smith-Barry. Occasionally, some agent of the Plan would set off a crudely fashioned bomb, known as an "infernal machine." For many months the Castle made no advance against the Plan, even though more than half of Smith-Barry's 253 ground tenants were evicted in the process. Whenever the tenants began to lose heart, Dillon or O'Brien would arrive in the town to awe the waverers back into line; and Father Humphreys, the militant parish priest, helped the Parnellites by "working heaven and earth and, indeed, hell" to prevent the settlement between landlord and tenants that finally took place at the end of May, 1891.[37]

The Tipperary agitation reached an appropriate climax in the spring of 1891 when Carson was sent down to prosecute some of the men who had rioted in protest against Dillon and O'Brien's arrest the previous September. At the trial Carson skillfully cross-examined both Morley and O'Brien, who had been present

[36] DICS, Jones, 12 Aug. 1889, SPO. See also reports of Crime Special Branch and of Dublin Metropolitan Police on the Tenants' Defence League, *ibid*. Ridgeway wrote: "There is literally nothing going on, and the new Tenants Association seems to have fallen to the ground. If so, the mountain never gave birth to smaller mouse"; Ridgeway to Balfour, 3 Sept. 1889, Add. MS 49810.

[37] Ridgeway to Balfour, 23 April 1891, *ibid*., 49811. See also DICS, Crane, 7 Oct. 1889, 5 Feb., 5 April 1892, SPO.

at the riot. Meanwhile, a mob had gathered outside the court-house, and several men succeeded in setting fire to the building. During the judge's summing up Carson was hit on the head by a piece of rafter, and smoke soon filled the courtroom. After a hasty evacuation by spectators and officials, the courthouse along with all the pertinent records, went up in flames. The court re-convened in Cork the next day; but the trial ended in acquittal of the defendants, owing to a hung jury. Although annoyed by the behavior of Morley, whom he held responsible for the September riot, Balfour felt that the act of arson was "a most characteristic termination" and one that would bring to an end "this epic of disorder." And in Cork some of the local wits quipped that when-ever Carson and O'Brien met, the sparks were sure to fly.[38]

In the bitter contest waged at Tipperary neither side emerged victorious. The expenditure by the Castle, the nationalists, and by the landlord himself was enormous; and the punishment meted out to Smith-Barry by the Parnellites hardly inspired other Irish landlords to defy the Plan.

IV. CLANRICARDE

There was one landlord who spent most of his life defying not only social convention but ministers and nationalists alike. Lord Clanricarde, grandson of Canning on his mother's side, owned vast estates at Woodford and Portumna, which stretched from the shores of Lough Derg to the outskirts of Galway. Clanricarde personified all the classic features of absentee landlordism, and much more. He was a millionaire, a miser, a recluse, and a con-noisseur of *objets d'art*; and no man did more to injure the Unionist cause in Ireland. His eccentric habits, which were almost fictional in their variety, made him the ideal target for the Plan's promoters. Objecting to interference of any kind in the manage-ment of his estates—which, according to popular accounts, he had never seen—Clanricarde had earned notoriety by informing his tenants: "If you think you can intimidate me by shooting my

[38] Ridgeway to Balfour, 28 March 1891; Balfour to Ridgeway, 2 April 1891, Add. MS 49811, 49829; Hartington to Salisbury, 7 Oct. 1890, Salisbury MSS; *Hansard*, 3d series, Vol. 350, pp. 692-804; E. Marjoribanks, *The Life of Lord Carson* (hereafter *Carson*), London, 1932, I, pp. 118-20.

agent, you are mistaken."[39] At Portumna the rents were considered exorbitant even by the Castle, and the estate was one of the first to be chosen as a site for the Plan. Late in 1886 Beach had tried to reason with Clanricarde, and their relationship had ended abruptly in the famous Woodford evictions. Now it was Balfour's turn.

Hoping to prevent any such evictions at Portumna, Balfour first tried arbitration. Negotiations with the land agents began in the summer of 1888, and Dr. Healy, co-adjutor bishop of Clonfert, whom the nationalists derided as a "Castle Bishop," offered his services as mediator. Clanricarde, however, flatly rejected the reasonable terms suggested by Dr. Healy; and this response so annoyed Balfour that he decided to bring some pressure to bear on the landlord. First he drafted a memorandum recommending legislation of a coercive nature in such cases, and next he wrote to Clanricarde asking him to reconsider his attitude to arbitration. In cabinet Balfour defended the use of compulsory powers on the ground that the mismanagement of estates such as Portumna created "grave public evils" for the whole community. But his colleagues hesitated to approve such a procedure until all other expedients had failed. When Clanricarde continued to oppose rent reductions, Balfour was finally forced to withhold police protection from evictions at Portumna. Early in December Balfour and Salisbury summoned the idiosyncratic landlord for a private talk in London. Balfour found the latter "very civil and garrulous," but obstinate in the extreme; and his warnings about compulsory legislation had little effect. The talk proved fruitless, and convinced Balfour that the Government would first have to reconcile "the two rival *amours propres* of the peer and the priest" before order returned to Portumna.[40]

In exasperation, Balfour revived his plan for a special bill that would compel landlords "of the Clanricarde stamp" to surrender control of their estates to the Land Court until they had agreed

[39] See T. P. O'Connor, *Memoirs of an Old Parliamentarian*, II, pp. 120-25; Hurlbert, *Coercion*, II, pp. 364-70; R. Nevill, *The Life and Letters of Lady Dorothy Nevill*, New York, 1920, pp. 185-92.

[40] Rev. P. J. Joyce, *John Healy, Archbishop of Tuam*, Dublin, 1931, chap. 5; Balfour to Ashbourne, 8 Nov. 1888; Balfour to Ridgeway, 7, 29 Nov., 10 Dec. 1888, Add. MS 49827.

to arbitrate their differences with the tenantry. Clanricarde's behavior and the condition of his estate at Portumna, he argued, made such a move imperative. The nationalists were longing for evictions there; the tenants were paying no rents; the land was lying fallow; and many farmers had driven their cattle off their holdings in order to avoid seizure. What began in November as a bill encumbered with "quasi-judicial machinery" had become, by January, 1889, an act of "high policy." The chief secretary intended to treat unreasonable landlords in future on a "criminal or quasi-criminal basis." Although aware of the weaknesses of such a scheme, he preferred it to wholesale eviction or to the flagrant use of a dispensing power; and the Government could not legislate separately for every "stupid or selfish" landlord in the country. Under the new provisions the lord lieutenant could authorize the compulsory transfer of an estate to the High Court of Justice. Realizing that even with safeguards the measure would be "repugnant . . . to ordinary English prejudices," Balfour nevertheless maintained that it would not seriously imperil property rights. And, after all, some landlords deserved just this treatment: "What right has Clanricarde to be treated better than a lunatic or an orphan? How can that be spoliation when applied to a grown man which is not spoliation when applied to an infant?"[41]

Fortunately for Clanricarde and other harsh landlords the bill did not survive cabinet discussion. Too many objections were raised. Ashbourne opposed it on legal grounds, arguing that the Liberals might abuse this precedent in the future; while the Irish Attorney General Peter O'Brien declared that it came too close to a dispensing power. In the end, Balfour had to fall back upon those clauses in the Land Act of 1887 that authorized compulsory rent revision in certain cases. Ridgeway's protests against the ability of landlords like Clanricarde to endanger public order and to embarrass the Government were in vain.[42] Portumna remained in a state of turmoil long after Balfour had left the Irish Office,

[41] Balfour memoranda on Clanricarde, 8 Nov. 1888, St. Aldwyn MSS, and 30 Jan. 1889, Add. MS 49827.

[42] Ashbourne to Salisbury, 17 Feb. 1889, Salisbury MSS; Ridgeway to Balfour, 12 Feb. 1889; Balfour to P. O'Brien, 20 March 1889, Add. MS 49809, 49827.

and many tenants adamantly refused to abandon the Plan. Clanricarde had successfully defied both Beach and Balfour, and only in 1915, the year before his death, did he lose control of his Galway estates by compulsory court order. This encounter taught Balfour that a government identified with the interests of Irish landlords could not expect to restrict their power without jeopardizing the very bases of the Unionist alliance.

Balfour achieved more encouraging results on other Plan estates. At Killarney a landlords' syndicate saved Lord Kenmare from surrendering to the demands of the Plan ringleaders, who were eventually compelled to accept a settlement on the owner's terms.[43] On another test estate belonging to Lord Lansdowne at Luggacurren, in Queen's county, the Plan proved a costly indulgence for the tenants and landlord alike. Lansdowne, who was governor general of Canada at the time, made up his mind to fight the Plan. After the usual cycle of eviction notices, fortification of houses, sieges, and injuries—all of this accompanied by severe boycotting—the annual rental on the estate had fallen from an average of £5,000 to almost nothing in 1887. Even though most of the evicted farms possessed new tenants by 1890, the financial losses incurred by Lord Lansdowne forced him to sell off portions of the estate and discouraged him from accepting a second term as governor general because of the expense of the office.[44] On two other test estates, at Coolgreaney in county Wexford and at Kilrush in county Clare, the owners had to resort to systematic eviction in order to break up the Plan. Nowhere, in short, did the Plan of Campaign collapse without a fight and numerous evictions.

V. THE PLAN IN RETROSPECT

The Plan's achievements defy accurate analysis. There can be no doubt that its adoption on some 120 estates focused the public attention of both countries on high rents and bad landlords. But if the Plan had publicity value, it also possessed an aura of futility. Where the landlords chose to resist, and on the test estates

[43] Balfour to Ridgeway, 5 April 1889, *ibid.*, 49827.

[44] For further details, see Hurlbert, *Coercion*, ii, pp. 219-41; Lord Newton, *Lord Lansdowne*, London, 1929, pp. 44-55, 497 ff. By 1888 Lansdowne's net rental from two estates had fallen from £23,000 to £500.

in particular, the tenants always suffered most. Moreover, even when the landlord capitulated to the Plan, the bad feeling engendered by the agitation, as well as the neglect of the holdings, meant that the tenants' material condition was not greatly improved. If the tenants were taught the art of combination, they did not find the lessons free.

The Plan also cost the Parnellites a huge sum of money. Having promised to support all tenants evicted on Plan estates, the organizers spent £40,800 on the maintenance of evicted tenants in the year 1890-1891 alone. With the party split came a sharp falling off in receipts, and this expenditure in the next year dropped to £21,700. At the height of the Plan struggle the evicted tenants were receiving some £3,600 every month in the form of direct grants.[45] From 1887 to 1893 the total cost of the operation, including overhead, must have exceeded £200,000.[46] The drain on the financial resources of the Irish party was thus steady and exhausting. After the split, the Paris funds that were earmarked for the victims of the land war were kept beyond the reach of Parnell's opponents; and the evicted tenants were left almost stranded. J. F. X. O'Brien, a prominent anti-Parnellite, described the situation as grave. "We are on the eve of a general collapse of the Plan of Campaign," he wrote to an American supporter; and the only way to prevent the spread of what he called "dry rot" among the tenant combinations was to increase the flow of money from America.[47]

The problem of providing for the evicted tenants, whether with the Paris funds or with the help of Irish-Americans and the Liberal party, remained to plague the Irish party long after the debates in Committee Room 15. And the fate of these unfortunate tenants—some of whom were not reinstated until 1907—became a major bone of contention between the two rival factions. To complicate matters, there was no unanimity on the question of offering relief to those tenants who had been evicted before the

[45] These figures are based on the accounts kept by the evicted-tenants committee of the anti-Parnellite party. See J. F. X. O'Brien to T. A. Emmet, 13 July 1891, and confidential memorandum on Irish party funds enclosed in E. Blake to T. A. Emmet, 14 Nov. 1893, Emmet MSS, AIHS.

[46] Davitt estimated the cost of operating the Plan for seven years at £230,000. See *The Fall of Feudalism*, p. 529.

[47] J. F. X. O'Brien to T. A. Emmet, 13 July 1891, Emmet MSS, AIHS.

Plan's inception. Parnell discussed the plight of the evicted tenants with John Morley in November, 1890. But in his famous manifesto, designed to rally support to his cause, he deliberately misstated Morley's position in order to heap further abuse on the Liberal alliance.

Admittedly, the Plan lowered rents on many estates. But to suggest that it halved the eviction rate is to exaggerate the merits of the scheme.[48] On the test estates, for example, the Plan produced a sharp increase in the number of ejectments, and it almost precipitated a series of mass evictions in the spring of 1889. What kept the eviction rate lower than in previous years was not just the Plan but the Government's sensitivity to public opinion in England. This is not to deny any connection between the two. But domestic considerations also bulked large in the decision to reduce evictions. The Land Act of 1887 afforded tenants greater protection against dispossession; land purchase was another means of reducing rents and thereby arrears; and in most cases after 1886 Dublin Castle supervised eviction proceedings. All clearances on the test estates had to be personally approved by Ridgeway and Balfour. Wherever the rental on an estate appeared unreasonable to the administration, the local officials received orders to do everything in their power to discourage eviction. And in England, where the Liberal Unionists felt many qualms about evictions, every type of pressure was exerted on the Irish Office to reduce their number.

And why did the Liberal and Radical Unionists swim against the prevailing currents of coercion and eviction in this manner? The answer has been supplied by J. L. Hammond in his passionate indictment of Balfour's regime.[49] Unlike their ministerial colleagues, the Liberal Unionists could see unmistakable signs of working-class sympathy in England for the Irish tenantry. To many British industrial workers, who tended to regard every Irish landlord as a Clanricarde, the Plan of Campaign resembled their own pilgrimage toward recognition of the right of combination. And at a time when the trade unions in England were entering upon a new and activist phase in their career, the reports that crossed the Irish Channel—of Plan organizers being im-

---

[48] See C. C. O'Brien, *Parnell and His Party*, p. 206.
[49] See *Gladstone and the Irish Nation*, pp. 573-75.

prisoned, of tenants evicted and starving because they had joined the Plan, and of landlords importing "landgrabbers" from Ulster to reoccupy the evicted holdings—found a receptive audience in England. To educate the electorate on such topics the Gladstonian Liberals imported Irish members, who shared their platforms in the constituencies, and they sent representatives to witness eviction scenes in Ireland. No policy could have done more to provoke the leaders and champions of organized labor in England than the Government's refusal to admit the tenants' right to combine and to bargain collectively for rent abatements. As one of the Plan's organizers said at the outset: "What they call a conspiracy now, they will call an Act of Parliament next year." Balfour's insensitivity to such strictures, his unflinching belief in the moral and political correctness of his cause, may have made him the undisputed heir to the party leadership; but it cost the Conservatives an incalculable amount of support and sympathy, not only in Great Britain but throughout the civilized world.

Needless to say, there were many Irishmen who did not enjoy their role as Campaigners. District inspectors in various parts of the country reported that the tenantry were not as enthusiastic about the antirent combination as the nationalist press asserted: only fear of intimidation prevented many of them from recanting. Some Plan members actually paid their rents in secret. And, occasionally, a tenant facing eviction tried to make a show of resistance by imploring the police to handcuff him as he emerged from his house in order to convince the spectators that he had put up a fierce struggle. On several test estates the tenants openly confessed their disgust with the Plan; but once they had paid their money into the "war chest," it was too late to pull out.[50] The real victim of the Plan was, of course, Irish agriculture, which could ill afford an agitation on such a scale. But to men obsessed with the idea of nationhood such considerations mattered little if at all.

Whatever the merits and demerits of the Plan, it caused the Irish administration and the Government prolonged anxiety; and

[50] Balfour to W. G. Matthews, 7 Sept. 1888, Add. ms 49827; DICS, Jones, 4 Sept. 1888; DICS, Bourchier, 13 Dec. 1887, SPO.

the combined forces of Dublin Castle, landlords' syndicates, the cabinet, and the Vatican could not eradicate this conspiracy. For the Government there was only one redeeming feature. As Ridgeway pointed out, Irish officials ought to dread the day when the landlords regained their full confidence. "As times become more prosperous," he wrote to Balfour, "landlords and agents will get out of hand and will insist on their pound of flesh —only danger has made the great bulk of them tractable."[51] The Plan of Campaign retarded this process; and it remains an impressive tribute to the tenacity and resourcefulness of the Irish people during the agrarian phase of the Home Rule movement.

For the Parnellites the era of "Tory coercion" had far-reaching consequences. While Parnell was in a state of semieclipse as leader, and while his coolness toward the Plan sorely strained the patience of his lieutenants, Balfour's regime, with its taint of martial law, created a common foe that closed the ranks of the Irish party during these years. If the Crimes Act frightened some of the "smaller fry" in the National League and the Plan, it also hardened the resistance of the Dillons and the O'Briens. Plank beds and prison uniforms, indeed the whole range of Government activity against the nationalist agitation, proved as effective a means of holding the party together as had Parnell's commanding personality in the past.[52] If anything united the tenantry at this time, it was not only the Plan but the series of evictions carried out on the test estates with battering rams, emergency men, and military precision. The Government—Balfour least of all—never understood the centripetal effect of their policies upon the nationalists. General Buller, who was blind to nuances of any order, exaggerated the divisive tendencies within the Irish party when he informed Hicks Beach in October, 1887, that Parnell was facing a "grave split in his upper ranks," while some "forty-six of his smaller fry" were demanding either more pay or their release from parliamentary duties.[53] The repressive machine that Balfour controlled with such thoroughness thus ef-

[51] Ridgeway to Balfour, 14 Feb. 1889, Add. MS 49809.

[52] This point is argued cogently in Lyons, *The Fall of Parnell*, pp. 19, 30.

[53] Buller to Beach, 19 Oct. 1887, St. Aldwyn MSS.

fectively stifled any disruption in the ranks until the verdict was handed down in the O'Shea divorce case.

VI. THE WINNING OF THE LAND WAR

Among the many visitors to Ireland after the passing of the Crimes Act was an American journalist named William Hurlbert. While in England he ingratiated himself with Balfour and other influential Unionists by professing his willingness to educate the American public about the "true" nature of Irish nationalism.[54] In 1888, after visiting Dublin Castle and the main battlesites of the Plan, and after interrogating landlords, tenants, league agents, priests, magistrates, and jarvey drivers, Hurlbert published the results of his tour in diary form, entitled *Ireland Under Coercion*. Although sympathetic with the Irishman's desire to manage his own affairs, he refused to condone the use of illegal means to attain this end. When Hurlbert used the word coercion, it was not the Crimes Act he had in mind, but the iron grip of the league and the Plan upon the freedom of the tenantry. In no other country could he recall having seen a population so thoroughly intimidated and contemptuous of the law, and he blamed this state of affairs on the "secret tribunals," the "personal cowardice," and the "greed" of nationalist agitators. Without the Crimes Act, he maintained, the law of the country would be that of the league or the jungle. What Ireland needed most, he concluded, was simply "Balfour, Balfour and more Balfour."[55]

Such an encomium naturally invites scepticism. Just how decisive, the critic may well ask, was Balfour's victory over the forces of agrarian disorder? The answer must be that Balfour, Ridge-

[54] See Balfour to E. Barrington, 13 Aug. 1888, Salisbury MSS. Balfour did his best to facilitate Hurlbert's "researches into recent Irish history" in the hope that Hurlbert's opinions would carry some weight in America. Hurlbert was a Harvard graduate and former editor of the *New York World*.

[55] Hurlbert, *Coercion*, I, pp. 17-38, II, pp. 325-44. Hurlbert left the British Isles "under a cloud" owing to his involvement in a breach of promise suit brought by an English woman of easy virtue. He was eventually acquitted in an English court, but the suit ruined him financially and both he and his wife left America to live in Italy. See Hurlbert's tract, *England Under Coercion*, Genoa, 1903; and Balfour to S. K. McDonnell, 24 Nov. 1891, Add. MS 49803.

way, the Castle bureaucracy, the Crimes Act, and economic recovery combined to restore respect for the law in almost every district of the country. In spite of such setbacks as Mitchelstown, Mandeville's death, O'Brien's breeches, the Pigott fiasco, and New Tipperary, there were definite signs by 1889 that the administration was defeating the league and the Plan. The paralysis of the legal machinery that Balfour inherited in 1887 had virtually disappeared. There was no clear line of division between the era of agrarian anarchy and that of peace; and the problem of gauging this improvement is aggravated by the ease with which certain districts suddenly relapsed into turmoil. But in terms of over-all improvement the summer of 1889 marked the watershed between a countryside dominated by the National League and one obedient to Dublin Castle.

Evidence for this change came from many sources. First and most important were the monthly reports of the district inspectors attached to the Special Crimes Branch of the RIC. The function of these officers was to gather information about the league, the Plan, and every secret society in their districts, and to expedite prosecutions whenever circumstances permitted. In general these inspectors were responsible and shrewd men, and much of their data was derived from a widespread network of paid informers.[56] Intelligence reports also came from the divisional and resident magistrates, whose knowledge of a county was usually less detailed than that of the Special Branch officers. Although some magistrates tended to gloss over unpleasant facts in their reports in order to impress their superiors, men like Captain Slacke were the exception rather than the rule. In addition, the Castle and the Irish Office in London received information from RIC headquarters, as well as from such miscellaneous and unreliable sources as "friendly" bishops, irate landlords, land agents, gombeen men, and cranks with a penchant for letter writing.

Nothing was more characteristic of the improvement in the crime rate than its gradualism. In such counties as Kerry, Clare, and Cork, lawlessness continued to flourish long after 1887. Elsewhere, Unionists had cause for satisfaction. In 1886 the total

[56] Their monthly reports are contained in cartons, for which no index exists, in Dublin Castle under the title, Crime Department, Special Branch, SPO.

number of outrages, including a high percentage of threatening letters, amounted to 1,056. By 1889 that figure had fallen to 535. In June, 1887, there were 4,901 persons either wholly or partially boycotted; by the end of 1889 there were 152 such cases; and in January, 1891, the records showed not a single instance of total boycotting in the country.[57]

In the summer of 1888 Balfour assured his uncle: "There is a remarkable unanimity of opinion from all quarters and all classes that a notable improvement has come over the country." The statistics of agrarian crime, he contended, were not the only means of measuring this change. Progress could also be discerned "in the altered demeanour of the people and in those nameless indications which show that the social storm is subsiding." The chief secretary attributed these results to three factors: the Crimes Act, the Papal Rescript, and a good harvest. But at the same time he was not blind to the existence of areas where the league was firmly entrenched. By the end of the year he was able to write from Dublin: "Everyone here is in high spirits. Rents are paid better than they have been for *years*. This is partly due to the administration of the law, but it is also due in part to the excellence of the harvest, and the improvement in prices."[58]

Yet the land war was not over. Clare remained the last stronghold of agrarian discontent and a haven for the veterans of Captain Moonlight's campaigns, but even there outrages dropped by fifty per cent between June and July, 1890.[59] The chief concern of Castle officials continued to be the Plan of Campaign; and yet the tenacious hold of the Plan on certain estates did not prevent Ridgeway from reporting to Balfour in March, 1888: "Everyone says that the country is rapidly improving, and after making due allowance for Irish exaggeration, there must be truth in it."[60] The improvement came in spurts. There were times when the nationalists appeared to have recouped some of their losses or when an important trial ended in acquittal. But by 1889 the worst of the struggle was past. Many of the suppressed

[57] *Hansard*, 3d series, Vol. 341, p. 36; *Return of Outrages*, RIC headquarters, 1885-1892, SPO.

[58] Balfour to Salisbury, 17 Aug., 28 Dec. 1888, Salisbury MSS.

[59] DICS, Gambell, 2 May, 31 July, 4 Sept. 1890, SPO.

[60] Ridgeway to Balfour, 16 March 1888, Add. MS 49808.

branches of the league had atrophied from disuse, and both nationalist funds and morale were low. So read the reports of magistrates and district inspectors scattered over the country. Irishmen, it seemed, had finally discovered the "hollow *éclat*" to be gained by breaking the law. In May, 1889, the Special Branch officer for the southwest division wrote:

"That ardent desire to earn martyrdom by imprisonment which we heard so much about last year has given place to a wholesome dread of the plankbed. There is apparently now as much un-willingness on the part of the average patriot to go to gaol for the good of his country, as to suffer imprisonment for drunken-ness and such like common place offences, as he knows the punish-ment will be similar whichever act he breaks."[61]

What pleased Balfour most was the infrequency of second and third offenders under the Crimes Act. Only a few nationalists chose to brave the rigors of prison life more than once; and these men were the Dillons, the Harringtons, and the O'Briens, who emerged from jail more determined than ever to defy British rule. Few Unionists, however, were naive enough to think that the zeal of the "hard core" patriots would erode under prison conditions.[62]

"The present lull," Ridgeway wrote to Balfour in June, 1889, "is becoming quite alarming. The outrages this month will be fewer than any month for several years."[63] Such proof of success, added to a mild revival of market prices, led Balfour to consider relax-ing the Crimes Act. The last few years, he believed, had taught most Irishmen a stern lesson, and the rod might safely be put aside, or at least out of sight. Only Clare, Cork, and portions of several other counties were to remain proclaimed under the more stringent clauses of the act.

The timing of this concession raised several questions, as he informed his uncle: "If we do it *now*, it may of course be alleged that we have done it because of recent bye-elections. If . . . we wait until Jan. 1 . . . it may be said that we did it in order to meet Par-liament. On the other hand, if we wait till the period when no nationalist can tell a lie about it, we shall wait forever!" Salisbury

[61] DICS, Jones, 3 May, 10 Oct. 1889, SPO.

[62] See Salisbury's speech on the subject of improvement in Ireland: *Hansard*, 3d series, Vol. 333, p. 29.

[63] Ridgeway to Balfour, 7 June 1889, Add. MS 49810.

preferred January 1. "It is the least splashy of the two alternatives," he wrote, "which is a great advantage. I am very glad you are able to do it—as the step will be an answer to many lies."[64] In the end, delay proved the wiser choice, and the news that eleven counties had been partially unproclaimed under section two of the Crimes Act appeared in the *Dublin Gazette* on January 24, 1890. The essentials of coercion, however, remained intact: only those provisions relating to assault and taking forcible possession were suspended. In June, 1891, another spate of unproclaiming took place, whereby the conspiracy clauses of the act were nullified in those areas where the league had ceased to be a threat.[65]

The Crimes Act may have curbed the land war, but it certainly did not solve the Irish Question. Because the forces of disaffection were still dangerous, the Castle bureaucracy and the magistracy were warned against overconfidence. The time for leniency, Balfour urged, had not yet arrived. Ridgeway maintained that only the fear of another prosecution prevented men like O'Brien from breaking the law: "When he believes that he can sin with impunity, he will sin."[66] In the event, O'Brien's monumental efforts to build New Tipperary after his release from Galway jail proved Ridgeway wrong. But the fact remained that public indifference to the land war was mounting on all sides. Colonel Turner noted that the agitators were longing for provocation, "for prosecutions, for a display of coercion, for baton charges, and to be deprived . . . of the right of free speech; and they find that nobody takes the slightest interest in or notice of their proceedings."[67] Balfour could not have asked for more than this.

Although the Conservative leaders were always at pains to deny that their measures in Ireland had anything to do with coercion—Salisbury once called this word a "scandalous misuse of language"—the nationalists considered the Crimes Act as coercive a measure as their country had ever experienced. And

[64] Balfour to Salisbury, 31 Oct. 1889, Salisbury MSS; Dugdale, *Balfour*, I, pp. 170-71.

[65] See *Times*, 4, 15 June 1891; Ridgeway to Balfour, 25 March, 14 June, 10 July 1891, Add. MS 49812. Out of 3,019 persons in Irish jails in 1891 only twenty-one had been imprisoned under the Crimes Act.

[66] See memorandum, Crime Special Branch, 25 April 1890, SPO.

[67] Turner to Sir Andrew Reed, I.G., RIC, 21 April 1890, *ibid.*

most Irishmen rightly considered themselves experts on the subject. William O'Brien once made an interesting comparison between the regimes of Forster and Balfour. The contrast between the Liberal chief secretary's "dove-like" prison arrangements and Balfour's "privations and petty abominations" led him to assert that the softer treatment was the more effective or dangerous because it tended to undermine the morale of its victims. In Kilmainham jail Parnell and his colleagues had luxuriated in privileges that not only weakened the will to fight, in O'Brien's opinion, but lost them the vital sympathy of the public. Whereas Balfour's reliance on prison uniforms, hard labor, plank beds, and other austerities only fortified the mettle of the prisoners and raised public feeling to heights of indignation.[68]

There can be little doubt that Balfour erred in making martyrs of those imprisoned under the Crimes Act. Admittedly, the harsh prison rules discouraged many of the rank and file and such sensitive souls as Scawen Blunt from repeating their offenses. But in an age of mounting political awareness among the working classes, it was unwise to ignore the capital that Home Rulers could and did make out of O'Brien's martyrdom or Mandeville's death. Any indiscretion by a prison warder was bound to make headlines in the Home Rule press. In this sense the Unionist cause was injured by Balfour's proverbial indifference to public opinion and newspapers.[69]

 It should be noted that even before the breakup of Parnell's party some Irish nationalists were beginning to despair of achieving Home Rule by constitutional means. Much of this disenchant-

[68] O'Brien, *Recollections*, New York, 1905, pp. 392-93.

[69] C. C. O'Brien has argued in *Parnell and His Party* (p. 210) that the Crimes Act did no more than "answer certain internal needs of the tory party" while building up, "at small expense, the personal reputation of Arthur Balfour as a strong man." If one were to accept this contention, then much the same charge could be leveled against Gladstone's coercive legislation of 1881-1882, not to mention all the other ministries in the nineteenth century responsible for peace preservation acts, arms acts, and crimes acts. In order to assign such motives to the Conservatives and their "strong man" it is necessary first to conjure away the fact of the land war and the statistics of boycotting, moonlighting, and conspiracies against rent. Such a conjuring act, however, requires not only practice but considerable bias.

ment with Parnellism was the result of Balfour's coercion. In October, 1889, a Special Branch officer observed that the physical-force party was "becoming daily more convinced that the Parnellite agitation is a failure in coping with the present firm action of the Government and that the prospect of establishing national independence through that channel presents insuperable difficulties." Ridgeway shared these fears. Months before the O'Shea divorce he was convinced that the extremists would detach themselves from the Parnellite party and resort to direct action. The resurgence of several secret societies moved him to predict that the "real revolutionists" would supplant the National League in the near future. But such pessimism was short lived, if in the long run prophetic.[70]

The decline in the crime rate, the ability of landlords to let more evicted holdings, and the rise in prices all indicated material improvement. "The change for the better," one district inspector reported in 1890, "is most striking and cheerful."[71] Thanks also to the impact of the Parnellite schism, the country had not been so tranquil for more than a decade. But to Balfour, whose mission was not just to pacify but to conciliate Ireland, the campaign was only half-finished. The administration, he wrote in January, 1891, ought never to forget that "the body politic is so liable to disease that a very slight occasion may cause a new outbreak of it."[72] Despite the divorce and its aftermath, what Balfour described as "the organized hypocrisy of the so-called constitutional movement" remained; and in order to prevent a relapse in the patient's condition, he was already hard at work on a comprehensive program of conciliation.

[70] DICS, Jones, 5 Oct. 1889, SPO; Ridgeway to Balfour, 12 Sept. 1888, Add. MS 49808.

[71] "Then [in 1887] there was avowedly no respect for the law or for authority—men said they were anxious to go to gaol—the police were daily insulted, and no person allowed to speak to them, and boycotting and intimidation were rampant. Now all that—though not completely cured—is changed. Crimes Act prisoners are beginning to give bail; men who have once been imprisoned under the act are not anxious to do a second term. . . ." DICS, Jones, 1 July 1890, SPO.

[72] Balfour to Turner, 2 Jan. 1891, Add. MS 49829.

CHAPTER XIII

Collusion

I. THE PAPAL RESCRIPT

THE IRISH ADMINISTRATION had more subtle ways of dealing with the agitation in Ireland than by coercion pure and simple; and there were occasions when the inherent limitations of the Crimes Act made the indirect approach a matter of necessity. Apart from the landlords' syndicates, the two most impressive examples of Government subterfuge concerned the Vatican and the *Times*. In both cases high hopes of crushing Parnellism through these flanking movements soon gave way to disillusion if not despair.

Since the Catholic Church had supplied so much of the cadre for the land war, some ministers thought it high time that the Pope be informed about the illegal conduct of his servants in Ireland. Salisbury's ministry was not the first to approach the Holy See in connection with the Irish Question. Both Peel and Gladstone had tried to exert pressure on the Irish hierarchy by way of Rome. The Errington mission, which had been sent to the Vatican in 1881 in order to influence ecclesiastical appointments in Ireland and elsewhere, offered the nearest precedent. And it was one with which the Conservative cabinet were only too familiar. Errington, they knew, had made "desperate efforts" to block Walsh's promotion to the archbishopric of Dublin. Ironically, it was Walsh who worked so astutely to render the nationalist agitation acceptable to the Pope during the years of the land war. But failure over the Walsh affair had not dampened the ardor of Gladstone and Granville about the utility of a secret emissary at Rome.[1]

In the spring of 1887 the question of sending a special mission to Rome came up in cabinet. Although Balfour tended to favor this idea, he warned that any news leak about such a mission

[1] Transcripts of Sir George Errington's correspondence with Lord Granville and Gladstone, 1881-1885, are in the Salisbury MSS and in the Balfour Papers, Add. MS 49690.

would certainly "alienate or shock" Protestant feeling, especially in Ulster, which was "more bound to us by community of religion than by anything else. . . . " For political reasons this section of opinion could not be ignored. But this did not mean that Balfour had rejected the plan. "Undoubtedly," he informed Buller, " . . . the inconvenience of allowing the whole Romish hierarchy in Ireland to ally themselves with the forces of disorder is so great, that I would readily run some risk if I saw a chance of obviating it."[2] Within a matter of months the cabinet had agreed to run that risk in the hopes of curbing the political activities of Irish prelates and priests. And Pope Leo XIII, who fervently wished to reassert the authority of the Holy See, proved a receptive audience for Unionist agents primed with dossiers about clerical activity in the land war.

The Government used several channels to transmit information to the Vatican. One of their most valuable agents was Salisbury's friend the Duke of Norfolk, whose connections in the Catholic hierarchy and "sound" views on the Union eminently qualified him to act as a private ambassador to Rome.[3] In December, 1887, he was appointed to lead a delegation of English Catholics to Rome as part of the jubilee celebrations. With him went Captain Ross, a prominent Catholic Unionist who performed most of the brain-work for the mission.[4] Soon after his arrival, Norfolk gave the Pope a personal report on the agitation in Ireland, as Balfour had charged him in London. From Rome the Duke informed Salisbury that the Holy See admitted priestly excesses in Ireland, realized the necessity of reducing this evil, but hesitated to do so publicly. The Pope expected, moreover, that the Government would prove their good intentions by promoting higher education for Irish Catholics. And Norfolk, for his own part, urged that such a concession be made at once.[5]

[2] Balfour to Buller, 6 April 1887, *ibid.*, 49826.

[3] Henry Fitzalan Howard, 15th Duke of Norfolk, 1847-1917; Special Envoy to the Vatican 1887; Postmaster General 1895-1900; served in South Africa 1900.

[4] Later Lt. Col. Sir John Foster Ross of Bladensburg, 1848-1926; A.D.C. to Lords Spencer and Carnarvon in Ireland; Secretary to British missions to Holy See 1887, 1889-1890; Chief Commissioner Dublin Metropolitan Police 1901-1914; K.C.B. 1903; K.C.V.O. 1911.

[5] Norfolk to Salisbury, 29 May 1887, 2 Jan. 1888, Salisbury MSS.

During the first months of 1888 Norfolk and Ross worked hard to convert Leo XIII to a Unionist point of view about Ireland. Two pamphlets, one on the land question and the other on the working of the Crimes Act, were carefully prepared, translated into Italian, and distributed among the college of cardinals. Evidence about the activities of Irish priests had already reached Rome from other quarters. Back in December, 1886, two Irish bishops, Dr. Healy of Clonfert and Dr. O'Dwyer of Limerick, had volunteered information to the Prefect of Propaganda. And in the following summer the Pope had sent a special envoy to Ireland, Msgr. Persico, to collect proof of clerical activity in the Plan and boycotting. After causing both the Parnellites and the Irish hierarchy much discomfort, Persico returned to Rome laden with facts and impressions, many of them sympathetic to the nationalist cause.[6]

In view of these efforts to enlighten the Pope about the Irish Question, it was more than a coincidence that on April 20, 1888, the famous Rescript was issued, condemning the Plan and boycotting as illegal and forbidding clerical participation in either. More drastic than the "De Parnellio" letter of 1883, the edict shocked the Irish world and revived memories of O'Connell's brush with papal authority over the veto question. This time the Parnellites felt privately, as O'Connell had once expressed openly, that they would prefer in future to take their politics from Constantinople rather than from Rome. The Rescript embarrassed the Irish hierarchy and delighted the Unionist party. Disappointed with the failure of their own intrigues at Rome, the nationalists accused the Government of "drawing a veil" over the Pope's eyes in order to succor rackrenting landlords. Captain Ross had done his work well, according to Norfolk, who gave him credit for the timing of the Rescript.[7] If the Government had not actually inspired the edict, they had helped Leo XIII to make up his mind.

[6] For further details of the Norfolk Jubilee delegation see Vol. A. 68 and E. Barrington to Norfolk, 9 Nov. 1887, *ibid.* See also Joyce, *John Healy, Archbishop of Tuam*, pp. 138 ff. For accounts of the Persico mission and the Rescript, see C. C. O'Brien, *Parnell and His Party*, pp. 213-25; W. O'Brien, *Evening Memories*, Dublin, 1920, pp. 345-59.

[7] Norfolk to Salisbury, 22 June 1892, Salisbury MSS.

PANIC AMONGST THE PIGS!
The Papal Rescript of April 1888 forbids clerical participation
in the Plan of Campaign.

The initial enthusiasm in Dublin Castle over the Rescript soon
gave way to discouragement. The effects of the order upon the
priesthood were slow to manifest themselves. Ridgeway complained in July, 1888, that many priests continued to promote
the Plan, although they were taking greater precautions to

conceal this fact. But as the months passed, magistrates and district inspectors began to notice that the Rescript had at least slowed down the momentum of the Plan. The first new outbreak of the Plan, after the papal decree, did not occur until September. Special Branch officers in the southwest remarked on the "wholesome effect" of the Rescript. And from the southeast division a district inspector confidently reported: "The pronouncement from Rome has come on the people like a thunderclap. . . . The Fenians are glad of it, as they do not like the priests, and they fancy this will be a blow to them. There are some priests much staggered by it, but very many are glad though not saying so publicly." Tradesmen and the more prosperous class of farmers, he added, welcomed the Rescript with open arms.[8] In London the prime minister also radiated confidence, expressing his hopes to a papal emissary that all "good and honest" persons would be moved to obey the civil law.[9] And from the Viceregal Lodge in Dublin Salisbury received a glowing picture of the country since the decree had come into effect.[10]

Such impressions belied the facts. The militant clergy continued to defend their parishioners' interests by means of the Plan; Archbishop Croke, unlike his colleague Walsh, did not hesitate to snort at the papal order; and the Parnellites, meeting in the Mansion House, Dublin, on May 17, passed several resolutions denying the right of the Vatican to judge political matters in Ireland. Moreover, by raising the question of church and state in Ireland, the Rescript proved in the end a costly indulgence. The edict drove a wedge into the body politic, forcing the Fenians and other extremists away from the restraining influence of the church; and by loosening the ties between the forces of order and disorder in Ireland, it anticipated to some extent the effects of the church's stand during the Parnellite split two years later.[11]

What the Government needed, once the Rescript had been issued, was a means of supplying the Vatican with news of its violation in Ireland; and after Norfolk's return, the cabinet

---

[8] DICS, Gambell, 5 Sept. 1888; DICS, Bourchier, 7 June, 5 Sept. 1888, SPO.

[9] Salisbury to Prince Ruffo Scilla, 9 May 1888, Salisbury MSS.

[10] Londonderry to Salisbury, 13 May 1888, *ibid*.

[11] DICS, Jones, 3 Oct. 1890, SPO.

considered the possibility of a more permanent agency at Rome. Salisbury went so far as to suggest accrediting an official envoy to the Vatican; but he found the Liberal Unionists "so nervous" on the subject that he desisted.[12] Eventually, the death of the Bishop of Malta solved the cabinet's quandary. A delegation was appointed to settle the question of the succession in Malta, with the object of using this excuse as a point of departure for further dealings with the Vatican about Ireland. The idea pleased both Salisbury and Balfour. Sir Lintorn Simmons was chosen to head the mission,[13] and Ross, by now a major, went along as his secretary. When Simmons arrived in Rome in the spring of 1889, Balfour began to send him information about Rescript violations in Ireland. Ross acted the part of intermediary, passing on reports about "good" or "bad" priests to the Prefect of Propaganda; and when vacancies in Irish Sees occurred, he forwarded advice about those candidates most palatable to the administration. In 1890 Balfour informed Ross that some Irish bishops, "though not technically violating the Papal Rescript," were condoning the Plan by implication; and he also cited instances of priests collecting funds for the Tenants' Defence League and exhorting tenants to boycott nonmembers of the Plan. The Vatican thus became an important, if secondary, theater of operations for the administration in their fight against the Plan and the league. And the Rescript, even if defied at Tipperary and elsewhere, greatly complicated the task of the Plan's organizers and of those spiritual leaders like Croke and Walsh who were committed to the nationalist cause. The Government, on the other hand, considered Ross's activities at Rome sufficiently useful to keep him there after the Maltese mission had returned.[14]

There was a second string to the Government's relations with the Vatican. In the minds of some Unionists the question of higher education offered a more constructive means of inducing the

[12] Salisbury to Lord Dufferin, 28 Dec. 1888, Salisbury mss.

[13] 1821-1903; Field Marshal and Colonel Commandant Royal Engineers; military delegate Berlin Congress 1878; Governor of Malta 1884-1888; Envoy Extraordinary to Vatican 1889-1890. See also memorandum of Count Strickland on diplomatic relations with the Holy See, 30 Jan. 1889, *ibid.*

[14] Norfolk to Salisbury, 13 June 1889, *ibid.*; Balfour to Ross, 22 Jan. 1890; Balfour to Norfolk, 17 March 1890, Add. ms 49828.

Holy See to exert its authority over wayward Catholics in Ireland. What their plan amounted to was a bribe in the form of a Catholic college. In this connection a group of influential English and Irish Catholics approached Balfour in October, 1887. Led by the Duke of Norfolk, and including the "Castle Bishops" Drs. Healy and O'Dwyer, the deputation asked the chief secretary to open "direct dealings" with the Vatican on the subject of establishing such a college in Ireland and providing it with a generous endowment. This concession, however, should be made only "when, by the efforts of the Holy Father, the Irish priesthood shall have learnt the ten commandments."[15] A similar delegation of prominent Catholics had approached Salisbury the year before, arguing that an Irish university approved by the Pope would be welcomed by the moderates in the Irish hierarchy who were anxious to throw off the yoke of Archbishop Walsh and his political friends. Such a concession had the support of several ministers. Beach had always regarded state grants to secular education in Ireland as a wise investment, and it did not matter to him whether the school or college concerned was denominational or not. Churchill also shared this view, though he had greater faith in the ability of the hierarchy to control the destiny of Parnellism and was therefore eager to conciliate the bishops as quickly as possible. Beach, however, never minimized the obstacles that stood in the way of a final settlement of the education question. Concessions of this kind, as he knew from bitter experience, tended to alienate Government supporters both in England and Ireland, while the slightest change in the status of the endowed schools always raised "a red flag" for the Presbyterians in particular.[16]

Obstacles to a Catholic university also loomed in the cabinet. Salisbury was less than lukewarm on the subject; and Balfour confessed that he could never understand how Catholics expected to strengthen their faith by exposing themselves to a liberal education. One thing he was certain about: the Government ought never to consider a concession of this nature except on a strictly *quid pro quo* basis. The Irish hierarchy would have to be informed that no state aid could be forthcoming so long as the church condoned or ignored the land war. Not even the Rescript, however,

[15] Balfour to Salisbury, 28 Oct. 1887, Salisbury MSS.
[16] Beach to Salisbury, 22 April 1887, *ibid.*

could induce the Government to move decisively in the direction of a Catholic university. The objections of Unionists in both countries proved strong enough to offset the influence of Norfolk, his Catholic sympathizers, and the moderates in the Government. In this important area of conciliation words took the place of action, and bigotry stifled good intentions as well as political scruples.

II. THE SPECIAL COMMISSION

In the summer of 1888 the Unionist leaders decided to put Parnell, his colleagues, and the New Departure on trial before a commission of English judges. Few governments have ever committed an error of such magnitude, and those Unionists who approved this course fully deserved the abuse that was heaped upon them by contemporaries and posterity. There is no better example of the degree to which the Irish Question forced men to abandon their normal standards of conduct and to revel so exultantly in their prejudices. It was more than ironical that the idea of a special commission should commend itself to the man who had fought against proclaiming the National League and who had championed bold reforms for Ireland. But whatever the personal involvement of Chamberlain in this trial—and Captain Harrison, the vindicator of Parnell, has compiled an impressive case against him—Lord Salisbury and his colleagues were also at fault. They knew only too well that crime of one sort or another had always "dogged the footsteps" of agitators in Ireland. But the temptation of ruining their political opponents at a single blow proved too much for them. The cabinet longed to see Parnell defend himself in an English court against the charges of complicity in murder and outrage brought by the *Times,* and they were willing to do all within their legal power—and perhaps more—to help the paper prove its case.[17]

The origins, procedure, and findings of the Special Commission constitute such familiar ground that they need no detailed study

[17] See H. Harrison, *Parnell, Joseph Chamberlain, and Mr. Garvin,* London, 1938, pp. 164-202, and Harrison, *Parnell, Joseph Chamberlain and "the Times,"* Dublin, 1953. See also Morley, *Gladstone,* III, chap. 3; W. S. Churchill, *Churchill,* II, pp. 405-28; R. B. O'Brien, *Lord Russell of Killowen,* pp. 210-58; J. MacDonald, *A Diary of the Parnell Commission,* London, 1890.

THE CHALLENGE

Accused by the *Times* of complicity in criminal agitation,
Parnell is forced to defend himself before the Special Commission.

here. Suffice it to say that, as in the Dreyfus case, there was more
at stake than the guilt—or innocence—of one man. Ministers
and their allies were determined to discredit Home Rule as well as
its chief apostles, and to accomplish this end they sought to prove

that the New Departure represented nothing more than the old methods of intimidation and rebellion in Irish history. When the *Times* published the facsimile letter linking Parnell, by implication, with the Phoenix Park murders, Unionist disgust knew no bounds. Although Parnell immediately denounced it as a "villainous and barefaced forgery," he wisely refrained from taking legal proceedings in an English law court. Government members, already inflamed by the debates on the Crimes Bill, challenged him to disprove the charges; and Lord Salisbury described Parnell as a man "tainted with the strong presumption of conniving at assassination." There may indeed have been more than a grain of truth in Tim Healy's charge that the *Times*, with ministerial approval, had rushed the letter into print in order to convince the Liberal Unionists, who showed signs of faltering over the Crimes Bill, that coercion was the only way to deal with criminals in constitutional disguise.[18]

Healy

When a fresh batch of incriminating letters came to light in the course of a libel action brought against the *Times* under curious circumstances by a renegade Parnellite F. H. O'Donnell, then Parnell's position began to look hopeless. The leading counsel for the *Times* in this suit was the plump, industrious, and somewhat obtuse attorney general, Sir Richard Webster. He undertook the case in spite of audible demurs from members of the Bar, who held that the chief law officer of the Government had no business defending the *Times* in a private action that was closely bound up with his status as a cabinet minister. But the attorney general saw no reason why he should be disqualified simply because he believed in the validity of the charges pressed by his client. Like his cabinet colleagues, moreover, Webster shared Chamberlain's conviction that the *Times* possessed more than enough evidence to prove the criminal inspiration of Parnellism.[19] The paper won its case early in July, and when Parnell demanded a select committee to examine the charges, the Government countered with a proposal to appoint a special commission. After prolonged obstruction and repeated use of the closure, ministers carried their bill, which set up the machinery of inquisition. The

[18] Healy, *Letters and Leaders of My Day*, I, pp. 271-72.
[19] See Viscount Alverstone, *Recollections of Bar and Bench*, New York, 1914, pp. 143-44.

tribunal was composed of three judges who were by no means sympathetic with Irish nationalism, and in October the "huge fishing enquiry" began.

All these events have been common knowledge for many years. But there are aspects of the case that have remained in obscurity to tease the imagination of every student of the period. The discretion exercised by ministers about the commission, even in their private communications, makes the task of piecing the story together all the more difficult. Here and there a small ray of light illuminates the movements of certain Unionists, but the image or impression is soon lost in the darkness of official silence. If a few tantalizing clues about the Government's relations with the *Times* have survived, too often they lead to conclusions based upon conjecture rather than fact. Nevertheless, enough evidence exists to suggest that confidence about the proceedings in the new law courts was conspicuously absent, not only in the Unionist coalition but also in Dublin Castle. In view of the widespread fears engendered by the Special Commission among certain Conservatives and Liberal Unionists, Government whips were forced to strain their powers to the utmost in order to prevent abstentions at division time.

The fact was that Home Rulers were not alone in regarding the commission as a poor substitute for a select committee of the House of Commons or a court of law. Many Liberal Unionists opposed the tribunal as a dangerous and insidious device, and Lord Hartington tried to discourage ministers from their course of action. Among Conservatives, even Lord Cranbrook balked initially at the use of parliamentary machinery for a quasi-legal purpose, although he soon gave in to the more compelling argument of "political necessity or expediency."[20] Churchill, greatly to his credit, denounced the commission from start to finish; and in July, 1888, he sent a long and prescient memorandum to W. H. Smith, warning against the creation of a "revolutionary tribunal" the findings of which would in no way alter the situation in Ireland. "Prudent politicians," he concluded, "would hesitate to go out of their way to play such high stakes as these."[21] But ministers had long since hardened themselves to the aspersions that flowed from

[20] Gathorne Hardy, *Cranbrook*, II, p. 298.
[21] Maxwell, *W. H. Smith*, II, pp. 227-31.

this quarter, and they chose to ignore the advice. Another prominent Unionist also deprecated the idea of a special commission. Lord Lytton, ambassador to Paris, wrote at this time to his confidante in London, Lady Dorothy Nevill: "I can't think what the *Times* has to gain, beyond a heavy bill, by spreading out its case at such length and in such detail, over ground which the public already knows by heart, and cares nothing about. If it can prove its charge on the Parnell letters, it will smash Parnell, and, if it fails to do this, it will have done no good to itself or any one else."[22]

More important than such disparaging remarks was the surprising behavior of the attorney general. Toward the end of August, Webster informed W. H. Smith, who was taking the waters at Aix les Bains, that he could not act as leading counsel in the Special Commission, on the grounds that it was "improper" for a minister to prosecute his political opponents. He wrote: "I have been going through the charges which will come before the Commission and I have come to the distinct conclusion that I ought not and must not appear before the Commission. To act as Counsel for the *Times* in an ordinary action brought by O'Donnell . . . is one thing; but this enquiry will embrace a number of charges against several Members of Parliament and will examine into the working of the Land League in England, Ireland, and America."[23]

The leader of the House, thinking that it was a little late for Webster to parade such scruples, replied by telegram that the final decision must rest on Webster's conscience and on his sense of duty to the *Times* and to the Government. Smith then forwarded Webster's letter to Salisbury, contending that with the attorney general out of the way the Government would at least have a much freer hand in dealing with the evidence collected by the commission. No pressure, he felt, ought to be put on Webster. But a second blow followed almost at once. Sir Henry James, whom the *Times* had retained as second counsel, and who had suspected that the facsimile letter was a forgery as early as January, 1887, also tried to excuse himself from the commission for much the same reasons as Webster. James argued rather

[22] D. Nevill, *Under Five Reigns*, London, 1913, p. 194.
[23] Webster to Smith, n.d. Aug. 1888, Salisbury MSS.

weakly that his role in the tribunal would exclude him from debating the issue in the House of Commons.[24]

Lord Salisbury was "very much disgruntled" by these signs of mutiny. The withdrawal of these two men, he feared, would not only have a serious effect upon the outcome of the commission, but would also place the *Times*'s witnesses in an awkward position. His reply to W. H. Smith conveyed a sense of the urgency that he attached to the whole undertaking:

"Now the simultaneous refusal of these two men to go on would have the worst possible effect. There will be no persuading the outside world that they have not run away from the case because on scrutinizing the evidence they satisfied themselves that the case was bad. The effect of this impression which will be of course heightened by Parnell's scribes will be disastrous upon all the Irish witnesses. They will be convinced that Parnell's is the winning hand and they will forswear themselves like mad. Again—where is the *Times* to supply the place of these two men? There is very little more left: men have made their engagements —this is a case which will require the devotion of all a man's time. There is great danger that owing to this surprise the *Times* will have to put up with some younger and inferior man. And this is a case in which everything depends upon cross-examination: for the Irish witnesses may be too much frightened to speak out, and the real truth will never be got out of them except by the screw of cross-examination."[25]

The attorney general, he concluded, was by no means so indispensable a debater in the House of Commons: a substitute could always be found to take his place in the debates on the commission. W. H. Smith forwarded a copy of this letter to Webster, who, however, continued to hold out obstinately for another fortnight. But the latter's contention that Parnell ought to have recourse to the ordinary courts of law fell upon deaf ears. By September 15 Webster had yielded to the entreaties of his colleagues, presumably on the condition that he be allowed to take part in the ensuing debates on "Parnellism and crime." To the Solicitor General Sir Edward Clarke he confessed his intense dislike of the commission: "Every day I curse Chamberlain and

[24] Smith to Salisbury, 29, 30 Aug., 2 Sept. 1888, *ibid.*
[25] Salisbury to Smith, 4, 9, 15 Sept. 1888, *ibid.*

the Unionists for their obstinacy, but perhaps they are wiser than I am." And in his memoirs he hinted at the severe pressure which the cabinet brought to bear and which he "could not well resist."[26] Sir Henry James followed suit by ending his own resistance to appearing as counsel for the *Times*. The Government had survived their crisis in connection with the Special Commission; and Salisbury was able to inform his nephew on September 20: "I suppose you heard from Smith of Webster's attempt to get out of his collar. We have kept the harness tight on him—but I am afraid he shows signs of gibbing still."[27]

Balfour himself was by no means free of doubts about the Special Commission. Although appreciative of the *Times*'s intentions, he realized the disadvantages of a commission and was somewhat sceptical of the newspaper's case. The legal proceedings made him uneasy. Some technicality, such as the intimidation of witnesses or the absence of certain documentary evidence, could, he felt, easily shake the foundations of the *Times*'s case. The fact that Parnell had in the past disdained a suit for libel against the paper did not impress him. Every man, in his opinion, had the right to repudiate such charges in a court of law: but failure to do so did not mean that the accusations were necessarily true. Irish nationalists, after all, had abused and vilified the chief secretary every day "in the grossest manner"; and yet he had never brought any suit for damages. If the *Times* succeeded in proving their charges, Balfour believed that the Irish party would be "blown to pieces," but he saw too many uncertainties to be confident of this result.[28] And in a speech at Eridge Park he prepared a loophole by asserting that the case against the Parnellites would not be "one whit weakened" even if all the *Times*'s charges turned out to be a "baseless accusation."

No aspect of the Special Commission caused the Government more anxiety than the nature of their obligation to the *Times*.

[26] Alverstone, *op.cit.*, pp. 144-45; Clarke, *The Story of My Life*, pp. 274-75.

[27] Salisbury to Balfour, 20 Sept. 1888, Salisbury MSS. Besides Webster and James, the *Times* was represented at the commission by J. P. Murphy, Q.C., John Atkinson, Q.C. (later Irish solicitor general and attorney general), W. Graham, and S. Ronan.

[28] Balfour to J. Hogg, 23 July 1888; Balfour to O'Brien, 21 July 1888, Add. MS 49827.

The charges contained in the articles entitled "Parnellism and Crime" vitally affected Unionist policy in Ireland. Were ministers therefore going to offer the paper every form of assistance in preparing their case, or did they intend to applaud the proceedings from the sidelines? The choice was made easier for them because the Home Rulers were bound to accuse the Government of collusion, no matter what the extent of their help to the paper and regardless of the commission's findings. To most of the cabinet, then, the question of assisting the *Times* became one of degree rather than kind. But the problem still posed difficulties, and Balfour asked his uncle whether or not the Government could legitimately transmit special information to the *Times*: "If we do *not* it may get wasted—if we do shall we not find ourselves in a somewhat embarrassing position?" Salisbury replied that there was no general answer to this query. Each case would have to be decided on its individual merits. "There may be grounds," he added, "for not stirring, if the evidence in question is not of a conclusive kind: or if the mode of getting it cannot be explained. If—on the other hand—it has come naturally into our hands—& still more if it clearly fixes some one's guilt, we shall be fulfilling an obvious and elementary duty in facilitating the proof of it before the Commission."[29]

The policy eventually pursued by the Irish administration was to make available to the *Times*'s solicitors the criminal files in Dublin Castle, and on occasion to grant interviews with Crimes Act prisoners, when there was a reasonable prospect of strengthening the case against the Parnellites. In addition, leave was granted to a large number of police constables, district inspectors, and magistrates, who were chosen to testify before the commission on the subject of politically inspired crime. But there was no unanimity either in Dublin Castle or in the cabinet on the question of whether or not evidence from Government sources was admissible, let alone prudent, and matters were further complicated because much of the Castle's information came from informers whose activities necessitated anonymity.

As the Special Commission continued its hearings, a growing sense of apprehension began to penetrate Dublin Castle. For

[29] Balfour to Salisbury, 17 Aug. 1888, Salisbury mss; Salisbury to Balfour, 22 Aug. 1888, Add. ms 49689.

early in November, 1888, Ridgeway learned that the letters upon which the *Times* had built their case had originally belonged to Richard Pigott. In that small world of writers, journalists, and patriots for which Dublin was so celebrated, the name of Pigott had long been synonymous with impoverished depravity. This hack journalist, the author of endless begging letters to the rich and famous, was known to be not only a blackmailer but a dealer in pornography and a bitter enemy of the Parnellites. Despised and despising, he was destined to become the Titus Oates of Irish history. Having absorbed some of these details, Ridgeway gave his chief the first definite word on the spurious nature of the letters, and predicted that the counsel for the defense would have no trouble in exposing them as forgeries. Such a result, he feared, would not only "neutralize a verdict against Parnell and Co. on other points," but would utterly demoralize every department in the Castle. According to Ridgeway, the *Times*'s solicitor Joseph Soames had completely bungled his preliminary investigations:

"The *Times* has been so extraordinarily reckless that one is naturally inclined to deny it credit for ordinary caution and common sense. They have never made any enquiry here regarding Pigott's character and antecedents before or since they accepted his information. By an accident Harrel placed in Soames' hands the papers regarding Pigott which I enclose to you. Soames seemed to pay little or no attention to them. Harrel had at that time no idea that Pigott had anything to do with the letters."[30]

Six months earlier Soames had boasted about making a "great haul" of Land League papers in Dublin, and Ridgeway had written confidently to Balfour: "The result is to make the *Times* case quite safe in the coming action, and, if Soames is not over-sanguine, to break Parnell's reputation. . . . Altogether the case looks very promising. If it is successful then I would suggest that advantage be taken of public feeling for a general advance all along the line on our part. If we could strike at the National League in Dublin and at *United Ireland*, I really believe that we should finally triumph and the movement would be overcome."[31]

And now the unpleasant truth was known. It was too late to repair the damage: all that Balfour could do was to inform his

[30] Ridgeway to Balfour, 9, 15 Nov. 1888, *ibid.*, 49809.
[31] Ridgeway to Balfour, 15 May 1888, *ibid.*, 49808.

colleagues in the Government of the imminent blow and advise Ridgeway how to sustain morale in the Castle. The attorney general thus had every reason to postpone discussion of the letters in the commission. And during the intervening months, ministers had ample time in which to prepare themselves for Pigott's unmasking.[32]

The *Times* spent thousands of pounds in compiling evidence of criminal intent and deed against the Parnellites; but it required only a little imagination to examine the credentials not only of Edward C. Houston, the secretary of the Irish Loyal and Patriotic Union, but of the man who supplied him with proof of Parnell's sinister operations. And if the owners of the paper already knew the facts about Pigott and still persisted in their charges, they deserved all that ensued, and more. To convince the commissioners of Parnellite iniquity, the *Times* lined up a cast of witnesses that included Captain O'Shea, Major Henri le Caron, the notorious antinationalist spy, the inept Captain Slacke, and numerous other officials connected with Irish administration. Sir Richard Webster, a poor speaker at best, handled the case with more bluster than skill; but he managed at least to stave off examination of the letters for four months. It was a time of forensic marathons. Witnesses and counsel alike reveled in long-winded speeches: Davitt's speech lasted for seven days; Sir Henry James droned on for twelve; and Sir Charles Russell required seven days to encompass the whole of Irish history. Witnesses came and went, the evidence against the Irish party mounted steadily, but no startling facts came to light until the week of February 14, when Soames went on the stand to testify about the sources of the *Times*'s information. Gradually the links in the chain were fitted together, as three more witnesses followed in significant order: J. C. Macdonald, the manager of the *Times*, Houston, and then Pigott. Soames admitted having paid Houston some £30,000 for "all purposes"; and the latter revealed that he had tried in vain to peddle the letters elsewhere but that only the *Times* would touch them. Attention within the court room and outside centered on the letters attributed to Parnell. And when Sir Charles Russell

[32] Webster subsequently admitted that he first learned of Pigott's complicity in mid-December; but circumstantial evidence would place the date at least one month earlier. See *Hansard*, 3d series, Vol. 334, p. 565.

finally succeeded in breaking Pigott down by the simple expedient of comparing handwriting and spelling, the Unionist
debacle was at hand. Russell, who had a flair for melodrama, prolonged the Unionists' embarrassment most adroitly. On February
22 he revealed Pigott as an absurdly clumsy forger who had
managed to dupe the *Times*.

The sequel is well known. Under police escort Pigott returned
to Anderton's Hotel, where he was staying; on the following
evening he called on Labouchere and signed a written confession;
and on Sunday the 24th he walked out of the hotel never to return.
Pigott had cheated his enemies out of their last satisfaction by
taking flight—in spite of his penniless state and in spite of a
police escort composed of an RIC constable and two detectives
from Scotland Yard. Five days later he committed suicide in
a Madrid hotel. Many Unionists who had heard rumors of
forgeries and of Pigott's seedy past were staggered nevertheless
by the turn of events in the central law courts. Lord Lytton made
a futile gesture by applying to the French government for a
warrant to arrest the fugitive Pigott, and then asked Lady
Dorothy Nevill in a letter the question that was on everyone's
lips: "How could the *Times* have been such a fool as to lean such
a heavy stake on such a rotten reed?" The scandal, he concluded,
would cause "infinite harm to us Unionists, whom it covers with
confusion."[33]

Nowhere was this confusion more acute than in Ireland, where
a profound gloom settled upon the loyalist population. In the
Castle many officials were shocked by the news; the *Freeman's
Journal* exulted in the *Times*'s humiliation and referred to the
Government as the "Pigottist Party"; while Unionists in both
countries talked despondently of a dissolution. A vivid account of
morale in the Castle was supplied by Ridgeway, who wrote Balfour
two days before Pigott's collapse under cross-examination:

"The state of things here is really very funny. There is utter
consternation in the Law Room. The Attorney General has for
the last two or three days refused to look at a paper. We cannot
get him to do anything. He is utterly demoralised by the present
phase of the Parnell Commission and regards a change of Gov-

[33] D. Nevill, *op.cit.*, pp. 194-95.

PENANCE!

The exposure of Pigott's forgeries in February 1889 shatters
the *Times'* case against Parnell.

ernment as a certainty. Of course all this is very undignified,
but if Pigott comes out of the ordeal all right it will be only a
passing inconvenience. If, however, the *Times'* case as regards
the letter is smashed up, I fear that we shall have serious diffi-

culties with the Attorney General and I think it would be well if in that case you were to get him over to London and restore his nerve. The curious thing is that all along we have anticipated a collapse of this part of the case with equanimity. I do not therefore understand this panic."[34]

Ridgeway tried hard to exhort his subordinates, the law officers most of all, to continue prosecuting Crimes Act offenders, but Irish officials did not recover their nerve for several months. From Dublin the demoralization spread rapidly to the Irish Office and to the cabinet in London. Balfour, with his usual detachment, observed just after the blow had fallen: "To a person of cynical mind there is something extremely entertaining in the present posture of affairs with regard to the Parnell Commission. That the *Times* has been stupid beyond all that history tells us of stupidity is surprising enough. It is perhaps even more surprising that the results of their stupidity should have spread such dismay among our own people."[35] One thing was certain, he maintained: the Government were not going to resign over the forgeries.

Ridgeway's forewarning about the forged letters, however, had not diminished the impact of the blow in some quarters. Unionists were both angry and humiliated, and in a vengeful mood. "What a state of things when the fate of an Empire depends on . . . a Pigott," Ridgeway wrote after the suicide. And then he tried to console Balfour with the afterthought: "I am sure that if the Parnellites get rope enough, they will spoil their case. They *always* do. They have no *taste*. Luckily they have not all the wisdom and self-control of Parnell."[36] As for Parnell, never had his stock stood so high in England. His vindication was as utter and complete as the *Times*'s humiliation. And the standing ovation he received in the Commons on March 1 —the first such demonstration since Warren Hastings' acclamation over seventy years before—was echoed by Liberals and Irishmen alike throughout the British Isles.

In public Lord Salisbury preserved a mask of indifference to these results of the commission. During Pigott's cross-examination

[34] Ridgeway to Balfour, 20 Feb. 1889, Add. ms 49809.
[35] Balfour to Ridgeway, 22 Feb. 1889, *ibid.*, 49827.
[36] Ridgeway to Balfour, 2 March 1889, *ibid.*, 49809.

he had endeavored to calm the Queen with reassuring words: the Irish journalist, he insisted, was only a "thorough rogue" whose testimony no one ought to take seriously.[37] And in his speeches the prime minister stressed the irrelevance of the letters compared with the other charges pending against the nationalists. In one of his addresses Salisbury attained what Hammond has called the "high water mark of . . . patrician insolence," by observing that Pigott's exposure proved only that one nationalist could forge the signature of another.[38] Home Rulers never forgave him for equating Parnell with the author of the forged letters. But to his intimates Salisbury did not conceal his alarm about the course of events. A note of increasing weariness with politics began to appear in his private correspondence. Intellectually, he confessed, he was "dead tired." The cumulative strains of two offices were taking their toll, and W. H. Smith's recurrent ill-health aggravated his worries. The "violence and unscrupulousness" of the Opposition depressed him more and more; and while dissuading Smith from his desire to resign in February, 1889, he wrote: "We are in a state of bloodless civil war. No common principles, no respect for common institutions or traditions, unite the various groups of politicians who are struggling for power. To loot somebody or something is the common object, under a thick varnish of pious phrases. So that our lines are not cast in pleasant places."[39] Smith remained at his post; and Salisbury gradually emerged from his fit of depression. Rumors of an impending ministerial resignation served to revive his fighting spirit, although he confessed to Alfred Austin: "As to internal affairs—they do not look promising. The life of the Ministry and the life of the G. O. M. are both ebbing—the question is which will ebb the fastest. On the answer to that question the fate of Ireland—and possibly of England—depends."[40]

[37] Salisbury to Queen Victoria, 21 Feb. 1889, Salisbury MSS.

[38] *Gladstone and the Irish Nation*, p. 594.

[39] Maxwell, *W. H. Smith*, II, pp. 240-41.

[40] Salisbury to Austin, 21 March 1889, Salisbury MSS. After Pigott's suicide Balfour wrote to Ridgeway: ". . . things will probably go pretty smoothly now. I have never felt personally discouraged, and I hope that you will try and explain to our weak-kneed brethren in Dublin that the Government are not likely to dissolve for many years to come"; 4 March 1889, Add. MS 49827.

One of the results of the Pigott crisis was the degree to which it strengthened the Government's ties with the *Times*. Although the exact nature of their commitment after February, 1889, will most likely never be known, the cabinet did decide to give the *Times* "all possible help" at the beginning of the fateful week of February 14. What additional steps the Government took to assist the newspaper remains buried with those who agreed in the decision. But it is evident that Balfour considered the Government's record up to February "quite clean." The nationalists, he knew, would make every effort to implicate the Government in the *Times*'s reverse, but he affected not to be worried: " . . . the more violent the attack upon us . . . the better for the cause."[41] The reaction to Pigott's exposure and flight was not long in coming. In the House of Commons ministers came under heavy attack from the Opposition benches. Harcourt, in a truculent mood, flayed the attorney general for his role as "*quasi*-Public prosecutor," while Morley accused the Government of conniving with the *Times* in order to secure a verdict in their own favor. In Ireland the *Freeman's Journal* joined in the chorus of invective with an editorial on the conspiracy between "the Pigottists of the cabinet and the Pigottists of the *Times*." With his usual composure Balfour repudiated these charges in Parliament, describing them as "shocking . . . scandalous . . . unfounded calumny." From the outset, he asserted, ministers had adopted an impartial attitude toward the Special Commission and had volunteered no information to either party in the case unless specifically requested. Balfour ended his speech by accusing the Home Rule party in turn of suborning and intimidating witnesses at the trial. The net effect of these excited debates was to make Unionists profoundly uneasy about the nature of the Government's assistance to the *Times*. And in the public eye, ministers had not succeeded in removing the stigma of collusion.[42]

[41] Balfour to Ridgeway, 1 March 1889 *ibid.*; Ridgeway to Balfour, 14 Feb., 31 May 1889, *ibid.*, 49809. Balfour had told Peter O'Brien when he was in London of the Government's decision.

[42] *Hansard*, 3d series, Vol. 334, pp. 415 ff.; *Freeman's Journal*, 15 Feb.-25 March 1889.

III. THE SPECIAL COMMISSION REPORT

For the Special Commission's sponsors there were further insults and insinuations in store. After 128 days of hearings, at which 98,000 questions were asked of 450 witnesses, the judges delivered a verdict based on evidence that filled eleven volumes. Their report, presented on February 13, 1890, dismissed those charges against Parnell that had grown out of the forged letters, and found the leading members of his party guilty of associating with boycotters, moonlighters, and the Clan-na-Gael in America, and guilty also of inciting to intimidation and to the nonpayment of rents. These acts of incitement had in turn led to outrages. But no more direct connection between Parnellism and crime could be established by the commissioners.[43] In other words, nothing new had been discovered about the New Departure.

The Opposition had no intention of allowing the commission report to pass through Parliament unchallenged. The resentments and frustrations that had been festering for months now found release in a series of angry attacks upon the Unionist leaders and their policies. Harcourt demanded that the *Times*'s publication of the facsimile letter be treated as a breach of privilege; and the Government managed to defeat this motion by a paltry majority of forty-eight. Parnell then moved a vote of censure against the whole range of Government policy in Ireland. Balfour was not only pursuing a program of "petty and systematic exasperation," but he was so "circumscribed . . . cabined, cribbed, and confined by the peaceable disposition" of the Irish people that he was forced to arrest harmless newspaper boys for peddling copies of *United Ireland,* and to evict innocent tenants on Plan estates. The acrimonious debate on Parnell's motion dragged on for three nights, and the clerks in the Irish Office were kept busy dredging up statistics of agrarian crime over the past fifty years so that ministers could support their case for the criminal inspiration of Irish nationalism. Once again it took Balfour to extricate the Government from an awkward position. With a succession of deft gibes he coolly dismissed the main charges levied by the nationalists. This was the twelfth vote of censure concerned with Ireland he

[43] See Report of the Special Commission, 1888, *HC 1890*, Vol. 27, pp. 477-640.

could recall since his appointment as chief secretary, and he confessed that he saw no difference among them. He emphatically denied that the Plan of Campaign was comparable to trade union activities in England, and boasted that no new outbreak of the Plan had taken place during the previous year. As for the deterrent effect of the Crimes Act, he announced that only eighty of the 1,614 persons imprisoned under that measure had been sent to jail more than once.[44]

The Government survived Parnell's censure by a majority of sixty-seven; but worse was still to come. Somehow ministers had to acknowledge the judges' report in a way that would allow the Opposition the least possible room for exploiting the forged letters. Three choices of action confronted them: ministers could ignore the report altogether; they could move a vote of censure against those Parnellites whom the commissioners found guilty of inciting to illegal acts, or, lastly, they could introduce a compromise resolution accepting the report and thanking the judges for their diligent work. At a cabinet council on Saturday, February 15, the ministers after much wrangling approved Cranbrook's suggestion that corresponded with the third line of procedure. But over the week end Beach had a talk with Churchill, who strongly objected to any show of gratitude for the commission's findings. When the cabinet reassembled on Monday, Beach shifted his ground and urged that the choice really lay between the first two alternatives. Owing to a mix-up in arrangements, Lord Salisbury, who was recuperating from a severe bout of influenza, missed the meeting. A tense discussion followed in which the idea of a vote of censure was dropped: the "practical difficulties" in the way of such a solution were deemed insuperable. Beach emerged as the only advocate of a "do-nothing" policy, such was his fear of provoking the Parnellites any more than necessary. The rest of the cabinet, however, voted in favor of the motion drafted on Saturday; and that same night W. H. Smith gave notice in the House of a resolution accepting the report and thanking the judges for their "just and impartial conduct."[45]

During the fortnight's interval before the debate on this motion,

[44] *Hansard*, 3d series, Vol. 341, pp. 315-32, 594-607.

[45] Smith to Salisbury, 17, 18 Feb. 1890, Salisbury MSS; *Hansard*, 3d series, Vol. 341, p. 444.

an air of uneasiness pervaded the Government. Unionists prepared their defenses for the occasion with serious misgivings as to the outcome. Balfour, who was least affected by the general gloom, wrote to his convalescent uncle warning him about the state of morale and the prospects of the impending debate:

"The defence of the Opposition next week will largely turn on the alleged alliance of 1885. Randolph is very likely to take the opportunity of alleging that there *was* such an alliance—with details! *You* will be the man attacked: will you think over the case in reference 1) to anything that occurred in London in the summer and autumn of 1885 between either the leaders or the whips of the party. 2) Carnarvon and the Parnell interview: Did you know of the interview before it took place? This is a hurried scrawl— prompted by the fact that Beach, who has been asked to reply to W. E. G. thinks . . . *that our position is so weak that we must take a very moderate line about the proven charges.* I for one will *not*: but you see the matter is pressing."[46]

Balfour's prediction was accurate. The debate that began on March 3 turned largely on the Government's role in launching the commission, their relations with the *Times*, and their alliance with the Parnellites in the summer of 1885. In moving an amendment denouncing the "odious, grave, and false" charges against the Parnellites, Gladstone made an eloquent appeal to the individual conscience of every Unionist. But the debate soon degenerated into an exchange of insults.

The Opposition interrupted Government spokesmen so frequently that several speeches became nothing more than extended conversations with members opposite. While the Unionists attempted to defend the Commission as a "holy cause," their opponents called it a "foul conspiracy." Armed with the words "calumny" and "collusion," the Home Rule party concentrated their attacks on Pigott and the Government's relations with the *Times*. Sexton spent three hours indicting Unionist policy, and Sir Charles Russell asserted that Pigott's name "would have stunk in the nostrils of any Dublin citizen." Ministers were accused of deliberately playing down the forged letters that they had at one time accepted as valid, and Harcourt exonerated all

[46] Balfour to Salisbury, 26 Feb. 1890, Salisbury MSS.

of Parnell's supporters by declaring that "revolutions, however mild, are not made of rose-water."[47]

On the night of March 10 the Government defeated Gladstone's amendment to the question by a majority of sixty-one. But the excitement was not over. Lord Randolph Churchill had yet to deliver his indictment of the Special Commission—that "tremendous instrument of oppression." His speech on March 11 arose out of an amendment that he had encouraged his friend and disciple Louis Jennings to move. The motion sought to condemn those responsible for the charge of Parnellite complicity in murder, but it was not intended as a vote of censure against the Government. At the last minute Churchill changed his mind and asked Jennings to withdraw the amendment. Jennings' refusal to do so did not deter Churchill from speaking to the main question, and he rose to address the House determined to punish the Government for their folly. Too much bitterness, too many months in isolation had left their mark upon his sensitive nature, and the despair and disgust that welled within him soon found expression in a memorable outburst. First came the clinical reference to the commission as a "mountainous parturition"; next, the warning of a nemesis that awaited every government which used such devious methods; and finally, the ringing question: "What, with all your skill, with all your cleverness, has been the result?" And ministers shuddered in their seats as Churchill, jabbing his finger at them, forced out the words: "A ghastly, bloody, rotten, foetus—Pigott! Pigott!! Pigott!!!"[48]

This time "Randolph" had gone too far: the Unionist press the next day was unanimous in proclaiming that fact. Home Rulers rejoiced in a speech that had caused far more havoc among Government supporters than had any of their own harangues. Dissension among the Conservatives and Liberal Unionists was just what they had hoped for. Immediately after this belligerent speech, Jennings declared that he could no longer move his amendment now that others had chosen to "stab the Government in the back." Jennings' disenchantment and subsequent rupture with Churchill was symptomatic, to a lesser

[47] *Hansard*, 3d series, Vol. 341, pp. 1670-96; Vol. 342, pp. 165 ff.
[48] *Ibid.*, Vol. 342, pp. 511-16. See also W. S. Churchill, *Churchill* II, pp. 412-22.

degree, of a discontent that prevailed in other sections of the party. According to George Curzon, at least half the Conservative rank and file favored some motion like Jennings' but dared not disobey the whips unless some prominent Unionist took the initiative. Leonard Courtney, the incorruptible chairman of committees and a devoted Unionist, had contemplated moving such an amendment himself but was persuaded to drop the idea. Courtney nevertheless succeeded in registering his protest against the commission by voting, along with several other Conservatives, for Jennings' motion, which had been moved in another member's name. Admittedly, the dissident vote was small, but it reflected widespread disillusionment within the Government.[49]

Those Unionists who joined in denouncing Churchill's speech were somewhat sobered by the appearance in the *Morning Post* of the entire memorandum on the Special Commission, which Churchill had sent to W. H. Smith in July, 1888. Lord Randolph had had the last word, but his own vindication did not endear him any further to his former colleagues. The Government's intransigent attitude to the report, its refusal to admit the damage done by Pigott, served in the end not only to antagonize Irish public opinion, but to accelerate the swing of the electoral pendulum in England toward the Gladstonian Liberals.

The Special Commission report raised two other problems for the cabinet. First, what action was the House of Lords to take in regard to the judges' findings? And second, ought the Government to help defray the expenses of the *Times*'s witnesses? In the first place, several Unionist peers were eager to introduce a resolution in the Lords similar to that in the Commons. Lord Cranbrook was the chief exponent of this plan; Salisbury was lukewarm because the report did not directly concern any member of the Upper House; and W. H. Smith directly opposed this idea on the grounds that it might lead to a collision between the two houses. Cranbrook gave way to Smith's plea for a postponement, but the militant peers won out, for on March 21 Lord Salisbury moved a resolution virtually identical with that in the Commons. Salisbury praised the judges for having unearthed a number of "absolutely new" facts that ought to fascinate any student of

[49] G. P. Gooch, *Life of Lord Courtney*, London, 1920, pp. 282-83.

"the philosophy of Government and of revolutions." Relegating Pigott's letters to a minor position, he devoted most of his speech to the commission's other findings which proved that the Parnellites had had "their hand upon the throttle-valve of crime." To argue, moreover, as did Gladstone, that agrarian crime could be excused because it had led to such reforms as the Land Act of 1881 was to assert "more completely and more recklessly than any school of Jesuits had ever ventured to propose it" that the end justifies the means. The Liberal peers who spoke in the debate protested against the commission and the resolution that condoned it, but they did not bother to divide the House on the question, and the Unionists achieved their hollow victory in the Lords.[50]

The second item on the cabinet's agenda aroused much apprehension among ministers. Buckle, the *Times*'s managing editor, had written bluntly to Salisbury asking about the possibility of a Government subsidy for legal costs. The *Times*, he claimed, had spent some £60,000 simply on witnesses who had testified before the commission. Although Salisbury confessed to W. H. Smith that he would like to see some of this money repaid to the paper, he doubted if the Commons would even consider such a proposal. On February 22 the cabinet met in his absence and decided unanimously that it would be both "impossible and impolitic" to ask the House for such a vote of credit. Lord Chancellor Halsbury was particularly averse to the suggestion, declaring that the *Times* would be lucky to receive even £6,000 compensation under the ordinary court rules governing witnesses' costs.[51] And to clinch matters, Balfour wrote to his uncle deploring such a grant to the *Times* on grounds that were not intended for the eyes of posterity: "I do not want to give the *Times* people a sense of ill usage: and I think I could tell you some things which (if judiciously communicated to them) might convince them that their own conduct left no choice in the matter. But the communication will have to be oral."[52]

[50] See Cranbrook to Salisbury, 21-23 Feb. 1890; Smith to Cranbrook, 23 Feb. 1890; Salisbury to Cranbrook, 22 Feb. 1890, Salisbury MSS; *Hansard*, 3d series, Vol. 342, pp. 1362-67.

[51] Salisbury to Smith, 20, 24 Feb. 1890; Smith to Salisbury, 22 Feb. 1890, Salisbury MSS.

[52] Balfour to Salisbury, 22 Feb. 1890, *ibid.*

Ministers never dared raise the question in Commons, and Buckle had to go disappointed. It was estimated that the *Times* spent over £200,000 on the commission from start to finish. Parnell subsequently received a settlement of £5,000 in a suit for damages that he brought against the paper. In terms of reputation, however, the loss to the paper was incalculable.[53]

A large part of the Government's relations with the *Times* between 1888 and 1890 still lies in "twilight" and will probably never be "illumined by the calm lamp of the historian."[54] Too many clues are missing to make the story complete; and in the memoirs and biographies of those men responsible for the commission there is a noticeable acceleration of pace when these events are considered. Sir Richard Webster, for example, skims over his own role in the proceedings with almost indecent haste, and other accounts of the Unionist leaders at this time are so discreet as to be most misleading. Yet some inferences can be drawn without indulging the imagination. It was more than a coincidence, for instance, that Balfour should have secured the *Times*'s consent, in the critical month of February, 1889, to publish official versions of nationalist "lies" about coercion in Ireland. The Irish administration, furthermore, had already opened its files to the *Times*'s solicitors; and a large number of police and magistrates had been relieved of their duties in Ireland so that they might testify in London. Moreover, in a moment of weakness W. H. Smith, who was not called "Old Morality" without reason, had admitted that Walter, the owner of the paper, had come to see him about the commission in the capacity of an "old friend." As a matter of fact, the cabinet had considered awarding Walter a peerage in the spring of 1888, when Smith had advised Salisbury that the present moment was the most favorable for such a move. "The public," he maintained, "would not now connect it in any marked manner with 'Parnellism and Crime,' but if you wait until the trial comes off, it will take the appearance of being either a reward or a consolation."[55] Instead of a peerage Walter received the Special Commission. Then, too, the cabinet,

[53] See *The History of the "Times," 1884-1912*, London, 1947, III, p. 89.
[54] W. S. Churchill, *op.cit.*, II, p. 426.
[55] Smith to Salisbury, 21 May 1888, Salisbury MSS. Walter died in 1894 without ever having received the desired promotion.

just after Pigott's collapse, had decided to give the *Times* "all possible help," although the exact nature of that aid is still unknown. The circumstances of Pigott's flight from London and arrival in Spain must also arouse some suspicion of connivance on the part of the Home Office. And last but most significant, the Government's blatant use of the attorney general as well as of extralegal machinery to prosecute their political opponents leaves no doubt as to the meaning of collusion. It was precisely because the public knew something about the strong ties, personal as well as political, which connected the ministry and the *Times* that the Unionist leaders had to be so careful in their dealings with the paper. After February, 1889, however, the Government could do little more to help their ally than focus attention on those charges that still remained to be proved. And the fact that the great majority of people in England and Ireland cared only about the dramatic vindication of Parnell tended to obscure not only those other charges but also the strenuous exertions of ministers to advertise them.

For lending their moral and material support to what became a witch hunt the Government suffered heavily in prestige at home and abroad. It is hard to excuse ministers for their clumsy attempts to prove by arbitrary means what informed persons had known for years. Hammond emphasized the Government's blindness to the Irish scene when he observed: "Successful violence was indeed the one permanent fact of Irish history."[56] But the truth was that the leading Conservatives were not totally unaware of this fact. In 1888 they believed that it was high time to expose the criminal content of Parnellism so as to deny it any chance of success in the future. This was not the only justification of the Special Commission. To explain Unionist conduct one must look beyond the Irish Sea, for the men who sponsored the commission were inordinately concerned with the integrity and the future of the British empire. They sought to indict Parnellism before an imperial, not just an English, audience; and a passionate conviction that their goals were in the national interest drove them to adopt such extreme methods. A disintegrating force, one that challenged the very premises upon which the empire rested, had erupted close to the epicenter of the imperial

[56] *Gladstone and the Irish Nation*, p. 579.

system; and the Unionist leaders were willing to pay any price in order to bring discredit upon those who threatened the vast, vulnerable network of colonies, dominions, and protectorates. In their view the Parnellites were striking a treacherous blow at one of the major sources of England's pre-eminence, and this at a time when the country could least afford to indulge such a divisive force. The perversion of justice embodied in the commission could thus be rationalized by the need to impress the great powers of Europe with the image of an ever-greater Britain, which was by no means on the verge of imperial disunity, economic decline, and national self-effacement. Such were the wider implications of the Special Commission.

For the Government and for Ireland the results of the commission were not wholly negative. As Leonard Courtney perceived, the fiasco of the forged letters moved the Conservative leaders to recommend constructive measures for Ireland that, in ordinary circumstances, would have been repugnant to many of their supporters. Balfour himself had always intended to supplement coercion with relief measures, but he had still to convince the bulk of the party, and especially the loyalists in Ulster, of their necessity. He was well on the way to failing in this mission when the Pigott scandal broke, provoking widespread resentment against the Unionists. Like the nationalists, the Liberal Unionists never allowed the Government to forget their blunders; and in this sense the Special Commission served to educate Conservative Unionists about the necessity of conciliation. It was a lesson long overdue.

CHAPTER XIV

Government Policy and the Fall of Parnell

I. MINISTERIAL WOES

BY-ELECTIONS are by no means infallible guides to the popularity of government policy in one field or another, but there can be no doubt that the Special Commission helped to swing the marginal vote in England toward the Liberals. Up to the summer of 1888 both British parties had shared almost equally the fortunes of the electoral game. But from the time of the Special Commission to the general election, the Unionists lost over fifteen seats while registering only one gain. Even more indicative, the Unionist majority in Parliament dropped from 118 in 1886 to sixty-six at the time of the dissolution in 1892. These reverses quickly punctured the complacency of ministers and their supporters: Unionists of all complexions came to dread every new trial of strength. The problem of morale was all the more acute in Ireland, where loyalists awaited the results of each English by-election as though their lives and property were at stake. Ridgeway described Irish interest in these contests as "astounding"; and the visible sagging of spirits in the Castle after each Government defeat caused him endless annoyance. On the occasion of a by-election at Deptford, at the end of February, 1888, where Scawen Blunt stood as a Gladstonian Liberal, the under secretary wrote to Balfour: "People really seem to believe that the fate of the Union depends on the capricious vote of these few thousand Cockneys and Navvies. But as they do think so, I devoutly hope that we shall win."[1] The Conservative candidate did win, although he polled only 275 votes more than Blunt, who was still sitting out his sentence in Kilmainham jail. Whenever possible, Balfour warned Dublin Castle of an impending defeat and took pains to deny that the Irish Question had any bearing whatsoever on the outcome. For his own part he was "perfectly indifferent" to these

---

[1] Ridgeway to Balfour, 29 Feb. 1888, Add. MS 49808.

electoral results, except as they affected the "spirits and perhaps the loyalty" of officials in Ireland.[2]

In the hope of strengthening the "union of hearts" the Parnellites resorted to "barn-storming" tactics in England. Members of the Irish party would descend upon English constituencies in groups of four or five and exhort the local voters to support Gladstone, Progress, and Home Rule. The introduction of a brogue and a new note of acrimony into the provincial hustings in England not only enhanced the Liberal cause but acutely discomfited Government supporters. Although Balfour always felt nothing but contempt for those Irishmen who canvassed voters from "pothouse to pothouse," he regretted that Unionist members could never be induced to sacrifice their own holidays to such pursuits. What struck him as highly ironical was the tendency of these itinerant Parnellites to forsake the question of Home Rule and to emphasize in their speeches such issues as the wheel and van tax or elective county councils.[3] But the Parnellites knew what they were doing. Home Rule, after all, could not be won in Irish constituencies but only in those of England, Wales, and Scotland. According to Dillon, the Irish party spent some £4,000 every year on electioneering in England. The money went to finance the printing and distribution of pamphlets as well as to pay for traveling expenses; and Dillon was convinced that the "steady work of education in the English constituencies" had spread the cause of Home Rule far and wide among British voters. It was in part a tribute to the tenacity of the Irish party that Gladstone should confess in 1890 that he had never in his life known such interest to be taken in elections as in the past five years.[4]

The string of Liberal victories not only re-enforced the cause of Home Rule but aggravated the Government's problems of patronage. Salisbury, for instance, had to plead with the Queen in the summer of 1888 to postpone raising a Conservative M.P. to the peerage because of the precarious state of the constituency in

[2] Balfour to Ridgeway, 18 Feb., 1 March 1888; Balfour to P. O'Brien, 9 March 1889, *ibid.*, 49826-827.

[3] Balfour to P. O'Brien, 29 June 1888, *ibid.*

[4] Dillon to T. A. Emmet, 15 April 1893, Emmet MSS, AIHS; *Annual Register, 1890*, p. 205.

question. "A defeat just now," he argued, "would be very damaging: and would moreover be a serious impediment to the Government of Ireland. Every electoral defeat here gives a fresh impulse to the National League."[5] Needless to say, it was not just the Special Commission, Mitchelstown, or prison scandals that decided these contests. Many voters were apathetic about the Irish Question and cared far more about low wages in times of reviving prosperity, free education, the budget, liquor licenses, local government, or even foreign affairs. Conservative party agents sent out to assess the role of the Special Commission in these elections invariably reported that local issues and the personal popularity of the candidates had determined the outcome. Salisbury, on the other hand, attributed these reverses not to the "mere mismanagement" of party agents but to the existence of a strong, irresistible "Socialist current." The success of the London dockers' strike, he believed, had inspired the working classes with the "wildest hopes." To share the country's private wealth seemed to be the prevalent cry, and compared with this tempting goal, the Irish Question was, for the mass of workers, only a small cloud on the horizon.[6]

There were other reasons besides by-elections for the sharp decline in Unionist morale during the spring and summer of 1890. For one thing, W. H. Smith's health was again in danger. The attacks of eczema had grown more severe, and the suffering they caused had depleted his reserves of strength. Consultations among the Unionist leaders and with his doctor revealed grave doubts about his ability to continue as leader of the House. Word of his bad health leaked out to the press and speculation about a successor grew rife: Balfour, Hicks Beach, Goschen, Hartington, and even Churchill were rumored as possibilities. But the cabinet decided that Smith could not be spared at this juncture; and after a cruise on his yacht, the "Pandora," and with his doctor's approval, he returned to his post in June, albeit in a weakened condition.[7] A second and more crucial reason for the Government's

[5] Salisbury to Queen Victoria, 23 June, 29 Aug. 1888, Salisbury MSS. Sir Archibald Campbell, the member in question, was raised to the peerage as Baron Blythswood in August, 1892.

[6] Salisbury to Queen Victoria, 16 March, 18 Oct. 1889, *ibid.*

[7] Smith to Salisbury, 31 May 1890, *ibid.*; Maxwell, *W. H. Smith*, II, pp. 272-74.

malaise was that the legislative machinery of the Commons was creaking and groaning to a halt. By early spring ministers foresaw trouble ahead for their whole legislative program. Alarmed by the slow progress being made in Parliament, Salisbury tried to rally Conservative support for Government measures at a party meeting in the Carlton Club on March 20. There he warned against the dangers of obstruction and insisted on the necessity of passing a land purchase bill for Ireland, as well as the Tithe Bill and a measure to promote free or assisted education. Unfortunately, Goschen's local taxation duties bill antagonized the temperance party, which resented the idea of any compensation for owners whose liquor licenses would be revoked; and the increase in the spirits tax aroused the ire of distillers and brewers alike. The cumulative effects of the Special Commission and coercion in Ireland had put the Opposition in a vindictive mood, and Government bills were being dissected clause by clause.

On June 8 Salisbury informed the Queen that the situation in the House of Commons was so serious that certain important bills might have to be postponed. To keep Parliament sitting into September was out of the question. Four days later another meeting of Conservative members was held at the Carlton Club, where the prime minister warned of a legislative collapse if the Opposition did not let up on their attacks. The only practicable way out of this impasse, he suggested, was to carry over several bills from this session to the next. There was some grumbling about this plan, but most of the party agreed with Salisbury that postponing the Tithe and Land bills until 1891 would never do. In the Commons ministerial efforts to appease the Opposition failed; and prolonged wrangling forced W. H. Smith to announce that the compensation clauses in the local tax bill were being withdrawn. Opposition leaders exulted and predicted a general election in July. At the same time Lord Cranbrook warned Salisbury that the Conservatives in the Commons were "thoroughly demoralised" and almost "reduced . . . to pulp"; he expressed his fear that they might "go to pieces" if drastic steps were not taken.[8] Government supporters, in fact, were exhausted; they yearned for release from their parliamentary chores; and country houses, spas, and the Riviera beckoned irresistibly. So lax and irregular was the at-

[8] Cranbrook to Salisbury, 24 June 1890, Salisbury MSS.

tendance of Unionists at Westminster that Government majorities dropped to forty-five and less.

An additional source of discontent came from within the Unionist alliance: this was the chronic grumbling about party patronage or the flow of honors. Neither W. H. Smith nor Salisbury ever managed to convince party supporters, whether Conservative or Liberal Unionists, that the "distribution of loaves and fishes" was as generous and equitable as possible under the circumstances. The supply of honors was never adequate to meet the demands of the Unionist alliance. And the Liberal Unionists, in particular, asked a high price in terms of patronage for their services in the House of Commons.[9] Lord Salisbury, in a typical flash of humor, once stated the quandary in which he was placed by the incessant requests for honors. In replying to an appeal from Beach for a specific appointment, he wrote that he would do his best. "But all my colleagues are in an honour-giving frame of mind—and I have *no* vacancies in the K.C.B.—and only 4 in the C.B. What are they among so many? These two grades are a positive elixir of life—a prophylactic against influenza and all other epidemics. Nobody dies who is either K.C.B. or C.B. I shall bring it under the notice of the hospitals."[10] In view of such ministerial afflictions the threat of a Liberal victory, seemingly so remote after July, 1886, now loomed close and menacing. The ministry, as Churchill had once prophesied, was indeed a "ricketty infant."

By late June Unionist morale had gone rapidly from bad to worse. Obstruction by Home Rulers held up the business of the House; on several critical occasions the Speaker denied the Government use of the closure; and there was still Supply to come. The situation was grave; and Smith informed his cabinet colleagues that their more contentious bills would have to be withdrawn and carried over to the next session of Parliament. Sensing a Unionist disaster, Chamberlain urged ministers to give no quarter and to rally the combined parties together in a supreme effort to pass the troublesome local tax bill: the only alternatives

[9] Smith to Salisbury, 13 Oct. 1888, *ibid.* Salisbury wrote in reply: "The Unionists are not quite a fifth of our force in the H. of C. They have had a great deal more than a fifth of the big appointments"; Salisbury to Smith, 19 Oct. 1888, *ibid.*

[10] Salisbury to Beach, 1 May 1891, St. Aldwyn MSS.

he saw were either resignation or a dissolution. In cabinet Goschen magnanimously offered to drop his bill and to resign as the author of all the Government's woes. But as Smith said, with an Opposition "rendered desperate by hunger," such a course was unthinkable. What made the Government's position all the more precarious was that the two most important and controversial measures of the session—Balfour's Land Purchase Bill and Hicks Beach's Tithe Bill—aroused either indifference or active dislike among the Conservative rank and file. "There is nothing in all our programme that they care to wait for," Smith complained, "unless it be to save the Government from disaster and themselves from an Election."[11]

Such a disaster was only narrowly averted. Anxious meetings among Conservative and Liberal Unionist leaders and whips produced a compromise solution; and at a cabinet council on June 25 ministers agreed to jettison these two bills, along with the Employers' Liability Bill, owing to obstruction and to the lack of any "popular enthusiasm" in the country. According to the gloomy prophecies of W. H. Smith, the most "drastic measures" would have been required to pass the eighty clauses of Balfour's bill by August, and he judged such a procedure so unwise as to be futile. Balfour reported to his uncle at the height of the crisis: "I don't know that more can be done: for all the King's Horses and all the King's men won't make Smith cheerful till he has been to a German Bath."[12]

Outside the Government the most anxious observer of these events, apart from Chamberlain, was Queen Victoria. Marshaling all her wrath against the Opposition, she wrote Lord Salisbury a letter that left no doubt as to her own inclinations: "She need not say that he knows he possesses her confidence, and how anxious she is to support him in every way. He knows also that it is of more than vital importance that the Socialist Homeruling Party, which really contains no one of respectability, and who could not stand alone, should not be allowed to have the *failure* which their attempt at governing would entail, because it would upset the whole country and the whole world, and destroy all confidence in British policy abroad. But the Queen does think that Mr. Smith's state of health and nerves renders him unfit for the

[11] Smith to Salisbury, 18, 24, 27 June 1890, Salisbury MSS.
[12] Balfour to Salisbury, 23 June 1890, *ibid.*

position of leader and that Mr. Goschen, or, still more Mr. Balfour ought to have that place. Mr. Smith should remain, if possible, in the Government but not in the House of Commons."[13]

Apart from ensuring that no dissolution took place in July, Lord Salisbury paid little heed to this royal advice. Early in that month he replied that he had opposed the decision to abandon temporarily the Tithe and Land bills "to the utmost of his power," but that the cabinet had disagreed with him. Under ordinary circumstances the existence of so "grave a difference of opinion" between the premier and his colleagues would necessitate a dissolution. But in view of the "abnormal" situation such an action would inflict "great injury on both the party and the country," and for the next two years the Government "must get on as well as they can." Reluctantly the Queen accepted this decision. The first consideration must always be to keep the Gladstonians out of office, as she put it, for "the safety of the Empire and imperial and national interests."[14]

The prospect of a legislative collapse raised serious misgivings in the minds of many Conservatives and Liberal Unionists about the Government's ability to survive another session. In the Commons members of the Opposition were clamoring to know ministerial intentions about the order of business. Ministers procrastinated, refusing to commit themselves to a definite time schedule for the next two months. But the Home Rule party persisted in their questions, and on July 10 the Government's humiliation was virtually complete when Smith announced that at least three major bills would have to be postponed until the special session in November. Some indication of the Government's plight can be gained from Balfour's strong appeal in August to Akers Douglas, the chief whip, to produce more party members at division time. As Balfour explained to W. H. Smith, "I have told Douglas he must bring up what men he can. If the Irish on their part bring any of their men back from Dublin we shall be in a considerable difficulty. The Tory party has . . . already vanished into an invisible vapour which will not condense again until we meet in November."[15]

As for the November session, W. H. Smith had already warned

[13] *Letters of Queen Victoria*, 3d series, I, pp. 617-18.
[14] *Ibid.*, pp. 618-19.
[15] Balfour to Smith, 16 Aug. 1890, Add. MS 49829.

Salisbury that the Government faced a grim prospect at Westminster. If the legislation pending proved to be no more popular in the country and just as repugnant to the Opposition, and if obstruction continued then the only choice in Smith's mind was to "throw up the sponge, bring about a General Election, and the repeal of the Union." This was precisely what Home Rulers had in mind. In the press and on platforms throughout the country they boasted of their intention to impede Government business at every turn. Elated by their recent electoral successes, the Opposition were hoping to force ministers into a dissolution before Christmas. In the words of Harcourt, the Opposition had only to "complete the rout of a defeated foe and the pursuit of a flying enemy." It was small wonder, then, that Unionists awaited the opening of Parliament with feelings of uneasiness. In an evasive speech at the Guildhall on November 10 Salisbury neatly sidestepped the Irish Question altogether, while belittling the results of by-elections. Although measures were taken to shorten the debate on the address, Salisbury was too cynical to expect any relief from obstruction. The Speaker, he predicted, would prove reluctant to use the closure because "his temperature is evidently not high enough for any effective action. It is of no use trying to boil eggs in cold water."[16] The outlook for ministers was bleak. If the Unionists had not spent all their "vital energy" on coercion in Ireland, as Harcourt alleged at Derby, they had, nevertheless, lost the sympathy of a large section of the electorate; and only a major windfall could save them from the disaster toward which they were heading.

II. THE DIVORCE AND ITS AFTERMATH

In the winter of 1890-1891 the verdict in the divorce case of O'Shea v. O'Shea rescued the Government from certain humiliation. The story of the divorce trial and of Parnell's subsequent fall from political as well as spiritual grace has been recounted in detail elsewhere.[17] Whatever Captain O'Shea's motives in filing

[16] Smith to Salisbury, 27 June 1890; Salisbury to Smith, 11 Nov. 1890, Salisbury MSS. The Speaker was Arthur Peel, who held this office from 1884 to 1895.

[17] For details of the O'Shea divorce action and its aftermath, see Lyons, *The Fall of Parnell*; H. Harrison, *Parnell Vindicated*, London, 1931; and C. C. O'Brien, *Parnell and His Party*, pp. 279-313.

a petition for divorce on the grounds of adultery in December, 1889—whether personal, mercenary, or political, or a combination of all three—the decision was made in the full knowledge of what the political repercussions might be. According to Henry Harrison, the devoted friend and vindicator of Parnell, the divorce suit was the culmination of a deliberate attempt to crush Parnell and his cause, the villains of the piece being Chamberlain and O'Shea, who were full of "gall and wormwood" over the debacle of the Special Commission.[18] This is not the place to enter into speculation about O'Shea's many intrigues and the alleged degree of his connivance at the adultery, while waiting for his wife's wealthy aunt Mrs. Benjamin Wood to die. Suffice it to observe that Captain O'Shea's assertion in court that he had had no definite proof of his wife's infidelity until 1889 stretches one's credulity too far. Between the years 1882 and 1884 Mrs. O'Shea gave birth to three children, two of whom survived. All three, it must be presumed, belonged to Parnell, Captain O'Shea having ceased to live regularly with his wife well before 1880. Harrison's case for a Chamberlain-O'Shea axis may sound highly plausible, but it must remain an hypothesis until by some miracle the necessary evidence is brought to light. If Chamberlain's guilt by association with O'Shea stands "not proven," however, the implications of charging the Irish leader with adultery were not lost on either man. As O'Shea observed to his political mentor in August, 1890, "He who smashes Parnell smashes Parnellism."[19]

With the exception—and it was an important one—of the solicitor general, cabinet ministers were mere bystanders during the divorce trial and its aftermath. Alternately fascinated, amused, and repelled by the rupture of the Home Rule alliance and by the internecine strife within the Irish party, most Government supporters were content to let the antagonists fight the matter out in Committee Room 15 of the House of Commons, and later in Ireland and overseas. But not all Unionists shared this passive view, and a study of their behavior during the supreme crisis of Parnellism offers some valuable insights into the workings of both the Unionist mind and the Irish administration.

[18] See H. Harrison, *Parnell, Joseph Chamberlain, and Mr. Garvin*, pp. 202-28.
[19] Garvin, *Chamberlain*, II, p. 404.

Ironically enough, Balfour was directly approached by Captain O'Shea about the divorce proceedings in a letter dated December 26, 1889. O'Shea wrote informing him that he had filed a petition for divorce two days earlier, naming Parnell as corespondent, and he enclosed a communication from one of the "Castle Bishops," Dr. O'Dwyer of Limerick, concerning the charges of adultery. O'Shea's letter also revealed that Chamberlain was "acquainted with the facts." No more blunt invitation to Balfour to exploit this information for political purposes could be imagined. But the chief secretary was not naive enough to risk any form of collaboration with O'Shea. His answer, written from Dublin Castle, was both terse and cool. Declining to make capital out of a subject "necessarily painful" to all those concerned, he evinced sympathy for the deceived husband, but stated in unmistakable terms his aversion to introducing "political and party feeling into private affairs, from which . . . they should be wholly dissociated."[20] Such was Balfour's reaction to this clumsy attempt to involve the administration in the divorce case. Needless to say, the revelations in the O'Shea letter, especially after the Pigott fiasco, must have given Balfour considerable reassurance about the future of the Union. During the divorce hearings and the subsequent debates in Committee Room 15, Balfour chose to keep his thoughts on the subject of adultery to himself and to his immediate family. The spectacle of chaos and conflict in the Irish party and of the Gladstonians caught in a dilemma largely of their own making amused him immensely, but he refrained from scolding Parnell in public for having broken the seventh commandment. That infraction, according to Balfour and his associates, was the least of Parnell's many sins.

In the second place, and far more significant, there was the personal involvement of the solicitor general in the divorce proceedings. One of the ablest and best-known barristers of his day, Sir Edward Clarke, Q.C., served his party well by acting as O'Shea's chief counsel in the case. Clarke was not only a successful lawyer: he was also a staunch Unionist, albeit a man of independent mind who rarely hesitated to voice his own opinions to party superiors no matter how unwelcome the advice. In the summer of 1888 he had warned his cabinet colleagues against too

---

[20] Dugdale, *Balfour*, I, pp. 182-83.

close an association with the *Times* in their campaign against
"Parnellism and Crime"; and he had spurned an offer to assist
Webster in the Special Commission. But any qualms he may have
had about mixing politics and private practice vanished altogether in December, 1889, when he accepted Captain O'Shea's
brief. Clarke knew a strong case when he saw one, and if there
were many questions left unanswered by O'Shea's evidence, he
had no doubts on the score of Parnell's guilt. He was also the last
man to ignore the effect that a decree *nisi* would have upon
Parnell's career and his cause. After all, there was the recent and
lurid precedent of the Dilke case, in which the charges of adultery,
although vehemently denied by the respondent, had been sufficient
to destroy the career of a man destined for high office. Clarke
knew only too well that the evidence against Parnell—the liaison
with Mrs. O'Shea having been an open secret in certain circles
for years—was far more convincing, if less ugly, than that compiled by Mrs. Crawford and her solicitors against Sir Charles
Dilke. In 1886 the guardians of "social purity" had not waited
for definitive proof of guilt before condemning out-of-hand
Chamberlain's erstwhile friend.

Captain O'Shea, in fact, had arrived at Clarke's offices by a
tortuous route, which began with his approach to Soames of the
Times. No choice of counsel could have been less opportune, and
that "very dull but respectable solicitor" was soon disqualified
on the grounds of his connection with "Parnellism and Crime."
Next, O'Shea made an even more foolish move by trying to engage
as counsel the son of Mr. Justice Day of Special Commission fame.
Eventually the wayward captain was directed to Clarke. At no
time did he seek legal assistance outside the Unionist camp; and
the final selection of the solicitor general supplied Home Rulers
with all the evidence they needed to accuse the Government of
another and more contemptible effort to discredit Parnell.

Once Clarke had seen all the evidence collected against Mrs.
O'Shea and Parnell, he ceased to worry about the strength of his
client's case. And when Mrs. O'Shea's counsel announced on the
first day of the trial that he would take no part in the proceedings,
would call no witnesses, and would conduct no cross-examination,
Clarke appeared surprised and must have been relieved. Parnell,
as is well known, never even bothered to engage counsel. The

solicitor general's confidence in O'Shea's case is the more surprising because a lawyer of such astuteness should have seen through the tissue of lies and distortions that O'Shea had perforce to construct in order to appear as a husband duped by his wife for more than seven years. The evidence would suggest that O'Shea had, in fact, known of the liaison as early as 1881, and that, after several domestic "scenes," he not only allowed his wife to set up a separate establishment with Parnell but actually connived at the arrangement until the death of Mrs. Wood in May, 1889. Such, at any rate, was the convincing charge leveled by Henry Harrison. Whatever Clarke's personal impressions may have been about O'Shea's connivance, the fact remains that the important question of the paternity of Mrs. O'Shea's three children born after 1882 did not trouble him in court. The two youngest children were described as Captain O'Shea's and he was awarded custody. And yet Clarke admitted in his memoirs twenty-five years later that these two daughters were "unquestionably" Parnell's.[21]

On the opening day of the trial Mrs. O'Shea's counsel unwisely entered counterallegations against O'Shea, which ranged from connivance in the adultery to cruelty toward the respondent. These charges were not defended. Instead, they served to open up the case ex parte and afforded O'Shea a chance to testify and to make a mockery of the facts, while Clarke revealed how Parnell's cunning had defiled a marriage that had been one of "sustained and great affection." He made use of ridicule by describing one of the horses stabled by Parnell at Eltham, named "Home Rule," as an "old crock, and only fit to go in the shafts." And he dwelt at length on the story of a cook, who testified that Parnell, having been surprised by O'Shea's unexpected arrival at Eltham, made a hasty exit from Mrs. O'Shea's bedroom via a rope fire escape, and then came round to the front door as if in the act of paying a call. The public took up this anecdote with relish, and Unionist references to fire escapes invariably brought howls of laughter from their audiences. In arguing his case the solicitor general displayed much skill in glossing over inconsistencies, in reconciling irreconcilable facts, and in representing O'Shea as completely

[21] Clarke, *The Story of My Life*, pp. 291-95; Lyons, *op.cit.*, pp. 48 ff.

innocent of the countercharges.[22] It was fortunate for Clarke's legal reputation that he had no defense counsel with which to contend. Almost any lawyer, provided with the facts in Parnell's possession, could have easily torn away the fabric of deception that Clarke wove around O'Shea's private life. But Parnell, once the divorce petition had been filed, was determined to marry Mrs. O'Shea and to legalize a connection that had always had all the meaning of marriage to him, and he refused to risk losing the divorce decree in order to salvage his own name. All other considerations, notably his promises and reassurances to members of the Irish party that they had no cause to fear the verdict of the divorce court, took second place behind his consuming desire, as Mrs. O'Shea later expressed it, "to acknowledge and claim me as his wife before the whole world." His decision to place private above political considerations could not have been an easy one, for in gaining a wife he lost far more than a majority of his party.

In the absence of any defense no one doubted the outcome of the divorce case. The judge, having described Parnell as a man "who takes advantage of the hospitality offered him by the husband to debauch the wife," found the charges of adultery proven, granted O'Shea a decree *nisi* along with custody of Parnell's children, and ordered the costs to be borne by the corespondent and by Mrs. O'Shea if her estate proved large enough. Parnell stood convicted by public opinion as well, and in the most unflattering light; whereas the nimble O'Shea had gambled and won an impressive victory for himself and, as it happened, for the Unionist party. The Queen reflected the prevailing temper of many Unionists when she described Parnell in her Journal as "not only a man of very bad character, but . . . a liar, and devoid of all sense of honour or of any sort of principle."[23] No doubt the verdict must have given Sir Edward Clarke much pleasure. That he had some notion of the wider implications of the case can be judged by his conversation—which he might have done well to suppress in print—with David Plunket, M.P., a former solicitor general for Ireland, during the debates in Committee Room 15. Clarke observed: "I knew I was throwing a bombshell into the Irish camp, but I did not know it would do quite so much mischief."

[22] *Times,* 17-18 Nov. 1890.
[23] *Letters of Queen Victoria,* 3d series, I, p. 656.

And Plunket replied: "Ah, you didn't know that when it burst they would pick up the pieces and cut each other's throats with them."[24]

The Unionist press responded to the divorce scandal with unusual fervor. For the *Times* revenge against Parnell was particularly sweet, and for several days in succession the leading editorials gloated over the exposure of the Irish leader. The trial itself and each fresh development in the crisis received the fullest coverage, and the *Times*'s correspondents reported in loving detail the reaction to the divorce from every corner of the Irish world. The paper's attitude to the revelations in court about Parnell's double life was summed up on November 18 in an editorial that was worthy of the archexponent of militant Unionism:

"Domestic treachery, systematic and long-continued deception, the whole squalid apparatus of letters written with the intent of misleading, houses taken under false names, disguises and aliases, secret visits and sudden flights make up a story of dull and ignoble infidelity, untouched, so far as can be seen, by a single ray of sentiment, a single flash of passion, and comparable only to the dreary monotony of French middle class vice, over which M. Zola's scalpel so lovingly lingers." The *Times* was also quick to note the dilemma in which Parnell's moral lapse had placed the Liberal party. Did Gladstone and his colleagues intend to make an exception of this case and to continue their alliance with a man so disqualified from "asserting the moral ascendancy" that ought to belong to a political leader?

That question was soon to be answered. The divorce had clearly placed both the Irish party, with their Roman Catholic affiliations, and the Liberal leaders, with their reliance upon the nonconformist vote, in an extremely awkward position. The latter group were the first to speak out against Parnell's fitness for public office. Through spokesmen moderate as well as fanatical, from J. J. Colman, the mustard magnate, to the fiery Hugh Price Hughes, the "nonconformist conscience" proved itself to be on the side of the angels.[25] The nonconformists were especially sensitive to the

---

[24] Clarke, *The Story of My Life*, p. 293.

[25] See J. F. Glaser, "Parnell's fall and the nonconformist conscience," in *IHS*, Sept. 1960, Vol. 12, No. 46, pp. 119-38.

interaction between public and private morality: as Hughes re-minded an audience in St. James's Hall, devotion to God came before that to Ireland, and "what is morally wrong can never be politically right." Literally besieged by letters, sermons, and petitions from this section of the party, as well as from several prominent English Catholics, Gladstone was forced to choose between loyalty to his supporters in Great Britain and Parnell. From the annual meeting of the National Liberal Federation in Sheffield both Harcourt and Morley reported that feeling was running high against Parnell's continued leadership. The Home Rule alliance appeared to be undermined from all sides. While nonconformists insisted that "Parnell must go" and threatened to swing their vote to the party of Balfour and coercion at the next general election if he did not, the hierarchy in Ireland stood by in embarrassed silence. The Liberal leaders soon found that the only course left open to them was to request Parnell's im-mediate, if temporary, retirement as leader of his party. But the uncrowned king of Ireland showed no signs of abdicating. Members of the Irish party had already received notice of the usual meeting before the beginning of the parliamentary session; and on November 25, 1890, Parnell was re-elected chairman of the party by acclamation. The situation was further complicated by the passing of several resolutions in Dublin, just after the divorce, enthusiastically supporting Parnell.

Confronted with a fateful choice, Gladstone at first temporized, and then, under heavy pressure from Harcourt and Morley, drafted the famous letter, addressed to Morley, which stated that Parnell's retention of the leadership would render his own position as head of the Liberal party "almost a nullity." Gladstone had also taken the precaution of informing Justin McCarthy, the vice-chairman of the Irish party, about his views on the question of the leadership. He thus relied upon both the Morley letter, which was to be shown to Parnell before the party meeting on November 25, and on McCarthy's personal representations to dissuade Parnell from remaining as leader. By accident or design both devices miscarried, and Parnell was re-elected chairman before Gladstone's decision could be communicated to him. When Parnell flatly refused to make the sacrifice that the Liberals were asking, Gladstone, by now much incensed, brought the crisis to a head by authorizing the publication of the Morley letter. This decision—which can only be called hasty—directly challenged not only Parnell, but the right of the Irish party to determine their leader without interference from Westminster. The letter appeared in the *Times* on November 26 and precipitated the agonizing debates in Committee Room 15, which ended with the splitting of the Irish party on December 6 into two bitterly hostile factions. Some forty-five members left the room and elected Justin McCarthy their chairman. The remainder of the party, numbering twenty-six, stayed behind with Parnell, who, with that pride and single-mindedness which was at once his greatest strength and weakness, vowed to fight relentlessly against his former colleagues and subordinates. The fact that Parnell had been increasingly neglectful of his duties as leader of the Irish party and that he had not crossed the Irish channel for five years did not enhance his cause. Nevertheless, for many members of the party, those who had made up "the 86 of '86," this was the most crucial decision of their careers. To choose between the man who had made the Irish parliamentary party possible and the Liberal alliance, with all that it implied for the future of Home Rule, was not easy.[26]

From Dublin Ridgeway sent his reflections on the Irish predicament to Balfour: "How could the G. O. M. have been such a fool! It seems grotesque that a great policy should be thrown away because Parnell had carnal relations with Mrs. O'Shea. But a policy based, as this was, on sentiment and not on principle, was certain to break up sooner or later. And what fools the Parnellite majority has been! If they had only stood by Parnell, the storm of cant would have passed over and the G. O. M. would have had him again at Hawarden." The under secretary asserted that there was no one with any "prescience" in the Irish party save Parnell and Davitt: all the others had hastened to express their confidence in Parnell before "waiting to see how the Methodist cat jumped." "O'Brien and Dillon will be in a fearful fix," he prophesied; and he ended on the affirmative note: "It is a great joy to see the other side making such fools of themselves."[27]

[26] Morley, *Gladstone*, III, pp. 428-45; Lyons, *op.cit.*, chaps. 3-5.
[27] Ridgeway to Balfour, 29 Nov. 1890, Add. MS 49811.

The crisis in the Irish party was aggravated because six of their most eminent members, among them Dillon and O'Brien, were in America. By the end of November, five of these delegates had decided that Parnell's continued leadership was "impossible" and they cabled this news to their colleagues at Westminster. Both Dillon and O'Brien refused to abandon hope of a reconciliation between the two wings of the party, and throughout the struggle these two took a moderate line against Parnell, in sharp contrast to such vindictive critics as Healy, Sexton, and Davitt. Parnell lost no time in taking the fight to Ireland, where he launched a series of appeals to the "hill-side people" in the hopes of receiving the mandate necessary to his political survival. On December 3 the standing committee of the Irish hierarchy finally declared against Parnell: the loss of clerical support proved to be one of the most telling blows in his fight for the leadership. Throughout Ireland rival delegations from the two factions taunted and abused each other; political meetings degenerated into name-calling and "shillelagh rallies"; tempers flared and blood flowed on both sides; the offices of *United Ireland* changed hands twice as the Parnellite forces ultimately recaptured the premises after a dramatic struggle. The anti-Parnellites began publishing their own paper, *"Suppressed" United Ireland*, and they organized a rival association to the National League called the National Federation. When Parnell stormed the offices of *United Ireland* Ridgeway described him as "another Cromwell," and he expressed his fears that the Irish leader would fall completely into the hands of the extremists. Several notorious members of the Irish Republican Brotherhood had been seen hovering around Parnell, and if their presence scared the moderates away, then the Parnellite cause would be lost.[28]

During the early months of the new year the leading members of the Irish party struggled to arrive at a modus vivendi in the neutral environment of Boulogne and later Calais.[29] As the bidding went back and forth among the various factions concerned, with the terms of a compromise fluctuating almost daily, the possibility of agreement grew steadily more remote. Too many forces, not

[28] Ridgeway to Balfour, 10-11 Dec. 1890, *ibid.; Times,* 11-12 Dec. 1890.
[29] For an account of the Boulogne negotiations, see Lyons, *op.cit.,* chap. 8.

to mention conflicting personalities, were pulling in different directions to permit a reunion of Irish hearts. Although the mediators offered him the most favorable terms imaginable, Parnell refused to allow his own sacrifice at what he considered so cheap a price. At length Dillon and O'Brien gave up in despair; they had failed to restore even the semblance of unity. On February 12 they landed in Folkestone, where they surrendered to the police. Despondent about the prospects for Home Rule, they had little choice but to serve out the sentences pending against them since November. The temporary removal of these two moderates meant that the field was left wide open for a series of collisions in Ireland between the extreme elements on either side.

From the Unionist point of view the Irish crisis was more than a boon: it completely altered the political scene at Westminster. Where ministers had once dreaded the thought of meeting Parliament, there now seemed no reason why the Government could not complete their full term of office without anxiety. The obstruction of Government measures in the Commons seemed to collapse almost overnight; the debate on the address lasted but one day; Balfour was left without his traditional sparring partners from the Irish section of the House; the number of questions about Irish affairs dwindled to a mere trickle; and the Government's majority on the first reading of the Land Purchase Bill soared to 138. The comparative tranquillity in the House both pleased and disappointed Balfour. He found the spectacle of the Irish party in turmoil "extraordinarily amusing"; but to Ridgeway he confessed a certain nostalgia for the battles of the past: " . . . the situation is so novel that I feel quite out of my element." "*Now* the rapidity with which Parliament does its work is almost embarrassing," he wrote, "and we do not know how to spend our evenings after five o'clock."[30]

By December 9 the Government had arrived at their announced goal, with each of their major bills ready to be considered in committee once the House had reassembled in January. In the meantime, and with mixed feelings of relief and contempt, Government supporters watched the reports of the political feud in the Irish party and listened to the rumors that scurried up and

---

[30] Dugdale, *Balfour*, I, p. 184.

down the corridors of Westminster. Exuding satisfaction, the *Times* reminded its readers that "the finest of faction fights is proceeding as merrily as honest men could desire." "When they are candid," the paper added, "the candour of these Irishmen is wonderful."[31] Most members of the Unionist coalition regarded Parnell's past conduct with Mrs. O'Shea as sordid, but adultery was nothing compared with the manifold sins of the Irish party, and their attention was absorbed by the war to the knife that was currently raging in Ireland. Here were the so-called nationalists showing their true colors: a party of quarrelsome ingrates reflecting the instincts of the mob; here was a preview of what Home Rule would mean for Ireland should the Liberals win the next general election. The "hollow truce" between Liberals and Parnellites was now exposed. A. V. Dicey, the noted jurist and paladin of Unionism, warned in a letter to the *Times* against an outbreak of Pharisaism over the seventh commandment. So much emphasis had been laid on the fact of Parnell's adultery, he cautioned, that people seemed to forget that Parnell was also a "traitor and a liar." Unionists would be well advised, he wrote, to stand aloof from the "miserable struggle" within the Irish party. "We need not decide whether the pot be blacker than the kettle; we have only to take care that we do not dirty our hands by touching either the one or the other."[32] And Balfour privately admitted to W. T. Stead, the former editor of the *Pall Mall Gazette,* that he took a much graver view of Parnell's political conduct between 1879 and 1887 ("since when he may almost have been said to have retired from active political life"), which made the O'Shea affair a matter of "relative insignificance."[33] And so the talk went in Unionist circles.

To stress the division in the enemy's ranks, Salisbury addressed a large Unionst rally in Lord Hartington's constituency at Rossendale. Most of the speech concerned the Parnellite crisis and the inability of the Gladstonians to come forward with any workable scheme for Home Rule. While regretting that adultery should be connected with a prominent politician, Salisbury wished that the seventh commandment "had not eaten all its brethren."

[31] *Times,* 16 Dec. 1890.
[32] *Ibid.,* 9 Dec. 1890.
[33] Balfour to W. T. Stead, 22 Nov. 1890, Add. MS 49829.

Too little attention had been paid in recent years to numbers six and eight. In other words, public indignation over boycotting, intimidation, and murder had been noticeably absent. After questioning the right of men like Healy and Sexton to "appear as the champions and the apostles of domestic purity," he challenged Gladstone to declare what his intentions were for a second Home Rule bill. Citing the internecine strife in Committee Room 15 as an inauspicious foretaste of what was to come under Home Rule, he asserted that the divisions in the Irish party went much deeper than a mere question of adultery: "powerful furies" were arrayed against each other in the conflict. The Home Rule alliance had always been a sham because the gap between Gladstone's solution and Parnell's aspirations for complete separation could never be bridged. Although he denied any real concern about the outcome of the factional fight, he confessed a personal preference for "the man who is fighting desperately for his life to the crew whom he made and who are turning against him." The speech ended, amidst prolonged cheers, with an exhortation to all Unionists to perform their duty to Ireland—an obligation admittedly neglected by their forefathers—by ensuring "stability, order, peace, and contentment."[34] It was the same old appeal for a firm and impartial administration of the law that Salisbury had enunciated four years before in St. James's Hall.

III. ELECTORAL DIVERSIONS

One of the first tests of the degree to which the Parnellite split had affected the domestic political scene came at Bassetlaw in Nottinghamshire, where a by-election was held on December 15. Liberals, Conservatives, and Irish members alike regarded Bassetlaw as something of a political barometer; and as the polling day approached, party agents worked hard to secure a victory for their side. Gladstone spoke in the constituency on behalf of the Liberal candidate, and more than a dozen M.P.'s appeared on the scene to promote one or other of the candidates. After the votes had been counted, the Conservative candidate Sir Frederick Milner was revealed as the victor, having retained the seat for the Government by a margin of 728. Ministerial spirits, so long depressed by electoral reverses, now rose sharply; and the *Times*

[34] *Times,* 4 Dec. 1890.

celebrated the result by calling it a personal defeat for Gladstone despite the fact that the Home Rulers had used "every device known to faction" in order to win.[35] The Liberal leaders, in fact, were considerably sobered by this setback and regarded it as a severe blow to the party and to the future of Home Rule.

As for Salisbury, there was no restraining the elation that permeated his letter of appreciation to Milner: "Allow me to offer you my most hearty congratulations on the contest which you have led to so brilliant an issue. It has been magnificently done. In this weather we may say of you—

> Now is the winter of our discontent
> Made glorious summer by the sun of York.

It was just the sustenance for our failing spirits that was urgently wanted."[36] However little effect the Irish crisis may have had upon the outcome, both British parties, and Gladstone in particular, interpreted the result as an ill omen for Home Rule. But the defeat of a Liberal Unionist at West Hartlepool in January, 1891, helped to restore the confidence of Gladstonian Liberals in their cause.

If by-elections in England stirred strong emotions among party leaders and agents, there was even greater urgency, not to mention violence, connected with those that took place in Ireland after the Parnellite split. Unionist opinion was sharply divided as to how the chaos within the Irish party might best be exploited. Balfour made himself unpopular among many loyalists in the south by urging them not to contest these by-elections—largely for fear of driving the nationalist factions into reunion; rather, he wanted them to save their energies for the general election. Although Parnell's candidates lost three elections in a row, the leader himself was undaunted and vowed to fight on to the bitter end. His sudden death on October 6 added an even more irreconcilable note to the political feuding. At the crucial by-election early in November to fill Parnell's seat in the city of Cork, the local Unionist association ignored the protests of Ridgeway and Balfour by running their own candidate, who came in a poor third. John Redmond, the heir to Parnell's mantle, was soundly de-

[35] *Ibid.*, 25 Nov.-17 Dec. 1890.
[36] Salisbury to Milner, 17 Dec. 1890, Salisbury MSS.

feated by an anti-Parnellite butter merchant, and he was not returned to Parliament until the end of December after defeating Davitt at Waterford. All efforts at reconciliation between the two factions having broken down, the strife continued in an atmosphere that was hardly conducive to the survival of the parliamentary party that Parnell had created almost single-handedly.[37]

In the meantime, rumors were current in England that ministers intended to dissolve Parliament in the new year in order to take advantage of their opponents' misfortunes. There was no truth in this report. As Balfour explained to A. V. Dicey, he was no believer in "that kind of political dexterity which sees in every misfortune that happens to your adversaries a convenient opportunity for exercising the prerogatives of the Crown and inflicting on the country all the disturbances and inconveniences of a general election."[38] Ministers were, in fact, quite content to bide their time and to watch the outcome of the struggle in Ireland; while Gladstone tried hard to convince the English electorate that Parnell "had now the support of the Tory Press and most of the Tories in England." Such charges often repeated by Liberals and anti-Parnellites, began to wear on the nerves of ministers. Lord Cranbrook, for one, found the imputation too repugnant to endure, and asked Salisbury to clarify the Government's position in his forthcoming speech before the Primrose League. Salisbury willingly complied, and on April 21, in his address as grand master of the league, he scoffed at the idea of a Tory-Parnellite alliance, reminding his audience of the Special Commission and how the Government had been roundly condemned for refusing to express regrets that Parnell's virtue had been impugned. The *Times* had rendered an "enormous service" to the public by educating them about the "facts" of Irish nationalism, especially in the matter of Parnell's close ties with those who advocated

[37] See *Times*, 12-23 Dec. 1890; Lyons, *op.cit.*, pp. 159-77.

[38] Balfour to Dicey, 1 Jan. 1891, Add. MS 49829. Balfour wrote to Ridgeway on 10 Dec. 1890: "Gossip says that Parnell still has other cards up his sleeve. I do not know how this may be. Well informed persons assert that Gladstone has several times dined with Parnell and Mrs. O'Shea and has corresponded with the latter upon questions of political interest! It is added, however, that Parnell will not make this fact public—at all events until the decree of divorce is made absolute"; *ibid.*

physical force. Since 1885, he asserted, the "gloss" of the Irish party had worn away, and Englishmen could at last appreciate the "seamy character of Irish heroism." According to the *Times*, Salisbury on this occasion was "in his happiest vein, easy, dignified, and urbane." And presumably the fretful Lord Cranbrook was also satisfied.[39]

IV. CONSERVATIVE REFLECTIONS ON PARNELL'S FALL

The Government's reaction to Parnell's death on October 6 was on the whole subdued, for the event was overshadowed by the news of W. H. Smith's sudden demise on the same day. There was no cheering or celebrating among ministers: instead, a sober calculation as to the effects of Parnell's loss upon the Home Rule movement. Balfour took some pains to minimize the importance of the event. Apart from providing a "fruitful field for the labour of political prophets," it would not, he felt, alter the balance of forces either in Ireland or in Parliament.[40] The chief secretary, in fact, showed far more concern over the death of W. H. Smith. To Ridgeway he wrote: "I am much upset at this announcement of poor Smith's death—it is a great personal blow. Parnell's death . . . may in one sense produce more startling political results, but Smith's loss is irremediable." Ridgeway, in reply, doubted that the absence of Parnell from the scene would substantially benefit the anti-Parnellites. The open breach in the Irish party, he observed, had advanced the Government's position in a number of ways. Thanks to the split, the Land Purchase Bill had been passed, the dispute at Tipperary was virtually settled, Dillon and O'Brien had become "objects of distrust with the extreme party," the nationalists had been deprived of their leader, and, most important of all, events in Ireland since the divorce decree had proved that Home Rule was nothing more than "Priest Rule." Ridgeway's sanguine report ended with his wish for the "complete disruption" of the Irish nationalists before the general election; and his only regret was that the dissolution loomed so near.[41]

[39] Cranbrook to Salisbury, 20 April 1891, Salisbury MSS; *Times*, 22 April 1891.

[40] Balfour to D. H. Madden (Irish Attorney General), 9 Oct. 1891, Add. MS 49830.

[41] Balfour to Ridgeway, 7 Oct. 1891; Ridgeway to Balfour, 10 Oct. 1891, *ibid.*, 49830, 49812.

On October 11 Ridgeway spent some four hours watching from different vantage points the funeral procession that conveyed Parnell's coffin to its grave in Glasnevin cemetery. The clergy had urged their parishioners not to attend the ceremony, and yet thousands of Irishmen, many of them having traveled long distances, thronged the streets of Dublin on that somber day. They came, as Ridgeway recounted, with a "sad, stern look" on their faces to pay homage to their late chief. The sight moved him: he had expected nothing "so dignified or genuine." He saw no disorder, not even drunkenness. And there was not a priest in sight. The sheer size of Parnell's adherents impressed him deeply —he estimated the crowds at 100,000—but what thrilled him was the "defiance" by so many of the clerical ban. Dillon, O'Brien, and the other anti-Parnellite leaders had stayed away, and Ridgeway thought they had made a "fatal mistake" in so doing; but he attributed their behavior to priestly orders. "In short," he wrote exultantly to Balfour, "Parnell dead has done what Parnell living could not do—he has struck a staggering blow at Priestly domination."[42]

The issue of clerical meddling in Irish politics was one very close to the hearts of Unionists, and to those of the Conservative leaders in particular. For years, if not centuries, the influence of the priesthood had aroused strong passions on both sides of the Irish Sea. In his protest against Archbishop Cullen's order forbidding clerical support of the Tenant League in the early 1850's, Gavan Duffy had exclaimed: "Exclude priests from politics! It was for this object that English intrigue laboured for the last half century." And he accused ministers and their representatives at Rome of "whispering, lying, intriguing, with sleepless activity" in order to achieve this end.[43] To many Irishmen in 1891 these words were particularly appropriate. Most Unionists, on the other hand, interpreted the struggle after the divorce as a test of strength between the priests and the Fenians, and between these two evils it was difficult to choose. While the Unionist camp rejoiced at the breakup of the Gladstone-Parnell alliance, there was considerable anxiety about the revival of either Fenianism or clericalism in Ireland.

[42] Ridgeway to Balfour, 12 Oct. 1891, *ibid.*
[43] Gavan Duffy, *The League of North and South*, London, 1886, p. 339.

For those whose concern was more practical, the activity of the priesthood in the land war and during the Irish party split furnished invaluable propaganda. Ridgeway, for example, wanted to use the phrase "Home Rule means Rome Rule" as an electioneering cry in Ulster. But in Salisbury's mind there were important, even sacrosanct, principles at stake, such as the distinction between individual liberty and virtual enslavement. The prime minister's Anglican instincts moved him to speak out in the strongest terms against the evil of clerical influence in secular affairs. Whether he would have spoken with equal conviction had the offenders belonged to the Church of England is another matter. At a meeting of the Primrose League he admitted that it was by no means easy to draw a clear line between the spiritual and temporal influence of the clergy. But he saw in the internecine struggle in Ireland a contest between "the sympathies, money, and conspiracies" of America, which were backing Parnell, and the "secular efforts" of the priesthood and hierarchy, which provided the mainstay of the anti-Parnellites. In a characteristically Cecilian aside he confessed his profound reverence for the lawn sleeves and crozier of an archbishop; but when he saw behind that crozier "the familiar features of Mr. Schnadhorst," then his respect vanished altogether. At all costs the Protestant and loyal men of Ulster, he asserted, must not be allowed to fall under this "hybrid secular ecclesiastical power."[44]

This declaration of war against the priest in politics was followed some months later by an even blunter attack. Parnell was dead, John Redmond had just lost the by-election at Cork, and Unionists in both England and Ireland felt that the priests were rapidly capturing the Home Rule movement. In his address at the Guildhall on November 9 the prime minister referred to the scenes of chaos and factional fighting currently on display in Ireland. As further evidence of the unfitness of Irishmen for self-government he spoke of the "curse of ecclesiastical domination. . . ." The sentence was left unfinished because the qualifying remark that followed was drowned out by loud applause.[45] Although Salisbury devoted most of his speech to foreign affairs, the reference to Irish clericalism was not forgotten by ardent

[44] *Times*, 22 April 1891.
[45] *Ibid.*, 10 Nov. 1891.

Catholics. It was an unfortunate expression for a party leader to make where Catholic supporters of the Government were concerned. And this fact the Duke of Norfolk drove home in a long and vigorous protest to the premier. In his letter Norfolk asked him to make some redress in public for this offensive remark, otherwise the Government might lose most of their Catholic "friends" at the next election. Salisbury, in his reply on November 20, tried to clarify his statement and at the same time to mollify his indignant friend. Refusing to alter the "essence" of his remarks, because he had always felt "strongly" on the subject, he revealed that the reporters had missed the latter part of his reference to "ecclesiastical domination in *purely secular* affairs" owing to a burst of cheering. This domination he regarded as "a most serious evil," almost as great a one as "lay domination in spiritual affairs." And he proceeded to elaborate this point in a passage of some significance:

"The evil lies in this—that the clergy, from their office, from the message they bear, and the sacraments they control, obtain a vast influence over their flocks. In spiritual matters—questions of faith and morals—that is all good: their training and their mission fit them for it. But their training and mission do not give them the slightest fitness for advising on questions of secular expediency, which are often of vast moment. If they use, and strain, the tremendous organized influence conferred upon them by their spiritual quality, in order to forward some purely political aspiration, they are guilty of mis-using that influence; and therein they are guilty of a breach of trust—just as much as a man would be, who received a sum of money to build a church with, and used it to build a country house, for himself. I consider that this guilt is equally incurred by the teachers in *all* religious communities, who come forward with what they believe and represent to be a divine message, and who use for purely earthly ends the influence which they derive from it."

When the priesthood, Salisbury continued, opposed a candidate for public office on the grounds of "some breach of the moral law," then he considered such an action open to the gravest abuses. Neither Croke nor Walsh nor those clergy acting under their orders were justified in condemning Parnell's fitness for office before his death, and all the less so afterwards. "Parnell's *party*," he went on, "have not committed adultery: and the fact that Parnell did, does not justify the Irish clergy in placing themselves at the head of so purely a secular movement as that for Home Rule. If they choose to do it, they have no right to complain, if they meet with as little ceremony as if they were really laymen." Such was Salisbury's personal "confession of faith." Beyond making it clear that he was concerned only with "arraigning the men, and not the order" he would not go. And Norfolk was left with little substance for consolation.[46]

Salisbury, as his daughter was careful to point out, never held any brief for those who passed judgment on their fellow men on moral issues.[47] And the fact that the hierarchy in Ireland had reacted to Parnell's moral lapse only after Gladstone had formally repudiated the Irish leader magnified his distaste for clerical excesses in Ireland. Whether aversion to priestly influence in politics was one of Salisbury's "innately British characteristics" or not, there could be no question about the degree to which the activity of priests in the by-elections had alarmed Unionists about the fate of Protestants under Home Rule. The tocsin had sounded in Ulster, where fear of Catholicism was not just an electoral device to be hauled out periodically after every dissolution of Parliament.

From a personal point of view the Parnellite debacle showed ministers in an unfavorable light. Speaking in the Lords one week after the divorce verdict, Salisbury amused the Unionist majority by declaring that escape seemed to be the specialty of Irish members at the time: some nationalists preferred to flee by water—a reference to Dillon and O'Brien, who had sailed to France—and others chose fire escapes.[48] Home Rulers never forgave Salisbury for such gibes, even though none of the language used by Unionists in public over the divorce ever equalled, in venom, the remarks of Tim Healy. It was once said that Healy had been baptized with the leftovers of the Passion vinegar, and during the campaign against his old leader he more than lived up to this reputation. Lord Hartington, perhaps least qualified

[46] Norfolk to Salisbury, 19 Nov. 1891; Salisbury to Norfolk, 20 Nov. 1891, Salisbury MSS.
[47] Cecil, *Salisbury*, IV, p. 398.
[48] *Hansard*, 3d series, Vol. 349, p. 27.

of all to throw stones at adulterers, remarked on the divorce to the Queen: "I never thought anything in politics could give me as much pleasure as this does."[49] And there were many other Unionists, including Lord George Hamilton and the bellicose Ulsterman Colonel Saunderson, who relied upon the revelations of the divorce court in order to entertain their audiences. Some of the less pleasant aspects of the factional fight that ensued in Ireland supplied grist to the Unionist mill, which was busy manufacturing arguments against Home Rule. In April, 1891, Lord Salisbury informed a gathering of the Primrose League in Covent Garden:

"I have no sympathy with the man who plasters lime in Mr. Parnell's eyes, but neither have I any sympathy with the man who drives spectacle-glasses into Mr. Tim Healy's eyes. I can but look on at a respectable distance at these very unusual methods of propagating political opinion, and express the hope that the Union of Ireland and England may never mean the extension of Irish methods to English political life. . . . The revelation of the experience of five years is that we know the Irish cause to be what it is. The English people know the seamy character of Irish heroism, and they know that the character of the men to whom they are asked to hand over their friends and brothers in Ulster is such as to cover with disgrace any nation who for any cause made such tremendous sacrifices and exertions."[50]

If one accepts Hammond's partisan complaint that Salisbury possessed the "most caustic tongue" in English politics, then a special category must be created for Balfour. The debates in Committee Room 15, which had many of the ingredients of tragedy, caused the chief secretary nothing but amusement. Lord Vansittart has described Balfour in his memoirs as viewing events "with the detachment of a choir-boy at a funeral service."[51] But the choirboy's reaction really depended upon who was being buried. There was nothing detached about his response to the news of W. H. Smith's death. On the other hand, he enjoyed watching the predicament of the Irish party and their Liberal allies. As he wrote to his uncle Lord Eustace Cecil early in

---

[49] *Letters of Queen Victoria*, 3d series, I, p. 658.
[50] *Times*, 22 April 1891.
[51] Vansittart, *The Mist Procession*, London, 1958, p. 218.

December, 1890, "What an amusing crisis this is. However it turns
out nobody can deny that we have had our fun for our money."[52]
Salisbury, at least, was capable of expressing his admiration,
however grudging, for Parnell's courage and stamina. He had
done so at Rossendale. And if Lady Gwendolen Cecil is to be believed, the premier, in the privacy of Hatfield, felt sympathy for
a man deserted "for reasons of state" by those who owed everything to his "genius." Parnell's fight against "overwhelming odds"
during the last few months of his life "appealed to every militant
fibre" in the prime minister. This much could not be said of his
nephew, who watched the entire drama unfold without betraying
any emotion save a smile.

The Irish party split thus transformed the political landscape
both in Ireland and at Westminster. The Government's troubles
were by no means over, but the schism brought on a semiparalysis
of the Irish party in the Commons, and it also seriously affected
the flow of money from the Irish nation overseas. The National _N. B_
League, the National Federation, and the Tenants' Defence
League were all desperate for money, and they tried to compete
for the funds that Parnell had frozen in Paris and to win the
support of Irishmen the world over. After the Boulogne negotiations, when the last chance of reconciliation had faded away, a
steady stream of appeals for money went out to America and to
other Irish "colonies" abroad. In response, a group of influential
Irish-Americans formed the Irish National Federation of America,
which proved its worth by raising money for the anti-Parnellites'
election expenses in 1892 and thereafter. In addition, some
federation funds were used to relieve the evicted tenants whose
monthly grants had been reduced by more than fifty per cent
since the split. For a time the financial position of the anti-Parnellites was most precarious, and, as one of their leading members
informed the treasurer of the American federation, the fight
against Parnell's "mad career of destruction" might not be continued unless immediate support was forthcoming from the United
States. Admittedly, the gravity of the situation was exaggerated
in order to frighten Irish-Americans into generous contributions.
Nevertheless some Irish landlords, especially those owning estates

[52] Balfour to Lord Eustace Cecil, 4 Dec. 1890, Salisbury MSS.

still invested by the Plan, were not slow to exploit the financial distress of the nationalists, and they held off arbitration with their Plan tenants until the shortage of funds had softened the latter sufficiently for them to accept "ruinous terms."[53]

The split in Parnell's party diverted the energies and interests of many Irishmen from the land war to the power struggle within the parliamentary party; and agrarian outrages rapidly declined in number and severity. According to one district inspector, the country was "visibly settling down" by October, 1891; the secret societies were "crumbling away"; and the desire for "perpetual excitement" had almost vanished. If Parnell's fall exposed the latent tensions within the Home Rule movement, the tenantry were growing tired of endless agitation. They wished to be left alone to cultivate their holdings in peace. One district inspector reported to the Castle: "This is the end of an epoch in Irish History and before another commences there will be a period of *comparative* indifference. The hearts of the people are with material rather than ideal prospects. Nationalism has been thrown into the shade and the people are looking to the more practical side of politics just now."[54]

Although less catastrophic than events in Ireland after 1914, the breakup of Parnell's party set the Home Rule movement back many years and introduced a new sense of frustration and bitterness into the country. The revolution that had taken place in Irish politics could best be illustrated by the sight of policemen trying to protect Dillon and O'Brien from the fury of a Parnellite mob during the election in Cork. The wheel had come full circle; and Ireland had another martyr to add to its already large collection. Not all of Parnell's achievements died with the man. His devotion to Ireland as a nation advanced the cause of Home Rule, with the indispensable help of Gladstone, to an entirely new plane—that of the possible. And if the man responsible was missing, the myth, properly embellished by his disciples, lived on in the minds of old and young Ireland alike.

[53] Sir T. Esmonde to E. Kelly, 9 July 1891, Emmet MSS, AIHS.
[54] DICS, Jones, 1 Oct. 1891; DICS, Crane, 4 July 1891, SPO.

CHAPTER XV

Conciliation

To THE general public, conciliation makes duller reading than coercion. The facts and figures of rent adjudication, poor law valuation, land tenure laws, or public works projects cannot hope to compete in terms of drama with emotionally charged accounts of riots, murder, arson, boycotting, and the "brutality" of policemen or prison warders. It is part of the perversity of human nature that men will remember Mitchelstown and forget the Congested Districts Board. But it is also the fault of skilled publicists that the more negative acts of coercion have been engraved on the minds of succeeding generations while the constructive works of the Salisbury administration in Ireland have been consistently overlooked. The end result of Home Rule propaganda has been that Balfour's name remains to this day synonymous with coercion or the ruthless suppression of individual liberty. To many Irishmen—and not a few historians—he is still "Bloody Balfour": a tyrant in the guise of a dilettante, who enjoyed arresting newsboys, jailing priests or members of Parliament, and harrying innocent tenants off Plan estates. Such was the popular image of Arthur Balfour.

No one can rightly dispute Balfour's intimate association with the Crimes Act. At times he seemed to personify coercion itself. But what has been ignored is the fact—inconvenient to those who wish to divide English administrators in Ireland into "good" and "bad" men—that Balfour also brought the substance of conciliation to Ireland. And he did so not out of any desire to throw sops to the nationalist party, but because he had always considered it essential to apply coercion and conciliation simultaneously to Ireland. This strategy was a matter of conviction with him; it was not the result of political opportunism. No man understood better the futility of trying to govern that island by means of an erratic alternation of "kicks and kindness." The misconceptions that surround Unionist policy in Ireland are contained in the time-honored statement that the process of "killing Home Rule with kindness" began in 1895 with Lord Salisbury's third ministry. No assertion could be further from the truth. Balfour's "good works" may not have been as radical as Parnell would have liked, but his conciliatory measures did serve as the foundation for what came to be known as "constructive Unionism." Under Balfour's aegis a new phase in Anglo-Irish relations began, and it lasted with but one brief interruption until the resignation of George Wyndham in 1905. It is all too easy to belittle the value of land purchase, fair rents, relief works, or the Congested Districts Board, when compared with the nationalists' objective of Home Rule. But it must be remembered that these measures were never intended as a mere substitute for an Irish parliament. Instead, they were designed to remove what was regarded as a trumped-up demand for self-government toward which the overwhelming majority of Irishmen were presumed to be either indifferent or actively hostile. Conciliation, in short, was supposed to cure an essentially "bread and butter" question.

There was nothing sensational about the remedial legislation that Ireland received in the years from 1887 to 1892. The first steps in the direction of conciliation were cautious, hesitant, and usually molded into final form by Liberal Unionist pressure, which was constant throughout this period. A number of Conservatives and most Irish landlords, in fact, despised the whole idea of conciliation and complained that they were being betrayed by piecemeal concession to the tenantry. Home Rule sceptics, on the other hand, argued that relief works were a waste of time and money and that Ireland needed not new bridges, piers, and railway lines, but fiscal and legislative autonomy.

Above and beyond the babble of political controversy, however, stand three vital facts. In the first place, any division between Balfour's coercive and conciliatory activities tends to distort the essence of his policy, which was a deliberate blending of both. These apparently contradictory cures were inseparable in his own mind. He meant them to be interactive or complementary, in the sense that coercion struck at the symptoms while conciliation treated the causes of Irish discontent. Thus the policies were different sides of the same coin. And any separation made in these pages between them is artificial. Second, the remedial measures passed in these years brought substantial relief to thousands of tenants, especially to those who lived in the south and west. Lastly, the material condition of Ireland forced ministers to indulge in greater state regulation of individual welfare. The Government, in other words, helped those Irishmen who had proved incapable of helping themselves. Conservatives might excuse this paternalistic legislation on the grounds that Ireland was a "backward" country, but the fact remained that political circumstances pushed them further in this direction than they would have gone if left to their own devices.

I. THE LAND ACT OF 1887

One of the chronic failings of Englishmen in this decade was their inability to appreciate the impact of a prolonged depression upon an economy almost wholly given over to agriculture. While the rural population in England was steadily losing members to urban industrial centers, the number of cultivators in Ireland declined through emigration and a falling birth rate, but not through a comparable transition from agriculture to industry. Only in the province of Ulster, where the textile and shipbuilding industries were sufficiently prosperous to attract migratory labor, and in other urban areas of the country could agriculture be considered an alternative occupation. Few English politicians besides Gladstone realized the plight of the Irish tenantry in the 1880's. The Jubilee year witnessed an upswing in the British economy, with exports slowly reviving and unemployment declining; and in 1888 there was a boom in the British shipbuilding industry. But this mild recovery left agricultural Ireland virtually untouched. The diminishing costs of transport combined with enormous increases in production overseas drove the price of grain and other foodstuffs down by as much as thirty per cent. The agricultural depression in England was severe enough: after a disastrous drought in 1894 the market price of grains reached a record low. But in England agricultural laborers could and did find jobs in the cities. This was not the case in Ireland, where industry could not absorb those men dislocated by changes in the world market and where landlords who adjusted their rents to the fall in prices were the exception rather than the rule.[1]

Having appointed the Cowper Commission to inquire into the state of Irish agriculture and industry, ministers were slow to arrive at conclusions long anticipated by Parnell and his party. What was more reprehensible, they ignored nationalist warnings that the winter of 1886-1887 would be especially severe for the tenantry, owing to inadequate food supplies and the likelihood of many evictions. Admittedly, Beach had been working on a new land bill when the Churchill crisis broke; and when Balfour succeeded him as chief secretary, he assumed the burden of guiding two controversial measures through the House. The scope of this undertaking can be measured by the fact that the parliamentary session of 1887 was the longest in fifty years, and that the average time of rising for the Commons during this session was 2:15 A.M. Government whips worked feverishly through the night trying to keep a majority together.[2] After two and a half months, one procedural rule concerning the closure had passed and members were still debating the second reading of the Crimes Bill. In addition, the Land Bill provoked as much dissension in Parliament—certainly more within the Unionist coalition—as did the Crimes Bill.

The passing of the Land Act proved beyond any doubt the tenuous nature of the ties that bound together the Unionist coalition on all issues other than Home Rule. During the debates on this measure Conservatives found themselves in the awkward position of having to reconcile the self-interests of landlords with the reforming instincts of Liberal Unionists, and they ended by abjuring their own pledges on the subject. Part of the price that ministers had to pay for the support of their allies was the inclusion of certain "liberal" provisions in their legislative program. The Liberal Unionists lived in constant fear of losing their virtue as a party firmly wed to Liberal principles. They retained their own whips and party organization, refused to sit with the Conservatives on the Government side of the House, and insisted that the Government treat Ireland's needs in a generous spirit. Chamberlain, in particular, applied his experience of fiscal and

[1] See Clapham, *An Economic History of Modern Britain,* III, pp. 1-78.
[2] See Viscount Chilston, *Chief Whip,* pp. 127-29.

commercial problems to the Irish Question. Even though he had never traveled widely in Ireland, he diagnosed the country's economic ills with a facility denied to many of the bureaucrats in Dublin Castle. It was Chamberlain's talk about promoting Irish industries, technical education, and public transport that had so impressed Balfour in the autumn of 1886; and in spite of his involvement in the Special Commission, Chamberlain continued to take an active interest in remedial measures. These two men of completely contrasting temperament and background were the chief architects of "constructive Unionism," and it was due to their cooperation that the Unionist party could go to the polls in 1892 with more than a "blank record of resistance" to Gladstone's crusade for Home Rule.

The Land Bill that Balfour launched in the spring of 1887 was a thinly disguised version of Parnell's Tenants' Relief Bill, which had been rejected the previous autumn. Ministers never intended it to be anything more than a temporary expedient that would rectify some of the defects in the Land Act of 1881. Imagine their consternation, therefore, when the measure antagonized Irish landlords and Liberal Unionists, not to mention the Home Rule party, and provided the Parnellites with an excuse for prolonged obstruction. In barely recognizable form the bill left the committee stage in the Commons, and its reception on both sides of the House showed that the Irish committee of the cabinet had been slack about sounding public opinion on the subject. Unlike coercion, which tended to polarize opinion into two main camps, conciliation, as ministers learned to their dismay, had the effect of splintering opinion into numerous segments each with its own special brief.

The truth was that ever since Gladstone's first venture into the land question, Lord Salisbury and his colleagues had resented these encroachments upon landlords' rights. From tampering with the laws governing property ownership in Ireland there was but a short step to the pursuit of similar ends in England, and this prospect Salisbury would not tolerate. The Land Acts of both 1870 and 1881 had, in his opinion, only aggravated the enmity between owner and occupier, while compulsory rent arbitration was nothing short of disaster. At the same time, his devotion to landlords' rights was tempered by feelings of contempt for those Irish landlords who in 1881 had surrendered to a Liberal majority what they would never have sacrificed had a Conservative government been in power. As he confessed to Lord Beaconsfield in January of that year, he had little time for the Ulster members who abandoned their principles with such ease.[3] Salisbury was not blind to the steady fall in prices between 1881 and 1887, but his attention in these years was largely confined to the depression in English agriculture, as his sympathetic remarks on the subject at Newport in 1885 attested. As for Irish economic troubles, time and a degree of common sense, he believed, would settle the outstanding problems. But the fact remained that as a result of increasing imports of cheap foods from the Argentine, Russia, and the United States, Britain was growing less dependent upon Irish exports. And this state of affairs was borne out by the decline in value of Irish agricultural produce from £72 million in the period 1866-1870 to £54 million in 1884-1888. Such was the trend that the Cowper Commission had been appointed to study.

After five months of inquiry, the commissioners recommended the admission of all leaseholders to the benefits of the act of 1881, the reduction of the contractual term for judicial rents from fifteen years to five, and the adjustment of rents to agricultural prices in each part of the country. The cabinet regarded the last two suggestions with a mixture of contempt and fear lest they become the starting point for nationalist demands, while the provision for leaseholders was considered an unfortunate necessity. The idea of revising judicial rents every time there was a price fluctuation was anathema to ministers, who insisted on the sanctity of contracts and dreaded anything resembling a "produce rent" based on market conditions. Originally, Balfour had planned to extend the Ashbourne act and to supplement the act of 1881 only where it would facilitate land purchase. But he was soon disembarrassed of this notion. Some means had to be devised to prevent harsh landlords from evicting tenants whose arrears were the result of circumstances beyond their control. How to restrain landlords of the Clanricarde type without alienating the entire class in Ireland became the central question. Early in March Balfour wrote to his uncle from Dublin, ex-

[3] Salisbury to Beaconsfield, 2 Jan. 1881, Salisbury MSS.

plaining some of the obstacles he faced in drafting a viable land bill:

"There is but one Irishman whose tongue I am afraid of—and that is Ashbourne. I had rather carry on serious business in the middle of a Manchester Cotton Mill than within reach of that man's voice! I find that Beach rather than Buller is the radical: —and apparently it is to Beach that we owe it that Cowper's Commission has reported in favour of breaking the 15 years term. Buller spits at the landlords of course; but he agrees with me on four principles (1) That the Land Act of 81 is an abomination (2) That the only final solution is *purchase* (3) That we ought to be very reluctant to break leases (4) That it would be fatal to break the 15 years term."[4]

To Balfour the land question required two different approaches. The most important involved a "big purchase scheme"; but that solution would have to be postponed until another session. The second was a measure "of immediate practical importance" that would offer relief to tenants impoverished by the recent depression. To achieve the second end he suggested abolishing the inconvenience of the "first eviction," which was a legal formality marking the commencement of the six-month period during which the tenant could "redeem" or come to some arrangement with his landlord about paying arrears. Balfour estimated that out of the total number of tenants thus evicted each year, only twenty-five per cent failed to redeem and were permanently driven from their holdings. The great majority were readmitted as "caretakers" and sooner or later offered terms of redemption acceptable to their landlords. A written notice would in future take the place of the first eviction. He also wished to dispense with the "absurd" provision that no eviction was complete until the bailiffs had removed every stick of furniture from a tenant's dwelling.

But the most controversial portion of the Land Bill, known as the equitable jurisdiction clauses, was aimed at sparing tenants whose insolvency was not their fault from eviction. These clauses gave the tenant a choice between two procedures: either he could be declared bankrupt in the Court of Bankruptcy, in which case his arrears would be treated in much the same way as a money debt, that is, liable to liquidation within a certain period; or, if

[4] Balfour to Salisbury, 9 March 1887, *ibid.*

he disliked the stigma of bankruptcy, he could take his case to the county court judge and obtain a stay of eviction against his landlord. The judge, if he saw fit, could also spread the tenants' debts over a reasonable length of time; and in the event that the landlord refused to accept this judgment, he could be compelled to appear before the county court judge in order to have the ruling upheld. Both the bankruptcy and equity clauses were aimed directly at unreasonable landlords, and for this reason Balfour anticipated serious trouble from Government supporters in Parliament. He described the clauses as a "method for compelling landlords, who act like lunatics, to be treated as such," and hoped that the "mere threat of it" would teach harsh landlords the merits of leniency.[5]

From the outset Salisbury made it clear that the main features of the bill did not please him. It was always the Irish tenant and never the landlord, he complained in the House of Lords, who was excused from respecting a contract. Any extension of the Land Act of 1881 clashed openly with Conservative principles of political economy and had been forced upon ministers "by a false position which we did not create." Another outspoken critic of the bill was Chamberlain, who called it an instrument with which to collect unfair rents and deplored the landlord flavor of its provisions. Only a campaign to convert all tenants into proprietors would solve the land question, he thought, but in the meantime relief was urgent, and he advised the cabinet not to spurn concessions at a time when the Home Rulers were about to launch a mass protest against coercion.[6] Unfortunately, Irish landlords viewed concession in a different light: it was their rights and privileges, after all, that Chamberlain wished to scatter to the winds. Ministers were thus caught between the crossfire of the two extreme wings of the Unionist coalition, and the prospect of any consensus on the subject seemed more remote than ever. Lord Salisbury revealed his own fears about concession when he warned his fellow peers against the dangerous "tendency to throw any Jonah into the sea in the hope of abating a storm."

The introduction of the Land Bill required careful timing.

[5] Balfour to Salisbury, 20 Feb. 1887, *ibid.*; Balfour to Buller, 15 March 1887, Add. ms 49826.

[6] Garvin, *Chamberlain*, ii, p. 304.

Ministers scheduled the second reading of the measure in the House of Lords to coincide with the same stage for the Crimes Bill in the Commons, hoping thereby to bribe the Opposition into curtailing their obstruction of the coercion bill. The nationalists were duly warned that the tenantry would receive no relief until the Crimes Bill had passed through the lower House. But these tactics proved of no avail: the Home Rulers resisted coercion tenaciously. On March 31 Lord Cadogan, the Government spokesman on Irish affairs in the Lords, introduced the Land Bill. His task was by no means an easy one, because he had to make the concessions look small to the landlords, who were "in a susceptible condition," and substantial to the Liberal Unionists, who needed to justify themselves "in the eyes of their constituents for voting for the 'coercion bill.' "[7] Cadogan announced that the Government had no intention of tampering with the judicial rents, but wished instead to deal with leaseholders, evictions, insolvent tenants, and landlords on Plan of Campaign estates who needed temporary relief from the payment of rates. When he had finished his speech, peers on both sides of the House began to condemn the bill as entirely "lopsided." Why, the landlords asked, should the bankruptcy clauses protect only the tenants and not themselves from insolvency? Balfour advised his uncle that Ashbourne was beginning to "funk" about the bill. When Opposition peers demanded rent revision and nothing less, Salisbury replied that the price fall in Ireland did not justify any alteration of the judicial rents. And after castigating landlords who indulged in wholesale eviction, he warned that the Land Bill was meant to discipline harsh landlords just as the Crimes Bill was aimed at punishing tenants who broke the law.[8]

Because of continued obstruction in the Commons, the Lords took the Land Bill at a leisurely pace. The equitable jurisdiction clauses were attacked from every quarter. A staunch Conservative Lord Kilmorey called them "twenty times more injurious than any Plan of Campaign." Lord Salisbury argued that the agricultural depression had seriously affected two crops that were not widely grown in Ireland, namely, wheat and barley; while

[7] Salisbury to Queen Victoria, 31 March 1887, Salisbury MSS.

[8] Balfour to Salisbury, 12 April 1887, *ibid.; Hansard,* 3d series, Vol. 313, pp. 1355 ff.

the price fluctuation for oats, livestock, butter, wool, and potatoes had been, in his opinion, unexceptional. But many Unionists disagreed with him; and a committee of Irish peers led by the Duke of Abercorn tried to work out a substitute for the bankruptcy clauses that would satisfy both themselves and the Liberal Unionists. The disputes within the Government over this bill drove the prime minister to exclaim: "I feel that I am living in an enchanted land, and I do not know what conclusions to form. . . . " What he steadfastly denied was that the majority of rents fixed by the land courts since 1881 were obsolete or unfair.[9]

The Liberal Unionists, however, insisted that concession over judicial rents could not be avoided. Eventually, after a series of tense parleys with Hartington and Chamberlain, the Irish committee of the cabinet arrived at a compromise solution whereby county court judges would be empowered to alter judicial rents at their discretion. Balfour and Salisbury still hoped to save the fifteen-year term, and to leave unchanged the rental of the holdings, by permitting the judges to grant only individual abatements according to prevailing prices. But even this plan to save the integrity of the judicial rents was shortlived. Reports from Ireland did not substantiate Salisbury's view of a mild recession. Landlords and tenants alike were short of cash. As an Irish judge observed: " . . . if present prices continue, reductions are necessary, and lots of tenants as well as landlords are clean broke all through the south of Ireland." Since rent revision seemed inevitable to landlords like the Duke of Abercorn, the most pressing problem was to draw a limit to reduction; otherwise, "the door would be open to absolute confiscation." But Balfour and his colleagues were still unconvinced.[10]

On July 11 the chief secretary introduced the Land Bill in the Commons in a speech that was at times almost apologetic. Having outlined the main provisions of this amending measure, he declared his unconditional opposition to revising judicial rents. If the act of 1881 was going to be "torn up by the roots," he declared, then one could never again hope for finality in Irish

[9] Salisbury to Abercorn, 26, 30 May 1887; Abercorn to Salisbury, 21 May 1887, Salisbury MSS.

[10] Abercorn to Salisbury, 6 Aug. 1887; Balfour to Salisbury, 19, 30 May 1887, *ibid.*

land legislation. Even Balfour was somewhat chastened by the hostile reception that the bill received. On the question of revising judicial rents Liberal Unionists were as angry as Home Rulers, and the equity clauses were labeled "unjust, demoralising, unworkable, ineffectual."[11] So intense were the attacks on the Government's position that the measure, upon Gladstone's suggestion, was withdrawn for further consideration in cabinet. The outcome was surrender on the key issue of judicial rents. In the words of Lord Cranbrook the cabinet "submitted rather than approved" the decision to revoke the fifteen-year term; and on July 19 Salisbury broke this news to a group of disheartened supporters at the Carlton Club. Dismay within the Conservative party was bitter, if muted, and several die-hard landlords openly objected. Cranbrook told the prime minister that "nothing but loyalty to him, and the Union" kept him from opposing the bill. "The Liberal Unionists must not drag us too far," he asserted, "or we may swamp principles as precious as the Union." Lord Salisbury justified the concession with the argument of sheer necessity; but to Beach he admitted that the bill "has been pain and grief to me"; and later, at Hatfield, he declared in somber tones: "It is the price which we have to pay for the Union and it is a heavy one."[12]

The amended bill provided for the revision of all judicial rents affected by the price fall between 1881 and 1886. Parnell, who had advocated triennial revision of these rents, was now fully vindicated, while the morale of Government supporters sagged visibly. The controversial bankruptcy clauses were jettisoned; the jurisdiction of county court judges in rent cases was extended; more than 100,000 leaseholders were admitted to the act of 1881; and ministers, after "delicate and protracted negotiations" with the Liberal Unionists, agreed to adopt a "produce rent" equivalent to the sliding scale recommended by the Cowper Commission. The new judicial rents were to be based on the prevailing prices and labor conditions in each district and would be valid for three years.[13] In Balfour's opinion the system was "rough, ready, and

[11] *Hansard*, 3d series, Vol. 317, pp. 385 ff.

[12] Gathorne Hardy, *Cranbrook*, II, pp. 285-86; Cecil, *Salisbury*, IV, pp. 149-50.

[13] For details of the Land Act, see *HC 1887*, Vol. 2.

rude but expeditious"; but he saw no alternative. To speed the bill through the House of Commons he asked Buller to suspend all evictions until the measure had become law.[14] Obstruction continued, nevertheless, and ministers were taunted for having reversed their stand. When the bill returned to the Lords for amendment, a group of Unionist peers tried to adulterate the concessions. Their efforts were in vain, however, because W. H. Smith impressed upon Salisbury the dangers of tampering with the Commons' version. It was already mid-August, he wrote, and members were tired, if not exasperated; and he was having difficulty in holding the Unionist forces together with the holidays overdue.[15] The Lords' amendments were promptly rejected by the Commons, and on August 18 the Land Bill became law.

Lord Salisbury, in the course of his Mansion House speech, described the recent parliamentary session as "a maximum of garrulity and a minimum of legislation." But he expressed his hope that the Crimes Act and the Land Act together would help to restore order and prosperity in Ireland. The Parnellites, in general, regarded the Land Act with disdain. William O'Brien called it a "miserable mockery of justice"; while Parnell would have preferred an "across the board" abatement of rent, relief from arrears, and compulsory land purchase in order to force landlords to sell. If reaction to the Land Act was mixed, there could be no ambiguity about the Government's surrender of a vital principle in this their first attempt at conciliation. Devonshire House, rather than Hawarden, had extracted this concession from the Conservatives. In the end, the gloomy prophecies of landlords about the effect of a sliding scale turned out to be greatly exaggerated. Balfour maintained that the rent reductions would be much less than his colleagues imagined. And events proved him right. Judicial rents fixed before 1886 were reduced by no more than fifteen per cent, and in most cases the abatements ranged between six and twelve per cent.[16] The real trouble lay in the number of cases awaiting adjudication in the land courts. In September, 1887, the backlog of business amounted to

[14] Balfour to Buller, 2 Aug. 1887, Add. MS 49826.

[15] Smith to Salisbury, 19 Aug. 1887, Salisbury MSS.

[16] In one instance the rent was raised five per cent above the 1885 level. Balfour to Salisbury, 21 Sept. 1887, *ibid.*

13,000 cases—a condition Balfour called scandalous. In order to cope with these arrears and also with litigation arising out of the Land Act, he appointed ten new subcommissioners. The reluctance of ministers to admit the need for rent revision, added to their unjustified fears about the results of a sliding scale, caused them much embarrassment. Having failed to consult Liberal Unionist opinion, they produced a bill unpalatable to both friend and foe. The fact was that ministers gained nothing but insults by enacting Parnell's bill one year too late. Henry Harrison has recorded a conversation in 1887 with an Ulster landowner who expressed his bitter feelings about the "Conservative surrender" of that year. According to the latter, Gladstone's Land Bill of 1886 had offered the landlords advantageous terms for the sale of their estates. "But the Tories said: 'Stick to us, and help us to smash old Gladstone and we'll see you through,' so we had to refuse it." This landlord and many others in Ireland, Harrison alleged, soon had cause to "repent in sackcloth and ashes," as their rights were gradually stripped away "like leaves off an artichoke."[17] And in view of the hasty concessions made by ministers in 1887, the landlords had some reason to talk about betrayal.

II. LAND PURCHASE

As Balfour declared both publicly and in private, the Land Act of 1887 was only a temporary expedient and did not seek to resolve the ancient antagonism between owner and occupier. The only lasting solution for that conflict in the minds of the Government and their Liberal Unionist allies was land purchase. To convert the great majority of Irish tenants into peasant proprietors by means of guaranteed loans payable in easy installments had become the ultimate goal of the Conservatives after 1881. Balfour called it "the one permanent hope for Ireland"; most of the cabinet regarded purchase as the "final solution" to the land question; and Lord Salisbury, who had been converted to purchase by the act of 1881, argued that without this policy the clash of interests between landlord and tenant would go on forever, "even if the present paroxysm of lawlessness" were to abate. Ministers saw in peasant proprietaries a means not only

[17] Harrison, *Parnell, Joseph Chamberlain, and Mr. Garvin,* p. 147.

of ending the iniquity of "dual ownership"—which they blamed on Gladstone—but of undermining the demand for Home Rule.[18] As Balfour explained to a supporter in 1890:

"The landlords are called the 'English garrison,' but while dual ownership exists, they no more add strength to England than the garrisons of Suikata [*sic*] and Tokar added strength to Egypt. On the contrary, the whole of our Home Rule controversy has been hampered and embarrassed by having to defend not only the Union but the landlords. Abolish dual ownership and the influence of the landlords will . . . be greatly augmented. There will be no cause of friction between them and their neighbours; they cannot be made the theme of platform oratory; and they will then for the first time really become an efficient support of the English connexion."[19]

By 1887 the majority of Conservatives believed that purchase would restore stability and perhaps even prosperity to Ireland, while it would also convince the tenant-owners that the Union was essential to their welfare. Instead of evacuation under pressure of the land agitation, landlords would be able to sell voluntarily with ample reward for the loss of their estates. Land purchase, it was hoped, would disconnect Fintan Lalor's agrarian engine from the rest of the train and sidetrack the Home Rule carriages forever.

The Conservatives' reliance on purchase revealed much about their interpretation of the Irish Question. As they saw it, Irish nationalism derived its chief inspiration and energy from the hostility between tenants and landlords. Consequently, they expected land purchase to deprive the Parnellites of the most important ingredient in their campaign for self-government. "I am not prepared to deny," Balfour once stated, "that as much misery and distress may exist in Ireland should dual ownership be abolished, as if the present system remained. But the political and social difficulties will . . . be greatly diminished or altogether removed."[20]

Needless to say, the Unionists did not embrace land purchase

[18] Balfour to Lord de Vesci, 3 April 1889, Add. MS 49827; Salisbury to Sir James Caird, 22 Nov. 1887, Salisbury MSS.
[19] Balfour to Sir Stafford Northcote, M.P., 1 May 1890, Add. MS 49828.
[20] Balfour to E. J. Wakefield, 26 March 1887, *ibid.*, 49826.

for purely altruistic reasons. At a time when the writings of Henry George on the evils of private property and the merits of the single tax had reached a wide public, and when Davitt and other nationalists were promising the tenantry that the land would be theirs once Home Rule had passed, it was natural that the party representing "landlordism" should promote sales while selling was still possible. Expropriation they saw as the only alternative to purchase; and if the administration waited too long before acting, the chances were that Irish landlords would be lucky to escape with the clothes on their backs. Or so the more pessimistic Unionists thought. Besides providing a safeguard against outright confiscation, land purchase also suited Conservative tactics at home. It served as a convenient and relatively cheap instrument with which to match the Liberal program, and after 1886 it became the mainstay of Unionist arguments against Home Rule. Moreover, ministers assumed that since Gladstone had trampled so maliciously on landlords' rights, the state now had an obligation to rescue that class from an impossible situation by providing Treasury securities for purchase.

Land purchase raised a number of questions, both theoretical and practical, and one in particular never failed to cause a commotion. This problem concerned the principle of compulsion. Ought landlords like Clanricarde to be forced by court order to part with their estates at a reasonable price? Balfour had already tried to answer this question by means of special legislation, but his plan had come to grief in cabinet. Parnell insisted that no measure was complete unless it contained some provision for compulsory sale; and Chamberlain would have vested his proposed county councils in Ireland or the Land Commission with power to buy up estates. In a memorandum on land purchase Salisbury recommended a form of limited compulsion whereby sale would be made mandatory in any parish upon a successful petition to both houses of Parliament by the individuals or authority concerned. In this way a Clanricarde or a Colonel O'Callaghan would be forced to sell his estate without jeopardizing the position of every landlord in the country. Compulsion, then, was ultimately desirable, but for the time being impracticable. Other ministers argued that such power could too easily be abused, especially by a government dedicated to Home Rule, and that the landlords would never submit to this violation of their rights. Balfour soon realized that only a bill based on voluntary purchase could survive in Parliament and hold the Unionist alliance together; and when he finally abandoned compulsion, he received a note from his uncle expressing the widespread relief that was felt within the party. Had the bill included a compulsory clause, he added, "it would have broken up the Cabinet, the Party, & the Union."[21]

There was also the problem of offering terms sufficiently attractive to tempt the tenants into buying their holdings. No government could compel this class to enter into purchase on what they considered landlords' terms. Lord Salisbury at Newport had admitted that one could not "force the hand of nature." What all Unionists did agree upon was that land purchase would work only if the price of a holding did not exceed its "fair" rent. "All the constabulary, with the British Army behind them," Salisbury remarked, "will not induce him to pay more." And in March, 1887, he told Cranbrook that he would like to combine coercion with the power to buy up landlords at arbitration prices, to issue debentures on the security of the land and rates, and to resell in small lots with deferred payment. "You will never force the tenants to buy," he concluded, "until you offer to let others of their own class buy their holdings over their heads."[22] To create the necessary incentive for purchase among the peasantry, a fair price was essential. And since the average price of land in Ireland stood at slightly less than twenty years' purchase of the rent, Lord Ashbourne and his successors fixed the payment at forty-nine years and four per cent interest.

The sceptics, whether nationalists or landlords, laughed at the idea of thousands of peasant proprietors' paying their annuities regularly. Even if the tenants could be induced to start purchase proceedings, they would surely default on their payments just as they had on their rents. Some Parnellites feared that purchase would injure the Home Rule agitation, and for that reason they adopted an equivocal or hostile attitude toward the scheme. Branches of the National League were often ordered to boycott

[21] See Salisbury's memorandum, "Suggestions for a Bill to enable Tenants to purchase the Holdings they occupy in Ireland," 4 Oct. 1887, Salisbury MSS; and Salisbury to Balfour, 1 Nov. 1889, Add. MS 49689.

[22] Salisbury to Cranbrook, 9 March 1887, Salisbury MSS.

tenants who showed a desire to buy their holdings. In an extravagant mood Parnell had once said that the tenant who became the owner of his holding would soon "turn the sands into gold." There were landlords, on the other hand, who welcomed land purchase because the land war and Home Rule agitation had made investment in land a nonpaying proposition. Lord Lansdowne was only one of a number of Irish landlords who had resigned themselves to the sale of their estates. "The British public," he informed Salisbury, "is indifferent to the ruin of the landlords and will not spend a penny to avert it. . . . " Having lost most of his rent to the Plan of Campaign, Lansdowne had come to realize that purchase offered the only way to escape financial ruin, and he urged the prime minister to educate public opinion on this subject. He attributed the unpopularity of purchase to the ignorance of Englishmen about the pernicious effect of Gladstone's land legislation; and because the agricultural scene in Ireland was so "hopelessly demoralized," he warned that ministers had to choose between "the collapse of the Union and a great agrarian revolution."[23] From a Government point of view there was no time to be lost, for Dillon, O'Brien, and other nationalists were stumping the country assuring the tenants that in a few years they would be able to claim their holdings free of charge. Land purchase was deceptive, these Parnellites urged, because the price would be based on "rack rents" and the landlords would demand too many securities to make ownership worthwhile.

In practice the mechanics of purchase raised several other questions. First, the Government had to select a reliable middleman to receive the tenants' annuity or rent charge. Since purchase was designed to eliminate the landlord from the scene, direct repayment of the loan to the landowner would hardly alter the old relationship between owner and occupier. The use of some intermediate or local authority was therefore essential to the proper working of purchase. But there were differences of opinion about what authority should be used. Chamberlain wanted a land purchase solution to coincide with an Irish local government bill, so that the county councils could buy and administer estates using a land bank specially created for the purpose; whereas Salisbury preferred that the old boards of guardians,

[23] Lansdowne to Salisbury, 7 Dec. 1887, 1 Feb. 1888, *ibid.*

long experienced in levying rates, should supervise the payment
of annuities. In spite of this disagreement over means, Salisbury
acknowledged his indebtedness to Chamberlain for the main
features of the purchase plan that he formulated in October, 1887.[24]

Next came the problem of funds. Since English capitalists were
on the whole reluctant to invest money in Irish land stock, the
Treasury would have to guarantee any debentures issued for
land purchase. Alternatively, under Chamberlain's scheme, the
funds would be raised on Irish securities. But the real difficulty
concerned maintaining the land debentures at par value. In
order to avoid unnecessary risks to the British taxpayer, Balfour had decided to use as the negotiable medium bonds pur-
chasable by the public rather than cash dividends. The trouble
was that this land stock remained consistently below par as a
result of the depression; and the landlords showed a justifiable
aversion to being paid in bonds that only depreciated in value.
Ministers kept hoping for a sharp rise in the market, but they
waited in vain. Safeguards were another vital feature of land
purchase: both the local authority and the landlords had to be
guaranteed against loss. Under the Ashbourne act the tenant
was required to deposit one-fifth of the purchase money in advance. But Balfour was anxious to abolish this deposit in order
to attract more buyers, while providing several other securities
against default. By 1895, however, only twenty-two tenants had
failed to pay their annuities under the various acts facilitating
purchase, so that much of the fuss about fancy safeguards was
superfluous.[25]

Lord Salisbury showed no qualms about the landlord flavor of
his ideas on purchase. Gladstone, he believed, had placed the landlords in such an anomalous position that they deserved special
treatment—or, as he once said, they "merited tenderness." Balfour, on the other hand, perceived that too much "landlordism"
in any bill would impair its appeal to the tenants, and he worked
hard to improve the terms of purchase. The Liberal Unionists,
in general, supported this position, although Lord Hartington

[24] Salisbury to Smith, 16 Oct. 1887, *ibid.* See also Salisbury's memorandum on purchase, 4 Oct. 1887, *ibid.*

[25] Salisbury to Balfour, 3 Oct. 1887, *ibid.*; Pomfret, *The Struggle for
Land*, p. 273.

and his followers treated the question of compulsory purchase with greater caution than did Chamberlain. Not every Unionist, however, saw a panacea in land purchase. Lord John Manners, one of Salisbury's oldest friends, despaired of restoring order to the chaos of Irish agriculture. Purchase, he was convinced, would never reduce the mutual hatred of owner and occupier, and he advised W. H. Smith: "If the process could be reversed and the landlords enabled to buy out the tenants, I should have more hope; but the barrel has been set trundling in one direction, and must, I suppose, trundle till it stops—and drops."[26]

Some self-styled experts on the land question predicted that purchase would fail because the tenants lacked thrift and industry and reproduced too rapidly. The lack of sunlight, furthermore, diminished the productive capacity of the soil and forced the people into migratory labor during the summer months. And the distance between the producer and his market was so great that it would raise the cost of transportation beyond the means of the average tenant-owner. In spite of such pessimistic forecasts, the Ashbourne act had proved a success. During the first three years after its passage tenants purchased more than half a million acres, with just under fifty per cent of these sales taking place outside Ulster. Such results, if not spectacular, at least encouraged the Government in 1888 to supplement this measure. Reports from Ireland, moreover, emphasized the general contentment and order in those districts where tenants had already purchased under the act.[27]

The Land Purchase Act of 1888 added, in effect, another £5 million to the Ashbourne act. Neither the prime minister nor Balfour rejoiced over the measure, which they regarded as an unhappy compromise. Salisbury lamented the absence of a clause that would compel harsh landlords to sell, and Balfour had decided that the Ashbourne act was no longer sufficient—partly because it was Ashbourne's, but also because it lacked the necessary inducements for the tenantry. What with coercion, the Special Commission, and the Local Government Bill, the political calendar was already overcrowded, and Balfour realized that

[26] Manners to Smith, 24 July 1889, Hambleden MSS. Manners had become the 7th Duke of Rutland on his father's death in 1888.

[27] Ridgeway to Balfour, 18 Nov. 1889, Add. MS 49810; DICS, Crane, 7 Feb. 1890, SPO.

this was no time to introduce a controversial measure. If he attempted to alter the provisions of Ashbourne's act, he feared that "the better would prove the victorious enemy of the good . . . " and he trusted that the old machinery would suffice until the parliamentary schedule allowed time for a more radical departure. Because of Ireland's exclusion from the Local Government Act, Chamberlain's plan to integrate land purchase with local administration never materialized. Applications for purchase had exceeded the amount provided by the Ashbourne act, and, even more encouraging, two-thirds of these purchasers belonged to the poorest class of tenant. As for defaults in payment, there was no need for alarm because the arrears on annuities were less than one per cent. The Land Purchase Bill passed through the Commons without alteration, although Gladstone tried in vain to attach a clause relieving tenants from arrears. As Goschen admitted, the measure was "not a final and permanent" solution to the land question. Ministers thus held out the promise of better things to come.[28]

Another year passed before Balfour re-entered the field of land purchase, and even then obstruction and delays in Parliament prevented his measure from becoming law until 1891. The new measure was supposed to crown all earlier attempts at promoting purchase, and Balfour devoted much thought to the problem of increasing the attractions for both vendor and buyer without alienating either. By 1890 some 23,348 tenants had applied for advances amounting to £9,127,388 under the acts of 1885 and 1888, but the limits of purchase were by no means exhausted. Balfour wanted his second venture in land purchase to be an "heroic measure"—one that would include some system of compulsory sale. But once again he was defeated by the landlord interest, which refused even to contemplate such a proposal. As Ridgeway complained when he saw the draft bill in the autumn of 1889: "The Union will never be safe, so long as landlords like Clanricarde are treated as if they were sane and reasonable men."[29]

[28] Salisbury to Balfour, 20 Sept. 1888, Salisbury MSS; Balfour to A. V. Dicey, 20 Nov. 1888, Add. MS 49827; *Annual Register, 1888*, pp. 208-17.
[29] Balfour to Ridgeway, 2 Oct. 1890; Balfour to Goschen, 16 Sept. 1889. Ridgeway to Balfour, 8 Oct. 1889, Add. MS 49828-829, 49810.

Balfour's bill was heroic in few respects save the size of the funds involved. Its provisions included the creation of a land department to supervise the sale of property. Unlike the Ashbourne act, Balfour's required no deposit, although an insurance clause stipulated that the tenant pay a higher rent charge for the first five years as protection against default. The bill contained several other safeguards or "collateral securities," which Ridgeway called "wonderfully ingenious." But the question remained whether or not they would work. Lord Salisbury approved the tenants' insurance fund, but suspected that the bill would antagonize the landlords because it tried too hard to please the buyer. Balfour replied that the landlords derived greater benefits from this measure than from Ashbourne's, and at one stage he was prepared to repeal the latter act altogether.[30] Balfour's bill made available the sum of £33 million in loans, guaranteed by the imperial Exchequer as well as by Irish local resources, and provided for the reimbursement of landlords in government stock bearing two and three-quarters per cent interest. By the end of November the cabinet had assented to Balfour's draft bill, which had been divided into two distinct parts, one dealing with purchase and the other with the so-called "congested districts" in the west.

Lord Salisbury's attitude to the new Land Bill was never more than lukewarm. He did not worry about the possibility of the landlords being driven from the country; on the contrary, he feared that too few tenants would take advantage of the measure. The bill was "not a good thing in itself," he wrote to an Ulster member, "it is only a remedy for worse evils, rendered necessary by the improvident and disastrous legislation of the last quarter of a century." And he continued in this vein: "I do not in the least anticipate that it will put an end to the class of landlords. . . . But what we hope for from it is not that it will fill the country with peasant proprietors, but that it will establish them in greater or less numbers in various parts of the country, scattered all over it, so that the present uniformity of condition and feeling which enabled agitators to turn the whole political and social force of the occupiers against the landlords will be arrested and broken,

[30] Salisbury to Balfour, 4 Oct. 1889, Salisbury mss; Balfour to Salisbury, 9 Oct. 1889; Balfour to Goschen, 30 Jan. 1890, Add. ms 49828.

and will lose its formidable effect."[31] In purchase, he believed, lay the means of dissolving the ties that bound the agrarian and political agitations together.

When Balfour introduced his Land Purchase Bill in the Commons on March 24, the "almost bewildering complexity" of its provisions left members either sceptical or mystified. Comments in the Unionist press were favorable but rarely ecstatic: the *Daily News* called the bill "Mr. Balfour's Puzzle"; and the intricate safeguards were widely attributed to the financial wizardry of Goschen. Even friendly critics complained that the scope of the bill was too narrow, objected to the excessive precautions therein, and wondered if the English electorate, not to mention the Irish tenant, would ever be able to understand it. The Home Rule press described it as Gladstone's abortive Land Bill of 1886 warmed-over, and scoffed at the Government's claim that no risk to the Treasury was involved. And the *Freeman's Journal* charged that the main object of the bill was to inflate the price of land in Ireland.[32]

The debates on the bill were in general languid, but the objections raised were nonetheless grave. Parnell, in moving the bill's rejection on April 21, argued that the courts ought to reduce all rents by at least twenty per cent, and that ministers cared only about enabling the largest absentee owners, who made up less than ten per cent of the landlord class, to "get out" of the country at an exorbitant price. The gravamen of his charge was that the bill would affect only one-fourth of the 600,000 tenant farmers in the country, and that it exhausted Irish credit without materially benefiting Ireland. Even Gladstone deplored the complexity of the bill, although Balfour made a brilliant speech in its defense, handling the many criticisms raised with consummate skill. The chief secretary once confided to a friend: "I am more or less happy when being praised; not very uncomfortable when being abused, but I have moments of uneasiness when being explained."[33] But this bill required considerable explanation, and he availed himself of the chance to address an overseas audience on the subject in the *North American Review*. In answering

[31] Salisbury to Col. Thomas Waring, M.P., 2 May 1890, Salisbury MSS.
[32] *Annual Register, 1890*, pp. 82-87, 116-26.
[33] I. Malcolm, *Lord Balfour, A Memory*, London, 1930, p. 95.

Parnell's attacks, he stressed the importance of simplifying the system of land tenure to the point where the occupiers were also the owners. It was too late to reverse the trend of Gladstone's land policies: one could only go forward by promoting purchase, and this the Government sought to accomplish in a bill that contained more flexible terms of repayment for the buyer. In addition, the loans repaid by the first group of tenants using this act could be reissued to the next set of purchasers, so that the original grant was self-perpetuating. If anything, the new bill erred on the side of generosity; and Balfour ended his article by explaining Parnellite objections to the bill as motivated by their desire to advance the "political revolution" in Ireland: "No wonder that those who think social anarchy the fitting prelude to home rule should oppose with all their energies a method by which the weakest part in the social fabric may be effectually strengthened."[34]

In Parliament the bill moved into committee at a snail's pace. The difficulties experienced by the Government during this sterile session have been recounted in detail above. Suffice it to say that from March to July obstruction blocked progress on the Land Bill, the Tithe Bill, and the even more unpopular Local Taxation Bill. There was much talk of a dissolution and of almost certain victory for the Home Rule alliance. In mid-June the cabinet reluctantly agreed to jettison their most important measures. The only alternative was dissolution, and, as Hartington advised Salisbury, "an election now would be fatal to us."[35] Moreover, W. H. Smith's ill-health was causing much anxiety, and the possibility of his resignation was never far distant. Many Unionists in the Commons were "demoralized" by the decision to postpone these bills; and the Queen implored Lord Salisbury to do all in his power to keep Gladstone out of office. The Government's troubles were increased by Lord Randolph Churchill, who attacked the Land Bill on the grounds that Ireland needed elective county councils before purchase. At the same time a number of Irish landlords began to criticize the inadequacy of the securities. "The

[34] See *North American Review*, July, 1890, Vol. 151, No. 104, pp. 1-13. Parnell's attack on the bill is contained in *ibid.*, Vol. 150, No. 403, pp. 665-70.

[35] Hartington to Salisbury, 17 June 1890, Salisbury MSS.

fact is that they are not very wise people," Balfour wrote to a friend, "and that they are entirely in the hands of their lawyers and land agents who, naturally enough, do not like a measure which will diminish their occupation."[36]

On December 2 Balfour moved the second reading of his slightly altered Land Purchase Bill, while the Parnellites were indulging in mutual recriminations in Committee Room 15. The drama of the Irish party on the verge of disintegration may have stolen the limelight from the Land Bill, but it accelerated the passage of that measure which Parnell and his followers "ostentatiously" supported. With the advent of the Christmas holidays the Government's legislative ordeal was almost over; "the year of small achievements" had come to a close. The combined effects of influenza and the Parnellite split reduced obstruction of the Land Purchase Bill to a minimum. When Parnell moved an amendment increasing the benefits offered to the tenantry, Ridgeway wrote to his chief from Dublin: "Have you thought of conceding Parnell's amendment or something like it? It would greatly revive his prestige and I think enable all the P. of C. disputes to be settled. Then Othello's occupation would be gone. Now is the time, while Dillon and O'Brien are in prison, to dish the Plan . . . by some concession. When the Plan is dead it will never be revived and the agrarian agitation will cease—at any rate until the General Election."[37] Balfour, however, did not share this optimistic view, and Parnell's amendment was defeated. On August 5, some eighteen months after its introduction, the measure received the royal assent.

In spite of its ingenuity, the Land Purchase Act of 1891 never lived up to advance expectations. The tenants, in the first place, preferred the Ashbourne act simply because they could understand it. The elaborate securities of the new measure made them suspicious and they feared the cost and trouble of litigation. Furthermore, nationalist agitators covered the act in a "cloud

[36] Cranbrook to Salisbury, 24 June 1890; Balfour to Salisbury, 23 June 1890; Beach to Salisbury, 6, 16 Nov. 1890, *ibid.* See also Balfour to Ridgeway, 2, 13 April 1890; Balfour to E. B. Iwan-Müller, 17 June 1890, Add. MS 49828.

[37] Ridgeway to Balfour, n.d. May 1891, *ibid.,* 49812.

of misrepresentation and deliberate falsehood."[38] The landlords, on the other hand, suspected that the value of government land stock would depreciate, and since these bonds did not recover appreciably between 1891 and 1896, they had good reason not to sell. By 1898 the number of applications for purchase had declined to less than one-fifth of those made each year under the acts of 1885 and 1888. The machinery of Balfour's act had come to a virtual standstill.[39]

Balfour attributed the collapse of purchase to other causes. The relative tranquillity that followed prosecutions under the Crimes Act had made the tenants apathetic. What with sliding-scale rents, equity clauses, and the easing of eviction laws, they had little wish to change their status. The imminence of the general election as well as the prospect of a second Home Rule bill also tended to "clog the wheels of the machine." The Parnellite split, moreover, gave the tenants more important things to worry about than the acquisition of their holdings on landlords' terms. For such reasons Balfour believed that land purchase had reached the point of stagnation.[40] Only the Liberal victory of 1892 prevented him from having another try in this field.

III. THE CONGESTED DISTRICTS BOARD

The second part of the Land Purchase Act of 1891 represented a new departure for Conservative policy in Ireland. A special board was created in order to provide relief and to stimulate the economy in the poorest districts of the country. If there were critics who called the plan "moonshine" or who, like Dillon, opposed the scheme ostensibly because it placed the financial burden on Irish local resources, at least the Government's intentions were not condemned. It was not easy to define those areas most in need of relief. The very term "congested" was a nineteenth-century euphemism used to describe areas where the inhabitants were never far from starvation, or where, as Lord Salisbury explained to the Queen, "a dense population of half starving multitudes"

[38] See reports of DICS, Crane, 7 April 1890, and DICS, Jones, 31 May 1890, SPO.

[39] Pomfret, *The Struggle for Land,* p. 271.

[40] Balfour to J. G. McCarthy, 14 Nov. 1891, Add. ms 49830.

tried to live off the inadequate resources of the soil.[41] In Ireland such chronically depressed parishes were located along the western coastal regions and extended inland into the mountainous and boggy terrain that divides the fertile midlands from the sea. In these districts two out of three meals consisted of potatoes, and the tenants were entirely dependent upon the credit of a local shopkeeper to keep their families fed and clothed for at least four months of the year. George Wyndham conveyed a vivid picture of this "wasteland" in the west, when, early in 1901, he made a tour of inspection through Connemara. He recorded some of his impressions for a close friend, the poet and author William Henley:

"We drove all day; descended to walk up crags and survey the scene, a maze of rocks & walls; a lace-work of sea indentations, islets & promontories. The sea on one hand, the bog & mountain on the other & between a fringe on which humanity is huddled to exist by *seaweed*. That is what brought them there. They manure with it the starved soil that has given potatoes for 50 years. To do this they light fires on the granite boulders until they crack, then carry the pieces to make walls round enclosures the size of a room which are humourously called 'gardens.' From these they extract the potato. Some wild colts & lean cattle roam like goats over the intricate waste. They burn the seaweed into kelp & they eat it. They can't talk English or scarce understand it. They weave their own clothes of thin & dirty flannel, sere as canvas. The women toil over the slippery rocks laden with creels of seaweed. The men lean & loaf & look with soft idle blue eyes at the sea. The place is a beautiful, stagnant desolation."

Wyndham's imagination was captivated by the timeless quality of these scenes and by the suffering and futility of life as he saw it in those inlets where "curlews cried" and "terns dipped and fluttered along the beach." And then, remembering his purpose there, he wrote like Balfour's prize pupil: "The problem is can you make the men fish; can you make the women work at lace,

[41] Salisbury to Queen Victoria, 8 Nov. 1889, Salisbury mss. Since the congested districts were so thinly populated, Salisbury's definition was inaccurate. Congestion was a misnomer derived from the high rate of emigration in the west and meant simply extreme poverty. See Royal Commission on Congestion in Ireland, first report, *H.C. 1906*, Vol. 32.

hand made curtains & tapestry? If you can, you may some day build up life: If you can't they must go. But there they are, dreaming & singing & drinking: making 'pot-sheen' & hitting each other on the head with the stones that abound."[42]

∝ In the spring of 1889 Balfour addressed himself to much the same problems that worried Wyndham, but then the situation was far more complex because no official agency of relief existed and even a partial failure of the potato crop could cause havoc at any time. Unless the Government took some action to build up agriculture and native industries in the congested districts, famine or the attrition of poverty and disease would soon remove the surplus population of the area. Such a calamity had to be prevented at all costs. But it was not easy to discover a solution to this chronic problem where so few precedents existed. Balfour would have preferred to reduce the surplus population through assisted emigration; but the United States as well as Canada had tightened their immigration laws since 1879, and the nationalists tended to regard any such schemes as equivalent to deportation. He explained to Ridgeway in May, 1889:

"Without doubt the congested districts supply us with the most insoluble part of the Irish difficulty. In other parts of Ireland it would probably be enough to restore obedience to the law and to facilitate the acquisition of the Freehold of their tenancies by the farmers—in the congested districts something more is required, and what that something more shall be is a most perplexing question. Railways, no doubt, will produce some benefit, but the chief advantage I anticipate from them is that of providing employment in the districts through which they are constructed, and thus tiding over the interval which must elapse before any more permanently beneficial scheme can come into operation."[43]

What complicated matters was the annual migration of "the whole male population" to Britain or to other parts of Ireland in search of seasonal work. Balfour despaired of finding a way to "loosen the tie which binds them to their wretched holdings." A scheme was needed to end the precarious margin of existence on which the populace lived from year to year. Once Balfour had

---

[42] Wyndham to Henley, 10 Feb. 1901, Henley mss, Pierpont Morgan Library (hereafter PML).

[43] Balfour to Ridgeway, 15 May 1889, Add. ms 49827.

found a feasible plan, however, long delays in Parliament, the suspicious attitude of the Parnellites, and the slowness of the peasantry to change their ways all acted as hindrances to the rehabilitation of this area.

Once again Chamberlain left his mark on Government policy in Ireland. Ever since 1886 he had advocated measures to improve the material condition of the country; and in 1888 he had declared that coercion offered no remedy for Ireland's real grievances, while conciliation in the form of economic and administrative reforms would not only benefit that country but also preserve "the old Liberal faith" of which the Liberal Unionists claimed to be the inheritor. It was impossible to change the Irish people, he added, but Parliament could and should change the conditions in which they lived by "stimulating the energy of the people and assisting in the development of its industries." Chamberlain's practical imagination permeated the brochure entitled "A Unionist Policy for Ireland," which was published by the *Birmingham Daily Post.* From land purchase and local government to railways and drainage, the essentials of constructive Unionism were set out in detail. And it would be foolish to deny the influence of this pamphlet on Balfour as well as on the thinking of Unionists in every quarter of the party. Admittedly, Chamberlain's plans to rebuild the Irish economy were drawn on a vast scale, too ambitious to be realized in every respect. They are reminiscent of the "municipal socialism" of his early career, only applied to a much larger, more depressed area, and one far removed from the world of heavy industry. Indeed, most of the legislation that Ireland received up to the first world war—Home Rule excepted—was anticipated in some form or another by this testament of "Birmingham Unionism" compiled in 1888.

The Congested Districts Board established by the Land Purchase Act of 1891 was designed to provide every type of assistance in the affected areas. The four main categories of this aid were: promotion of native industries by subsidies and technical education; the amalgamation and improvement of holdings through purchase; the resettlement of tenants upon these holdings which the Board had made into viable units; and, lastly, instruction in modern farming methods. The territory under the board's jurisdiction in 1891 amounted to 3,608,569 acres with a population of 500,000, and included parts of counties Donegal, Leitrim, Sligo, Mayo, Roscommon, Galway, Kerry, and Cork. Almost all the congested districts lay west of an imaginary line drawn between Londonderry and Skibbereen. One of the poorest areas was the island of Achill, where one thousand families lived off holdings with an annual value of £4 or less. Because some objective standard had to be found in order to classify a district as congested, it was decided to proceed on the basis of the Poor Law valuation in each electoral division. Wherever the total rateable value of a division, when divided by the number of inhabitants, amounted to less than £1/10/0 per person, it was designated as congested. This criterion was bound to result in major inequities, and county Clare, along with large sections of Galway, Cork, and Mayo, was excluded even though many of the inhabitants lived on the verge of starvation. It took years to redress some of these unjust omissions, but the board's success can be measured by the fact that the lands under its control amounted to 7,658,114 acres by 1910.[44]

Despite its Unionist inspiration, the board reflected as little party politics as was possible in Ireland. It was composed of two land commissioners, five Government-appointed experts, and the chief secretary, who was an ex officio member and bore no parliamentary responsibility for decisions taken by his fellow members. In the way of income the board received the annual interest on part of the Irish Church surplus, which amounted to £41,250. Although the board enjoyed a semi-independent status, all special applications to the Treasury were expected to pass through Dublin Castle before being forwarded to London.

Its duties were legion. Besides purchasing and developing estates, it encouraged scientific farming and breeding, promoted the fishing, spinning, and weaving industries, and supervised the construction of bridges, piers, and roads in these districts. These multifold duties gave the board a power and responsibility unique among Irish local authorities. In the eighty-four Poor Law unions that made up the original congested districts, inspectors studied conditions in minute detail and sent their findings to Dublin. These surveys were called "baseline reports" and proved

---

[44] For a complete study of the Board and its activities, see W. L. Micks, *An Account of . . . the Congested Districts Board for Ireland from 1891 to 1923* (hereafter *CDB*), Dublin, 1925.

invaluable in charting the progress of a union during its course of recovery. In most cases the reports took over a year to complete; but in the interval, funds were apportioned to those districts in need of immediate relief.[45]

The Congested Districts Board gradually increased the number and cost of its commitments: by 1912 its net income from all sources amounted to £532,440. Even the remnants of Parnell's party had to agree that the money spent was not wasted; their chief complaint, in fact, was that the board operated on too small a budget. One of its most notable successes took place in the fishing industry, where sales had been steadily declining and the gear could only be called primitive. In the past the private philanthropy of such persons as the Baroness Burdett-Coutts— who was known as "the Queen of Baltimore" for her efforts in building up native industries and relieving distress in and around that town—had paid for a few boats and tackle as well as for instruction.[46] But this form of assistance affected only a fraction of the coastline. Under the board's auspices new boats for deep-sea fishing were supplied on loan, curing stations were opened, and technical education offered. And with the extension of railway lines to the coast, the market for fresh as well as cured fish gradually began to expand. In Donegal and Galway the fishing industry attracted agricultural laborers, and within twenty years the total income from this source had trebled.[47]

Similarly, the board acted as a stimulus to agriculture in the west. The peasants were taught the rudiments of scientific farming by board instructors; and for the first time they began to spray their crops and to use artificial fertilizer. Native fear of innovation meant that concrete results were slow to appear; but within a decade the benefits of such assistance manifested themselves in bigger and more regular crops. The board also gave expert advice on the proper breeding of livestock and helped to introduce new breeds of cattle, horses, sheep, and poultry into the districts. Balfour even persuaded the Queen to donate one

[45] See Micks's own report on the Glenties union of co. Donegal, *ibid.*, pp. 241-58.

[46] C. Burdett Patterson, *Angela Burdett-Coutts and the Victorians*, London, 1953, pp. 209-10. See also *Times*, 18 Aug. 1887.

[47] Micks, *CDB*, pp. 54-65.

of the stallions from the royal stables for stud purposes.[48] Under the heading of industrial development the board encouraged the production of lace, tweed, and glass; while it also supervised harbor improvements and road building. The board was especially active in land purchase, and, although lacking adequate powers at first, it bought up, consolidated, and resold thousands of holdings in units that were large enough to sustain a family. A special guarantee fund was set up to provide security against default by purchasing tenants in the congested districts where the risk of loss was expected to be high. The board enlarged the holdings that it bought by acquiring adjacent land, and assisted the migration of tenants who had lived on these estates. Housing, drainage, roads, and fences were improved in order to make the holdings viable. In his draft bill Balfour had abandoned the principle of compulsion with the greatest reluctance.[49] But by 1909 the board had acquired compulsory powers in certain cases, and it was under these clauses that the Clanricarde estate at Woodford was finally purchased in 1915, after the landlord had disputed the legality of this action in every possible court.

When the Congested Districts Board was officially dissolved in 1923, over two million acres had been purchased under its auspices at a cost of more than £9 million; and on these holdings improvements worth £2,249,477 had been made. If the western seaboard was not transformed into a land of milk and honey, at least the living conditions of the inhabitants had been ameliorated, and some of the surplus population had been drained off by assisted migration rather than by death. The board fully deserved the many tributes that attended its efforts. Davitt praised the board; William O'Brien called it a boon to Irish industry; and Dillon described it as "the only really successful remedy" ever applied to Ireland.[50] And the *Times*—perhaps by way of atone-

---

[48] "Of course it is a mark of Her Majesty's sympathy and interest rather than the horse which we desire to have, and I think it would not only prove valuable to us but might also do good in Ireland generally"; Balfour to Sir Henry Ponsonby, 11 April 1892, Add. ms 49830.

[49] Balfour to Salisbury, 31 Oct. 1889, Salisbury mss.

[50] Davitt, *The Fall of Feudalism*, pp. 663-64; O'Brien, *An Olive Branch in Ireland*, London, 1910, p. 88. Davitt considered the board a form of

ment—published a series of exhaustive articles on the location, condition, and future of the congested districts.[51] Balfour considered the board one of his crowning achievements in Ireland and continued to take an active interest in its functions after he had left the Irish Office. "The experiment was a novel one," he confessed to Sir Henry Ponsonby, "but I have really some hope now that it will succeed, not indeed in entirely removing the evils with which it was intended to deal, but in mitigating their severity." In a less modest mood he remarked that the board had done more for Ireland than one hundred parliaments in St. Stephen's Green.[52]

IV. RELIEF WORKS

Whereas the Congested Districts Board had been established to deal with a more or less permanent problem, the relief works launched in 1890 were considered a temporary expedient to rescue the populace in the west from starvation. Strictly speaking, railway construction was not designed as part of this program; the measure authorizing the extension of certain "light railways" in the west was conceived long before the potato failure of 1890. But once the blight had appeared, railway construction became an integral part of the relief works. Established on an *ad hoc* basis, the program of relief brought employment and food to those districts where the crop failure ranged between twenty-five and seventy-five per cent. There was nothing new about the phenomenon of potato failure in the west. The whims of the weather, the absence of nutrient agents in the soil, and the habit of planting seeds from the same potato stock year after year meant that the threat of famine was never far distant. Balfour realized that there was no "perfectly satisfactory" remedy against this danger, but he intended to offer assistance whenever "the pinch of distress" was first felt.[53] In the summer of 1890 unusually

---

"enlightened state socialism." See also H. Sutherland, *Ireland Yesterday and Today*, Phila., 1909, pp. 50 ff.

[51] See *Times*, 1, 13, 15, 21, 22, 27 Oct., and 5, 12, 26 Nov. 1890.

[52] Balfour to Sir Henry Ponsonby, 11 April 1892, Add. MS 49830. An indication of success was the creation of a Congested Districts Board for the highlands and western islands of Scotland in August, 1897.

[53] Balfour to J. H. Tuke, 25 Aug. 1890, *ibid.*, 49829.

wet weather presaged the advent of a crop failure. Balfour's scientific curiosity was aroused by reports from the Castle, and samples of potatoes from the west were sent to Whittingehame for inspection and comparison with healthy seed potatoes. At the end of August he wrote to Salisbury that the impending crisis might be the most severe since 1847, although a much smaller population would be affected. As a result, the Irish Land Commission was ordered "to buy with all possible secrecy and despatch" a large supply of potatoes. According to Balfour, the Irish Board of Works could not be trusted in this matter because they were "all old women."[54]

In directing the program of relief works, Balfour kept two principles constantly in mind. The first was that the assistance provided by the state must on no account demoralize the population. By demoralization he meant exactly what Peel had meant: the local population must not expect a dole every time there were signs of crop failure. In the second place, the relief works must be supervised by a central authority so as to reduce waste and inefficiency to an absolute minimum. In 1879 and again in 1886 the distribution of relief had been attended by "gross abuses" and "reckless administration" of public funds. Relief and jobbery had been synonymous in Ireland. In 1879-1880 boards of guardians had failed to distribute the funds with which they were entrusted, and some of this money had been used instead for electioneering purposes. Such "scandalous fraud" was not to be repeated in 1890, if Balfour had any voice in the matter.[55]

Balfour, in fact, took over direct responsibility for the allocation of relief, and he devoted much time to ensuring that funds went to the needy, and not to local contractors who acted like parasites in times of famine. The Irish Office was virtually inundated with letters and reports from land commissioners, magistrates, district inspectors, parish priests, and unofficial sources, all of which provided a detailed, if often inaccurate, picture of Irish distress. The amount of exaggeration was enormous, but each report of hardship had to be carefully investigated. Balfour's most difficult task was to know whom to believe: the

[54] Balfour to Salisbury, 27 Aug. 1890, Salisbury MSS. See also Dugdale, *Balfour*, I, pp. 178-79.

[55] See *Hansard*, 3d series, Vol. 349, pp. 544-51.

unreliability of Irish local authorities in such matters was a commonplace. In the face of such indigence and corruption the administration of relief posed as many obstacles as had coercion. And Balfour's insistence upon a thorough appraisal of all scheduled works did not make him any more popular in those districts that were eventually denied relief.[56]

When challenged in Parliament about the scope of the Government's remedial efforts, Balfour readily admitted that the relief works were not intended primarily to increase the self-sufficiency of those living in the distressed districts. The Government, he argued, had first to help the tenant-farmers before they could be taught to help themselves; and these emergency measures were designed to "tide them over" during a period of crisis and to "give them a lift out of the mire of insolvency." The ultimate goal was self-help. But first the distressed tenants needed an income with which to buy both food and seed potatoes for next year's crop. For this purpose he asked the House in December, 1890, to approve a supplementary grant of £5,000 to relieve distress. This assistance, he emphasized, would be only temporary, and would cease once the tenants had improved their holdings sufficiently to preclude the likelihood of another famine. Outdoor relief would be administered in a sparing manner, and harbor and bridge construction, which employed predominantly skilled labor, would be kept to a minimum. After listing the projects that the Government contemplated, Balfour warned the House about the consequences of denying Ireland relief: "You throw a burden on the locality which it cannot bear. You lend it money which it cannot pay back; and it will sink deeper and deeper in the demoralising slough of insolvency which already has almost destroyed the powers of self-help in the poorer and congested parts of the country."[57]

The Government's much-publicized program of relief did not reach Ireland until the end of 1890, and in February of the new year Irish members complained that the public works were pro-

[56] See Relief of Distress papers, Crime Special Branch, and RIC returns on progress of Relief Works 1890-1891, SPO. Dublin Castle also prepared maps of those poor law unions in need of relief and subdivided these areas into categories of light, severe, or acute distress.

[57] *Hansard*, 3d series, Vol. 349, p. 560.

ceeding too slowly and in too limited an area. Railway construction, road works, the distribution of seed potatoes, and outdoor relief were the four main components of Balfour's program. To advise the "unreliable" county surveyors in judging the neediest areas and the type of works best suited for each, several officers from the Royal Engineers were assigned to Dublin Castle. A rigid system of inspection before, during, and after the works was introduced, and Balfour encouraged members of the RIC to supervise works in their districts. Almost every aspect of the relief works reflected a concern for economy, and Balfour adhered religiously to the precept that direct grants sapped the morale of the recipients.[58]

The most ambitious and expensive form of relief was the construction of some 280 miles of railroad in counties Donegal, Mayo, Galway, Kerry, Sligo, Clare, and Cork. In 1888 the Royal Commission on Irish industrial resources had recommended extending the existing railways in the west, as well as improving the system of arterial drainage, and Balfour had drafted several bills along these lines.[59] At one time Churchill had urged the Government to buy out the companies that controlled the railroads in Ireland as a means of strengthening the Union; and Salisbury had long favored a similar plan, perhaps with the Prussian model in mind.[60] But the Light Railways Act of 1889 stipulated instead that the Treasury cooperate with the railway companies in financing the new lines. A Treasury guarantee enabled promoters and speculators to raise the necessary capital at three per cent instead of the standard five per cent interest rate. One year passed and still no construction had begun; and it was at this time that Balfour first learned of the impending potato failure. The result was a

[58] See Balfour's memorandum on Relief Works, 2 Jan. 1891; Balfour to E. Stanhope, 26 March 1891; and Balfour to Col. Fraser, 16 Sept. 1890, Add. MS 49829.

[59] See the Reports of the Royal Commission on Irish Public Works, *HC 1887-1888*, Vols. 25 and 48.

[60] Churchill had written: "If the Government had the railways in this land, the power of the Government in Ireland either for strategic movements of troops and police, for patronage, for bribery by reduction of rates and construction of new lines would be increased one hundred fold"; Churchill to Salisbury, 2 Dec. 1886; Salisbury to Churchill, 2 Dec. 1886, Salisbury MSS.

new bill, which expedited and made more flexible the administration of the Light Railways Act, and ground was first broken on some of the new lines at the end of November. The longest extensions ran from Galway to Clifden and from Collooney to Claremorris, amounting to forty-nine and forty-eight miles, respectively. At an average cost of £5,000 per mile, the capital outlay involved was considerable, and Balfour did not have an easy time arriving at satisfactory terms with the Irish railway companies that had agreed to build and manage the lines. Sir Ralph Cusack, the wealthy and cantankerous director of the Midland and Great Western Railway Company, rejected the Government's original contract and thus delayed work on several important lines for more than three months. At one time Balfour threatened to suspend the contracts altogether unless some of the directors, whom he called "wretched, incompetent," saw reason.[61] By the time the dozen lines were completed, the total number of men employed had reached 8,000 and the expenditure stood at £1,130,000. Relying on the advice of local priests and the police as to the neediest persons in each community, Balfour was confident that the Government had "squeezed out" of this railway construction the maximum amount of unskilled labor available.

The man whom Balfour placed directly in charge of the railway works was William Lawies Jackson, financial secretary to the Treasury, whose experience with English railways stood him in good stead, although Ridgeway called him "a slow, overcautious, and unimaginative negotiator."[62] Jackson went to Ireland at the end of August, 1890, in order to complete arrangements for the new lines. The machinery of relief, Balfour pointed out to him, was designed to prevent the "iniquitous and demoralising extravagance" that had characterized the relief works in 1879-1880 and 1886. Work was to begin on the lines as soon as the first signs of famine appeared; labor would be recruited from nearby dis-

[61] Balfour to Cusack, 21 June, 22 Nov. 1890; Ridgeway to Balfour, 20 Sept., 16 Oct., 23 Nov., 1, 5, 10 Dec. 1890; Balfour to Ridgeway, 6, 16 May, 21 Nov. 1890, 11, 13, 26 March 1891, Add. ms 49828-829, 49811-812.

[62] 1840-1917; created Baron Allerton 1902; M.P. 1885-1902; Financial Secretary to Treasury 1886-1891; Chief Secretary for Ireland 1891-1892; chairman of Jameson raid inquiry 1896-1897. See Ridgeway to Balfour, 16 Oct. 1890, Add. ms 49811.

tressed areas; workers coming from a distance would be housed in temporary shelters; and plans for launching supplementary works would have to be drawn up to meet the eventuality of continued hardship. Whether by accident or design, the new lines did not run across any property invested by the Plan of Campaign; and Balfour rejoiced at this fact. In principle he was opposed to the hiring of any Plan tenants, evicted or otherwise, because he believed that the nature of the combination as well as the grants supplied by the Tenants' Defence League precluded any Government aid.[63] The chief secretary derived much satisfaction from the building of these railways, and the carping of critics who alleged that the cost was excessive and that the gauge was too wide to qualify as a "light railway" did not bother him. The fact was that these works not only provided employment at a time when the need for work was critical, but also brought an important boon to fishermen, who could now ship fresh fish to the market towns at low cost.

The relief works that supplemented railway construction consisted mainly of road improvements. New bridges and piers were also built, but Balfour was sceptical of these projects because they required skilled labor. The supplementary works lasted for more than a year; and the size of this operation forced Balfour to ask Parliament in March, 1891, for an additional grant of £55,831. The administration was under "severe pressure," Balfour explained, to start public works at the whim of every local authority, and many requests had been turned down. In any event, 7,392 persons were employed on these works at a cost of £3,000 each week. Payment was in cash or in Indian meal, according to the type of work; while wages were deliberately kept lower than on the railway sites. The services of the Royal Engineer officers proved invaluable, and the works were finished without undue delay or waste of money. Balfour was the first to admit that mistakes had been made: a certain amount of jobbery was unavoidable. But at least the people in the west no longer regarded relief "as an excuse for getting money for doing nothing; they have to do a day's work for a day's wages." All told, the railway

[63] Balfour to Jackson, 20 Aug., 1 Oct. 1890; Balfour to Ridgeway, 1, 10 Oct. 1890; Balfour's memorandum on Irish railway works, 4 Feb. 1891, *ibid.*, 49829.

and relief works together employed upwards of 16,000 men, and reports of improvement in the living conditions of the families affected by relief began to arrive in Dublin Castle as early as mid-December, 1890.[64]

With regard to the purchase of seed potatoes, the Government were forced to adopt a less ambitious policy. However resistant to disease in England or Scotland, the chances of any seed's surviving for long in the west of Ireland were very slim; thus Balfour knew that the Government could not incur the risk of ordering large amounts of seed potatoes only to be blamed when the new crop had failed. The type of seed best suited to the soil and climate varied from one county to another, and many farmers refused to change the stock that had been planted for generations. These circumstances forced Balfour reluctantly to throw the responsibility for purchasing new seeds on the local boards of guardians. And his reluctance was justified when he learned that in thirty-seven out of forty-six cases inspectors had found the seed obtained by these authorities deficient either in quality or quantity. But he considered the Government's reputation more important than such inherent shortcomings. The result was that Parliament granted loans for the purchase of seed potatoes in the autumn and winter of 1890, while the boards of guardians in Ireland as well as the House of Lords debated the merits of "Champions" and "Magnum Bonums." According to Balfour, the potato was to blame for many of Ireland's troubles. If only the people cared for lentils, he once exclaimed in a fit of exasperation to Sir James Caird, the distinguished agriculturist: "I wish to heaven we could induce the Irish to grow some food of a more trustworthy character than the potato. . . . The readiness to accept new ideas and to engage on new enterprises is precisely the characteristic most wanting in the population. . . . If it were not so they would long have refused to squat generation after generation on the bogs and mountains of the inclement West."[65]

[64] *Hansard*, 3d series, Vol. 351, pp. 778-91; Balfour's memorandum to Ridgeway on "Relief to Intermediate Paupers," 5 Dec. 1890; Balfour's memorandum on "Jurisdiction of Inspectors," 8 Jan. 1891, Add. MS 49829.

[65] Balfour to Sir James Caird, 5 Sept. 1890, *ibid.*

Outdoor relief or direct grants to the populace comprised the last category of Balfour's relief program. This form of assistance, which he believed most dangerous of all in terms of undermining morale, was to be confined to disabled or aged persons who were incapable of working for relief. Supplies of food and turf were stockpiled and distributed to those most in need; and two steamers were hired to convey both food and inspectors to the western islands, which had suffered so severely from the crop failure. But the administration of direct relief was based upon a "rigid enforcement" of the workhouse test, and therefore provided no more than the barest means of subsistence.

Direct relief also included privately sponsored charity. At the end of 1890 Balfour and the new viceroy, Lord Zetland, launched an appeal for funds to help the inhabitants in famine-stricken districts.[66] The area was divided into two sections, each with a magistrate in charge of relief. The British public responded immediately and generously: some £50,000 was collected under the auspices of the Irish Distress Fund, and in Dublin Castle a special office called the Distress Division supervised the distribution of this sum. Police officers collected the names of needy families, and Indian meal or flour was handed out on a merit basis. Food supplies, moreover, were sent to famished children in schools. Needless to say, the distress fund engendered much goodwill among the 13,000 families who were relieved in this way.[67]

While the plans for relief of distress were being completed, Balfour deliberately avoided visiting the congested districts. He was afraid that any official tour would make "all the Boards of Guardians and other authorities in those Western districts who are now beggars by profession suppose that public money was to be squandered like water on every kind of jobbery, as it has been on previous occasions."[68] But he could not postpone his trip forever. Early in October, 1890, Hartington confided his anxieties on this score to Salisbury. He hoped that Balfour would go to

[66] Lawrence Dundas, 3d Earl of Zetland, 1844-1929; M.P. 1872-1873; Lord Lieutenant of Ireland 1889-1892; created Marquess 1892.

[67] Balfour to T. J. Mulhall, 14 Jan. 1891; Balfour to W. L. Micks, 14 Jan. 1891, Add. ms 49829.

[68] Balfour to G. Wyndham, 5 Sept. 1890, *ibid.*

Ireland as soon as possible. "If anything should go wrong," he wrote, "there will be a terrible outcry about his absence however unreasonable it may be."[69] In order to forestall such an outcry and to see for himself the areas likely to be hit hardest by the famine, Balfour left for Ireland toward the end of the month. With him went a small party consisting of his sister Alice, Ridgeway, and George Wyndham.

The tour was divided into two parts, covering first Connemara and then Donegal, and it received wide publicity in the English as well as Irish press. Balfour insisted on traveling informally and dispensed with both protocol and bodyguards. At every town or village he was greeted with cheers, an occasional jeer, and protestations of loyalty to the Crown. During the two-week excursion he traversed some of the most impoverished parts of the country. The special correspondent of the *Daily Express*, who covered the tour, described the habitations that Balfour saw near Belmullet as "simply wigwams, with a roof of turf sods held together by a fishing net, fastened to the low mud walls by wooden pegs." At times the terrain proved too rugged for jaunting cars, and Balfour's party would alight and walk to the nearest cluster of cabins in order to ask questions about the potato harvest and farming techniques. Alice Balfour, who was "armed with a camera and an alpenstock," followed the same rough trails and set an example of stamina for the male members of the party. At Carrick in Donegal Balfour showed his Peelite instincts when he told a priest that "eleemosynary relief is destructive of the fibre of the people." His last stop before returning to Dublin was Portadown, where he delivered another speech promising relief and left with the cheers of the populace and the explosion of fog signals ringing in his ears. From a personal point of view the tour had been an unqualified success. Not only had the chief secretary learned a great deal about the land and the people in the congested districts, but he had been hailed as "Balfour the Brave" by a number of tenants—which was no mean accomplishment for the villain of Mitchelstown.[70]

[69] Hartington to Salisbury, 7 Oct. 1890, Salisbury MSS.

[70] See *Times*, 25 Oct. -8 Nov. 1890; "Mr. Balfour's Tours in Connemara and Donegal," Dublin, 1890; Alice Balfour to W. A. Knight, 17 July 1892, Knight MSS, PML. See also E. B. Iwan-Müller, *Ireland: Today and Tomorrow*, London, 1907, p. 19.

One of the conclusions Balfour drew from his tour was that only emigration and land purchase contained a permanent solution to the problem of the congested districts. Light railways and other public works, he had assured the people of Glenties, would "enrich permanently" the areas in which they were constructed. But the ultimate goal was reduction of the surplus population, and this object was not attained for many years. If assisted emigration could not eliminate poverty altogether, it could at least "render the next attack of the disease less virulent." And because Irishmen seemed to prosper so well in North America, he was unable to understand why the nationalists continued to regard such a proposal as an insult to the Irish people. This attitude annoyed Balfour intensely; and although the Land Act of 1891 contained provisions for loans to prospective emigrants, the Government treated the question with the same caution as they did the principle of compulsion in land purchase.

At Liverpool Balfour reported on his western tour to members of the National Union of Conservative Associations and described the grim conditions he had seen. He also made light of nationalist taunts about his "new capacity as a professional humanitarian."[71] Although Balfour's tour served to advertise the Government's good works, Home Rule gibes about "light railways" were abundant, and Ridgeway's patience was severely strained by "conceited wiseacres who rush through a country in a fault finding spirit." In addition, departmental feuds in Dublin Castle over the administration of relief vexed the under secretary, who informed his chief: "It is easy to see how easily a catastrophe could arise in this country with its loose congeries of independent Departments. The whole system is rotten and if you did not happen to be an all powerful member of the Cabinet, the catastrophe would have happened long ago."[72]

Despite these obstacles to success, the program of relief works achieved maximum results for the amount of money spent. The disaster of a famine was effectively averted, and the improvement in transport facilities brought convenience to countless inhabitants in the west. Such achievements cannot be measured in terms of pounds, shillings, and pence. But when parish priests began to

[71] *Times*, 8 Nov. 1890.
[72] Ridgeway to Balfour, 26, 28 March 1891, Add. MS 49812.

express their approval of the works, then Balfour knew that this aspect of conciliation had not been a waste of time or money.

Unionist conciliation also took the form of attempts to improve the system of arterial drainage or flood control in the country. Unfortunately, this aspect of "kindness" turned out to be one of the least productive. In Parliament the mortality rate of drainage bills was extremely high. In July, 1888, Balfour introduced three such bills in the Commons, and only one survived. A year later four bills dealing with drainage on the rivers Barrow, Bann, Shannon, and Suck were abandoned after they encountered persistent obstruction.[73] John Morley was fond of ridiculing Government efforts in this direction: "The Chief Secretary is to come bearing balm upon his healing wings in the shape of a Drainage Bill. He is going to minister to a mind diseased by light railways." The Government's "healing" powers, however, did not include flood prevention. Their attempts to improve drainage, especially in places where the bog or marshland was considered reclaimable, foundered on the question of local contributions. The nationalists accused ministers of trying to thrust too much of the financial burden onto the tenants who would be affected by these works, while ministers insisted that these tenants should bear some share of the cost. No satisfactory compromise could be reached; both the cabinet and officers in Dublin Castle were "lukewarm" on the subject; and Lord Salisbury threw "cold water" on the scheme because he thought it too expensive. In addition, the authorities responsible for arterial drainage were known to be rife with jobbery: in 1888 the expenditure on preliminary inquiries alone amounted to twice the sum voted for this purpose. Conciliation by drainage was thus expensive, risible, and futile.[74]

In the summer of 1891 the relief works gradually began to close

[73] Balfour had envisaged a Treasury grant of £380,000 to cover expenses in each of these "catchment" areas. Part of the financial burden was to be borne by the tenants and landlords whose lands would be affected by the improvements. Owing to Home Rulers' objections, all four bills were withdrawn in August and a private bill authorizing a grant to the Suck river project was eventually passed. See *Hansard*, 3d series, Vol. 338, p. 1790; Vol. 339, pp. 1120 ff.

[74] *Ibid.*, Vol. 333, p. 287; Balfour to Goschen, 23 Jan. 1889, Add. MS 49827; Irish Departmental Letter Books, 10 Nov. 1888, SPO.

down, and the last projects ended on November 28. The total cost of these works, excluding the railway lines, was £21,800; and if the new roads were scorned by nationalists, and if many of the bridges and piers eventually fell into disuse and became havens for puffins, petrels, and solitary fishermen, the fact remained that these memorials to "constructive Unionism" brought work and wages to thousands of tenants in a time of acute distress. The money that Balfour appropriated for these works was spent carefully, not haphazardly; and in his opinion the railways, public works, seed-potato loans, and Congested Districts Board all constituted a permanent boon to the Irish people. These remedial acts, moreover, were not just temporary cures for economic troubles: they were meant to enhance the value of the land and to teach the population the virtue of self-reliance. Balfour once admitted: "The exaggeration, the mendacity, and the jobbery which meet us whenever we have . . . public money to distribute render my task a difficult one." But he was confident that his program of "reproductive works" would reduce the severity of distress at a lower cost in money and morale than had ever been known in the past.[75]

It is not surprising that there were harsh critics of conciliation within the Conservative party, men who accused the cabinet of subservience to the Liberal Unionists and to Chamberlain in particular. Many rank and file members harbored feelings of resentment or distrust toward Chamberlain and complained that Ireland was receiving too much largesse from the Treasury. Lord Salisbury did his best to discourage or deny these charges by asserting that Government policy had not deviated from the line of his Newport speech in 1885 despite two general elections and two changes of government. As for Chamberlain's role in shaping legislation, his very need to boast of his influence proved that the fact was not self-evident and that it required "a good deal of special pleading to make it out."[76] Nevertheless, the Government's relief measures owed much of their inspiration to Chamberlain's fertile mind; and as coercion was slowly relaxed in Ireland, the two main blocs of the Unionist coalition found it much easier

[75] Balfour to W. Rathbone, M.P., 24 Jan. 1891, Add. MS 49829.
[76] Salisbury to H. H. Howorth, M.P., 3, 12 Dec. 1891, Salisbury MSS.

to cooperate with one another in planning the means by which England might escape from "the labyrinth of Irish disaffection."

Lord Palmerston once described the Irish as "the worst clad, the worst housed, and the worst fed people on the face of God's earth." Neither the Congested Districts Board nor relief works revolutionized living conditions in the west of Ireland. But at least Palmerston's statement was less true after 1891 than it had been in the time of the great famine. It is too easy to dismiss the program of public works as useless simply because many of the piers, roads, and railways became obsolete. Those sturdy monuments to Conservative conciliation that lie scattered through the west must be judged not by today's standards of utility but by the standards of Balfour's time. When every extra source of income might spell the difference between starvation and survival for the people of Achill, Letterkenny, Belmullet, or Clifden, these projects and the efforts of the Congested Districts Board to revive agriculture and industry cannot be lightly brushed aside. A decade later, in 1900, George Wyndham faced many of the same problems in the west, albeit to a lesser degree, and with his usual passion he imagined himself in the role of Hercules about to clean the Augean stables. "If one could turn the river of Imperialism into this back-water spawned over by obscene reptiles," he wrote to Henley after his tour of the congested districts; " . . . if one could change these anaemic children into full-blooded men!"[77]

If Balfour did not aspire to such heights, he knew that a policy wholly negative in character was doomed from the start. And in the guise of a "modern" physiocrat operating on Peelite principles, he made certain that he left behind in Ireland something more tangible than prosecutions and more productive than miles of stone walls.

[77] Wyndham to W. E. Henley, 10 Feb. 1901, Henley MSS, PML.

CHAPTER XVI

An Hibernian Aftermath

THE GOVERNMENT's last year in office was notable for the amount of attention paid to the Irish Question both in and outside Parliament and for the paucity of legislation that Ireland received. One reason for this state of affairs was the growing indifference of ministers and their supporters to conciliation. In their view the nationalists were too preoccupied with internal discord and financial worries, and the Gladstonians were too busy dreaming about the grandiose "Newcastle Programme"—which began with Home Rule and ended with triennial parliaments—to bother about the condition of Ireland on the eve of a general election. Furthermore, ministers themselves were showing signs of wear after the ordeals of the past few years. Ireland had been the dominant political issue since 1885, and now, with Parnell's party shattered and the leader dead, many Conservatives questioned the necessity of additional conciliation. There were enough troubles at home. The domestic scene was marred by labor unrest: the dockers' strike of 1889 had served to vindicate the "new unionism" that stood for activism in the political as well as industrial world. In a time of economic recovery unskilled workers were organizing, and this meant "hard times" ahead for both management and the ministry in power. Foreign affairs also helped to account for ministerial apathy about Ireland. The prime minister was devoting more time to his duties at the Foreign Office, if only because he found the task of dismembering Africa a more exhilarating occupation than discussing Irish measures. The Government's indifference toward conciliation increased in direct proportion to the proximity of the election; and by the beginning of 1892 both British parties were paying more attention to the constituencies than to events at Westminster.

I. THE SUCCESSION

In the meantime, several changes of personnel had interrupted the continuity of the administration. Lord Londonderry had resigned his office in the spring of 1889. Balfour's relations with him had always been somewhat superficial, because he wanted a viceroy whose functions consisted of forwarding requests for honors to London, receiving deputations, and giving sumptuous levees. For two years Londonderry had performed these duties admirably, if begrudgingly, but he soon tired of this role and expressed his wish to inform the House of Lords about Government achievements in Ireland. Eventually Balfour gave him permission to speak as a reward for his "non-interference." As he wrote to his uncle, Londonderry had "behaved so well throughout that the least that we can do for him is to give him an opportunity of talking about his performances!"[1] The Viceroy made his speech and was duly awarded a Garter for his services in Ireland. Upon returning to Dublin, however, he began to complain about the expense of his office. Having already threatened to resign in 1887 over a misunderstanding with the Queen and Salisbury, he was by no means deeply committed to his post. Ignoring Balfour's pleas to stay on, he made up his mind to resign just as the Pigott scandal was about to break. Rumors to this effect spread through the Castle, and in Parliament a Parnellite member asked if the report were true.

Finding a new viceroy proved no simple matter. "It is a very difficult post to fill now," Salisbury declared, "for most people of rank are so poor." Only rich men were eligible, because a lord lieutenant was expected to spend between £15,000 and £20,000 a year out of his own pocket. After weeks of searching and several refusals, Ridgeway suggested putting the lord lieutenancy into commission until such time as Parliament could abolish the office altogether. But in the end the Marquess of Zetland, who had refused the offer once, agreed to accept the post. Londonderry did not leave Ireland until the end of August, because, as Ridgeway alleged, his wife wanted to stay over for the Horse Show. Although Balfour was vexed by stories that the office had "gone begging around the peerage," he was also much relieved that the vacancy had been filled.[2]

---

[1] Londonderry to Salisbury, 31 Jan. 1888; Salisbury to Londonderry, 31 Jan. 1888; Balfour to Salisbury, 30, 31 Jan. 1888, 10, 21 April 1889, Salisbury MSS.

[2] Londonderry to Salisbury, 30 Aug. 1889; Salisbury to Londonderry, 29 Aug. 1889; Salisbury to Queen Victoria, 26 May, 8 April 1889, *ibid.*

The Government sustained a much more important loss in 1891, when W. H. Smith died on the same day as Parnell. Although most of his colleagues were prepared for a breakdown in Smith's health in the near future, the news of his death stunned them. A "terrible gap," as Salisbury expressed it, was left in the ministry's ranks. No one could have guessed in 1887 the extent to which this quiet, self-effacing man would soon command the respect and the affection of the House during one of the most arduous periods in its history. Cranbrook described him as "a man to rely upon and certainly showed a tact and power of gaining confidence which before he was tried could hardly have been expected." And there were countless tributes to his patience in adversity and to his gentle disposition.[3]

The choice of a new leader of the House involved some extremely delicate negotiations. It was a subject to which Balfour for one had given much thought—ever since, in fact, he had first learned of Smith's fragile health. In November, 1888, he had analyzed the probable consequences of Smith's retirement and the possibility of a coalition government with Hartington as leader in the Commons. The objections to either himself or Goschen as leader were, in his opinion, sufficiently strong to eliminate both. Personally, he found Goschen "so able, loyal, good tempered and good natured, so obviously honest, and so incapable of intrigue that, *faute de mieux*, he would . . . do very well both by his colleagues and the Party." But he was not altogether happy with this choice, and, besides, Goschen's "fussiness" and habit of "fidgeting" on the front bench irritated several of his colleagues. One good reason for Balfour's decision against a coalition government in 1888 was Chamberlain, who, he feared, would "rapidly drift back into the bosom of the True Radical Church" in the event that Hartington and his followers merged with the Conservatives.[4]

See also Ridgeway to Balfour, 16 March 1888, 10, 30 April 1889; Balfour to Ridgeway, 30 May 1889, Add. ms 49809, 49828. Balfour asserted that both Londonderry and Cadogan required "a fortnight's concentrated exertion" to prepare their speeches in Parliament.

[3] Maxwell, *W. H. Smith*, ii, pp. 319 ff.; Balfour to Salisbury, 27 Aug., 2 Nov. 1891; Cranbrook to Salisbury, 8 Oct. 1891, Salisbury mss.

[4] Dugdale, *Balfour*, i, pp. 201-03. See also Balfour to Salisbury, 23 Nov. 1888, Add. ms 49689.

Three years later the contest for "Elijah's Mantle" still lay between Goschen and Balfour. The prospect of a coalition was more remote than ever, and the only other candidate, Hicks Beach, had judiciously informed Salisbury of his wish to be excluded from consideration. As chancellor of the Exchequer and a Unionist of impeccable principles, Goschen had a strong claim to the succession. But his personality, past connection with the Liberal party, and failure to join the Carlton Club did not commend him to the Conservative rank and file. Salisbury wrote to the Queen that his appointment might conceivably "break up the Party."[5]

Balfour's claims were more convincing. His record in Ireland and his stature in Parliament made him the candidate of a majority of Conservative members. Reports from Akers Douglas, the party whip, as well as his own instincts, moved Salisbury to regard his nephew as an "inevitable choice." But Hartington had to be consulted on the matter, and since he was at Newmarket "all political arrangements have to be hung up," Salisbury observed, "till some quadruped has run faster than some other quadruped." His letter to Balfour continued: "But all the information that reaches me from every quarter shows clearly that the party—& the L.U.'s—expect you to take Smith's place. I do not think it wholly for your comfort or advantage. It will make you a target for very jealous and exacting criticism. But I do not think you can avoid or refuse it as matters stand. The feeling is so general that it would require a strong personal reason to justify you in declining it."[6]

During the fortnight following Smith's death Balfour kept in close touch with his uncle and even tried to defend Goschen against the rumors of his unpopularity that were circulating through the party. But Salisbury was always more susceptible to facts than to gossip, and he knew that Balfour's promotion was in the Government's best interests. Pressure to accept the leadership came from all sections of the party, and Balfour ultimately consented, although with "rather a wry face." His view of the honor was appropriately fatalistic: "The prospect is not exactly exhilarating:—a (temporarily) waning cause and a dying Par-

---

[5] *Letters of Queen Victoria*, 3d series, II, p. 76.
[6] Salisbury to Balfour, 14, 15, 16 Oct. 1891, Add. MS 49689.

liament. . . . " But he saw no other feasible alternatives to the succession. Salisbury wrote to Goschen, "as tenderly" as possible, explaining the reasons for Balfour's preferment, the announcement of which was delayed by altercation over his successor in Ireland. The new leader of the House and first lord of the Treasury had reached a pinnacle of success at an age young enough to arouse Churchill's jealousy. Balfour's own equanimity, however, was not disturbed by this rapid advance, and he began immediately to prepare for what his uncle had warned would be "rough water for the next twelve months."[7]

There was some difference of opinion about the man who should succeed Balfour as chief secretary. Balfour's first choice was W. L. Jackson, whose qualities he summed up for Salisbury's benefit with his usual mixture of asperity and shrewdness: "He has great tact and judgment—middle class tact and judgment I admit, but good of their kind. He justly inspires great confidence in business men: and he is that *rara avis*, a successful manufacturer who is fit for something besides manufacturing. A cabinet of Jacksons would [be] rather a serious order, no doubt: but one or even two would be a considerable addition to any cabinet."[8]

Goschen, on the other hand, objected to the appointment, not on the grounds of administrative skill wherein Jackson clearly excelled, but because he lacked the requisite personal qualities needed to win the confidence of the loyalists in Ireland. "His very cleverness in compromise and getting round opponents," he wrote to Salisbury, "would be a reversal of Balfour's successful *un*-compromising ways. Can you fancy him dealing with the religious question?" Moreover, he was not a "ready speaker" and would have trouble answering Morley and the leading nationalists in debate.[9] Other critics besides Goschen pointed to his lack of vigor and inability to hold the attention of the House. But Balfour persisted in his original choice. Jackson, he argued, had much experience of Ireland and Irish officials. He had been a key figure in relieving distress and had acted as unofficial "head" of the

---

[7] Salisbury to Balfour, 18 Oct. 1891, *ibid.*; Salisbury to Beach, 20 Oct. 1891, Salisbury MSS.

[8] Balfour to Salisbury, 27 Aug. 1891, *ibid.*

[9] Goschen to Salisbury, 22 Oct. 1891, *ibid.*

Irish Board of Works. Few chief secretaries ever had less to learn about Irish affairs upon their first appointment, he added, than Jackson. In view of the "serene" atmosphere in the Commons, Balfour saw no danger in this appointment and informed his uncle that there was no one better qualified to take the post. Salisbury accepted this recommendation, although he was still unconvinced that Jackson would be "strong as a fighting Secretary." Ritchie, the president of the Local Government Board, who was the only other serious competitor, remained in that position; and Jackson took command of the Irish Office early in November.[10]

Although no longer chief secretary, Balfour was determined to supervise the drafting and passage of the last Irish measures on the agenda. He also assumed responsibility for the Education Bill, which was expected to antagonize members on both sides of the House. As to leaving the post where he had scored his greatest triumphs to date, Balfour had somewhat mixed feelings. The leadership of the House, with all its administrative detail, would never provide the excitement and sense of battle that he had known in the last four years. And he did not care for the wire-pulling, placeseeking, and petty bickering that were so much a part of his new office. His strength lay in handling ideas, not men; to leading a coalition of divergent interests he preferred fighting the enemy and directing the campaign on every front. The very qualities that made him an outstanding chief secretary—his in-difference to criticism and his imperturbability in time of crisis—were to work against him as the leader of a party. In the midst of his preparations to quit Dublin he confessed to Goschen that he did not like the prospect of leaving Ireland. "It is odd, but never-theless true," he wrote, "that quite apart from the interest at-taching to the Irish administration, there have grown up ties with the grim old Castle, and this beastly town, which it is painful to sever; I feel as if I had had a good time which has for ever come to an end; and the thought is not agreeable. . . . "[11] But at least there was the consolation of knowing that the social and economic,

[10] Salisbury to Beach, 20 Oct. 1891; Salisbury to Queen Victoria, 22 Oct. 1891, *ibid.* Jackson was replaced at the Treasury by Sir John Gorst.
[11] Dugdale, *Balfour,* I, p. 185.

not to mention political, condition of Ireland was far different from what it had been in 1887.

II. IRISH LOCAL GOVERNMENT REFORM

The Local Government Bill of 1892 was the Government's last major venture in Irish legislation, and it proved a miserable failure. As far as the cabinet were concerned, it was an unwanted child, the result of their liaison with the Liberal Unionists. As far back as 1886 the Government had pledged themselves to carry such a measure, and only by pleading the excuse of social disorder had they managed to exclude Ireland from the Local Government Act of 1888. Churchill had been a staunch advocate of Irish local government reform when it suited his other plans; and Chamberlain had precipitated the fall of the Liberal ministry in 1885 on the question of a national council scheme. In 1888 his tract, "A Unionist Policy for Ireland," had included a plan for creating provincial councils in Ireland complete with power to legislate on local affairs. Ever since the last months of the Caretaker ministry the Conservative leaders had promised Irish local government reform, and yet, just as consistently, they had shelved the question. By 1890 the policy of procrastination had come to an end. Balfour was set on introducing some form of county councils in Ireland, and he urged his colleagues to accept this concession as part of the price they had to pay for Liberal Unionist support. The result of half-hearted deliberations on the question in cabinet was a bill encumbered with safeguards. From beginning to end the measure was a prolonged compromise between conflicting interests within the Government, and no attempt was made to draft a bill that would gratify public opinion in Ireland.

The prospect of elective councils in Ireland stirred feelings of dread among supporters of the Government. Salisbury reported that the Local Government Act of 1888 had made the party's "right wing . . . sore & uneasy"; and loyalists in Ireland were firmly opposed to what they called "raw democracy." The landlords who cherished the few powers remaining to them were convinced that such reform would mean an open invitation to the nationalists to seize private property. The Government, they asserted, might just as well establish a parliament in Dublin.

RIDING THE PIG

Balfour's policy of the "carrot and the stick" culminates in
the Local Government Bill of 1892.

Balfour dismissed these outbursts as "mere insanity" and retorted
that Unionists seemed to have lost all compunction about redeeming a pledge made five years ago. And he reminded these critics
that this would be a far safer bill than any likely to be produced
by the Liberals. To Salisbury he confided his fears about having
to conduct the bill through the Commons: " . . . it will probably
end in my having as many curses heaped on my devoted head as
I now have blessings by the 'Loyal Minority.' " But he was confident of one thing: the landlords would be more disposed to accept

unpleasant realities from him than from anyone else on the front bench.[12]

On the question of Irish local government the administration received advice from a number of quarters, but none was so interesting, if impracticable, as that sent by F. H. O'Donnell. According to this renegade Parnellite the only viable solution lay in creating four provincial assemblies with local legislative authority, which could unite for matters of national interest through the agency of a standing committee or "consultative senate" composed of delegates from each of the assemblies. The whole purpose of O'Donnell's plan was to "dish Gladstonism & Parnellism together." The real villains in Ireland, he reminded Salisbury, were "the Central Agitators, the Dublin Parnellite Ring," and he was convinced that provincial assemblies would emancipate the Irish people, who were genuinely loyal, from the tyranny of *"the Dublin Ring."* Salisbury forwarded these recommendations to his nephew, but the latter was unimpressed by O'Donnell's arguments.[13] The idea of county councils was hard enough to sell to party members without raising the far more objectionable issue of legislative assemblies in Ulster, Munster, Leinster, and Connaught.

In October, 1890, Balfour had promised that local government reform in Ireland would follow *"mutatis mutandis"* the system of elective councils in England and Scotland; but the Irish measure was not introduced until after the Parnellite split, and even then some of its features deviated widely from the act of 1888. Having immersed himself in facts about the operation of the Irish Local Government Board, Balfour set out to devise a bill that would "safeguard all the interests of the propertied classes." His first goal was minority representation. This provision he justified on the grounds that it was essentially "democratic" because it would guarantee the rights of Catholics in the north as well as Protestants in the south. Fancy franchises would not suffice, he felt, because they would only arouse the nationalists without affording real security to the loyalists. The task of applying minor-

---

[12] Salisbury to Balfour, 6 Feb. 1889; Balfour to Salisbury, 2 Nov. 1891, Salisbury MSS. See also Balfour to St. John Brodrick, M.P., 2 Sept. 1891; Balfour to the Duke of Argyll, 12 Dec. 1891, Add. MS 49830.

[13] See O'Donnell to Salisbury, 12 Nov. 1890, *ibid.*, 49689.

ity representation to local government when there were no comparable precedents either in England or Scotland was an awkward one, but by the end of November, 1891, Balfour believed that he had a workable plan, even if it was not the "best conceivable."[14] So novel a proposal was bound to anger the Opposition, but then neither the Irish loyalists nor many Conservatives would think of looking at a bill that did not contain some insurance against what they labeled "Catholic oppression."

Although Balfour had declared that his Irish bill would resemble the act of 1888 in almost every respect excepting the question of safeguards, these exceptions were the most significant part of the measure. Already he was encountering the difficulties of leading a coalition party. While the Irish loyalists remained disgruntled over the prospective safeguards, there were complaints from Conservative members about the unduly "Hibernian complexion" of the parliamentary agenda. These Conservatives wanted more attention paid to English affairs, even though they could not agree, as Balfour pointed out, on the precise forms that domestic legislation ought to take. Harried and advised from all quarters, Balfour was determined to press on with his plan to transfer the administrative functions of the grand juries to councils representing the various baronies and counties. In private Balfour considered the grand jury system "quite indefensible," but in Parliament he had perforce to say kinder things of these influential bodies.[15] The new bill replaced the presentment sessions with elected county and baronial councils (the latter being roughly equivalent to district councils in England). The chief duties of these councils would be to maintain the roads and highways and to appoint various local officials. The grand juries would retain their judicial functions, and the elected councils would have no control over the police, the administration of the Poor Law, or land purchase. The franchise for the councils would be the same as that for parliamentary elections, the only difference being

[14] Balfour to A. R. Barker, 10 Oct. 1890; Balfour to W. H. Long, M.P., 23 Nov. 1891, *ibid.*, 49829-830.

[15] Balfour to Col. Kenyon-Slaney, M.P., 2 Dec. 1891, *ibid.* See also Balfour to Goschen, 16 Sept. 1889; Balfour to Lord Waterford, 22 Oct. 1891, *ibid.*, 49828-830.

that women and peers received the vote. A minority-representation clause was also included.

The most controversial feature of the bill authorized the dissolution of a county or baronial council for malfeasance—that is, financial irresponsibility or the oppression of a minority group—upon the successful petition of twenty cesspayers to a judge of election. There was no precedent for such a drastic limitation either in the English or Scottish Local Government acts; and the reaction of Irish members to this clause left no doubt that Balfour's search for a measure "as little noxious as possible" to all parties had been in vain. Balfour's speech introducing the bill, moreover, was derided as "one prolonged apology." Jeers and laughter from the Home Rule benches greeted the clause permitting the dissolution of "peccant" county councils; and in trying to justify minority representation, Balfour revealed the weakness of his case by asserting that there were "very great advantages in doing a stupid thing which has been done before, instead of doing a wise thing that has never been done before."[16]

For the Opposition the Protestant and landlord flavor of the bill proved overpowering. Justin McCarthy ridiculed this attempt "to win and wean the Irish people from all their wild desire for Home Rule," and he advised Balfour in blunt language: "Take your Bill and put it in the fire." Home Rulers called the measure "a miserable and pitiable farce," "a monstrous imposure," "a sham," and "an unclean thing." According to Healy the bill ought to have been named "The Put-'em-in-the-Dock Bill." Balfour admitted that local government reform would never do as much for Ireland as had the Crimes Act, light railways, and the Congested Districts Board, but at least it would heal rather than aggravate prejudices in Ireland by bringing together the various classes—rich and poor, Protestant and Catholic—so that they could work toward a common object. Such sentiments did not impress Morley, who accused him of preferring coercion to county councils. In view of this hostile reception, Ridgeway urged Balfour to drop the dissolution clause at once.[17]

[16] *Hansard*, 4th series, Vol. 1, pp. 700-20.

[17] *Ibid.*, pp. 721-98; Ridgeway to Balfour, 19 Feb. 1892; Balfour to Ridgeway, 24 April 1892, Add. MS 49812, 49830.

Long delays in Parliament caused by debates on supply, the education question, and the Small Holdings Bill held up the second reading of the Irish Local Government Bill until May 19. The Home Rule party continued to heap scorn on the measure and insisted that the principal safeguards be abandoned. But Balfour was determined to have all his bill or nothing. Such precautions as the dissolution clause were essential, he believed, in a country where the nationalists were hoping to use local government reform "as a ladder by which to climb to Home Rule, and possibly through Home Rule to separation." As he said in Parliament, there was no point in comparing the "moral merits" of the two countries. Ireland was no worse than England: it was merely different. And he proceeded to underline the inherent political weakness of that other island:

"We all live a Party life. Party feeling is the breath of our nostrils. . . . We belong to Party. We are all accustomed to Party controversies; and that which is a mild attack in this country is a virulent and fatal disease in Ireland. It attacks the Irish constitution with a violence of which you have no conception. Even friends in Ireland, when they do fall out, use language to each other which would quite stagger the more steady-going politicians on this side of the Channel."[18]

The whole implication of Balfour's speech was that the volatile character of the Irish people did not suit them for self-government. The Opposition kept up their attacks and at length, on June 13, ministers announced their intention to drop the measure in order to end the session as soon as possible. The truth was, as George Wyndham remarked, that "nobody cared a damn" about the bill. With the general election so close there were more important issues at stake, and the objections of Ashbourne and Beach to the safeguards did not help matters. The prospect of Irish county councils thus evaporated, and there were few who mourned this loss.[19] On the eve of a general election in which Home Rule figured so prominently, ministers, by refusing to concede to Irish national sentiment some form of local self-government, waived their only

[18] *Hansard*, 4th series, Vol. 4, pp. 1715-25.
[19] Biggs-Davison, *Wyndham*, p. 63; Ashbourne to Salisbury, 14 Feb. 1892, Salisbury MSS; Hicks Beach's memorandum on Irish Local Government Bill, 31 Dec. 1891, St. Aldwyn MSS.

chance of blunting that demand. This miscalculation proved all too vividly the contempt in which Irish nationalism was held by the great majority of Unionists.

III. THE EDUCATION QUESTION

Within the sphere of conciliation the thorniest problem with which Balfour had to deal was the question of assisted education for Catholics. Whenever the Government showed any inclination to treat this problem, the Irish hierarchy invariably raised their demands, Protestant loyalists began to cry "treachery," while members of the Church of England and not a few nonconformists denounced any show of favoritism to Rome. Both Carnarvon and Beach had faced this irrational reaction in their time, and the latter had been fortunate to escape relatively unscathed from his part in carrying the Intermediate Education Act of 1878. In December, 1885, Carnarvon had tried in vain to crown his series of good works by establishing a Catholic university; and during his second term as chief secretary, Beach had negotiated with Archbishop Walsh on the subject of higher education for Catholics. In Ireland this question had always been something of a graveyard for good intentions. The Queen's colleges established by Peel in 1845 at Belfast, Cork, and Galway had been condemned as "godless" by O'Connell, the Vatican, and the Irish hierarchy; and the Catholic university founded in 1854 with Newman as rector failed to satisfy the hierarchy's desire for an institution comparable to Trinity College. Gladstone's bill in 1873 reforming the entire structure of university education on a nondenominational basis had been defeated in Parliament even though ministers treated the issue as one of confidence. No more successful in appeasing Catholic opinion was the Royal University of Ireland established in 1879, which was in essence merely an administrative body, designed to set examinations and award degrees. In spite of such ominous precedents, Balfour was determined to deal with this long-standing grievance.

There were two main aspects of the education question: on the elementary level financial assistance was needed to increase the incentive for teacher and pupil alike; and then there was the demand for a Catholic college or university equivalent in status and endowment to Trinity College. On both these issues Balfour insisted that the Irish hierarchy be made to pay as high a price as possible for any concessions. There was no point in proposing measures that alienated Protestant opinion if they conferred "a boon upon men who were separated from us by more than mere Party difficulties, and were using the whole influence of a great hierarchy" to aggravate civil disorder.[20] In 1887 Balfour wrote a memorandum for his uncle's perusal in which he outlined three possible methods of promoting higher education in Ireland. The first scheme, favored by Walsh, entailed a Catholic university that would be placed under "Episcopal management." The second involved a Catholic college coordinate with Trinity College and forming together a single university. Balfour ruled out this possibility on the grounds that the "violent opposition" of Trinity College would prove fatal to the plan. The last proposal was for a college endowed with an income of £33,000 a year that would be affiliated with the Royal University of Ireland. Those who advocated this college—and there were many Catholic loyalists among them—proposed a governing body of fifteen eminent Catholics who would be government nominees "in the first instance." While Balfour favored this third plan, he stipulated that first the Irish hierarchy should be told that " . . . it is impossible to ask Parliament or the country to make any sacrifice in favour of the Catholic Church in Ireland while all the resources of that Church are being exhausted in the cause of Socialism and Revolution. But as soon as this unhappy state of things is brought to an end, the matter will be taken seriously in hand." Balfour fully realized that the effect of this bribe upon "Irish Ecclesiastical politics" would be neither "striking nor immediate," but he was anxious to attract the support of not only the moderates in the Church but, far more important, of the Pope himself.[21]

It was Leo XIII to whom Balfour looked for help in controlling the Irish episcopacy. The Rescript was only a scrap of paper so long as the Holy See took no steps to enforce it; and Balfour's tactics were simply to hold out the prospect of a Catholic college in return for papal sanctions in the event of clerical disobedience. During the months after the Rescript had been issued Balfour

[20] Balfour to Buller, 11 May 1887, Add. MS 49826.
[21] See Balfour's memorandum on Irish Education, n.d. Oct. 1887, Salisbury MSS.

kept in touch with Norfolk and sent him his draft proposals for Irish higher education. It was imperative, he felt, to keep the Vatican informed about the Government's willingness to consider a concession in this field. What was withheld from publication in Vatican circles was that the chief secretary did not want the governing body of any new Roman Catholic college to dictate the curriculum. Instead, a committee composed of the various faculties, ranging from theology to medicine, would advise the council of Catholic governors on such matters. Balfour was adamant on this issue: " . . . if we draw too tight the bonds of Catholic orthodoxy," he wrote, "the interests of Education are bound to suffer."[22]

In the summer of 1889 Balfour decided that the land war had abated sufficiently to begin negotiations in cabinet about a Roman Catholic college; and at the end of August he announced in Commons the Government's intention to deal with this question in the near future. His remarks were deliberately vague and tentative because he was interested in sounding party and public opinion. In mid-September he wrote to Salisbury expressing his forebodings about the fate of the proposed college: "I think we shall have trouble, and my impression is that the trouble shall come rather from the no-popery middle class in England than from the Orangemen in Ireland. But I may be wrong. . . . It is curious that the row, if row there is, should have been deferred so long:—for I said nothing in the House which I had not before said on more than one occasion on the Platform; though for some reason or other Protestant sensibilities have never before taken alarm." The announcement, he continued, would at least afford ministers a useful "means of gauging public opinion"; and if the objections to a bill proved insuperable, the Government was honor-bound to inform both Norfolk and the Pope of this fact, "unless indeed the influence of Rome in enforcing its own decrees is so feebly exercised as to absolve us entirely from any feeling of obligation towards them."[23]

[22] Balfour to Norfolk, 11 Dec. 1888; Balfour to John Thomas Ball (former Irish lord chancellor), 30 Jan. 1889, Add. MS 49827.

[23] Balfour to Salisbury, 17 Sept. 1889, Salisbury MSS; Balfour's memorandum on Irish education, n.d. Jan. 1889; Balfour to Ridgeway, 18 Sept. 1889, Add. MS 49827-828.

In his letter Balfour had referred to the "outraged feeling" of party members, and this phrase was more than appropriate. The outcry from Government supporters was sharp enough to puncture his trial balloon. The proposal was mocked as being "Mr. Balfour's bribing University," and the chief secretary was called "a Jesuit in disguise." One nonconformist member wrote to Salisbury in October that the bill must be stopped because it had already cost the Government two by-elections, "& it will cost us the entire Ministry if introduced and no one will be conciliated in the least. They will get all they can & bite the hand that gives (viper-like)." Captain Middleton, the Conservative principal agent, wrote that he had heard no party member support it and a great number oppose it. "Altogether it looks ill" was Salisbury's comment. In addition, the college failed to win the approval of either Walsh or the Vatican; and Ridgeway reported from Dublin that the Presbyterians were insisting upon a share of the bounty that was being offered to their enemies. Once again an attempt to aid Catholic higher education had only heightened the fears and mutual aversion on both sides. At Glasgow Balfour defended his moribund plan against its numerous critics, disclaiming any intention of trying to bribe the Irish people or the hierarchy. His only wish was to introduce Irish Catholics to the liberal arts and sciences, and he failed to understand how this instruction could "advance the interests of any particular church, and least of all the church to which they belong."[24]

It was all very well for Balfour to exonerate himself in public from any ulterior motives in seeking education reform, but the fact remained that there was no likelihood of a Unionist concession on this score without some guarantees of good behavior on the part of Archbishops Walsh and Croke and their followers. Such guarantees the latter were unwilling to give. They regarded their own freedom of action as more important than the promise of a gift that they considered niggardly in the first place. Catholic Ireland did not receive a full-fledged university until 1908, and this long delay attested to the amount of prejudice that surrounded the subject.

[24] Balfour to Salisbury, 28 Sept. 1891, Salisbury MSS. Salisbury to Balfour, 23 Oct. 1889; H. J. Atkinson, M.P., to Salisbury, 18 Oct. 1889; Ridgeway to Balfour, 3 Sept. 1889, Add. MS 49689, 49810; Dugdale, *Balfour*, I, pp. 169-70.

The Government was more successful in the area of elementary education. In 1891 fees in elementary schools in England and Scotland had been abolished, despite the protests of numerous Government supporters as well as Cardinal Manning that free education would destroy the voluntary school system. This measure also set aside funds for the purpose of freeing education in Ireland. In February, 1892, W. L. Jackson introduced the National Education (Ireland) Bill, which was designed to end the payment of school fees and to increase teachers' salaries. The situation in Ireland, he explained, differed markedly from that in England and Scotland because the state contributed four-fifths of the cost of education in that country, as opposed to two-fifths in the rest of the United Kingdom. Moreover, there was no provision in the Irish schools system for compulsory attendance, which had operated in England since 1876; and Jackson's bill incorporated this feature as a means of checking the decline in the number of children at school. Lastly, the friction between the different faiths was increasing and could be seen in the trend away from "mixed schools." Jackson's object was to encourage as many children as possible to enter schools, and he hoped to promote regular attendance by restricting the employment of children under fourteen. The latter provision would apply only to towns and urban districts, which represented twenty-five per cent of the population. In rural areas child labor was essential, and the difficulties of enforcing the law outside the towns necessitated much flexibility in the measure. The £90,000 available for the current financial year was assigned to the teachers' pension fund; and with the £200,000 that would fall due in the following year under the act of 1891, fees would be abolished in most schools, whether Catholic or Protestant, and the remainder would go toward increases in teachers' salaries.[25]

The Irish Education Bill met an indifferent reception in the Commons, where the nationalists objected to the distribution of the funds and called the compulsory clause "gross interference" with parental rights. The second reading was postponed until May 30, at which time some of the Irish members offered to support the bill if the Government abandoned the principal safe-

[25] See *Hansard*, 4th series, Vol. 1, pp. 968-82; Vol. 5, pp. 225 ff.; and Balfour to S. K. McDonnell, 24 June 1891, Add. MS 49830.

guards in their Local Government Bill. In cabinet it was decided to drop the latter measure, but Balfour urged that the Education Bill be carried; and, after being rushed through the House of Lords, the bill became law on June 27, one day before the prorogation of Parliament. The principle of compulsory attendance had been heavily diluted, but all fees under six shillings a year per child were removed. If the Irish hierarchy complained about slights to the Christian Brothers Schools, and if Protestants berated ministers for selling out to the "papists," at least the teachers were grateful. The Government's "legislative orgy," as Cadogan described it, ended on this note. The dissolution was announced, and the fate of both the Union and the ministry was left in the hands of the electorate.[26]

[26] Balfour's memorandum on Irish education, n.d. Jan. 1889, *ibid.*, 49827; Balfour to Salisbury, 21, 28 Sept. 1891; Salisbury to Goschen, 7 June 1891, Salisbury MSS; *Annual Register 1892*, pp. 33-34, 105-06.

CHAPTER XVII

Resignation and Reflection

THE CAMPAIGN to educate the electorate about the virtue or vice of Home Rule began formally at Easter, although it might be said that both British parties had been trying to sell their views on this issue ever since 1886. The arguments on each side had not changed much in the course of six years, although the Parnellite split had considerably strengthened the Unionist case against Home Rule. Morley simplified the problem by asserting that the choice lay between "perpetual coercion" and Home Rule. His insistence that "justice to Ireland" take priority over English legislation, however, did not endear him to every section of the Liberal party. On the subject of Home Rule Gladstone's utterances were discreetly veiled, much to the annoyance of Unionists, who demanded that the voters be shown the prospectus of any new plan before making up their minds. Lord Salisbury in his election address dealt first with domestic questions, emphasizing the Government's signal achievements from the Local Government Act to the conversion of the national debt. When he arrived at the Irish Question, he employed all the rhetoric at his command to convey the gravity of the issues in dispute. For the loyal minority in Ireland this election would bring either salvation or "a sentence of servitude and ruin." Whereas mistakes could be made in other fields and easily rectified, this was not the case in Ireland, where the wrong decision would mean for every loyalist "the certainty of bitter and protracted struggle, culminating probably in civil war, and . . . ultimate condemnation to the doom which they dread beyond any other fate—the subjection of their prosperity, their industry, their religion, their lives, to the absolute mastery of their ancient and unchanging enemies." In earlier speeches he had denied Parliament the right to sell Irish loyalists into slavery and had warned of the dire consequences of forcing them into this position.[1]

[1] *Annual Register 1892*, pp. 108-12.

Spring Time in Leap Year

Salisbury and Balfour hesitate before plunging the country
into the general election of 1892.

The Unionist case against Home Rule in 1892 revolved around
four main arguments. These were the integrity of empire, the
security of England, the Ulster question, and the clerical issue.

394

The first three had seen active service in 1886. According to the imperial argument, Home Rule was nothing but a euphemism for separation; the loss of Ireland would be followed by that of India; and the process of disintegration would then be in full motion. Or, as Salisbury had expressed it: "If you fail in this trial, one by one the flowers will be plucked from your diadem of Empire, you will be reduced to depend upon the resources of this small, overpeopled island." As to national security, the existence of an independent and hostile Ireland would be an invitation to any belligerent power on the continent to use the island as a base from which to attack England. The Ulster question, with its corollary of protecting minority rights in the south, was the legacy of earlier conquests and transplantations, and it was aggravated by the relative prosperity of the textile and shipbuilding industries in the northeast. The presence of a large Catholic population had turned Ulster into a breeding ground of fanatics, and nothing was easier for Unionist politicians than to goad the Protestant citizens of Belfast or Londonderry into an "Orange frenzy" by a few allusions to the Boyne or to the prospect of a "papist parliament" in Dublin. The Ulster question attracted more attention in this campaign than it had in 1886; and a giant rally of Ulstermen in Belfast on June 17 gave some cogency to Unionist warnings that the Orangemen would not surrender their "rights" without a fight. Lord Randolph Churchill's war cry had not been forgotten.

The question of clerical interference in Irish politics was hardly new, but it had received an impressive stimulus from the events surrounding the O'Shea divorce, and ministers devoted many of their speeches to the theme that Home Rule meant Rome Rule. Oblivious to the roles of both nonconformist opinion and the Liberal leaders in precipitating Parnell's downfall, they reminded their audiences that it was the parish priest who had condoned the National League, who had aided and abetted the Plan of Campaign, and who had intimidated voters at the critical by-elections that followed the debates in Committee Room 15. Lord Salisbury attributed Parnell's defeat in these contests almost entirely to priestly machinations. He described Ireland as "an ultra clerical state" and declared that the Catholic majority contained "all that is unprogressive, all that is contrary to civilization and enlightenment in Ireland."[2] Gladstone quickly retaliated by accusing the prime minister of being a religious bigot, and he belittled the political influence of both the hierarchy and the priesthood. At Glasgow, however, he was presumptuous enough to scold the Government for having carried on underhand negotiations with the Pope through the agency of Sir Lintorn Simmons. This charge irritated Salisbury, who possessed a copy of the correspondence that had passed between Gladstone and his own secret agent in Rome, Sir George Errington, during the period 1881-1885. The whole cabinet knew that the Errington mission had dealt with such matters as ecclesiastical preferment in Malta and Ireland, official relations with France and Portugal, and with "emphatic proffers of friendliness" to the Pope himself. The *Times* re-enforced Unionist diatribes against the priest in politics by publishing two feature articles on the evils of Irish clericalism; and at east Manchester Balfour informed an audience about the contribution of the priesthood to the land war.[3] The public debate raging over the clerical question in Ireland may have added a sharper, more acrid note to the election, but it settled nothing.

There were more positive aspects to the electoral campaign fought by the Unionists. The improvement in Ireland since 1887 spoke for itself. And the restoration of respect for the law, according to Government spokesmen, meant that the way was open for a revival of trade and industry. Balfour contended that the remarkable advance in the material condition of the country during the past five years was ample proof that constructive Unionism offered a more rewarding and practicable solution to the Irish Question than Home Rule. It would be no exaggeration to say that the very neglect of Unionist conciliation in the speeches of Home Rulers and the constant appeals of nationalists to the memory of Mitchelstown, Mandeville, and New Tipperary were evidence in themselves of the beneficial effects of land acts, the Congested Districts Board, and relief of distress.

Before the polling began on July 4 the Gladstonian Liberals had predicted a majority for Home Rule of 25 to 120 seats. Unionist agents boasted of similar results for their own side.

[2] *Irish Unionist Alliance 1892*, II, pp. 413-14.

[3] Salisbury to Balfour, 4 July 1892, Add. MS 49690; *Times*, 29-30 June 1892.

But neither Salisbury nor Balfour had any illusions about the outcome of the election. Not only had the Government's majority dwindled from 116 to 66 since 1886, but the immunity of Conservatives to physical ailments seemed to be lower than that of their opponents. In the spring of 1891 five Conservative members had died in a three-week period—four of them having won their seats after a severe contest. And the loss of W. H. Smith, added to Hartington's elevation to the Lords two months later, did not help the Unionist cause in the Commons. The influenza epidemic in the winter of 1890 and other assorted diseases had thus thinned the party's ranks at Westminster; and in view of the "swing of the pendulum," Salisbury observed in October, 1891, that "the chances of my having to form another Administration are very shadowy. . . . " Balfour, convinced that domestic issues would determine the results in most parts of the country, echoed Salisbury's sentiments.[4]

The pessimism of the Conservative leaders was justified. When the polling had ended, the Home Rule party could count on 355 seats as against 315 for the Unionists. But the flaw in this verdict was that the Liberals were once again dependent on the Irish vote, which was now split into two factions of unequal size. It was indeed a "victory without power."[5] The Liberal Unionists had been somewhat mauled in the election, while the Conservatives had lost a number of county seats to the Gladstonians. The Unionist coalition, nevertheless, had the satisfaction of holding a decisive majority in English constituencies and of knowing that their opponents were suffering from grave internal discord.

Lord Salisbury greeted the news of the Liberal-nationalist victory with a calm that verged on relief. Only the defeat of his son Lord Cranborne at Darwen in Lancashire upset him visibly. On the whole he regarded the results as a blessing in disguise, and Cranbrook accused him of displaying "indecent joy at his release." When Balfour first learned of the loss of several Conservative seats by small margins, he wrote to his uncle: "This

---

[4] Salisbury to Queen Victoria, 17 April 1891; Balfour to Salisbury, 28 Sept. 1891, Salisbury MSS; Salisbury to Balfour, 1 Oct. 1891, Add. MS 49689. For an account of the Government's electoral misfortunes after July 1886, see *Times*, 29 June 1892.

[5] Gooch, *Courtney*, p. 296.

is provoking from some points of view but makes it at all events tolerably certain that we shall have a long holiday! I shall be able to prepare my new edition of 'Philosophic Doubt'!"[6] After much discussion in cabinet, ministers decided not to resign until Parliament had met and the Opposition moved a vote of no-confidence. A brief, nonpolemical Queen's speech was drafted; and when the new Parliament assembled, Asquith moved his hostile amendment to the address. After three days of contentious debate, the motion was carried on August 11 by a majority of forty, whereupon Balfour moved the adjournment. On the same day Lord Salisbury wrote that the Government's defeat would not jeopardize the Act of Union, even though he might have wished for a smaller Liberal majority. In opposition, the Unionists, he believed, would form a "much more united phalanx" and would be better prepared "to fight the battle out to the bitter end." Moreover, he continued: " . . . the general experience of all countries is that six years is about the extreme limit to which the strength given to men will carry them in the discharge of laborious offices; and that beyond that limit the danger is serious that the public service will be affected by their necessary loss of vigour. Therefore I am inclined to say very sincerely that all is for the best."[7]

Salisbury tendered his resignation on August 13. He took some pains to console the Queen, who disliked having Gladstone "that dangerous fanatic thrust down her throat." The Unionist coalition, he assured her, would defeat any new Home Rule scheme invented by Gladstone. To him defeat was only incidental. As he had already informed the Queen, there were "many compensations" in this verdict, because a change of ministry "would bring to the test many promises which are really hollow, and which the electorate must learn by experience to see through." And more than a year before, he had declared that it made no difference who won the election because the Irish Question would remain active for another generation, "ultimately, but gradually and patiently to be solved."[8]

[6] Gathorne Hardy, *Cranbrook*, ii, p. 334; Balfour to Salisbury, 5 July 1892, Salisbury MSS.

[7] Salisbury to H. Cecil, 11 Aug. 1892, *ibid.*

[8] *Letters of Queen Victoria*, 3d series, ii, p. 123; Salisbury to Queen Victoria, 3 June 1892, Salisbury MSS; *Annual Register 1891*, p. 100.

For ministers the last weeks in office were largely taken up with the chore of distributing patronage. The list of applicants seemed unending, and every award, as Salisbury knew only too well, hurt someone else. It was difficult enough to divide the spoils between Conservatives and Liberal Unionists without creating grievances in the other camp, but the persistence of Irish claimants surpassed the expectation of even the most hardened whips. According to Balfour, Irish honors were "fought for by the rival denominations in a manner of which we have no notion on this side of St. George's Channel, so that patronage really becomes a question of the highest political moment. . . . " Gladly would he sacrifice his salary to be relieved of this responsibility.[9] No such relief came, and Balfour could not afford to neglect the deserving servants of the Castle. Among those Irish officials who had already received awards were Ridgeway, with a K.C.B., the Lord Chief Justice Peter O'Brien, who became a baronet, and the Inspector General of the RIC Andrew Reed, who earned a knighthood. And in August, 1892, Chief Baron Palles was promoted to an English privy councillorship in the hope that this "compliment to his rigid inflexibility in the administration of the Law," as Ridgeway wrote, "might induce him to be a thorn in the side of those who may desire to tamper with the Law."[10] But the most indefatigable claimant for honors was George Brooke, the Dublin wine merchant and landlord of the Coolgreaney estate in county Wexford, who insisted that his triumph over the Plan of Campaign had benefited not only "the Community" but also the party. To advance his claims for a baronetcy Brooke recruited more than a dozen Irish peers to write on his behalf, and he reminded them that the struggle against the Plan had cost him £20,000. While fully appreciating Brooke's services to the landlords' cause, Balfour found his persistence rather tiresome. "I think he is the only one of your countrymen," he observed to Salisbury's private secretary, "who would think that a vigorous resistance to a lot of scoundrels who wished to pick his pocket was an adequate ground for giving him some public honour." Brooke's perseverance won him a baronetcy in the end—but not until 1903. To Salisbury

[9] Balfour to S. K. McDonnell, 21 July 1892; Balfour to W. Thorburn, M.P., 31 Aug. 1888, Add. MS 49827, 49830.

[10] Ridgeway to Balfour, 27 July 1892, Salisbury MSS.

such hunger for rewards was commonplace. In this respect no one understood the nature of political man better. Honors he once described as those "prizes which animate that class of superior wire pullers who are the very soul of our party organization. Starving the sheep dogs is even worse than starving the sheep."[11]

Amidst an inundation of requests for honors the second Salisbury administration came to an end. Although better known for their achievements in foreign affairs, and in particular for the partition of Africa, the Government could also boast of some success in domestic affairs, not the least being the improvement in Ireland. Within a fortnight of his resignation Salisbury had left for Puys and a much-needed vacation; and Balfour began to collect his thoughts for another book on the philosophy of religion, which appeared two years later under the title *The Foundations of Belief*.

Sir Henry Lucy, the sharp-witted commentator on political events and people, dedicated his *Diary of the Salisbury Parliament 1886-1892* to the "principal product" of the session, Arthur Balfour. And this tribute to the man whom he had once described as "a Parliamentary *flaneur*, a trifler with debate" and "a pretty speaker, with a neat turn for saying nasty things" was well deserved. The former dilettante had matured into a "civil Cromwell," or, as *Punch* called him, "Prince Arthur." There could be no doubt that Ireland had "made" Balfour, in both a personal and political sense. The experience of coercion and conciliation, the match of wits and endurance with Parnell and his party had developed in his character those latent qualities of intellectual toughness and dexterity that Salisbury had been the first to notice. By 1892 Balfour's achievements in Ireland had earned him the title of "favourite Minister of the day."[12]

This rapid advance in the political world was all the more remarkable because Balfour seemed at first to possess so few of

[11] Balfour to S. K. McDonnell, 9, 13 Jan. 1892; Abercorn to Balfour, 23 Nov. 1891; De Vesci to Balfour, 8 June 1892; Zetland to Balfour, 26 July 1892; Salisbury to Goschen, 26 Jan. 1889, *ibid*.

[12] Lucy, *A Diary of the Salisbury Parliament 1886-1892*, London, 1892, pp. 78-81.

the attributes ordinarily identified with success in the House of Commons. By his own admission he was not an orator in the classic tradition. Speeches fit for publication, he once said, "I could not deliver if I would, and would not if I could."[13] Furthermore, he lacked the warmth and "common touch" that were W. H. Smith's greatest assets. Yet his proverbial insensitivity to the opinions of others had contributed to his success as chief secretary. No matter how hard they tried, the Irish members could not penetrate his outer defenses. Instead of causing him annoyance by their personal attacks in Parliament and in the nationalist press, they found themselves being baited by the chief secretary. It was said of Balfour that "nothing altered his seraphic equanimity," and his unruffled calm in the midst of Parnellite fulminations against the Crimes Act impressed every onlooker.[14] A master of dialectic, he was always at his best or most dangerous when on the defensive, whereas his set speeches lacked the verve and incisiveness of his extemporaneous replies. What unperceptive critics called cynicism, arrogance, or a patrician temperament was really no more than a high degree of detachment, attained through inordinate self-discipline. The fact that he saw "much of life from afar," as Ramsay Macdonald once said of him, may have originated in his adolescent conviction that he would not live beyond the age of thirty. But whatever the cause of his valetudinarian obsession, this air of remoteness proved his most effective weapon in Parliament. For the nationalists as well as for many Unionists it took Mitchelstown to prove that Balfour was not the indolent weakling whom caricaturists loved to portray.

George Wyndham once wrote somewhat frivolously: "The truth about Arthur Balfour is this: he knows there's been one ice-age, and he thinks there's going to be another." What lay behind Balfour's pessimistic outlook was a streak of fatalism. How much of his apparent indifference to earthly cares was pose and how much pure instinct cannot be easily ascertained. Balfour, who was fond of inquiring into the meaning of life, had arrived at the conclusion that human beings were important only insofar as their feelings of vanity and egotism moved them to think so. Hating drudgery, tolerating politics, and enjoying leisure, he

---

[13] Balfour to J. R. Fisher, 21 Dec. 1891, Add. MS 49830.

[14] See Malcolm, *Lord Balfour*, p. 38.

had the facility of being able to forget the problems of the world the moment he went to bed. Insensible to the material rewards of success, he was hailed by his admirers as "fearless, resolved and negligently great."[15]

Unlike Carnarvon and Hicks Beach, he could never have been accused of "going green" in Dublin. Even if he had not possessed a natural immunity to this sentiment, the fact was that he never exposed himself long enough to the mood and scenery of Ireland. During his four and a half years as chief secretary he spent less than a total of six months in the country, and only once, on the occasion of his congested districts tour, did he venture into the west. He readily justified his long absences from Ireland on the grounds that the vast majority of a chief secretary's duties consisted of paper work, which could be dealt with just as easily in London.[16] In addition, while Parliament was in session his presence was required at Westminster; and in the autumn he faced a number of speaking engagements. What he did not say was that London provided him with access to Lord and Lady Salisbury in Arlington Street or Hatfield, and that in Scotland he had his estates and golf. Fortunately, the competence of Ridgeway meant that Balfour could avoid crossing the Irish Channel for months at a time without impairing the administration of the country.

From his Irish experience Balfour gained not only a reputation but an insight into human nature. Never before, he admitted, had he "so clearly understood how much more important in the eyes of ordinary men are *nominal* differences than real ones." This lesson many Englishmen as well as Irishmen would have to learn again, at a considerable cost in lives, after 1916. At the same time the meaning of nationalism and its import for the future completely escaped him. He could never credit the Parnellites and their supporters with motives any loftier than those of material gain at the expense of the propertied classes. In later years he paid generous tribute to Parnell's party, calling them one of the most talented and disciplined groups ever to sit in Parliament. But to him it was a shame that such prodigious talent had been

[15] Biggs-Davison, *Wyndham,* p. 40; Lord Rayleigh, *Lord Balfour,* Cambridge, 1930, pp. 16-20.

[16] Balfour to C. Bell, 6 Nov. 1888, Add. MS 49827.

wasted on so unworthy a cause. In 1889 Churchill had advised W. H. Smith: "You have to fight two battles: one in Ireland against crime, the other in Parliament against disorder. You must win both. The loss of one entails the loss of the other."[17] The Government's victory on both these fronts can be attributed as much to Balfour and to the support he received from his uncle as to the calamity that befell the Irish party in December, 1890.

Besides being the favorite nephew, almost son, of the prime minister, Balfour was endowed with superior intellectual powers. In Dublin Castle he supplied both resolution and the ability to make decisions. The ease with which he handled such problems as prosecutions, prison rules, test estates, Castle morale, diseased potatoes, parliamentary affairs, and Rome left a profound impression on his subordinates. "The last of the hereditary rulers of the Conservative Party," he sneered at the myth that politics was "an instrument of human progress."[18] Those people who espoused extreme positions invariably stirred feelings of contempt within him. As he confessed to his uncle in 1892: "I have never quite made up my mind whether I dislike the Orangemen, the Extreme Ritualists, the political disputers, or the R.C's the most. On the whole the last: but they are all odious."[19] Balfour, nevertheless, was unusually modest about his achievements in Ireland. To him the restoration of respect for the law and the policy of land purchase and light railways represented only a beginning. Speaking at Plymouth in 1890, he emphasized that much work still remained to be done: "It does not rest with one individual—with one Government . . . with one generation, completely to solve so ancient a controversy, so old an historic difficulty as . . . the Irish Question. All we can claim to have done . . . is to be in the process of solving it, and that claim we may put forward with something like moderation and justice."[20]

During his term as chief secretary—indeed, throughout his early career—Balfour received constant encouragement from Salisbury, who was always ready to offer criticism and advice. The idea

[17] Churchill to Smith, 16 April 1889, Hambleden MSS.

[18] H. Sidebotham, *Political Profiles from British Public Life*, New York, 1921, pp. 46-49.

[19] Balfour to Salisbury, 24 Dec. 1892, Salisbury MSS.

[20] *Times*, 11 Aug. 1890.

of the Ponsonby syndicate was officially born at Hatfield during one of Balfour's frequent visits there; and the interchange of ideas and information between uncle and nephew on domestic and international affairs helped to mold Conservative policy for a generation. On Ireland their views were almost identical. Salisbury was less sanguine than Balfour about the efficacy of conciliation at the height of the land war. "The cumbrous processes and precautions of English law," he had complained to Alfred Austin in 1887, "are an unwieldy armoury against modern forms of lawlessness." If Russia or Germany had to contend with the Irish Question, he had no doubt that their governments would make short shrift of the Parnellites.[21]

The two men had much more in common than family ties. They shared a sense of profound scepticism about democracy. "The question is," Salisbury had written in 1865, "whether England shall be governed by property and intelligence, or by numbers. . . . There is no middle term between the two. It is the great controversy of modern society, the great issue upon which the hopes of freedom and order, and civilisation depend."[22] In the ensuing years this outlook did not change appreciably; and after two extensions of the franchise he could only regret that the masses had become the "ignorant masters" of the intelligent few. Having confidence in the ability of aristocracy to govern and to govern well, he felt that the best a Conservative leader could do in a world that "had been going to the dogs" for many years was to retard the process of democratization and to prevent class war from breaking out in England. Only Salisbury's religious faith saved him from the despair into which this deep-seated pessimism might have led him.

Intellectual curiosity was a prominent trait in both uncle and nephew. The former, Churchill once complained, was "always in that damned laboratory" at Hatfield, experimenting with electric currents and lighting; and Balfour, when out of office, spent much of his time speculating on the relationship between religion and science. Both men could be outspoken to the point of indiscretion, and their gift for deflating adversaries commanded much respect. At times the Balfour of the 1880's resembled the caustic political observer of the 1860's, Lord Robert Cecil, who had vilified in the

[21] Salisbury to A. Austin, 27 Oct. 1887, Salisbury MSS.
[22] *Quarterly Review*, July 1865, Vol. 118, No. 235, p. 295.

Quarterly Review all those who treated Conservative principles as so much merchandise to be sold for votes. What Balfour lacked was his uncle's warmth and magnanimity. A penchant for metaphysical inquiry gave Balfour what Scawen Blunt called a certain "philosophic hardness of view." Indeed, he seemed to have buried such feelings as pity and sympathy deep within himself; and as a result, while Salisbury's heart was described as "pure gold," his gave the impression of being made of steel.[23]

Both Salisbury and Balfour had ambivalent feelings about politics. As Cecils they were born into the governing class, and yet they detested the professionalism, the publicity, and the personal ambition that were so intimately associated with the world of Westminster. Deploring these "sordid" aspects of the profession, Salisbury went so far as to warn his colleagues against excessive party organization. "However well-rigged we may be," he once observed, "we cannot sail without wind: and we do not make the wind. The wind bloweth where it listeth." There were times when both men wondered why they persisted in a career that they found "quite intolerable." Perhaps the answer was force of habit, a Cecilian sense of duty, or, as Salisbury once quipped, the realization that retirement "would give such infinite pleasure to their adversaries."[24]

For Lord Salisbury the Foreign Office remained first and foremost his great passion. It was there that he found the subdued drama, the magnitude of issues, and the relative seclusion in which he delighted. In marked contrast to these attractions, the premiership seemed an unpleasant chore that brought him face to face with every "exhibition of littleness." A reluctant prime minister par excellence, he tried to avoid this office—which he described as one "of infinite worry but very little power"—on three different occasions, each time in vain. As premier he left his cabinet colleagues such latitude in the management of their affairs that some of them complained of being neglected.[25] Massive in frame as well as intellect, he possessed a quality of wisdom born

[23] Blunt, *The Land War in Ireland*, p. 296; Hamilton, *Reminiscences*, II, p. 314.

[24] Salisbury to Smith, 2 Nov. 1889, Hambleden MSS; Salisbury to Lady John Manners, 8 March 1889, Salisbury MSS.

[25] Cecil, *Salisbury*, III, pp. 313-14. Both Carnarvon and Beach expressed discontent over Salisbury's apparent remoteness. See Balfour to Salisbury 19 Oct. 1891, Salisbury MSS.

of inner composure and a highly analytical mind. His reserve, dislike of publicity, and belief in diplomacy by patient and unspectacular means have all tended to obscure his stature as an astute statesman and party leader. Even in moments of crisis or defeat the party's trust in his judgment remained unshaken. An early Victorian in both training and spirit, Salisbury conceived it his duty to uphold the Anglican Church and the interests of aristocracy, and to serve with absolute loyalty the Queen, his country, and the Conservative party. As foreign secretary he worked to safeguard England's honor and prestige abroad; as party leader he dedicated his career to preserving those constitutional checks—the most important being the House of Lords—that could prevent or delay the advent of mass democracy or, worse, socialism. Like Burke, he insisted that "all change to be wholesome must be gradual"; and in view of the events that followed his death, from the party schism over tariff reform to world war and rebellion in Ireland, his pessimism was not altogether unjustified. "There was a tremendous air about this wise old statesman," wrote Winston Churchill; and Beach's tribute to this eminent Victorian, the last peer to become prime minister, was both terse and appropriate: "He was felt by all who worked with him to be essentially a great man."[26]

When it came to the Irish Question, the scepticism of Balfour and Salisbury about the contents of the Home Rule agitation was shared by most of their colleagues and supporters. In their view—one that Marx would have endorsed—the land war was not just an agrarian means to a political end: it was class war. The New Departure represented a façade behind which lurked the ancient forces of landlord-tenant antagonism. Parnellism supplied the peasantry with the means of expropriating the landowners without compensation, and all the talk about nationhood and a unique cultural heritage was only so much propaganda designed to hide the real aims of the agitators. Conservatives looked at the preceding centuries of conquest and intermarriage, and they scoffed at the idea of a pure, undefiled Irish people or nation. The highest culture that Ireland had ever known, they insisted, had been im-

[26] W. S. Churchill, *My Early Life, A Roving Commission*, London, 1930, p. 179; Hicks Beach, *St. Aldwyn*, II, p. 363.

ported from England. George Wyndham, whose imperial vision was steeped in legend, once described the heterogeneous nature of the Irish. Who were they?

" . . . They are part of the Aryan race: all that is left of the foremost waves of Aryan migration; bubbles left above high-water mark, fragile & rain-bow hued. 'Ireland a nation'—Yes & Ah! No. Ireland is the yeasty scum of all the most gallant waves of unrest that did *not know when to stop*. It is that, insulted by decivilized modernity; a *beach*, stones & seaweed, iridescent decay, an old boot, a piece of soda-water bottle chafed to chrysoprase, sodden wreckage, a curlew's cry, dead men's bones;—that is Ireland: the romance & call of the sea with no one to answer. But here and there the Norseman or Ultonian; here & there, the Gaul who sacked Rome & over-ran Asia Minor, the Neolithic carver; the Angevin & Norman who followed Strongbow; the Ironside who came with Cromwell, have left the phantoms of ruling Races. 'Pale Princes; death pale are they all.' "[27]

Racial integrity, then, was a myth. But socialism was not. For most Conservatives and for the Whig residue in the Unionist party the National League—which they deliberately referred to as the Land League—as well as the Plan of Campaign were far more indicative of Irish aspirations than was the so-called constitutional movement for Home Rule.[28] In this context Michael Davitt, the advocate of land nationalization, rather than Parnell, was the true representative of Irish nationalism because he had vowed to return the holdings confiscated in previous centuries to their rightful owners. Property was the rallying point of all those interests opposed to Home Rule, and many Unionists believed that a crude form of socialism was the motivating force behind both nationalism in Ireland and labor unrest in England. How wrong this diagnosis was only time would tell. Nothing could convince Balfour that the Parnellites were not operating under false pretenses, and he tried to teach the British public that the Crimes Act was not suppressing a legitimate demand for autonomy. On the contrary, he declared: "The Home Rule agita-

[27] Wyndham to W. E. Henley, 10 Feb. 1901, Henley MSS, PML.

[28] "I have long been impressed by the fact that at least half the force behind Home Rule is Socialistic, and the more this is understood the better for us"; Balfour to W. H. Hurlbert, 1 April 1889, Add. MS 49827.

tion, properly understood, is a very hollow affair consisting chiefly
. . . of two elements in conjunction, neither of which separately
have anything to do with Home Rule whatever—the old Fenian
element, namely, which desires separation, and the agrarian element which desires or did desire spoliation."[29] This agitation,
moreover, was maintained by and for a small fraction of the
population. For Balfour the struggle in Ireland was between the
forces of law and decency on the one hand and those of organized
rebellion and robbery on the other. "To allow the latter to win,"
he wrote in 1888, "is simply to give up civilisation."[30]

Long after he had left the Irish Office, Balfour continued to
deny the existence of a genuine national sentiment in Ireland.
Even Scotland, he maintained, had a stronger claim to nationhood.
Before a Scottish audience he once defined the prerequisites of
nationality as a "long, an independent, and a glorious history . . .
a religious and political evolution, the result of our own actvity."
Ireland lacked these attributes, and the existence of Ulster was
ample proof that no "single nationality" existed in that country.
This line of argument was tenuous enough, but in 1913 he went
further, and in an address on the subject of nationality and Home
Rule he denied that the Irish people had any reasonable ground
for complaint either in political or financial respects. The nationalists based their demand for Home Rule on the existence of a
"separate nationality"; but nationality was highly elusive and
subject to distortion, and he preferred to call it a "sentiment of
hostile and exclusive local patriotism." Even if the argument of
nationality were valid, there was more than enough room for
Ireland within the British empire, which was, after all, a "great
congeries of free countries." Patriotism or feelings of loyalty
to a part ought merely to strengthen allegiance to the whole; and
in view of the admixture of cultures and blood throughout the
British Isles, he denied Ireland's right to Home Rule on the ground
of a distinct heritage. The real reasons for Irish discontent in
the twentieth century were the "sectarian differences and agrarian
wrongs" of the sixteenth and seventeenth centuries, which had ir-
revocably tainted Irish patriotism with an anti-British flavor.
Thus Balfour did not deny the existence of a national self-con-

[29] Balfour to Prof. Henry Calderwood, 22 Oct. 1891, *ibid.*, 49830.
[30] Balfour to J. Roberts, 6 Feb. 1888, *ibid.*, 49826.

sciousness in Ireland, however artificial it might be, but he argued that this feeling was entirely compatible with the Act of Union, and that the only other alternative (Home Rule being impracticable) was complete separation, which would satisfy Irish patriotism "in its narrowest and most hostile form." The Home Rule movement struck Balfour as being unrealistic in its aims and unconstitutional in its methods; and any Home Rule bill, especially one that included Ulster, was simply a "rotten hybrid" scheme that could never offer a final solution to the Irish Question.[31]

Most of the cabinet shared Balfour's view of Irish nationalism. Bernard Shaw once wrote that self-government, like democracy, was not for the people's good but for their satisfaction. "There is indeed no greater curse to a nation," Shaw continued in his preface to *John Bull's Other Island*, "than a nationalist movement, which is only the agonizing symptom of a suppressed natural function." Unfortunately, only a few Conservatives realized that others besides themselves needed to perform this "natural function." Goschen once called Home Rule a "bastard nationalism"; and Salisbury accused the Parnellites of caring far more about land and economic issues than about nationhood. The nationalist agitation, he concluded, was based on "a wholesale system of fraudulent bankruptcy," its primary objective being to banish the landlords without compensation. The main difference between socialism and the Home Rule movement, in Salisbury's opinion, was the vigor and staying power of the latter. Working-class agitation in England broke out sporadically, but the Irish Question persisted with undiminished intensity. There was another difference too. Whereas mistakes could be made in Ireland without affecting the welfare of Englishmen, the latter would be the first to suffer from any mishandling of the labor question.[32]

Needless to say, there were some Conservatives and Liberal Unionists who differed from the bulk of their party by believing in the sincerity of Irish national aspirations. These men ranged in

[31] Balfour, "Nationality and Home Rule," in *Opinions and Arguments from Speeches and Addresses of the Earl of Balfour*, New York, 1928, pp. 48-68. See also Dugdale, *Balfour*, II, pp. 337-43.

[32] Cecil, *Salisbury*, IV, pp. 206-07. Salisbury believed that Parnellism was only "a transitory movement which would have its rise, its culmination, and its fall like all moral movements of the kind."

terms of time and temperament from Carnarvon to George Wynd-ham; they respected Ireland's grievances, both historic and con-temporary; and they wished to find some means of redressing these wrongs consistent with the integrity of empire. For them it was not just a matter of appeasing Ireland for reasons of political gain, but a question of principle which they refused to com-promise. The ideals of Carnarvon and Wyndham in this respect cost them their offices and left them open to Unionist charges of treachery. Their convictions and the courage with which they up-held them, however, were not forgotten by the moderates on both sides of the Irish Sea. In general, Unionists, Liberal as well as Conservative, continued to regard Irish nationalism as a fraud inspired by a combination of agrarian unrest, religious bigotry, and socialism. This tendency to denigrate the strength and the in-gredients of Irish nationalism was not confined to the era of Lord Salisbury, but sustained the far more militant Unionism of Carson, Craig, and Bonar Law.

Epilogue: 1892-1905

IF THE FIRST two years of Gladstone's ministry were not entirely monopolized by Irish affairs, Home Rule was the paramount issue upon which ministers staked their fortunes. The fate of both Gladstone and the Irish nation hung in the balance, and once again the octogenarian prime minister rose to the occasion in Parliament with feats of endurance as well as eloquence. In its main features the second Home Rule Bill resembled its predecessor, except that a reduced number of Irish members would remain at Westminster to vote on matters concerned with Ireland or the empire. Early in April, 1893, Balfour carried the Unionist campaign to Ireland, where he received tumultuous welcomes in Belfast and Dublin. He was followed a month later by his uncle, who assured crowds in Belfast and Londonderry that the House of Lords would never allow "this accursed bill" to pass.[1] In the meantime, the British public was being harangued in newspapers, pamphlets, and speeches by spokesmen of the Primrose League, the Irish Unionist Alliance, and every other organization dedicated to preserving the Union. Members of the stock exchange went so far as to burn a copy of the bill in front of the Guildhall. But the fact was that many Englishmen were either bored by the subject of Home Rule or resented this attention being paid to Ireland when pressing social and economic problems bulked large at home.

In the Commons the Home Rule Bill received cavalier treatment from the Opposition. In view of the Irish party split, Parnell's demise, and the Liberals' small majority, the Unionist leaders decided to point up all the "absurdities" in the measure and to obstruct its progress as long as possible. The resort to delaying tactics would force ministers to employ the closure repeatedly, and this in turn would justify the House of Lords in rejecting the bill. Such was Chamberlain's line of reasoning, and his relentless assaults on the measure earned him the epithet "Judas" from Irish members and the gratitude of his Conservative allies. After passing

[1] *Annual Register 1893*, pp. 304-07.

its second reading in April, the bill went into committee for four months. Beach summed up his colleagues' views when he called Gladstone's scheme neither union, nor federation, nor colonial self-government, but a "bastard combination of all three."[2] After blocks of clauses were carried by guillotine, the bill passed its third reading on September 1. One week later the House of Lords rejected the measure by a margin of 419 to 41. To all intents the bill was dead and buried.

Lord Salisbury was not in the least disturbed by talk of a popular campaign against the House of Lords. Aware that larger issues than the Act of Union were involved, he wished to use the Home Rule Bill to test the powers of his House. "What I dread," he wrote to Alfred Austin, "is that the House of Lords should be bullied or cajoled into allowing its independent right to become atrophied, while the name of a second chamber remains to it—thus leaving the House of Commons in unchecked supremacy."[3] The Lords may have vindicated their rights on this occasion, but in retrospect their victory seems more like a stay of execution. Gladstone's second Home Rule Bill had survived each stage in the Commons, and this fact was not lost on those who believed in the practice and not just the theory of representative government.

The debates on Home Rule had an unsettling effect in Ireland, where savings-bank deposits and stocks fell, evicted tenants clamored for relief, and the Castle's officials were "all at sixes and sevens." In addition, Ridgeway was stranded with a Home Rule administration. Morley, the new chief secretary, when not preoccupied with ministerial duties in London, was proving to be a "veritable schoolmaster" in Dublin Castle. The working hours and habits of each civil servant were closely watched and, even worse, fox-hunting was not permitted in the afternoon.[4] For such

---

[2] *Ibid.*, p. 109; Garvin, *Chamberlain*, II, pp. 567-75.

[3] Salisbury to A. Austin, 28 Oct. 1892, Salisbury MSS.

[4] "Morley is a veritable pedagogue. He rules all the officials with a rod of iron. *All*, including Harrel, Bourke, and others, have to keep fixed hours and work done or not, dare not leave their office till the clock strikes the prescribed hour. To prevent their disobeying with impunity they have to sign attendance books and if a day is required for rest or hunting, it is deducted from the annual leave. Morley's minutes are stinging—not merely tart! He flagellates all. All work is done by him—work which used not to be seen even by the Under Secretary. I guess that the Nationalists

reasons Ridgeway did not protest his transfer from Ireland at the end of 1892, and after a mission to Morocco he was appointed governor general of the Isle of Man.

The defeat of Home Rule and Gladstone's subsequent resignation forced the Liberals to rest content with more humble achievements in Ireland. The new prime minister, Rosebery, hardly ingratiated himself with Irish nationalists by asserting that England would remain "the predominant partner" for some time to come. In Parliament the Opposition managed to wreck Morley's land bills and launched a full-scale attack on the report of the Evicted Tenants Commission in March, 1893. The commissioners found the Plan of Campaign neither "fraudulent" nor "dishonest," and recommended that some authority be empowered to reinstate these tenants at a fair rent. Unionist spokesmen charged that the commission had been packed with nationalist sympathizers who wished to force a settlement down the landlords' throats. After several false starts, an Evicted Tenants bill passed the Commons in 1894 only to be rejected with "Bourbon obstinacy" by the Lords. The evicted tenants were left to seek their own redemption until 1907, when a relief measure was finally carried. Compared with that of their opponents, the Liberals' legislative record in Irish affairs could only be called barren.

In the sensitive area of financial relations between Great Britain and Ireland, much controversy was aroused after 1896 by the report of a commission set up to examine the equity of the Irish contribution to imperial expenditure. Most of the commissioners agreed that the Act of Union had imposed too heavy a burden on Ireland and that this excessive taxation amounted to approximately £2.75 million a year. Unionist ministers had reason to dispute the accuracy of the report and refused to take any action.[5] But the remarkable feature of the commission's findings was the sight of Irish landlords and nationalists sharing the same platform and using similar language to indict the British Treasury. In Ireland the agitation to redress this grievance mounted steadily, and some Irish Unionists even threatened to withdraw their sup-

---

insist on this and examine him occasionally to see whether he is keeping his promise"; Ridgeway to Balfour, 6 May 1894, Add. MS 49812.

[5] A. E. Murray, *A History of the Commercial and Financial Relations between England and Ireland* . . . , London, 1907, pp. 395-421.

THE ASSAULT!!

The Unionists use their majority in the House of Lords to defeat
the second Home Rule Bill. Chamberlain and Balfour help to
operate the battering ram personified by Salisbury's head.

port from the Government unless the surplus taxation was repaid.
Although nothing was done to relieve the tax burden, loyalists
and nationalists had at last found one point of common interest.[6]

While the material condition of Ireland steadily improved after
1892, despite an occasional potato famine in the west, the political
scene was characterized by internecine strife. Within the anti-
Parnellite party a power struggle developed between Healy and
Dillon. At the general election of 1892 seventy-one anti-Parnellites were returned, as opposed to only nine Parnellites led by
John Redmond. When Justin McCarthy resigned the chairmanship of the majority party in January, 1896, the contest over the
succession was fought in the best tradition of Irish factionalism.

[6] *Annual Register 1896*, pp. 223-27; Beach to Salisbury, 26 Dec. 1896,
Salisbury MSS.

414

Apart from the contrasting temperaments of Dillon and Healy, the clash involved two different conceptions of the party's role in achieving Home Rule. Dillon, the elitist, wished to emulate the Parnellite model of one-man rule and almost military discipline; whereas Healy, who had never cared for Parnell's autocratic methods, advocated rule by committee and wider powers to the constituencies. Dillon was elected chairman by a narrow margin, but Healy remained a dangerous threat until his expulsion from the party in 1900.[7]

D. V O'B.

It was over the issue of conciliation that Dillon fell out with his old comrade-in-arms William O'Brien. The new chairman had always feared the corrosive effects of Unionist "kindness" on the Home Rule movement, while O'Brien insisted that the Irish party had no right to deny impoverished tenants the fruits of Unionist generosity. O'Brien's sensitivity to conditions in the west moved him to found the United Irish League in January, 1898, as the instrument whereby "the land would be returned to the people." The league was also supposed to reunite the various remnants of Parnell's party; and early in 1900 this reunion took place when Redmond became chairman of the parliamentary party. The vindication of O'Brien's "olive branch" was short-lived, however, because friction between the party and the league reached an intolerable degree, and in 1903 O'Brien resigned from the party amidst much acrimony. The supremacy of the party was now established, and in the ensuing years Redmond dominated the political arena, while more extreme forces slowly gathered strength in a Gaelic setting.

What with the disintegration of Parnell's party machine, Gladstone's retirement as leader, and the return of a strong Unionist ministry in 1895, the cause of Home Rule had gone into eclipse. According to reports from the Special Crimes Branch, the land war was at a standstill; and the agrarian scene remained quiescent until the United Irish League began to agitate for land reform. The Irish policy of Salisbury's third ministry represented little more than an extension of those principles laid down by Balfour after 1887. The elements of continuity between the two periods were striking, not only in personnel and policy, but also in terms

---

[7] For further details, see F. S. L. Lyons, *The Irish Parliamentary Party 1890-1910*, London, 1951, *passim*.

of the growing alienation between ministers and the extreme section of the Unionist alliance. In the first place, Ashbourne continued as Irish lord chancellor until 1905; Balfour's brother Gerald became chief secretary in 1895 and was succeeded in 1900 by George Wyndham; the under secretary from 1892 to 1902, Sir David Harrel, had served as chief commissioner of police under Arthur Balfour; and the lord lieutenant from 1895 to 1902 was Cadogan, who had been spokesman for Irish affairs in the Lords after 1886. In addition, that great exponent of constructive Unionism, Chamberlain, had joined the cabinet and was fully prepared to regenerate Ireland along with the empire overseas.

Continuity also marked Unionist legislation after 1895. The Crimes Act remained in effect until 1906, although this was now mostly a matter of "keeping the rod in pickle" because its provisions were not widely used until agrarian crime flared up during the Boer War. From land purchase to local government reform, the formula of conciliation remained virtually unchanged. When the Unionists returned to office in 1895 with a majority of 133 seats, land purchase was the first item on their Irish agenda. The fourth measure since 1885 to convert occupiers into owners proved more controversial than expected, and Gerald Balfour received a somewhat rude initiation into his new post. The chief secretary was always being compared with his more illustrious brother and invariably suffered in the comparison. Although possessing a first-class mind, Gerald lacked the facile charm, the virtuosity in debate, and the commitment to politics that distinguished Arthur. Like his uncle, he had a gift for making "blazing indiscretions" in public. But the condition of Ireland in 1895 did not require another "Bloody Balfour": it was conciliation not coercion that mattered.

The Land Purchase Bill of 1896 was designed to remedy the defects of its predecessor by removing the elaborate safeguards that had helped to stifle sales. The new measure offered tenants the attraction of gradually diminishing payments and authorized £36 million in credit. These concessions did not appeal to the landlords, who criticized the bill at every stage and carried an amendment changing the provision for payment in cash back to land stock in view of the rise in the land market. This boom could not last forever, and by 1900 the landlords were beginning to regret their action.[8] Carson led some of the sharpest attacks on the measure and implied that ministers had repudiated their pledges to the landlords in order to enjoy the "sweets of office." On this occasion Arthur Balfour came to his brother's rescue with a crushing denial of the charge. Later he confessed his annoyance to Ridgeway: "The storm caused by the Land Bill is rapidly going down. There never was a more remarkable instance of the power which one able man has of doing infinite mischief. I really believe that if Carson had not put his finger in the pie, we should not have had the slightest difficulty with the measure either in Lords or Commons."[9]

After encountering further opposition in the Lords, where several amendments were carried in defiance of Government whips, the measure became law at the close of the session. The new act gave a stimulus to purchase that lasted until the land stock depreciated sharply during the Boer War. By 1903 the land market had arrived at another nadir, and ministers realized that a more drastic measure was needed in order to salvage the policy of purchase.

The most important measure of conciliation carried by either Arthur or Gerald Balfour did not fall in the area of land legislation. The Irish Local Government Act of 1898 went far to remove the stigma left by the farcical bill of 1892. Based on the British model, the measure created county councils, urban district councils, and rural district councils; elections were triennial, and women and peers were admitted to the franchise. The new councils took over the administrative and fiscal, but not judicial, duties of the grand juries and received funds from the Treasury as well as from local sources.[10] The act of 1898 was a fitting concession to mark the centenary of the insurrection, and it helped to complete the process of transferring local powers from the class of large landowners to the predominantly Catholic populace. The election to these councils of small farmers, shopkeepers, and publicans, however inexperienced in public affairs, was a giant stride toward democracy in Ireland, but at the same time this breach in the

---

[8] See Pomfret, *The Struggle for Land,* pp. 271-75. In 1896 land stock reached a peak of 113; by 1903 it had fallen to 93.

[9] Balfour to Ridgeway, 20 Oct. 1896, Add. ms 49812. See also *Hansard,* 4th series, Vol. 43, pp. 544-46.

[10] *Annual Register 1899,* pp. 240-42.

ancien régime did not spoil the nationalists' appetite for Home Rule.

Under the benevolent rule of Gerald Balfour the jurisdiction and income of the Congested Districts Board were increased, a Department of Agriculture and Technical Instruction was set up in 1899 to coordinate efforts at developing the country's natural resources, and a program of relief works was initiated to cope with the potato failure of 1897-1898. But none of these acts of "kindness" matched local government reform in reducing the proportions of the Irish Question. If poverty in the west remained almost as severe as ever, at least Gerald Balfour had succeeded in piloting several major bills through Parliament and continuing the precedent of state assistance in the congested districts. In keeping with Conservative principles, nothing was done to establish a Catholic university, despite much discussion on the subject. Last but not least, the Liberal Unionists had crossed the floor of the Commons in 1895 to join the Conservatives in a formal coalition, although they clung to their traditional independence in matters of party organization and finance.

While the Unionists were striving to kill Home Rule with kindness, Horace Plunkett was galvanizing Irish agriculture and industry by means of a cooperative movement. Anxious to unite moderate Unionists and nationalists in a program of social and economic reform, Plunkett founded the Irish Agricultural Organization Society in 1895, and this man of "creameries and dreameries" soon became a household hero in many parts of the country. His ideas about the regeneration of Ireland, which were embodied in the report of the famous "recess committee," eventually won some official recognition when the Department of Agriculture was established. The new vice-president of this department was Plunkett, whose proselytizing skill increased the number of recruits to the cooperative experiment among both landlords and tenants. By 1900 the IAOS controlled some 110 agricultural societies and 210 dairy societies, with a combined membership of 41,000. Credit banks were formed, moreover, to help tenant farmers finance improvements. In many districts the IAOS served to diminish old animosities among the tenantry and between landlord and tenant; and Plunkett's movement, which combined the principles of self-help with government aid, held out real hope for the future.[11]

Unfortunately, after 1900 the condition of Ireland deteriorated. Intimidation and outrage, often inspired by the United Irish League, reached proportions reminiscent of the land war; and again coercion was brought into play. In April, 1902, nine counties were proclaimed under various sections of the Crimes Act, and eleven Irish M.P.'s received prison sentences. The launching of a landlords' trust to protect individuals against the league goaded the agitators into extending their boycotting operations, and by September more than half the country including Dublin was proclaimed. The revival of aggressive nationalism was in part a reaction to the Boer War, in which many Irishmen found a cause close to their hearts. In Parliament nationalist members cheered the news of British military reverses, and in both countries Home Rulers denounced the militant imperialism of the ministry. The much-publicized visit of Queen Victoria to Dublin in the spring of 1900 accomplished little in the way of reconciliation. On this occasion Salisbury had written to Balfour: "No one can suppose that she goes to Ireland for pleasure."[12] And the mixed reception given to the Queen by the Dublin corporation was not forgotten amidst the abundant signs of goodwill shown by the populace.

The period 1900-1905 was notable for the degree of disunity that pervaded the Unionist alliance. Even before Chamberlain's tariff-reform policy split the ministerial party, a number of Irish Unionists had expressed their hostility to further concessions to the nationalists. The conciliatory measures associated with the Balfour brothers and the number of Irish appointments given to "tepid" Unionists like Plunkett or to avowed Home Rulers incensed men like Carson and Lord Ardilaun who suspected that the landlords were being sold out for political reasons. It was against this background of mounting unrest among Government supporters that Wyndham went to the Irish Office in the ministerial reshuffle following the "khaki" election.

The two reforms associated with Wyndham's name brought to

[11] *Ibid.*, p. 244. See also Sir Horace Plunkett, *Ireland in the New Century*, London, 1904, *passim*.

[12] Quoted in Balfour to Salisbury, 7 March 1900, Salisbury MSS.

a head the long-smoldering discontent of the extreme Unionists. If the extension of land purchase represented traditional Conservative policy, the devolution of administrative power to a central authority in Dublin did not. The principal element of discontinuity in Conservative Unionism was represented by Sir Anthony MacDonnell, who became Irish under secretary in the autumn of 1902. Having served as lieutenant governor of an Indian province, MacDonnell was no ordinary civil servant who unhesitatingly carried out the orders of his superiors. An Irish Catholic with Liberal inclinations, he stipulated that he be given some voice in policy-making. The combination of Wyndham's poetic imagination and MacDonnell's reforming zeal could result only in aggravating the dissension within the Unionist alliance.

When Balfour succeeded his uncle as prime minister in 1902, the state of social disorder in Ireland held out dim prospects for the policy of conciliation. And yet, despite renewed coercion, that same year witnessed another new departure in Irish history. Upon the invitation of Captain Shawe-Taylor a group of prominent landlords and nationalists formed the Land Conference, which aspired to solve the land question by abolishing the system of dual ownership. With the Earl of Dunraven as chairman, the Land Conference won the support of moderate elements in both camps and provided the basis upon which Wyndham and MacDonnell framed the Land Purchase Act of 1903. Unlike Wyndham's abortive measure of the previous year, this final installment of Conservative land legislation contained the inducements necessary to end the stagnation in the land market. The new scheme offered vending landlords a cash bonus of twelve per cent, reduced the interest rate on loans, and extended the term of repayment to sixty-eight and one-half years. Compulsory purchase was excluded, but several of Redmond's suggestions were incorporated; the bill survived the attacks of extremists in Parliament and became law in August. In 1909 this "revolutionary" measure was amended by the Liberals to include a provision for compulsory sale under certain circumstances. The acts of 1903 and 1909 together accounted for the creation of over 200,000 peasant proprietors, whose holdings amounted to one-half the arable land in Ireland.[13]

[13] *Annual Register 1902*, pp. 247-49; Pomfret, *The Struggle for Land*, pp. 272-308.

The Wyndham act accelerated the slow revolution in Irish land tenure and helped to reduce the number of social and economic ties between the two countries. Nationalists like Dillon opposed the measure for fear that any solution of the land question would damage the appeal of Home Rule, while Irish Unionists condemned land purchase as a form of "concealed confiscation." The landlords had every reason to worry about their own future, and their lamentations about the removal of Ireland's only "civilizing influence" through purchase contained a note of despair, shared by Ulster Unionists, about the viability of the Union once the land had been returned to "the people."[14]

The attempt to carry over the spirit of cooperation between landlord and nationalist into the sphere of administrative reform proved calamitous. For different reasons the Dillonites and the militant Unionists were hostile to the Wyndham act and feared the inspiration behind the Land Conference. Revenge was in the minds of both groups, and the devolution crisis provided the enemies of Wyndham and MacDonnell with an ideal excuse to kill the policy of kindness. At the end of 1904 it became known that the under secretary had assisted Lord Dunraven and his Irish Reform Association in drafting a plan to create two statutory bodies that would handle Irish finance and legislate on purely Irish affairs. Among those who approved the principle, if not the details, of devolution was Ridgeway, who considered this reform entirely compatible with the Act of Union. Through carelessness Wyndham mislaid the vital letter from MacDonnell informing him of his own role in the affair. This letter was found years later inserted in a volume of Congested Districts Board reports, which Wyndham had been reading at the time. Once he learned the details of devolution, Wyndham immediately repudiated the proposals in a letter to the *Times*. The scheme was abandoned, but the damage had already been done. Those Unionists who preferred coercion to conciliation cried "treachery" and "Home Rule on the sly." Resentment against the whole concept of "Balfourian amelioration" now found an outlet, and the much-hated MacDonnell was pilloried both in Parliament and in the press. Balfour treated rumors of his own involvement with the contempt they

[14] See W. O'Connor Morris, *Present Irish Questions*, London, 1901, pp. 15-20, 182-270.

deserved and did his best to exonerate Wyndham. Although Mac-Donnell defended his position resolutely, Wyndham could not stand the strain of incessant attacks and finally resigned in March, 1905.[15] Carson and his followers had thus wreaked their revenge; a promising career was abruptly terminated; and the reactionary Conservative W. H. Long became chief secretary. With the Unionists already split over tariff reform, Balfour had enough problems on his hands, but to the moderate Unionists Wyndham's resignation meant that the Government had "surrendered and gone over, bag and baggage, to the extremists."[16]

The days of Balfour's ministry and of Unionist ascendancy at Westminster were numbered. Through such policies as war in South Africa and educational reform the Government had made more enemies than friends. But by repudiating the forces of moderation in Ireland, Unionist ministers and their Ulster vanguard only hastened that solution of the Irish Question which they had sworn to prevent. In 1905 Ridgeway wrote a bitter article mourning the death of the Liberal Unionist party; this death had come, he maintained, as a result of the dangerous polarization taking place in British politics. There was no longer any middle ground, he asserted, between the Conservative policy of negation in Ireland and the Liberal policy of Home Rule. But Unionists like Ridgeway, who realized that the extremists on their own side were as harmful to the Union as were the nationalists, constituted an unpopular minority. The great majority of the party saw no point in granting to a peaceful Ireland concessions that only agrarian crime and parliamentary obstruction had extracted in the past.

In orthodox Conservative policy the devolution plan represented an unforgivable transgression. To the followers of Carson it was the culmination of that heresy which had started with Carnarvon in 1885. The irony was that Wyndham had been Balfour's protege just as Carnarvon had once been close to Salisbury. And in each case an under secretary sympathetic to Irish nationalism had

[15] F. S. L. Lyons, "The Irish Unionist party and the devolution crisis of 1904-1905," *IHS*, Vol. 6, No. 21, pp. 1-22; Dugdale, *Balfour*, I, pp. 415-24.

[16] Sir Joseph Ridgeway, "The Liberal Unionist Party," *Nineteenth Century*, Vol. 58, Aug. 1905, pp. 182-97.

helped to compromise his superior in the eyes of ministers and their supporters. If little place existed for heretics in the Unionist coalition of 1886, there was no room at all for "appeasers" after 1905, when the Liberal resurgence drove the party led by Balfour and Lansdowne into an intransigence born of desperation.

Conclusion

IN THE 1880's the Irish Question became the dominant issue in British domestic politics. The grievances and unrest of "the other island" had troubled English rulers for centuries, but after 1879 what gave this problem a new urgency, an irresistible momentum, was a complex of factors. Prolonged economic depression, a series of bad harvests, the secret ballot, the extension of the franchise to urban and rural workers, Davitt's Land League, and the organizing genius of Parnell—these were the forces that propelled the Irish Question into the forefront of British political life. The New Departure more than justified the observation of a Frenchman earlier in the century that "Irlande n'est plus en état de guerre civile; mais elle est toujours en révolution."[1] At first, both British parties failed to appreciate the implications of the New Departure, and the repressive legislation of 1881-1882 shows how little Gladstone himself understood the nature of constitutional agitation when conducted by Irishmen. By exploiting the indecision of Liberals and Conservatives alike, the Parnellites were able to achieve their goal of ascendancy at Westminster when they emerged from the general election of 1885 holding the balance in Parliament. Having warned against this very result, Gladstone appealed to the Conservatives for a bipartisan settlement of the question, was rebuffed, and then succumbed to messianic zeal and to the forces set in motion by his impetuous son Herbert. The espousal of Home Rule, which was no sudden conversion on Gladstone's part but the product of many years' reflection, created a new line of cleavage in British politics and proved how loose were the ties binding together that formidable compromise of interests which had been the Liberal party.

In the course of the political upheaval of 1885-1886 the Liberals suffered the amputation of both wings of their party, losing thereby not only much talent but also wealth. In these two respects the

[1] G. de Beaumont, *L'Irlande Sociale, Politique et Religieuse,* 5th ed.; Paris, 1842, I, p. 9.

Liberals' loss proved the Conservatives' gain. Gladstone learned too late that the Irish Question could never be freed from the trammels of party politics. The Home Rule movement was as much a party question as franchise reform or free trade had been, and any attempt to prevent its becoming "the strife of nations, the dividing line between parties" was doomed to fail.[2] Not only were the Conservatives in need of an issue that would rally all "moderates and defenders of property" to their cause, but Parnell himself fully intended to keep the Irish Question on a party level in order to force the Liberal and Conservative leaders to outbid each other in their efforts to gain his support.

For the Conservatives the effect of the Home Rule alliance after 1886 was threefold. First, the party's fortunes prospered, thanks to the voting strength and political acumen of their Liberal Unionist allies. In the second place, the Conservatives were compelled to "liberalize" their policies in order to hold together a coalition of many disparate interests. As the Land Act of 1887 illustrated, the Liberal Unionists were determined to exact a high price for their services. Lastly, there was a negative influence at work, which derived from the nature of the agitation in Ireland. Parnellism, as manifested both in Parliament and in Ireland, aroused all the most retrogressive instincts in the majority of Conservatives. In an era of increasing labor unrest and working-class organization the Home Rule movement appeared as an ingenious device that concealed motives of outright expropriation. Most Unionists failed to appreciate the dimensions of Irish national consciousness because they were far too preoccupied with boycotting, moonlighting, and the Plan of Campaign. In their view the land question remained the mainspring of discontent, and once that problem had been removed through land purchase the demand for Home Rule would collapse ignominiously. Even as moderate a Unionist as Leonard Courtney believed that by solving the land question the demand for Home Rule would abate and Irishmen would learn to behave.

Lord Salisbury had long been the spokesman for those Conservatives who feared an assault on private property. In 1867 he had warned that this attack by the masses was not far distant

[2] See *The Political Correspondence of Mr. Gladstone and Lord Granville, 1876-1886,* ed. A. Ramm, II, p. 423.

and that it would begin in Ireland, where the church would be the first target of the extremists, to be followed in short order by the invasion of property rights. Gladstone's Irish legislation of 1869-1870 only re-enforced his fears on this score. In the next decade, however, Salisbury's pessimism was reduced by the passage of time and by his absorption in foreign affairs. But the rise of Parnell and his party served to revive the old fears; and the Irish Question became a struggle between the forces of civilization and those of disorder. To Salisbury the issue was clear-cut: pure democracy was fighting to eliminate the property and privileges of the aristocracy. And if the "masses" defeated the "classes" in Ireland, England would be next. The elements of class conflict were unmistakable. Fifty years earlier, while touring Ireland with De Tocqueville, Gustave de Beaumont had noticed that the country bore a striking resemblance to the *ancien régime* in France. Condemning the Irish aristocracy as functionless because it enjoyed all the privileges without meeting any of the obligations of a ruling class, Beaumont asserted that in a time of rising democracy there was not a single Irish grievance that did not constitute a menace to the English aristocracy. Lord Salisbury was equally aware of this interaction.[3] Property was more sacred than party; and the rights of property were at stake in Ireland. Many Unionists, in short, believed that the Land League was nothing more than "treason, seeking support from socialistic greed."[4]

A sense of approaching doom at the hands of the avaricious working classes thus pervaded the thinking of Conservatives in this period. The Cecilian flavor of this pessimism was reflected in a letter written by Lord Salisbury's brother in the summer of 1887: "As far as I can see Conservatism is dead and as powerless

---

[3] Not only did Salisbury connect the agitation for redistribution of wealth in Ireland with a similar movement in England, but he lamented the passing of the House of Commons as an instrument of "impartial arbitration" owing to the triumph of democracy over rule by "Crown and aristocracy." In Ireland the landlords had lost much of their property "under a mockery of judicial forms, to satisfy the clamour of the secular enemies of their class and of England. . . ." See Salisbury's revealing article, "Disintegration," *Quarterly Review,* Oct., 1883, Vol. 156, No. 312, pp. 563-77.

[4] W. O'Connor Morris, *Present Irish Questions,* p. 149.

as the landed interest. Unionism is possible—but only by great concessions on the Conservative side—and a reconstruction in principles which must eventually be followed by a change of name. God help you through it all! I do not know which is most to be dreaded—the treachery and inconsistency of so-called friends or the Machiavellian hostility of avowed enemies."[5]

Needless to say, Conservative opposition to Home Rule was not based on the argument of property alone. There were imperial considerations that could not be ignored. Behind the phrase "integrity of empire" lay an abiding fear: if Ireland gained Home Rule, India would follow suit, and the empire would disintegrate as if by chain reaction. In addition, there were obligations to the loyalist minority in Ireland. Always sensitive to the ties of honor that bound the Government to protect the rights of Irish Protestants and Catholic loyalists, Salisbury was convinced that the nationalists would make life unbearable for all those opposed to Home Rule. To tamper with the Act of Union, he once warned, would be to precipitate a "death struggle between two islands born to be friends."[6] These were the assumptions, then, that moved Salisbury to declare that "rightly or wrongly" he had no intention of satisfying Irish national aspirations.

The ease with which Conservatives dismissed the Home Rule movement as a mélange of "hollow, sentimental follies" reveals much about their political philosophy. Salisbury and Balfour were adept at borrowing old ideas and even improving on them, but they lacked the capacity for or sympathy with new departures. The subtlety and flexibility of Gladstone's mind horrified them because these qualities were conducive to the most radical ideas. Their cautious, empirical approach obscured the essential conservatism in both Gladstone and Parnell. Perhaps it was an inherent flaw in Cecilian Conservatism that more importance was attached to the form of things than to their content; or that the Irish Question was treated as an administrative problem while the intangible forces that kept it alive were hardly considered. Influenced by economic determinism, the Conservatives tended to assume that Home Rule had nothing to do with national aspirations and everything to do with material grievances. The

[5] Lord Eustace Cecil to Salisbury, 12 Aug. 1887, Salisbury MSS.
[6] *Times*, 28 July 1887.

land question, chronic distress in the congested districts, and the need for a revival of native industries: these were the real agents of discontent; and if only the Treasury would act in a generous spirit, if only the tenantry would learn to help themselves, then the age-old problem of poverty could be alleviated. Allow the tenants to purchase their holdings on easy terms, encourage agriculture and the fishing industry, provide technical education for the young, improve communications in the west, and facilitate emigration in the congested districts as discreetly as possible; and after all these projects had been initiated, then Irishmen would soon reject the professional demagogues who harangued them about a separate national existence. Such were the arguments of Balfour, who at least proved that Unionism could be constructive as well as coercive.

Those who prescribed this cure failed to see that constructive Unionism, however diligently administered, could never stifle or exorcise what William O'Brien called "the indestructibility of the national sentiment." Irish nationalism was not just a tumor in the body of society, which could be removed by the latest surgical techniques of summary justice and land purchase. What Ireland needed in 1886, according to Salisbury, was not concession but a "licking." And when Balfour had applied that remedy, conciliation followed in cautious instalments. The series of land purchase acts culminating in Wyndham's measure may have solved the land question, but it did not end the Irish Question. If anything, Unionist "kindness" made many Irishmen, who in the past had been preoccupied with rent disputes and famine, far more aware of their national heritage. The fact that nationalist representation at Westminster never fell below eighty seats between 1886 and 1910 provided some indication of the Irishman's commitment to Home Rule.

Compared with the Conservative interpretation of the Irish Question, Gladstone's attitude was not only more courageous but farsighted as well. The Liberal leader saw beyond the "external symptoms" of the agitation in Ireland. "Will the Government," he asked in 1888, "ever continue to deal with signs and never look at the substance—will it for ever deal with external symptoms, and never search out the source and seat of the malady; to tear from a diseased and luxuriant vegetation here a twig and there a leaf, but never to ask themselves whether the proper course is not to bring it out by the roots?"[7] Goldwin Smith echoed these sentiments when he wrote that the Irish people had an irresistible craving for "objects of national reverence and attachment." In 1885 Carnarvon and Hart Dyke had had the imagination to see the validity of Irish national aspirations and the courage to argue that Home Rule could be reconciled with integrity of empire. The insensitivity of their colleagues to this approach forced both men to resign. Such was the result of their diagnosis of the Irish disease—a disease that George Moore once called "fatal to Englishmen and doubly fatal to Irishmen."

The Government's achievements in Ireland during this period were by no means totally negative. After Carnarvon's attempts to find a lasting settlement, and after Beach's tortuous efforts to keep the peace without benefit of special legislation, Balfour was able both to enforce the law and to pursue a policy of conciliation. His twin cures were derisively called a policy of "heavy punishment and light railways," but for the short term this prescription proved effective. In its essentials Balfour's policy differed only in degree from that of Peel, who had introduced remedial as well as coercive measures "for the permanent civilization" of the country. Both men believed in relief works based on principles of strict economy, and both relied on stipendiary magistrates to preserve order. Apart from Peel, the Conservatives were most indebted to J. S. Mill whose ideas on land reform helped to pave the way for the ultimate solution of land purchase.

The effect of Balfour's coercion was to harden the resolve of the nationalist party. Mitchelstown, the evictions at Glenbeigh or Woodford, the Rescript, the Special Commission, and countless prison scandals all served to aggravate the relations between the two countries and, in the long run, made it increasingly difficult for Irish nationalists to operate effectively within the limits of constitutional agitation. Although conciliation posed a more serious threat to Irish nationalism, most Conservatives, not to mention the Irish Unionists, preferred coercion because it involved no sacrifice of principle. From the tenants' point of view

---

[7] *Hansard,* 3d series, Vol. 322, p. 776.

land purchase acts, aid for the congested districts, and produce rents were welcome concessions. But something more durable was needed to satisfy a people still obsessed by the presence of an "alien garrison." The enforcement of the Crimes Act left a legacy of bitterness that could not be effaced either by the Congested Districts Board or by local government reform. The Conservatives, moreover, had been so mesmerized by the land question that they neglected the "urban question." The appalling working and living conditions in Irish towns and cities were scarcely affected by land purchase acts, loans to the fishing industry, or by training in modern farming techniques. It was the workers in the cities, as well as those school teachers and poets caught up in the Gaelic revival, who would play so decisive a role in the next phase of the nationalist agitation.

The attitude of the Conservative leaders on the subject of coercion was reminiscent of Mill's statement in his introduction to the essay *On Liberty*: "Despotism is a legitimate mode of government in dealing with barbarians, provided the end be their improvement, and the means justified by actually effecting that end." The only difference was that Salisbury considered coercion —not to mention despotism—too strong a word to describe the enforcement of ordinary legal obligations. Rule by summary justice was not only a well-tried formula but one that even Parnell respected. "It is a great mistake," the Irish leader once remarked, "to suppose that Ireland cannot be governed by coercion." And Peel, when chief secretary in 1816, had written: "I believe an honest despotic Government would be by far the fittest Government for Ireland." Balfour and Salisbury would have agreed with these appraisals, although they knew only too well that the exigencies of politics in an age of the mass electorate meant that the blow of coercion would have to be softened by conciliation. Many Liberal Unionists, on the other hand, found themselves identified with a policy of repression that was wholly repugnant to their Liberal creed. Only when Balfour turned to his program of conciliatory measures did their consciences know relief from feelings of mortification. To these Unionists it took the Land Purchase Act of 1891 to prove that "Bloody Balfour" also possessed statesmanlike qualities.

The larger implications of the Irish Question in this era are so numerous and complex that they can be mentioned only in passing. As Beaumont wrote in the 1830's: "L'Irlande est une petite contrée sur laquelle se débatent les plus grandes questions de la politique, de la morale et de l'humanité."[8] Apart from its effects—both collective and personal—on the careers of English ministers, the Irish Question, as embodied in the New Departure, introduced a disruptive force at Westminster that threatened the very basis of parliamentary procedure. The Irish party, moreover, served as a model of discipline and effectiveness for the leaders of the labor movement in Great Britain, and for a time the Social Democratic Federation was virtually sustained by the Home Rule movement, which provided both a cause and an object lesson in political tactics. The New Departure also accelerated the adoption of techniques of mass propaganda, from huge rallies to lantern slides, as seen in the Primrose League. What the Irish Question meant to domestic politics in England in terms of time wasted and bills lost through obstruction can never be ascertained. Neither Liberals nor Conservatives can be blamed for creating the Irish Question, but elements in both parties consciously allowed events in Ireland to obscure social and economic problems at home. It was easier for a Conservative to support coercion and even to sacrifice landlords' rights in Ireland than to approve measures that might, at his own expense, alleviate the condition of England question. The issue of Irish nationalism also embittered the British political scene. After 1879, and especially with the upheaval of 1885-1886, debates grew more acrimonious, political invective exceeded all bounds of propriety, and old friendships withered and died. The whole area of party strife was enlarged, and Salisbury confessed in 1891 that political feeling had never been so strong or vindictive within his memory. The Irish Question had repercussions upon English society as well as party politics. It was all too easy to equate Unionism with class and wealth and to see in Irish nationalism the cause of the oppressed and impoverished masses. The Irish Question was thus a tributary flowing into the mainstream of increasing class tensions in Britain.

In the sphere of imperialism, too, the Irish Question left its mark. According to Lord Salisbury the Home Rule movement "awakened

[8] Beaumont, *op.cit.*, i, p. 1.

the slumbering genius of Imperialism," and this assertion revealed much insight. No other single question in the late nineteenth century so sensitized British public opinion to the existence and preservation of empire. Many Unionists seriously believed that Irish nationalism, however bogus its inspiration, contained the seeds of imperial decay, and that Home Rule would give impetus to the forces of separatism in every part of the empire. To men like Salisbury, who believed that the key to England's greatness lay in its position as the hub of a trading and banking world, imperial integrity was far more than a catch phrase. Since Home Rule in their view was a euphemism for separation, any such concession, they felt, would diminish the country's prestige in the eyes of the rival great powers, and Irish autonomy would be hailed as the first symptom of a disintegrating empire. As a source of controversy between Great Britain and the United States the Irish Question again deserves mention. Irish-Americans not only helped to finance the New Departure, but by political lobbying they were able to keep relations between Washington and London constantly strained. To many Americans, whether of Irish ancestry or not, Balfour's administration of the Crimes Act appeared to be totally alien to English traditions of common law and constitutional rule. Burke had declared that the world was big enough for England and Ireland to flourish together: "Let it be our care not to make ourselves too little for it."

The Irish Question also helped to quicken the pace at which *laissez-faire* principles were abandoned in favor of increasing economic activity by the state. By the end of the century the amount of regulatory legislation for Ireland alone showed how far both parties had departed from the tenets of classical liberalism. In 1867 Mill had asserted that Ireland's grievances were so compelling that the country ought to be treated "like a spoilt child" for at least a generation. And the Unionist coalition did not lag behind Gladstone in this respect. Except in the amounts of money involved, the conception and administration of the Congested Districts Board would compare favorably with any modern program of assistance to so-called underdeveloped countries. Conservative Unionists took great pains to justify their legislation for Ireland on the grounds that the majority of the Irish population did not know the meaning of private enterprise and self-help.

In a highly industrialized and civilized society, such as England, these measures, they contended, were both unnecessary and demoralizing.

In some respects the Irish Question resembles a gigantic digression in the course of English history. For centuries it consumed the time and energies of England's rulers, not to mention the money as well as lives sacrificed in keeping Ireland subordinate to the imperial Parliament. Well might Lord Rosebery remark: "The Irish question has never passed into history, for it has never passed out of politics." That the Irish Question remained a powerful catalyst in British politics Salisbury admitted when he wrote to the Bishop of North Dakota in May, 1892:

"I am very glad to receive from you so full and valuable a recognition of the justice of the policy which we are pursuing with respect to a portion of this Empire. The mode of dealing with the Irish, of curing them of their inveterate political faults, and of obtaining from them the amount of public service which their very great abilities, properly directed, would be calculated to provide, is the most difficult problem of English policy at the present day. . . . We must hope that the steady persistence in a sound policy will gradually teach them the political wisdom which the rest of our race has, in a great measure, acquired. I am quite sure that in Ireland such a revolutionary proposal as Home Rule can have no other effect, if it were carried into execution, but to begin again the weary round of antagonism and repression which has constituted the history of English and Irish relations for many generations."[9]

It is doubtful whether Home Rule in 1886 or 1893 would have improved the standard of living in Ireland any more rapidly than did English rule. If Irishmen in this period were overtaxed, as the fiscal experts seemed to agree, they were also overrepresented at Westminster, owing to a depleted population; and Irish politicians could not ignore the fact that the country relied on England to absorb ninety per cent of its exports. Whatever the economic arguments for or against Home Rule, there can be little doubt that in terms of political maturity Ireland was better prepared for self-government in 1886 than at any time between 1891 and 1922. Such is the verdict of hindsight. It was a far different matter

---

[9] Salisbury to the Bishop of North Dakota, 21 May 1892, Salisbury mss.

in 1886, when Parnell was regarded by the Unionists as an arch-villain bent on destroying every vestige of British rule in Ireland, when Gladstone was condemned as having sold his principles in order to gain office, and when an avenging Chamberlain had sworn on "war to the knife."

To assert that the Conservatives had implicit faith in their ability to solve the Irish Question is to state the obvious. They also thought that there was ample time in which to prescribe their cure of resolute government and land purchase. Disraeli had once remarked apropos of Ireland's future, "What are fifty years in the history of a nation?" Among other lessons, the twentieth century would teach how little time was left.

Appendices

I. THE NATIONAL LEAGUE AND MITCHELSTOWN

North Berwick

"My dear Uncle Robert,

"I am here enjoying golf and comparative repose! I only got your letter after dictating what follows: but I think it deals with most of your points.

"At a Privy Council on Saturday (17 Sept) we signed the Orders suppressing certain Branches of the League in the main identical with those we had intended to deal with at our earlier meeting three weeks ago. The only alteration is that we have not touched Limerick, and that we have added the district of Kanturk to those previously decided upon in the county of Cork. We have thus suppressed the whole of Clare; the Dingle promontory of Kerry; the Loughrea district in Galway; Kanturk, Millstreet, and Mitchelstown in Cork; and the Rams-Grange Branch in Wexford. These will be sufficient for the present and until we see how the new system works.

"On Friday last I had up to Dublin the three Divisional Magistrates of the divisions concerned, together with one Resident Magistrate for the purpose of discussing how the Orders, under the Special Proclamation, to be issued next day were to be enforced. There appears to be considerable doubt, to say the least of it, as to the legal rights of the Police to break open doors on mere suspicion; and if after having done so they were unable to prove that the persons in the house or chapel were really assembled for an illegal purpose, an action for damages would be brought against them. This method therefore, of attacking a recalcitrant Branch must only be adopted as a last resource. What we ought to be able to do without difficulty and without risk is:

1. Disperse all *public* meetings of the suppressed branch, and prosecute the ring-leaders.

435

2. Stop any attempt to publish the Resolutions of suppressed Branches in Newspapers, or any Report of their proceedings.
3. To proceed against any persons who in furtherance of the objects of such a branch shall proceed to any overt action.

"These powers vigorously exercised should be sufficient either to root out or to render impotent and contemptible any branch against whom they are employed.

"There would be no difficulty in obtaining information of all that goes on at secret meetings. We have that already. Unfortunately it all comes through informers whose value would be destroyed if they had to be brought into court to prove their case. Nevertheless by a persistent use of such means as we have, I think we ought to be able to carry the business through.

"At the same meeting at which these matters were discussed I raised the point of the conduct of the police 'in the field,' so to speak; the defects of which had been brought into prominence at Mitchelstown. With regard to Mitchelstown, I am hesitating whether or not to have a formal departmental enquiry into the conduct of those responsible for the proceedings. But without deciding this question of policy, even in the absence of the results of such enquiry it is perfectly clear that there was great mismanagement displayed by Magistrates and officers. In their excuse it must be said that there was no suspicion that any difficulty was likely to arise. The Members of Parliament who were on the scene had not taken their tickets as if going to Mitchelstown but threw the police off the track by apparently making for another destination. The trial of O'Brien in Court had been over for some time, and no suspicion had apparently arisen that there was to be any premeditated attempt made to force on a collision with the police. It was for these reasons also that the Meeting had not been proclaimed as in my opinion it ought to have been. (And with regard to this I may say that I have laid down general instructions that no meetings are to be allowed in any place on the day for which a trial under the Crimes Act is fixed). When all allowance, however, is made for the circumstances to which I have alluded, it still remains true that the Resident Magistrates were not present when the riot took place, and that the Police

Officers do not appear to have behaved with judgment or presence of mind.

"The proper method of handling the Police in the face of a mob appears to be this.—They should be divided into two parties of unequal size. The larger one (probably the much larger one) should be armed only with batons and to them should be entrusted the duty of dispersing the mob or otherwise enforcing the law. The smaller party should act as a reserve; and if through the defeat of the baton party they are called upon to support it, they should not do so (as they did at Mitchelstown) by clubbing their rifles and acting as baton men armed with an inferior kind of baton, but they should either fire or charge with fixed bayonets as the exigencies of the particular case may seem to require. This is the general disposition of a police force in the face of a hostile mob which both humanity and efficiency seem to require; and on this point Buller and the three Resident Magistrates (all soldiers) who were present agreed. I desired them to draw up in concert a memorandum embodying in detail their views upon the subject; not for circulation, which is another name for publication in the "Freeman's Journal," but in order that they might orally communicate the same doctrine to their subordinates.

"I do not think Buller's presence in Dublin (he was away on leave) would have made much difference to the Mitchelstown affair. It was begun and ended in a quarter of an hour and was entirely unexpected apparently by the Authorities. But I have no doubt that it would have prevented the scandals attending O'Brien's arrest. These simply arose out of the total incapacity of Ashbourne to take a courageous decision and stick to it. They shilly-shallied for a whole day, apparently as to whether the Warrant should be used or not, and finally late on Sunday afternoon actually telegraphed to me on the subject! It is this helplessness of the ordinary Irish Official in the face of an emergency which is the cause of half our troubles. '*You* can take a decision,' said Buller to me, 'and *I* can take a decision, nobody else in Ireland can.' I am glad to say he has now come back, and will remain at his post at all events until within a few days of his successor's installation. I found him as usual extremely easy to work with, and most kind to me personally when we could meet face to face and were not involved in controversies by telegraph.

"I have left word that they are to proceed against any Member of Parliament in every case in which there is a serious incitement to lawlessness given, and a clear prospect of getting a conviction. I am a little anxious as to the possibility of some prison scandals . . . this Winter. The smallest failure would be made the most of, and I am afraid the Prison Board in Dublin is even more incompetent than the rest of the Irish Departments. What I have decided upon is to send all the prisoners who belong to the educated class to a particular prison (the name has escaped me) where there is a good Governor; a good Doctor; and no Nationalist Visiting Magistrates; with general instructions that they are to be treated in every respect like ordinary prisoners, but that most careful watch is to be kept upon their health. I am also going to have a Prison Inspector over from England to take a general survey of Prison management, on the other side of St. George's Channel so as to enable me to state with confidence in the House of Commons that the systems are identical in both Countries, not merely in theory, but also in practice.

Yours affectionately,

A. J. B."[1]

II. SHADOWING

In the 1880's the Special Crime Branch department of the RIC devised a system to facilitate the observation of suspect persons. Police officials compiled a list of the most prominent nationalists, whether active in Parnell's party or in secret societies, and divided these men into three categories according to their importance or potential as threats to law and order. The first or "A" list contained the names of the dozen top nationalists who were to be "shadowed" by plain-clothesmen in both countries. During Balfour's time Dillon and O'Brien, as well as four paid organizers of the National League, qualified for this special treatment by the police. The second or "B" list was composed in 1890 of thirteen men who were either active Parnellite members or promoters of the league and the Plan. These nationalists fell into the category

[1] Balfour to Salisbury, 21 Sept. 1887, Salisbury MSS.

of "ciphering": the police in each district watched the movements of these men and telegraphed their information to Dublin Castle. The third or "C" list consisted of local agitators and the remainder of Parnell's party, who traveled through the country less frequently. The procedure in this instance was called "noting," which meant that the police simply took note of any unusual activity and reported the matter to headquarters.

The classification of suspects was revised monthly, and Dublin Castle had to be informed immediately whenever a divisional commissioner decided to transfer a suspect from one list to another. The process of shadowing occasionally went to extremes. When Dillon prepared to go abroad in 1889 on a fund-raising tour, the Government took steps to hire a special agent, through the auspices of the Primrose League, who would report his more violent speeches in Australia and America.[1]

III. EVICTIONS

Early in 1889 Balfour wrote to his uncle about the need to improve the procedure at evictions:

"This elaborate resistance to evictions is becoming intolerable. It is rendered possible largely by the legal fiction that the Police have nothing to do but protect the Sheriff's officers, who are supposed to be the really responsible people. In consequence of this it has constantly happened (it happened yesterday in the Donegal evictions) that no proper appliances are provided by the Sheriff or the Agent, and the Police are kept under fire (so to speak) for hours before a house that ought to have been carried in a few minutes.

"The Donegal evictions, which are over today, would I believe, never have been finished if I had not on Friday night sent a telegram of which I enclose a copy. The threat of firing, and the threat of firing alone, caused the surrender of the more strongly fortified houses. This is a new departure: and one of our best officials here literally got *white* with terror when he was shown the text of the document. I think it *possible* though not *probable* that someday

[1] For further details see memorandum on shadowing, 27 June 1890; "Returns of Suspects Shadowed," 9 May 1890, Special Crime Branch; and "Returns of Persons on the General A List," 1, 22 Sept. 1890, Dublin Metropolitan Police, SPO. See also Balfour to Lord Harris, 24 Jan. 1889, Add. ms 49827.

or other there *will* be firing at one of these Plan of Campaign evictions. But *if* proper appliances be supplied to the Police, & if it be well understood that we mean business, the chances are very small of such a calamity. In any case we ought not, in my opinion, to go on as we are doing now.

"I have therefore broken through the trammels which the lawyers . . . have woven round the executive, and have written the enclosed minute. It is rather wordy: but it is intended to be shown to the Divisional Magistrates who like things explained fully!

"I may add that by 'proper appliances' I mean a suitable battering ram with a testudo arrangement: & possibly a fire engine. If there is anything in the proposed proceeding which you dislike, please let me know."

MEMORANDUM:

"Resistance to Evictions, especially on estates where the Plan of Campaign prevails, is no longer the isolated act of a lawless individual here and there, but is part of a regular conspiracy for providing topics to agitators and for showing as far as possible the weakness of the law. Hundreds of persons assemble at these scenes exhibiting every mark of open sympathy with the law-breakers, and cheering whenever the defenders of the elaborately fortified houses succeed in inflicting some injury upon the Police. Meanwhile, the local priest, who is probably an accomplice in the conspiracy, goes backwards and forwards between the Magistrate and the Tenants suggesting terms and initiating negotiations. The whole day is not unfrequently wasted over a single siege. The police are seriously injured with every sort of missile and weapon in the very presence of the Military, by whom nothing is done for their protection; and great expense is incurred by the State in carrying on operations in a manner which brings home to the mind of every spectator the fact that, if the final triumph of the law is certain, it is a triumph which may be almost indefinitely delayed.

"The ineffectiveness of the executive is without doubt due to the fact that the responsibility for carrying out the Evictions really rests with the Sheriff or the Landlord, as the case may be, and that the duty of the Magistrates and Police is simply to protect the officers of the law who are engaged in executing the legal process; not to execute it themselves. If therefore, as constantly happens, the mechanical apparatus at the disposal of the Sheriff is quite inadequate for the purpose of destroying the elaborate works which tenants have constructed, it has never been thought the business of the Police to remedy the deficiency, although they have been the persons who have chiefly suffered by it.

"In my opinion some change must be made in the procedure of those responsible for executing the law to meet a conspiracy which works by methods which, in substance, differ very little from Civil War: and henceforth the following principles must govern the action of the Divisional Magistrates and others concerned.

"I. The Military Forces present on these occasions are not to be regarded as there simply to over-awe the crowd; they are there also to protect the Police. The Military Forces should therefore be used without hesitation as soon as it becomes absolutely plain that there is no other method of preserving from violence or injury the Police who are engaged in protecting the Sheriff's Officers or bailiffs.

"II. The great waste of time which constantly occurs in conducting these sieges is due to the fact that while the besieged have made every preparation for resistance, the Sheriff and the Landlord have made no preparation for attack. If waste of time was the sole consequence of this carelessness, the matter might be left as heretofore in the charge of those principally concerned. But the result is not merely a waste of time, it is the certainty of a great hardship, and the probability of severe and possible fatal physical injuries being inflicted upon the Police. This is not to be tolerated, and therefore each Divisional Magistrate should be provided with such apparatus as may, in the event of serious resistance being offered enable him to overcome it at the cost of the least possible suffering to those under his command, and with the least possible chance of being obliged to resort to military aid.

"III. It should in all cases be made perfectly clear to the lawbreakers that they are to be effectually and promptly dealt with; and when this has once been thoroughly done, superfluous discussion and parleying should be dispensed with.

"IV. In every case where Evictions are likely to lead to resistance, the Landlord should be required to produce an opinion by leading counsel to the effect that the Warrants or Writs of Execution under which he proposes to act are regular."[1]

[1] Balfour to Salisbury, 8 Jan. 1889, Salisbury MSS.

441

BIBLIOGRAPHICAL NOTE

THE principal documentary sources used in this work are listed below. Apart from the secondary sources cited in the footnotes, relevant literature on the subject can also be found in J. Carty's *Bibliography of Irish History 1870-1911*, Dublin, 1940. Unpublished Crown Copyright material in the Public Record Office, London, has been reproduced by permission of H. M. Stationery Office.

ENGLAND

1. *Balfour Papers*

These papers in the British Museum are catalogued under Add. MSS 49683-49962. The bulk of Balfour's Irish correspondence is contained in six bound volumes, amounting to some 5,000 pages of transcripts compiled at the Irish Office.

2. *Carnarvon Papers*

The papers of the 4th Earl of Carnarvon are in the Public Record Office. The material most pertinent to this study is classified as P.R.O. 30/6/53-66.

3. *Hambleden Papers*

The correspondence of W. H. Smith, also located at the Public Record Office, contains many references to Ireland, although most of the material concerns domestic politics and procedural matters at Westminster.

4. *Iddesleigh Papers*

The papers of Sir Stafford Northcote, 1st Earl of Iddesleigh, were presented to the British Museum by Lord Iddesleigh in 1959. The number of letters from Lord Salisbury in the collection proved most useful for the purposes of this study.

5. *Ridgeway Papers*

The private papers of Sir Joseph West Ridgeway were made available through the kindness of Lord Tollemache of Helmingham.

6. *St. Aldwyn Papers*

The correspondence and notes of Sir Michael Hicks Beach, 1st Earl St. Aldwyn, are kept at Williamstrip Park, Coln St. Aldwyn, Glos. and contain material of importance to every student of politics in this period.

7. *Salisbury Papers*

The papers of the 3d Marquess of Salisbury are housed in the library of Christ Church, Oxford. Apart from the existence of many cabinet memoranda, the value of this collection lies in the range of subject matter as well as in the number of Salisbury's own letters transcribed by his daughter and biographer.

IRELAND

8.A. *Irish Crimes Records*

The monthly reports of Crime Special Branch officers, the returns of outrages reported to RIC headquarters, 1879-1893, and many other items concerned with the Irish administration are preserved in the State Paper Office, Dublin Castle. Of special interest were the Irish Departmental Letter Books, 1879-1892; "Intelligence notes on Prosecutions, 1887-1891"; biographical details of the Irish parliamentary party, Feb., 1887; and a "Summary of Warned National League Branches." Memoranda on outrages, shadowing, prosecutions, and the Plan of Campaign are catalogued under Crime Special and Crime Ordinary. The reports of Special Branch officers are annotated by Ridgeway, Balfour, and the Inspector General, RIC.

8.B. *Relief of Distress Papers*

These highly detailed reports of relief works are also in the State Paper Office, some of them listed under "Crime Special, Registered Papers 1891." The remainder may be found in "Constabulary Returns" and "Major Peacock's Returns on Progress of Works." There are also elaborate maps of the distressed areas, located principally in the congested districts.

NEW YORK

9. *Thomas A. Emmet Papers*

The papers of the president of the American Irish National Federation are available at the American Irish Historical Society.

This collection contains a number of interesting letters from prominent anti-Parnellite members about party finances and policy after the split.

10. *W. E. Henley Papers*

These papers are preserved in the Pierpont Morgan Library and are of interest, owing to Henley's close friendship with George Wyndham.

INDEX